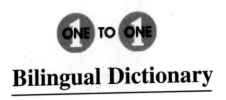

## Bilingual Dictionary

# English-Serbian
# Serbian-English
## Dictionary

Compiled by

### Vesna Kazanegra

## STAR Foreign Language BOOKS
### 55, Warren Street, LONDON W1T 5NW (UK)

© Publishers

First Edition: 2011

Published
**STAR Foreign Language BOOKS**
55, Warren Street, LONDON W1T 5NW (UK)
E-mail : starbooksuk@aol.com
www.foreignlanguagebooks.co.uk


Printed in India at
Star Print-O-Bind, New Delhi-110020

# About this Dictionary

Developments in science and technology today have narrowed down distances between countries, and have made the world a small place. A person living thousands of miles away can learn and understand the culture and lifestyle of another country with ease and without travelling to that country. Languages play an important role as facilitators of communocation in this respect.

To promote such an understanding, **STAR Foreign Language BOOKS** has planned to bring out a series of bilingual dictionaries in which important English words have been translated into other languages, with Roman transliteration in case of languages that have different scripts. This is a humble attempt to bring people of the word closer through the medium of language, thus making communication esay and convenient.

These dictionaries have been compiled and edited by teachers and scholars of relative languages.

# Bilingual Dictionaries in this Series

| | |
|---|---|
| English-Amharic / Amharic-English | Aschalew Mekonnen Bekele |
| English-Arabic / Arabic-English | Rania-al-Qass |
| English-Bengali / Bengali-English | Amit Majumdar |
| English-Bosnian / Bosnian-English | Boris Kazanegra |
| English-Cantonese / Cantonese-English | Nisa Yang |
| English-Chinese (Mandarin) / Chinese (Mandarin)-Eng | Y. Shang & R. Yao |
| English-Croatian / Croatain-English | Vesna Kazanegra |
| English-Dari / Dari-English | Amir Khan |
| English-Estonian / Estonian-English | Lana Haleta |
| English-Farsi / Farsi-English | Maryam Zaman Khani |
| English-Gujarati / Gujarati-English | Sujata Basaria |
| English-Hindi / Hindi-English | Sudhakar Chaturvedi |
| English-Hungarian / Hungarian-English | Lucy Mallows |
| English-Latvian / Latvian-English | Julija Baranovska |
| English-Lithuanian / Lithuanian-English | Regina Kazakeviciute |
| English-Marathi / Marathi-English | Sahard Thackerey |
| English-Nepali / Nepali-English | Anil Mandal |
| English-Pashto / Pashto-English | Amir Khan |
| English-Polish / Polish-English | Magdalena Herok |
| English-Punjabi / Punjabi-English | Teja Singh Chatwal |
| English-Romanian / Romanian-English | Georgeta Laura Dutulescu |
| English-Serbian / Serbian-English | Vesna Kazanegra |
| English-Slovak / Slovak-English | Zozana Horvathova |
| English-Somali / Somali-English | Ali Mohamud Omer |
| English-Tamil / Tamil-English | Sandhya Mahadevan |
| English-Thai / Thai-English | Suwan Kaewkongpan |
| English-Turkish / Turkish-English | Nagme Yazgin |
| English-Urdu / Urdu-English | S. A. Rahman |
| English-Vietnamese / Vietnamese-English | Hoa Hoang |

## More languages in print

## STAR Foreign Language BOOKS
55, Warren Street, LONDON W1T 5NW (UK)

# ENGLISH-SERBIAN

# A

aback *adv.* unazad
abaction *n* krađa stoke
abactor *n* kradljivac stoke
abandon *v.t.* napustiti
abase *v.t.* poniziti
abasement *n.* poniženje
abash *v.t.* postideti
abate *v.t.* smanjiti
abatement *n.* smanjenje
abbey *n.* manastir
abbreviate *v.t.* skratiti
abbreviation *n.* skraćenica
abdicate *v.t,* odreći se
abdication *n.* odricanje
abdomen *n.* stomak
abdominal *a.* stomačni
abduct *v.t.* oteti
abduction *n.* otmica
abed *adv.* u postelji
aberrance *n.* nenormalnost
abet *v.t.* nagovoriti
abetment *n.* nagovaranje
abeyance *n.* neizvesnost
abhor *v.t.* gnušati se
abhorrence *n.* gnušanje
abide *v.i* trpeti
abiding *a.* trajan
ability *n.* sposobnost
abject *a.* bedan
ablaze *adv.* goruće
ablactate *v. t.* odbiti dojenče
ablactation *n.* odbijanje dojenčeta
able *a.* moguć
ablepsy *n.* slepilo
ablush *adv.* pocrvenelo
ablution *n.* pranje

abnegate *v. t.* poricati
abnegation *n.* poricanje
abnormal *a.* nenormalan
aboard *adv.* ukrcano
abode *n.* prebivalište
abolish *v.t.* ukinuti
abolition *v.* ukidanje
abominable *a.* gnusan
aboriginal *a.* urođenik
aborigines *n. pl.* urođenici
abort *v.i.* prekinuti
abortion *n.* pobačaj
abortive *adv.* neuspeo
abound *v.i.* obilovati
about *adv.* otprilike
about *prep.* o
above *adv.* povrh
above *prep.* gornji
abreast *adv.* uporedo
abridge *v.t.* skratiti
abridgement *n.* skraćivanje
abroad *adv.* u inostranstvu
abrogate *v. t.* poništiti
abrupt *a.* naglo
abruption *n.* prekid
abscess *n.* apsces
absonant *adj.* neskladan
abscond *v.i* pobeći od zakona
absence *n.* odsutnost
absent *a.* odsutan
absent *v.t.* biti odsutan
absolute *a.* potpun
absolutely *adv.* potpuno
absolve *v.t.* osloboditi
absorb *v.t* upiti
abstain *v.i.* uzdržati se
abstract *a.* apstraktan
abstract *n.* rezime
abstract *v.t* sažeti
abstraction *n.* apstrakcija

| | |
|---|---|
| **absurd** *a.* apsurdan | **accordingly** *adv.* prema tome |
| **absurdity** *n.* apsurd | **account** *n.* račun |
| **abundance** *n* .obilje | **account** *v.t.* izvestiti |
| **abundant** *a.* obilan | **accountable** *a.* odgovoran |
| **abuse** *v.t.* zlostavljati | **accountancy** *n.* računovodstvo |
| **abuse** *n.* zlostavljanje | **accountant** *n.* računovođa |
| **abusive** *a.* uvredljiv | **accredit** *v.t.* opunomoćiti |
| **abutted** *v.* naslanjati se | **accrete** *v.t.* srasti |
| **abyss** *n.* bezdan | **accrue** *v.i.* nagomilati se |
| **academic** *a.* akademski | **accumulate** *v.t.* akumulirati |
| **academy** *n* akademija | **accumulation** *n.* akumulacija |
| **acarpous** *adj.* jalovo | **accuracy** *n.* tačnost |
| **accede** *v.t.* pristupiti | **accurate** *a.* tačan |
| **accelerate** *v.t* ubrzati | **accursed** *a.* proklet |
| **acceleration** *n.* ubrzanje | **accusation** *n.* optužba |
| **accent** *n.* naglasak | **accuse** *v.t.* optužiti |
| **accent** *v.t.* naglasiti | **accused** *n.* optuženik |
| **accept** *v.t.* prihvatiti | **accustom** *v.t.* privići se |
| **acceptable** *a.* prihvatljiv | **accustomed** *a.* naviknut |
| **acceptance** *n.* prihvatanje | **ace** *n.* as |
| **access** *n.* pristup | **acentric** *adj* bezsredišnji |
| **accession** *n.* pristupanje | **acephalous** *adj.* bezglav |
| **accessory** *n.* pribor | **acephalus** *n.* bezglavi fetus |
| **accident** *n.* nesreća | **acetify** *v.* oksidisati |
| **accidental** *a.* slučajan | **ache** *n.* bol |
| **accipitral** *adj.* sokolovski | **ache** *v.i.* boleti |
| **acclaim** *v.t.* odobriti | **achieve** *v.t.* postići |
| **acclaim** *n.* odobravanje | **achievement** *n.* uspeh |
| **acclamation** *n.* klicanje | **achromatic** *adj.* bezbojan |
| **acclimatise** *v.t.* prilagoditi se | **acid** *a* kiseo |
| **accommodate** *v.t* smestiti | **acid** *n* kiselina |
| **accommodation** *n.* smeštaj | **acidity** *n.* kiselost |
| **accompaniment** *n.* pratnja | **acknowledge** *v.* priznati |
| **accompany** *v.t.* pratiti | **acknowledgement** *n.* priznanje |
| **accomplice** *n.* saučesnik | **acne** *n* bubuljice |
| **accomplish** *v.t.* ostvariti | **acorn** *n.* žir |
| **accomplished** *a.* ostvaren | **acoustic** *a* akustično |
| **accomplishment** *n.* dostignuće | **acoustics** *n.* akustika |
| **accord** *v.t. slagati* se | **acquaint** *v.t.* upoznati |
| **accord** *n.* saglasnost | **acquaintance** *n.* poznanstvo |

acquest *n* tekovina
acquiesce *v.i.* prećutna saglasnost
acquiescence *n.* pomirenje
acquire *v.t.* steći
acquirement *n.* postizanje
acquisition *n.* akvizicija
acquit *v.t.* osloboditi
acquittal *n.* oslobađajuća presuda
acre *n.* jutro (jedinica za površinu)
acreage *n.* površina u jutrima
acrimony *n* ljutina
acrobat *n.* akrobata
across *adv.* preko
across *prep.* preko puta
act *n.* delo
act *v.i.* postupati
acting *n.* delovanje
action *n.* akcija
activate *v.t.* aktivirati
active *a.* aktivan
activity *n.* delatnost
actor *n.* glumac
actress *n.* glumica
actual *a.* stvaran
actually *adv.* zapravo
acumen *n.* sposobnost
acute *a.* oštar
adage *n.* poslovica
adamant *a.* nepopustljiv
adamant *n.* tvrdoća
adapt *v.t.* prilagoditi
adaptation *n.* prilagođavanje
adays *adv.* danju
add *v.t.* dodati
addict *v.t.* biti zavistan
addict *n.* zavisnik
addiction *n.* zavisnost
addition *n.* dodatak
additional *a.* dodatni
addle *adj.* pokvareno

address *v.t.* obratiti se
address *n.* adresa
addressee *n.* primalac
adduce *v.t.* navesti
adept *n.* veština
adept *a.* vešt
adequacy *n.* adekvatnost
adequate *a.* adekvatan
adhere *v.i.* držati se
adherence *n.* privrženost
adhesion *n.* adhezija
adhesive *n.* lepljiva materija
adhesive *a.* lepljiva materija
adhibit *v.t.* dopustiti
adieu *n.* pozdraviti se
adieu *interj.* zbogom
adjacent *a.* susedni
adjective *n.* pridev
adjoin *v.t.* graničiti se
adjourn *v.t.* odgoditi
adjournment *n.* odlaganje
adjudge *v.t.* dosuditi
adjunct *n.* dodatak
adjuration *n* preklinjanje
adjust *v.t.* prilagoditi
adjustment *n.* prilagođavanje
administer *v.t.* upravljati
administration *n.* uprava
administrative *a.* upravni
administrator *n.* administrator
admirable *a.* za divljenje
admiral *n.* admiral
admiration *n.* divljenje
admire *v.t.* diviti se
admissible *a.* prihvatljiv
admission *n.* pristup
admit *v.t.* priznati
admittance *n.* pristupanje
admonish *v.t.* upozoriti
admonition *n.* upozorenje

**ado** *n.* buka
**adobe** *n.* čerpić
**adolescence** *n.* mladost
**adolescent** *a.* mlad
**adopt** *v.t.* usvojiti
**adoption** *n* usvajanje
**adorable** *a.* neodoljiv
**adoration** *n.* obožavanje
**adore** *v.t.* obožavati
**adorn** *v.t.* ulepšavati
**adscititious** *adj* dopunski
**adulation** *n* preterano laskanje
**adult** *a* odrastao
**adult** *n.* odrasla osoba
**adulterate** *v.t.* falsifikovati
**adulteration** *n.* kvarenje
**adultery** *n.* preljuba
**advance** *v.t.* unaprediti
**advance** *n.* predujam
**advancement** *n.* napredovanje
**advantage** *n.* prednost
**advantage** *v.t.* iskoristiti
**advantageous** *a.* povoljan
**advent** *n.* pojava
**adventure** *n* avantura
**adventurous** *a.* pustolovan
**adverb** *n.* prilog
**adverbial** *a.* priloški
**adversary** *n.* protivnik
**adverse** *a* suprotan
**adversity** *n.* nesreća
**advert** *v.* skrenuti pažnju
**advertise** *v.t.* oglašavati
**advertisement** *n* oglas
**advice** *n* savet
**advisable** *a.* preporučiv
**advisability** *n* preporučivost
**advise** *v.t.* savetovati
**advocacy** *n.* advokatura
**advocate** *n* advokat

**advocate** *v.t.* zastupati
**aerial** *a.* vazdušni
**aerial** *n.* antena
**aeriform** *adj.* vazdušast
**aerify** *v.t.* isparavati
**aerodrome** *n* aerodrom
**aeronautics** *n.pl.* aeronautika
**aeroplane** *n.* avion
**aesthetic** *a.* estetski
**aesthetics** *n.pl.* estetika
**aestival** *adj* letnji
**afar** *adv.* izdaleka
**affable** *a.* ljubazan
**affair** *n.* afera
**affect** *v.t.* uticati
**affectation** *n* prenemaganje
**affection** *n.* naklonjenost
**affectionate** *a.* nežan
**affidavit** *n* pismena izjava
**affiliation** *n.* pridruženje
**affinity** *n* sklonost
**affirm** *v.t.* potvrditi
**affirmation** *n* potvrda
**affirmative** *a* potvrdan
**affix** *v.t.* pričvrstiti
**afflict** *v.t.* ožalostiti
**affliction** *n.* žalost
**affluence** *n.* bogatstvo
**affluent** *a.* bogat
**afford** *v.t.* priuštiti
**afforest** *v.t.* pošumiti
**affray** *n* kavga
**affront** *v.t.* uvrediti
**affront** *n* uvreda
**afield** *adv.* napolju
**aflame** *adv.* zapaljeno
**afloat** *adv.* plov'eći
**afoot** *adv.* pešice
**afore** *prep.* pre
**afraid** *a.* uplašen

afresh *adv.* ponovo
after *prep.* nakon
after *adv* nakon
after *conj.* pošto
after *a* poslednji
afterwards *adv.* kasnije
again *adv.* opet
against *prep.* nasuprot
agamist *n* neženja
agape *adv.* zapanjeno
agaze *adv.* zagledano
age *n.* doba
aged *a.* ostareo
agency *n.* agencija
agenda *n.* dnevni red
agent *n* agent
aggravate *v.t.* pogoršati
aggravation *n.* pogoršavanje
aggregate *v.t.* nagomilati
aggression *n* agresija
aggressive *a.* agresivan
aggressor *n.* agresor
aggrieve *v.t.* ožalostiti
aghast *a.* prestravljen
agile *a.* agilan
agility *n.* agilnost
agitate *v.t.* uzrujati
agitation *n* uzrujanost
agist *v.t.* iznajmiti pašnjak
aglow *adv.* užaren
agnus *n* jagnje
ago *adv.* pre
agog *adj.* nestrpljiv
agonist *n* takmičar
agonize *v.t.* mučiti
agony *n.* agonija
agronomy *n.* agronomija
agrarian *a.* agrarni
agree *v.i.* složiti se
agreeable *a.* saglasan

agreement *n.* sporazum
agricultural *a.* poljoprivredni
agriculture *n.* poljoprivreda
agriculturist *n.* poljoprivrednik
ague *n.* malarična groznica
ahead *adv.* ispred
aheap *adv.* u gomili
aid *n.* pomoć
aid *v.t* pomagati
aigrette *n.* kresta
ail *v.t.* bolovati
ailment *n.* oboljenje
aim *n.* cilj
aim *v.i.* ciljati
air *n.* vazduh
aircraft *n.* letelica
airy *a.* vazdušast
ajar *adv.* pritvoren
akin *a.* srodan
alacrious *adj* živahan
alacrity *n.* živahnost
alamort *adj.* smrtno
alarm *n* uzbuna
alarm *v.t* uzbuniti
alas *interj.* avaj
albeit *conj.* iako
albion *n* albion
album *n.* album
albumen *n* belančevina
alchemy *n.* alhemija
alcohol *n* alkohol
ale *n* pivo
alegar *n* sirće
alert *a.* oprezan
alertness *n.* opreznost
algebra *n.* algebra
alias *n.* pseudonim
alias *adv.* zvano
alibi *n.* alibi
alien *a.* stranac

alienate *v.t.* otuđiti
aliferous *adj.* krilat
alight *v.i.* osvetljen
align *v.t.* poravnati
alignment *n.* poravnanje
alike *a.* nalik
alike *adv.* jednako
aliment *n.* izdržavanje
alimony *n.* alimentacija
aliquot *n.* delitelj bez ostatka
alive *a.* živ
alkali *n.* baza
all *a.* sav
all *n.* ceo
all *adv.* svo
all *pron.* svi
allay *v.t.* ublažiti
allegation *n.* navod
allege *v.t.* izjaviti
allegiance *n.* vernost
allegorical *a.* alegorijski
allegory *n.* alegorija
allergy *n.* alergija
alleviate *v.t.* olakšati
alleviation *n.* olakšanje
alley *n.* uska ulica
alliance *n.* savez
alligator *n* aligator
alliterate *v.* koristiti aliteraciju
alliteration *n.* aliteracija
allocate *v.t.* dodeliti
allocation *n.* raspodela
allot *v.t.* odrediti
allotment *n.* dodeljivanje
allow *v.t.* dopustiti
allowance *n.* dozvola
alloy *n.* legura
allude *v.i.* aludirati
allure *v.t.* privlačiti
allurement *n* privlačnost

allusion *n* nagoveštaj
allusive *a.* skriven
ally *v.t.* ujediniti se
ally *n.* saveznik
almanac *n.* almanah
almighty *a.* svemoguć
almond *n.* badem
almost *adv.* umalo
alms *n.* milostinja
aloft *adv.* visoko
alone *a.* sam
along *adv.* uzduž
along *prep.* duž
aloof *adv.* daleko
aloud *adv.* naglas
alp *n.* planinski vrh
alpha *n.* alfa
alphabet *n.* abeceda
alphabetical *a.* abecedno
alpinist *n.* alpinista
already *adv.* već
also *adv.* takođe
altar *n.* oltar
alter *v.t.* izmeniti
alteration *n* izmena
altercation *n.* prepirka
alternate *a.* naizmenično
alternate *v.t.* zamenjivati
alternative *n.* alternativa
alternative *a.* alternativan
although *conj.* iako
altimeter *n* visinometar
altitude *n.* visina
alto *n* alt
altogether *adv.* sveukupno
aluminium *n.* aluminijum
alumna *n* svršena učenica
always *adv.* uvek
am sam
amalgam *n* legura žive

amalgamate *v.t.* mešati sa živom
amalgamation *n* mešanje
amass *v.t.* nagomilati
amateur *n.* amater
amatory *adj* ljubavni
amaze *v.t.* zadiviti
amazement *n.* zadivljenost
ambassador *n.* ambasador
amberite *n. vrsta* baruta
ambient *adj.* ambijent
ambiguity *n.* dvosmislenost
ambiguous *a.* dvosmislen
ambition *n.* ambicija
ambitious *a.* ambiciozan
ambry *n.* ormar
ambulance *n.* hitna pomoć
ambulant *adj* putujući
ambulate *v.t* kretati se
ambush *n.* zaseda
ameliorate *v.t.* poboljšati
amelioration *n.* poboljšanje
amen *interj.* amin
amenable *a* nadležan
amend *v.t.* popraviti
amendment *n.* amandman
amends *n.pl.* odšteta
amenorrhoea *n* amenoreja
amiability *n.* ljubaznost
amiable *a.* ljubazan
amicable *adj.* prijateljski
amid *prep.* među
amiss *adv.* loše
amity *n.* prijateljstvo
ammunition *n.* municija
amnesia *n* amnezija
amnesty *n.* amnestija
among *prep.* među
amongst *prep.* između
amoral *a.* nemoralan
amount *n* iznos

amount *v.i* iznositi
amount *v.* iznos
amorous *a.* zaljubljiv
amour *n* ljubavna afera
ampere *n* amper
amphibious *adj* amfibijski
amphitheatre *n* amfiteatar
ample *a.* opsežan
amplification *n* pojačanje
amplifier *n* pojačalo
amplify *v.t.* pojačati
amuck *adv.* besomučno
amulet *n.* amajlija
amuse *v.t.* zabavljati
amusement *n* zabava
an *art* neodređeni član
anabaptism *n* anabaptizam
anachronism *n* anakronizam
anaclisis *n* zavisnost od drugih
anadem *n* venac za glavu
anaemia *n* malokrvnost
anaesthesia *n* anestezija
anaesthetic *n.* anestetik
anal *adj.* analni
analogous *a.* analogan
analogy *n.* analogija
analyse *v.t.* analizirati
analysis *n.* analiza
analyst *n* analitičar
analytical *a* analitički
anamnesis *n* anamneza
anamorphous *adj* anamorfan
anarchism *n.* anarhizam
anarchist *n* anarhista
anarchy *n* anarhija
anatomy *n.* anatomija
ancestor *n.* predak
ancestral *a.* nasleđen
ancestry *n.* poreklo
anchor *n.* sidro

anchorage *n* usidrenje
ancient *a.* drevni
ancon *n* konzola
and *conj.* i
androphagi *n.* ljudožderi
anecdote *n.* anegdota
anemometer *n* anemometar
anew *adv.* iznova
anfractuous *adj* krivudav
angel *n* anđeo
anger *n.* bes
angina *n* angina
angle *n.* ugao
angle *n* stanovište
angry *a.* ljut
anguish *n.* bol
angular *a.* ugaoni
anigh *adv.* blizu
animal *n.* životinja
animate *v.t.* oživeti
animate *a.* živahan
animation *n* animacija
animosity *n* neprijateljstvo
animus *n* zlonamernost
aniseed *n* anisovo seme
ankle *n.* članak
anklet *n* ukras za nogu
annalist *n.* letopisac
annals *n.pl.* letopisi
annectant *adj.* spojni
annex *v.t.* dodati
annexation *n* pripajanje
annihilate *v.t.* uništiti
annihilation *n* uništenje
anniversary *n.* godišnjica
announce *v.t.* objaviti
announcement *n.* objava
annoy *v.t.* dosađivati
annoyance *n.* dosađivanje
annual *a.* godišnji

annuitant *n* rentijer
annuity *n.* renta
annul *v.t.* poništiti
annulet *n* prstenčić
anoint *v.t.* mazati
anomalous *a* nepravilan
anomaly *n* nepravilnost
anon *adv.* odmah
anonymity *n.* anonimnost
anonymity *n.* bezimenost
anonymous *a.* nepoznat
another *a* drugi
answer *n* odgovor
answer *v.t* odgovoriti
answerable *a.* odgovorljiv
ant *n* mrav
antacid *adj.* antacid
antagonism *n.* protivljenje
antagonist *n.* protivnik
antagonize *v.t.* protiviti se
antarctic *a.* antarktički
antecede *v.t.* prethoditi
antecedent *n.* prošlost
antecedent *a.* prethodni
antedate *n.* raniji datum
antelope *n.* antilopa
antenatal *adj.* prenatalni
antennae *n.* antene
antenuptial *adj.* predbračni
anthem *n.* himna
anthology *n.* antologija
anthropoid *adj.* čovekolik
anti *pref.* anti
anti-aircraft *a.* protivavionski
antic *n* lakrdijaš
anticipate *v.t.* predvideti
anticipation *n.* predviđanje
antidote *n.* protivotrov
antinomy *n.* kontradikcija
antipathy *n.* antipatija

antiphony *n.* antifonija
antipodes *n.* antipodi
antiquarian *a.* starinski
antiquarian *n* antikvar
antiquary *n.* starinar
antiquated *a.* zastareo
antique *a.* starinski
antiquity *n.* antika
antiseptic *n.* antiseptik
antiseptic *a.* antiseptički
antithesis *n.* antiteza
antitheist *n* ateist
antler *n.* rog
antonym *n.* antonim
anus *n.* čmar
anvil *n.* nakovanj
anxiety *a* uznemiren
anxious *a.* zabrinut
any *a.* svaki
any *adv.* ma koji
anyhow *adv.* u svakom slučaju
apace *adv.* hitro
apart *adv.* odvojeno
apartment *n.* stan
apathy *n.* apatija
ape *n* majmun
ape *v.t.* oponašati
aperture *n.* otvor
apex *n.* vrh
aphorism *n* aforizam
apiary *n.* pčelinjak
apiculture *n.* pčelarstvo
apish *a.* majmunski
apnoea *n* disajne smetnje
apologize *v.i.* izviniti se
apologue *n* basna
apology *n.* izvinjenje
apostle *n.* apostol
apostrophe *n.* apostrofiranje
apotheosis *n.* obožavanje

apparatus *n.* aparat
apparel *n.* odeća
apparel *v.t.* obući
apparent *a.* prividan
appeal *n.* žalba
appeal *v.t.* žaliti se
appear *v.i.* pojaviti se
appearance *n* izgled
appease *v.t.* umiriti
appellant *n.* apelant
append *v.t.* dodati
appendage *n.* dodatak
appendicitis *n.* upala slepog creva
appendix *n.* slepo crevo
appendix *n.* dodatak
appetence *n.* požuda
appetent *adj.* željno
appetite *n.* apetit
appetite *n.* nagon
appetizer *n* predjelo
applaud *v.t.* aplaudirati
applause *n.* aplauz
apple *n.* jabuka
appliance *n.* uređaj
applicable *a.* primenljiv
applicant *n.* kandidat
application *n.* primena
apply *v.t.* primeniti
appoint *v.t.* imenovati
appointment *n.* imenovanje
apportion *v.t.* raspodeliti
apposite *adj* prikladan
apposite *a.* primeran
appositely *adv* prikladno
approbate *v.t* odobriti
appraise *v.t.* proceniti
appreciable *a.* primetan
appreciate *v.t.* ceniti
appreciation *n.* zahvalnost
apprehend *v.t.* shvatiti

**apprehension** *n.* razumevanje
**apprehensive** *a.* pronicljiv
**apprentice** *n.* šegrt
**apprise** *v.t.* obavestiti
**approach** *v.t.* pristupiti
**approach** *n.* pristup
**approbation** *n.* odobrenje
**appropriate** *v.t.* primeniti
**appropriate** *a.* prikladan
**appropriation** *n.* prisvajanje
**approval** *n.* odobrenje
**approve** *v.t.* odobriti
**approximate** *a.* približan
**apricot** *n.* kajsija
**appurtenance** *n* pripadanje
**apron** *n.* kecelja
**apt** *a.* sposoban
**aptitude** *n.* sposobnost
**aquarium** *n.* akvarijum
**aquarius** *n.* vodolija
**aqueduct** *n.* akvadukt
**arable** *adj.* obradiv
**arbiter** *n.* sudija
**arbitrary** *a.* proizvoljno
**arbitrate** *v.t.* presuditi
**arbitration** *n.* arbitraža
**arbitrator** *n.* arbiter
**arc** *n.* luk
**arcade** *n* svod
**arch** *n.* svod
**arch** *v.t.* zasvoditi
**arch** *a* prepreden
**archaic** *a.* drevan
**archangel** *n* arhanđeo
**archbishop** *n.* arhiepiskop
**archer** *n.* strelac
**architect** *n.* arhitekta
**architecture** *n.* arhitektura
**archives** *n.pl.* arhive
**Arctic** *n* Arktik

**ardent** *a.* užaren
**ardour** *n.* vrućina
**arduous** *a.* energičan
**area** *n* područje
**areca** *n* ukrasna palma
**arena** *n* arena
**argil** *n* glina
**argue** *v.t.* raspravljati
**argument** *n.* rasprava
**argute** *adj.* oštrouman
**arid** *adj.* suv
**aries** *n.* ovan
**aright** *adv* pravilno
**aright** *adv.* pravedno
**arise** *v.i.* ustati
**aristocracy** *n.* plemstvo
**aristocrat** *n.* aristokrata
**aristophanic** *adj.* aristofanski
**arithmetic** *n.* aritmetika
**arithmetical** *a.* aritmetički
**ark** *n.* kovčeg
**arm** *n.* ruka
**arm** *v.t.* naoružati
**armada** *n.* armada
**armament** *n.* naoružanje
**armature** *n.* armatura
**armistice** *n.* primirje
**armlet** *a.* narukvica
**armour** *n.* oklop
**armoury** *n.* oružarnica
**army** *n.* vojska
**around** *prep.* oko
**around** *adv.* okolo
**arouse** *v.t.* pobuditi
**arraign** *v.* optužiti
**arrange** *v.t.* urediti
**arrangement** *n.* uređenje
**arrant** *n.* opak
**array** *v.t.* rasporediti
**array** *n.* red

arrears *n.pl.* dugovi
arrest *v.t.* zaustaviti
arrest *n.* hapšenje
arrival *n.* dolazak
arrive *v.i.* doći
arrogance *n.* oholost
arrogant *a.* ohol
arrow *n.* strela
arrowroot *n.* strelast koren
arsenal *n.* arsenal
arsenic *n* arsen
arson *n* podmetanje požara
art *n.* umetnost
artery *n.* arterija
artful *a.* lukav
arthritis *n* artritis
artichoke *n.* artičoka
article *n* članak
articulate *a.* raščlanjen
artifice *n.* smicalica
artificial *a.* veštački
artillery *n.* artiljerija
artisan *n.* zanatlija
artist *n.* umetnik
artistic *a.* umetnički
artless *a.* neumetnički
as *adv.* tako
as *conj.* kao
as *pron.* koji
asbestos *n.* azbest
ascend *v.t.* uzdizati se
ascent *n.* uspon
ascertain *v.t.* utvrditi
ascetic *n.* asket
ascetic *a.* asketski
ascribe *v.t.* pripisati
ash *n.* pepeo
ashamed *a.* posramljen
ashore *adv.* na obali
aside *adv.* po strani

aside *n.* strana
asinine *adj.* tvrdoglav
ask *v.t.* pitati
asleep *adv.* u snu
aspect *n.* aspekt
asperse *v.* ukaljati
aspirant *n.* pretendent
aspiration *n.* težnja
aspire *v.t.* težiti
ass *n.* magarac
assail *v.* nasrnuti
assassin *n.* atentator
assassinate *v.t.* ubiti
assassination *n* atentat
assault *n.* napad
assault *v.t.* napasti
assemble *v.t.* sastaviti
assembly *n.* sklop
assent *v.i.* pristati
assent *n.* pristanak
assert *v.t.* tvrditi
assess *v.t.* proceniti
assessment *n.* procena
asset *n.* imovina
assibilate *v.* asibilant
assign *v.t.* dodeliti
assignee *n.* punomoćnik
assimilate *v.* izjednačiti
assimilation *n* izjednačavanje
assist *v.t.* pomoći
assistance *n.* pomoć
assistant *n.* asistent
associate *v.t.* sarađivati
associate *a.* udružen
associate *n.* saradnik
association *n.* udruženje
assoil *v.t.* oprostiti
assort *v.t.* svrstavati
assuage *v.t.* ublažiti
assume *v.t.* pretpostaviti

**assumption** *n.* pretpostavka
**assurance** *n.* uverenje
**assure** *v.t.* uveriti
**astatic** *adj.* nestabilan
**asterisk** *n.* zvezdica
**asterism** *n.* sazvežđe
**asteroid** *adj.* zvezdolik
**asthma** *n.* astma
**astir** *adv. u* pokretu
**astonish** *v.t.* začuditi
**astonishment** *n.* čuđenje
**astound** *v.t* zapanjiti
**astray** *adv.,* zalutao
**astrologer** *n.* astrolog
**astrology** *n.* astrologija
**astronaut** *n.* astronaut
**astronomer** *n.* astronom
**astronomy** *n.* astronomija
**asunder** *adv.* nadvoje
**asylum** *n* azil
**at** *prep.* u
**atheism** *n* ateizam
**atheist** *n* ateista
**athirst** *adj.* žedan
**athlete** *n.* sportista
**athletic** *a.* atletski
**athletics** *n.* atletika
**athwart** *prep.* popreko
**atlas** *n.* atlas
**atmosphere** *n.* atmosfera
**atoll** *n. koralno* ostrvo
**atom** *n.* atom
**atomic** *a.* atomski
**atone** *v.i.* popraviti
**atonement** *n.* pokajanje
**atrocious** *a.* okrutan
**atrocity** *n* okutnost
**attach** *v.t.* pričvrstiti
**attache** *n.* ataše
**attachment** *n.* prilog

**attack** *n.* napad
**attack** *v.t.* napasti
**attain** *v.t.* postići
**attainment** *n.* dostignuće
**attaint** *v.t.* osramotiti
**attempt** *v.t.* pokušati
**attempt** *n.* pokušaj
**attend** *v.t.* prisustvovati
**attendance** *n.* pohađanje
**attendant** *n.* pratilac
**attention** *n.* pažnja
**attentive** *a.* pažljiv
**attest** *v.t.* potvrditi
**attire** *n.* odeća
**attire** *v.t.* obući
**attitude** *n.* stav
**attorney** *n.* zastupnik
**attract** *v.t.* privući
**attraction** *n.* privlačnost
**attractive** *a.* privlačan
**attribute** *v.t.* dodeliti
**attribute** *n.* karakteristika
**auction** *n* licitacija
**auction** *v.t.* licitirati
**audible** *a* glasan
**audience** *n.* publika
**audit** *n.* revizija
**audit** *v.t.* revidirati
**auditive** *adj.* slušni
**auditor** *n.* revizor
**auditorium** *n.* gledalište
**auger** *n.* burgija
**aught** *n.* išta
**augment** *v.t.* povećati
**augmentation** *n.* povećanje
**August** *n.* Avgust
**august** *n* avgust
**aunt** *n.* tetka, strina, ujna
**auriform** *adj. u* obliku uha
**aurora** *n* zora

**auspicate** *v.t.* proricati
**auspice** *n.* proricanje
**auspicious** *a.* povoljan
**austere** *a.* strog
**authentic** *a.* autentičan
**author** *n.* autor
**authoritative** *a.* zapovednički
**authority** *n.* vlast
**authorize** *v.t.* ovlastiti
**autobiography** *n.* autobiografija
**autocracy** *n* autokratija
**autocrat** *n* autokrata
**autocratic** *a* autokratski
**autograph** *n.* autogram
**automatic** *a.* automatski
**automobile** *n.* automobil
**autonomous** *a* autonoman
**autumn** *n.* jesen
**auxiliary** *a.* pomoćni
**auxiliary** *n.* pomoćnik
**avale** *v.t.* umanjiti
**avail** *v.t.* pomoći
**available** *a* raspoloživ
**avarice** *n.* škrtost
**avenge** *v.t.* svetiti se
**avenue** *n.* avenija
**average** *n.* prosek
**average** *a.* prosečan
**average** *v.t.* naći srednju vrednost
**averse** *a.* protivan
**aversion** *n.* averzija
**avert** *v.t.* sprečiti
**aviary** *n.* kavez za ptice
**aviation** *n.* avijacija
**aviator** *n.* avijatičar
**avid** *adj.* pohlepan
**avidity** *adv.* pohlepno
**avidly** *adv* lakomo
**avoid** *v.t.* izbegavati
**avoidance** *n.* izbegavanje

**avow** *v.t.* priznati
**avulsion** *n.* nasilno odvajanje
**await** *v.t.* čekati
**awake** *v.t.* probuditi
**awake** *a* budan
**award** *v.t.* nagraditi
**award** *n.* nagrada
**aware** *a.* svestan
**away** *adv.* daleko
**awe** *n.* strahopoštovanje
**awful** *a.* užasan
**awhile** *adv.* časkom
**awkward** *a.* nezgodan
**axe** *n.* sekira
**axis** *n.* osovina
**axle** *n.* osovina

# B

**babble** *n.* brbljanje
**babble** *v.i.* brbljati
**babe** *n.* dete
**babel** *n* metež
**baboon** *n.* pavijan
**baby** *n.* beba
**bachelor** *n.* neženja
**back** *n.* nazad
**back** *adv.* unazad
**backbite** *v.t.* ogovaranje
**backbone** *n.* oslonac
**background** *n.* pozadina
**backhand** *n.* bekhend
**backslide** *v.i.* ponovo pasti u greh
**backward** *a.* unazad
**backward** *adv.* unazad
**bacon** *n.* slanina
**bacteria** *n.* bakterija
**bad** *a.* loše
**badge** *n.* značka

badger *n.* jazavac

badly *adv.* gore

badminton *n.* badminton

baffle *v. t.* zbuniti

bag *n.* torba

bag *v. i.* nateći

baggage *n.* prtljag

bagpipe *n.* gajde

bail *n.* jemstvo

bail *v. t.* jemčiti

bailable *a.* sposoban za jemstvo

bailiff *n.* sudski izvršitelj

bait *n* mamac

bait *v.t.* namamiti

bake *v.t.* ispeći

baker *n.* pekar

bakery *n* pekara

balance *n.* ravnoteža

balance *v.t.* uravnotežiti

balcony *n.* balkon

bald *a.* ćelav

bale *n.* bala

bale *v.t.* pakovati u bale

baleful *a.* štetan

baleen *n.* kitova kost

ball *n.* lopta

ballad *n.* balada

ballet *sn.* balet

balloon *n.* balon

ballot *n* glasački listić

ballot *v.i.* glasati

balm *n.* melem

balsam *n.* balzam

bam *n.* prevara

bamboo *n.* bambus

ban *n.* zabrana

ban *n* anatema

banal *a.* banalan

banana *n.* banana

band *n.* grupa

bandage *n.* zavoj

bandage *v.t* zaviti

bandit *n.* razbojnik

bang *v.t.* lupiti

bang *n.* prasak

bangle *n.* narukvica

banish *v.t.* proterati

banishment *n.* proterivanje

banjo *n.* bendžo

bank *n.* banka, nasip

bank *v.t.* nagomilati

banker *n.* bankar

bankrupt *n.* bankrot

bankruptcy *n.* stečaj

banner *n.* zastava

banquet *n.* banket

banquet *v.t.* ugostiti

bantam *n.* kokoška

banter *v.t.* zadirkivati

banter *n.* zadirkivanje

bantling *n.* dete

banyan *n.* indijska smokva

baptism *n.* krštenje

baptize *v.t.* krstiti

bar *n.* šipka

bar *v.t* zabraniti

barb *n.* bodlja

barbarian *a.* divljački

barbarian *n.* divljak

barbarism *n.* divljaštvo

barbarity *n.* surovost

barbarous *a.* varvarski

barbed *a.* bodljikav

barber *n.* berberin

bard *n.* bard

bare *a.* nag

bare *v.t.* razgolititi

barely *adv.* jedva

bargain *n.* cenkanje

bargain *v.t.* cenkati se

| | |
|---|---|
| **barge** *n.* barka | **bath** *n* kupanje |
| **bark** *n.* kora | **bathe** *v. t* kupati se |
| **bark** *v.t.* lajati | **baton** *n* palica |
| **barley** *n.* ječam | **batsman** *n.* udarač u kriketu |
| **barn** *n.* ambar | **battalion** *n* bataljon |
| **barnacles** *n* školjke | **battery** *n* baterija |
| **barometer** *n* barometar | **battle** *n* bitka |
| **barouche** *n.* fijaker | **battle** *v. i.* boriti se |
| **barrack** *n.* baraka | **bawd** *n.* podvodačica |
| **barrage** *n.* brana | **bawl** *n.i.* vika |
| **barrator** *ns.* svadljivac | **bawn** *n.* štala |
| **barrel** *n.* bačva | **bay** *n* zaliv |
| **barren** *n* neplodnost | **bayard** *n.* vrsta konja |
| **barricade** *n.* barikada | **bayonet** *n* bajonet |
| **barrier** *n.* barijera | **be** *v.t.* biti |
| **barrister** *n.* advokat | **be** *pref.* biti |
| **barter1** *v.t.* trampiti | **beach** *n* plaža |
| **barter2** *n.* trampa | **beacon** *n* svetionik |
| **barton** *n.* seosko dvorište | **bead** *n* perla |
| **basal** *adj.* osnovni | **beadle** *n.* poslužitelj |
| **base** *n.* baza | **beak** *n* kljun |
| **base** *a.* osnovni | **beaker** *n* pehar |
| **base** *v.t.* zasnovati | **beam** *n* snop |
| **baseless** *a.* neosnovan | **beam** *v. i* zračiti |
| **basement** *n.* podrum | **bean** *n.* grašak |
| **bashful** *a.* stidljiv | **bear** *n* medved |
| **basic** *a.* osnovni | **bear** *v.t* nositi |
| **basil** *n.* bosiljak | **beard** *n* brada |
| **basin** *n.* bazen | **bearing** *n* ležaj |
| **basis** *n.* osnova | **beast** *n* zver |
| **bask** *v.i.* uživati | **beastly** *a* zverski |
| **basket** *n.* korpa | **beat** *v. t.* udarati |
| **baslard** *n.* ornamentni nož | **beat** *n* udarac |
| **bass** *n.* bas | **beautiful** *a* lep |
| **bastard** *n.* kopile | **beautify** *v. t* ulepšati |
| **bastard** *a* vanbračan | **beauty** *n* lepota |
| **bat** *n* slepi miš | **beaver** *n* dabar |
| **bat** *n* motka | **because** *conj.* jer |
| **bat** *v. i* udariti motkom | **beck** *n.* mig |
| **batch** *n* serija | **beckon** *v.t.* namignuti |

| | |
|---|---|
| **beckon** v. t dati znak | **belief** n verovanje |
| **become** v. i postati | **believe** v. t verovati |
| **becoming** a pristojan | **bell** n zvono |
| **bed** n krevet | **belle** n lepotica |
| **bedevil** v. t opčiniti | **bellicose** a ratoboran |
| **bedding** n. posteljina | **belligerency** n ratno stanje |
| **bedight** v.t. ukrasiti | **belligerent** a ratoboran |
| **bed-time** n. vreme za spavanje | **belligerent** n zaraćena strana |
| **bee** n. pčela | **bellow** v. i urlati |
| **beech** n. bukva | **bellows** n. meh |
| **beef** n govedina | **belly** n trbuh |
| **beehive** n. košnica | **belong** v. i pripadati |
| **beer** n pivo | **belongings** n. svojina |
| **beet** n repa | **beloved** a drag |
| **beetle** n buba | **beloved** n dragi |
| **befall** v. t zadesiti | **below** adv dole |
| **before** prep pre | **below** prep ispod |
| **before** adv. ranije | **belt** n pojas |
| **before** conj pre nego | **belvedere** n vidikovac |
| **beforehand** adv. unapred | **bemask** v. t maskirati se |
| **befriend** v. t. sprijateljiti se | **bemire** v. t uprljati |
| **beg** v. t. moliti | **bemuse** v. t zbuniti |
| **beget** v. t začeti | **bench** n klupa |
| **beggar** n prosjak | **bend** n savijanje |
| **begin** n početi | **bend** v. t saviti |
| **beginning** n. početak | **beneath** adv niže |
| **begird** v.t. opasati | **beneath** prep ispod |
| **beguile** v. t obmanuti | **benefaction** n. dobročinstvo |
| **behalf** n korist | **benefice** n dar |
| **behave** v. i. ponašati se | **beneficial** a koristan |
| **behaviour** n ponašanje | **benefit** n korist |
| **behead** v. t. odrubiti glavu | **benefit** v. t. imati korist |
| **behind** adv iza | **benevolence** n blagonaklonost |
| **behind** prep iza | **benevolent** a blagonaklon |
| **behold** v. t opaziti | **benight** v. t biti neprosvetljen |
| **being** n postojeći | **benign** adj blag |
| **belabour** v. t izlupati | **benignly** adv dobroćudno |
| **belated** adj. zakasneo | **benison** n blagoslov |
| **belch** v. t podrigivanje | **bent** n sklonost |
| **belch** n podrignuti | **bequeath** v. t. zaveštati |

bereave *v. t.* ucveliti
bereavement *n* ucveljenost
berth *n* vez
beside *prep.* pored
besides *prep* u poređenju sa
besides *adv* sem toga
beslaver *v. t* balaviti
besiege *v. t* opsedati
bestow *v. t* zbrinuti
bestrew *v. t* zasipati
bet *v.i* kladiti se
bet *n* opklada
betel *n* betel
betray *v.t.* izdati
betrayal *n* izdaja
betroth *v. t* veriti
betrothal *n.* veridba
better *a* bolji
better *adv.* bolje
better *v. t* poboljšati
betterment *n* poboljšanje
between *prep* između
beverage *n* napitak
bewail *v. t* žaliti
beware *v.i.* čuvati se
bewilder *v. t* zbuniti
bewitch *v.t* začarati
beyond *prep.* izvan
beyond *adv.* dalje
biangular *adj.* dvougli
bias *n* kosina
bias *v. t* naginjati ukoso
biaxial *adj* dvoosni
bibber *n* pijanac
bible *n* biblija
bibliography *n* bibliografija
bibliographer *n* bibliograf
bicentenary *adj* dvestagodišnji
biceps *n* biceps
bicker *v. t* prepirati se

bicycle *n.* bicikl
bid *v.t* ponuditi
bid *n* ponuda
bidder *n* ponuđač
bide *v. t* čekati
biennial *adj* dvogodišnji
bier *n* mrtvačka nosila
big *a* velik
bigamy *n* bigamija
bight *n* omča
bigot *n* pobornik
bigotry *n* revnost
bile *n* žuč
bilingual *a* dvojezični
bill *n* priznanica
billion *n* milijarda
billow *n* talas
billow *v.i* talasati se
biliteral *adj* biliteralan
bilk *v. t.* prevariti
bimonthly *adj.* dvomesečni
binary *adj* binarni
bind *v.t* vezati
binding *a* obavezujuć
binocular *n.* dvogled
biographer *n* biograf
biography *n* biografija
biologist *n* biolog
biology *n* biologija
bioscope *n* životopisac
biped *n* dvonožac
birch *n.* breza
bird *n* ptica
birdlime *n* lepak za ptice
birth *n.* rođenje
biscuit *n* keks
bisect *v. t* prepoloviti
bisexual *adj.* biseksualan
bishop *n* biskup
bison *n* bizon

bisque *n* porcelan
bit *n* komadić
bitch *n* kuja
bite *v. t.* ugristi
bite *n* ugriz
bitter *a* gorak
bi-weekly *adj* dvonedeljni
bizarre *adj* bizaran
blab *v. t. & i* izbrbljati
black *a* crno
blacken *v. t.* potamneti
blackmail *n* ucena
blackmail *v.t* uceniti
blacksmith *n* kovač
bladder *n* bešika
blade *n.* oštrica
blain *n* plik
blame *v. t* kriviti
blame *n* odgovornost
blanch *v. t. & i* blanširati
bland *adj.* blag
blank *a* prazan
blank *n* praznina
blanket *n* pokrivač
blare *v. t* trubiti
blast *n* eksplozija
blast *v.i* razoriti
blaze *n* plamen
blaze *v.i* goreti
bleach *v. t* izbeleti
blear *v. t* zamagliti
bleat *n* blejanje
bleat *v. i* blejati
bleb *n* plik
bleed *v. i* krvariti
blemish *n* mana
blend *v. t* umešati
blend *n* mešati
bless *v. t* blagosloviti
blether *v. i* besmislica

blight *n* štetan uticaj
blind *a* slep
blindage *n* bunker
blindfold *v. t* staviti povez preko očiju
blindness *n* slepilo
blink *v. t. & i* treptati
bliss *n* blaženstvo
blister *n* žulj
blizzard *n* mećava
bloc *n* blok
block *n* panj
block *v.t* blokirati
blockade *n* blokada
blockhead *n* glupan
blood *n* krv
bloodshed *n* krvoproliće
bloody *a* krvav
bloom *n* cvet
bloom *v.i.* cvetati
blossom *n* procvat
blossom *v.i* procvetati
blot *n.* mrlja
blot *v. t* umrljati
blouse *n* bluza
blow *v.i.* duvati
blow *n* duvanje
blue *n.* plava boja
blue *a.* plav
bluff *v. t* blefirati
bluff *n* strmina
blunder *n* omaška
blunder *v.i* omašiti
blunt *a* tup
blur *n* mrlja
blurt *v. t* izbrbljati
blush *n* rumenilo
blush *v.i* porumeneti
boar *n* vepar
board *n* odbor
board *v. t.* ukrcati

boast *v.i* hvaliti se
boast *n* hvalisanje
boat *n* brod
boat *v.i* ploviti
bodice *n* prsluk
bodily *a* telesni
bodily *adv.* u celosti
body *n* telo
bodyguard *n.* telohranitelj
bog *n* močvara
bog *v.i* zaglibiti
bogle *n* avet
bogus *a* prividan
boil *n* ključanje
boil *v.i.* ključati
boiler *n* bojler
bold *a.* hrabar
boldness *n* hrabrost
bolt *n* reza
bolt *v. t* zabraviti
bomb *n* bomba
bomb *v. t* bombardovati
bombard *v. t* bombardovati
bombardment *n* bombardovanje
bomber *n* bombarder
bonafide *adv* dobronamerno
bonafide *a.* u dobroj nameri
bond *n* veza
bondage *n* ropstvo
bone *n.* kost
bonfire *n* lomača
bonnet *n* kapa
bonus *n* bonus
book *n* knjiga
book *v. t.* uknjižiti
book-keeper *n* knjigovođa
book-mark *n.* obeleženo mesto
book-seller *n* prodavac knjiga
book-worm *n* knjiški moljac
bookish *n.* knjiški

booklet *n* brošura
boon *n* blagodat
boor *n* seljak
boost *n* podizanje
boost *v. t* pojačati
boot *n* čizma
booth *n* kabina
booty *n* plen
booze *v. i* pijančiti
border *n* granica
border *v.t* graničiti
bore *v. t* bušiti
bore *n* bušotina
born *v.* roditi
born *rich adj.* rođen bogat
borne *adj.* nošen
borrow *v. t* pozajmiti
bosom *n* grudi
boss *n* šef
botany *n* botanika
botch *v. t* zakrpiti
both *a* oba
both *pron* oba
both *conj* oba
bother *v. t* dosađivati
botheration *n* dosađivanje
bottle *n* boca
bottler *n* punilac flaša
bottom *n* dno
bough *n* grana
boulder *n* stena
bouncer *n* izbacivač
bound *n.* granica
boundary *n* međa
bountiful *a* darežljiv
bounty *n* darežljivost
bouquet *n* buket
bout *n* nastup
bow *v. t* pokloniti se
bow *n* luk

bow *n* naklon
bowel *n.* crevo
bower *n* senica
bowl *n* činija
bowl *v.i* kuglati se
box *n* kutija
boxing *n* boks
boy *n* dečak
boycott *v. t.* bojkotovati
boycott *n* bojkot
boyhood *n* dečaštvo
brace *n* spona
bracelet *n* narukvica
brag *v. i* hvalisati se
brag *n* hvalisanje
braille *n* brajeva azbuka
brain *n* mozak
brake *n* kočnica
brake *v. t* kočiti
branch *n* grana
brand *n* marka
brandy *n* vinjak
brangle *v. t* prepirka
brass *n.* mesing
brave *a* hrabar
bravery *n* hrabrost
brawl *v. i. & n* svađa
bray *n* njakanje
bray *v. i.* njakati
breach *n* prodor
bread *n* hleb
breaden *v. t. & i.* napraviti od hleba
breadth *n.* širina
break *v. t* prekinuti
break *n* odmor
breakage *n* lom
breakdown *n* slom
breakfast *n* doručak
breakneck *n* opasan
breast *n* grudi

breath *n* dah
breathe *v. i.* disati
breeches *n.* pantalone
breed *v.t* roditi
breed *n* pasmina
breeze *n* povetarac
breviary *n.* molitvenik
brevity *n* kratkoća
brew *v. t.* variti
brewery *n* pivara
bribe *n* mito
bribe *v. t.* podmiti
brick *n* cigla
bride *n* nevesta
bridegroom *n.* mladoženja
bridge *n* most
bridle *n* uzda
brief *a.* kratak
brigade *n.* brigada
brigadier *n.* brigadir
bright *a.* svetao
brighten *v. t* razvedriti
brilliance *n* blistavost
brilliant *a* blistav
brim *n* obod
brine *n* rasol
bring *v. t* doneti
brink *n.* rub
brisk *adj* žustar
bristle *n* čekinja
british *adj* britanski
brittle *a.* krt
broad *a* širok
broadcast *n* emisija
broadcast *v. t* emitovati
brocade *n* brokat
broccoli *n.* brokoli
brochure *n* prospekt
brochure *n* brošura
broker *n* broker

brood *n* leglo
brook *n.* potok
broom *n* metla
bronze *n. & adj.* bronza
broth *n* supa
brothel *n* bordel
brother *n* brat
brotherhood *n* bratstvo
brow *n* obrva
brown *a* braon
brown *n* braon boja
browse *n* pregledanje
bruise *n* modrica
bruit *n* glasina
brush *n* četka
brustle *v. t* pucketati
brutal *a* brutalan
brute *n* nečovek
bubble *n* mehurić
bucket *n* kanta
buckle *n* kopča
bud *n* pupoljak
budge *v. i. & n* mrdnuti
budget *n* budžet
buff *n* volovska koža
buffalo *n.* bizon
buffoon *n* lakrdijaš
bug *n.* buba
bugle *n.* vojnička truba
build *v. t* graditi
build *n.* građa
building *n.* zgrada
bulb *n.* sijalica
bulk *n* hrpa
bulky *a* glomazan
bull *n* bik
bulldog *n* buldog
bull's eye *n.* meta
bullet *n* metak
bulletin *n* bilten

bullock *n* june
bully *n* siledžija
bully *v. t.* zastrašivati
bulwark *n* bedem
bumper *n.* branik
bumpy *adj* neravan
bunch *n* hrpa
bundle *n* snop
bungalow *n* bungalov
bungle *v. t* pobrkati
bungle *n* petljanje
bunk *n* ležaj
bunker *n* bunker
buoy *n* bova
buoyancy *n* potisak
burden *n* teret
burden *v. t* natovariti
burdensome *a* tegoban
bureau *n.* biro
Bureacuracy *n.* birokratija
bureaucrat *n* birokrata
burglar *n* provalnik
burglary *n* provala
burial *n* pokop
burn *v. t* goreti
burn *n.* opekotina
burrow *n.* jazbina
burst *v. i.* prasnuti
burst *n* prasak
bury *v. t.* zakopati
bus *n* autobus
bush *n* grm
business *n* posao
businessman *n* biznismen
bustle *v. t* žuriti
busy *a* zauzet
but *prep* ali
but *conj.* osim da
butcher *n* mesar
butcher *v. t* klati

**butter** *n* puter
**butter** *v. t.* namazati puterom
**butterfly** *n* leptir
**buttermilk** *n* surutka
**buttock** *n* stražnjica
**button** *n* dugme
**button** *v. t.* zakopčati
**buy** *v. t.* kupiti
**buyer** *n.* kupac
**buzz** *v. i* zujati
**buzz** *n.* zujanje
**by** *prep.* kod
**by** *adv.* blizu
**bye-bye** *interj.* zbogom
**by-election** *n.* naknadni izbori
**bylaw,** *bye-law n.* lokalni propis
**bypass** *n* zaobilaznica
**by-product** *n* nusproizvod
**byre** *n* štala
**byword** *n* izreka

# C

**cab** *n.* taksi
**cabaret** *n.* kabare
**cabbage** *n.* kupus
**cabin** *n.* koliba
**cabinet** *n.* kabinet
**cable** *n.* kabel
**cable** *v. t.* vezati kablom
**cache** *n* skladište
**cachet** *n* pečat
**cackle** *v. i.* kokodakati
**cactus** *n.* kaktus
**cad** *n* nitkov
**cadet** *n.* kadet
**cadge** *v. i* prositi
**cadmium** *n.* kadmijum
**cafe** *n.* kafić

**cage** *n.* kavez
**cain** *n* bratoubica
**cake** *n.* torta
**calamity** *n.* nesreća
**calcium** *n* kalcijum
**calculate** *v. t.* izračunati
**calculator** *n* digitron
**calculation** *n.* proračun
**calendar** *n.* kalendar
**calf** *n.* tele
**call** *v. t.* pozvati
**call** *n.* poziv
**caller** *n.* pozivač
**calligraphy** *n.* kaligrafija
**calling** *n.* poziv
**callow** *adj* nezreo
**callous** *a.* okoreo
**calm** *n.* mir
**calm** *n.* spokoj
**calm** *v. t.* smiriti
**calmative** *adj.* sredstvo za umirenje
**calorie** *n.* kalorija
**calumniate** *v. t.* klevetati
**camel** *n.* kamila
**camera** *n.* kamera
**camlet** *n.* kamelot
**camp** *n.* kamp
**camp** *v. i.* kampovati
**campaign** *n.* kampanja
**camphor** *n.* kamfor
**can** *n.* limenka
**can** *v. t.* konzervirati
**can** *v.* moći
**canal** *n.* kanal
**canard** *n.* lažna vest
**cancel** *v. t.* otkazati
**cancellation** *n.* otkazivanje
**cancer** *n.* rak
**candid** *a.* iskren
**candidate** *n.* kandidat

candle *n.* sveća
candour *n.* iskrenost
candy *n.* slatkiš
candy *v. t.* zasladiti
cane *n.* trska
cane *v. t.* šibati
canister *n.* kanister
cannon *n.* top
cannonade *n. v. & t* kanonada
canon *n.* kanon
canopy *n.* baldahin
canteen *n.* kantina
canter *n* laki galop
canton *n* kanton
cantonment *n.* naselje od baraka
canvas *n.* platno
canvass *v. t.* raspraviti
cap *n.* kapa
cap *v. t.* poklopiti
capability *n.* sposobnost
capable *a.* sposoban
capacious *a.* prostran
capacity *n.* kapacitet
cape *n.* rt
capital *n.* kapital
capital *a.* glavni
capitalist *n.* kapitalista
capitulate *v. t* kapitulirati
caprice *n.* hir
capricious *a.* kapriciozan
Capricorn *n* jarac
capsicum *n* paprika
capsize *v. i.* prevrnuti
capsular *adj* čaurast
captain *n.* kapetan
captaincy *n.* čin kapetana
caption *n.* naslov
captivate *v. t.* zarobiti
captive *n.* zarobljenik
captive *a.* zarobljen

captivity *n.* ropstvo
capture *v. t.* uhvatiti
capture *n.* hvatanje
car *n.* automobil
carat *n.* karat
caravan *n.* karavan
carbide *n.* karbid
carbon *n.* ugljenik
card *n.* kartica
cardamom *n.* vrsta biljke
cardboard *n.* karton
cardiacal *adjs* srčani
cardinal *a.* kardinalan
cardinal *n.* kardinal
care *n.* briga
care *v. i.* brinuti
career *n.* karijera
careful *a* oprezan
careless *a.* neoprezan
caress *v. t.* milovati
cargo *n.* teret
caricature *n.* karikatura
carious *adj.* truo
carl *n.* momak
carnage *n* pokolj
carnival *n* karneval
carol *n* pesma
carpal *adj* koji se tiče zapešća
carpenter *n.* stolar
carpentry *n.* stolarija
carpet *n.* tepih
carriage *n.* kočija
carrier *n.* nosač
carrot *n.* šargarepa
carry *v. t.* nositi
cart *n.* kolica
cartage *n.* putarina
carton *n* karton
cartoon *n.* crtani film
cartridge *n.* patrona

carve v. t. rezbariti
cascade n. kaskada
case n. slučaj
cash n. gotovina
cash v. t. unovčiti
cashier n. blagajnik
casing n. kućište
cask n bure
casket n kovčeg
cassette n. kaseta
cast v. t. baciti
cast n. bacanje
caste n kasta
castigate v. t. kazniti
casting n bacanje
cast-iron n izdržljiv
castle n. dvorac
castor oil n. ricinusovo ulje
casual a. ležeran
casualty n. žrtva nesreće
cat n. mačka
catalogue n. katalog
cataract n. katarakt
catch v. t. uloviti
catch n. ulov
categorical a. kategoričan
category n. kategorija
cater v. i. snabdevati hranom
caterpillar n gusenica
cathedral n. katedrala
catholic a. katolički
cattle n. stoka
cauliflower n. karfiol
causal adj. uzročan
causality n uzročnost
cause n. uzrok
cause v.t uzrokovati
causeway n nasip
caustic a. oštar
caution n. oprez

caution v. t. upozoriti
cautious a. oprezan
cavalry n. konjica
cave n. pećina
cavern n. pećina
cavil v. t cepidlačiti
cavity n. duplja
caw n. graktanje
caw v. i. graktati
cease v. i. prestati
ceaseless a. neprestan
cedar n. kedar
ceiling n. plafon
celebrate v. t. & i. slaviti
celebration n. slavlje
celebrity n. slavna osoba
celestial adj nebeski
celibacy n. celibat
celibacy n. bezbračnost
cell n. ćelija
cellar n podrum
cellular adj. ćelijski
cement n. cement
cement v. t. cementirati
cemetery n. groblje
cense v. t kaditi
censer n kadionica
censor n. cenzor
censor v. t. cenzurisati
censorious adj kritičan
censorship n. cenzura
censure n. kritika
censure v. t. kritikovati
census n. cenzus
cent n cent
centenarian n stogodišnjak
centenary n. stogodišnjica
centennial adj. stogodišnji
center n centar
centigrade a. sto stepeni

centipede *n.* stonoga
central *a.* centralni
centre *n* centar
centrifugal *adj.* centrifugalni
centuple *n. & adj.* ustostručiti
century *n.* vek
ceramics *n* keramika
cerated *adj.* voštana mast
cereal *n.* žitarica
cereal *a* žitni
cerebral *adj.* moždani
ceremonial *a.* svečan
ceremonious *a.* obredni
ceremony *n.* ceremonija
certain *a* određeni
certainly *adv.* sigurno
certainty *n.* izvesnost
certificate *n.* sertifikat
certify *v. t.* potvrditi
cerumen *n.* ušna mast
cesspool *n.* septička jama
chain *n.* lanac
chair *n.* stolica
chairman *n* predsednik
chaise *n* stolica
challenge *n.* izazov
challenge *v. t.* izazvati
chamber *n.* komora
chamberlain *n.* viši dvorski službenik
champion *n.* šampion
champion *v. t.* braniti
chance *n.* šansa
chancellor *n.* kancelar
chancery *n* arhiv
change *v. t.* promeniti
change *n.* promena
channel *n* kanal
chant *n* pesma
chaos *n.* haos
chaotic *adv.* haotičan

chapel *n.* kapela
chapter *n.* poglavlje
character *n.* karakter
charge *v. t.* puniti
charge *n.* punjenje
chariot *n* kočija
charitable *a.* dobrotvorno
charity *n.* milosrđe
charm *n.* šarm
charm *v. t.* šarmirati
chart *n.* grafikon
charter *n* povelja
chase *v. t.* juriti
chase *n.* potera
chaste *a.* nevin
chastity *n.* nevinost
chat *n.* čavrljanje
chat *v. i.* čavrljati
chatter *v. t.* brbljati
chauffeur *n.* šofer
cheap *a* jeftin
cheapen *v. t.* pojeftiniti
cheat *v. t.* varati
cheat *n.* varanje
check *v. t.* proveriti
check *n* provera
checkmate *n* mat
cheek *n* obraz
cheep *v. i* pijukati
cheer *n.* bodrenje
cheer *v. t.* bodriti
cheerful *a.* veseo
cheerless *a* neveseo
cheese *n.* sir
chemical *a.* hemijski
chemical *n.* hemikalija
chemise *n.* ženska košulja
chemist *n.* hemičar
chemistry *n.* hemija
cheque *n.* ček

cherish *v. t.* negovati
cheroot *n.* vrsta cigare
chess *n.* šah
chest *n* grudi
chestnut *n.* kesten
chew *v. t* žvakati
chevalier *n* konjanik
chicken *n.* kokoš
chide *v. t.* psovati
chief *a.* glavni
chieftain *n.* poglavica
child *n.* dete
childhood *n.* detinjstvo
childish *a.* detinjast
chill *n.* jeza
chilli *n.* čili
chilly *a* prohladno
chiliad *n.* hiljada
chimney *n.* dimnjak
chimpanzee *n.* šimpanza
chin *n.* brada
china *n.* Kina
chirp *v.i.* cvrkutati
chirp *n* cvrkut
chisel *n* dleto
chisel *v. t.* klesati
chit *n.* klica
chivalrous *a.* viteški
chivalry *n.* viteštvo
chlorine *n* hlor
chloroform *n* hloroform
choice *n.* izbor
choir *n* hor
choke *v. t.* gušiti se
cholera *n.* kolera
chocolate *n* čokolada
choose *v. t.* izabrati
chop *v. t* seći
chord *n.* akord
chorus *n.* refren

Christ *n.* hrist
Christendom *n.* hrišćanstvo
Christian *n* hrišćanin
Christian *a.* hrišćanski
Christianity *n.* hrišćanstvo
Christmas *n.* Božić
chrome *n.* hrom
chronic *a.* hroničan
chronicle *n.* letopis
chronology *n.* hronologija
chronograph *n* hronograf
chuckle *v. i.* prigrušeno se smejati
chum *n* pobratim
church *n.* crkva
churchyard *n.* groblje
churl *n* grubijan
churn *v. t. & i.* mućkalica.
churn *n.* mućkati
cigar *n.* cigara
cigarette *n.* cigareta
cinema *n.* bioskop
cinnabar *n* cinober
cinnamon *n* cimet
cipher *n.* cifra
circle *n.* krug
circuit *n.* kruženje
circumspect *adj.* obazriv
circular *a* kružni
circular *n.* cirkular
circulate *v. i.* cirkulisati
circulation *n* cirkulacija
circumference *n.* opseg
circumstance *n.* okolnost
circus *n.* cirkus
cist *n.* kripta
citadel *n.* tvrđava
cite *v. t* citirati
citizen *n* građanin
citizenship *n.* državljanstvo
citric *adj.* limunski

city *n* grad
civic *a* građanski
civics *n.* građansko pravo
civil *a* civilni
civilian *n* civil
civilization *n.* civilizacija
civilize *v. t* civilizovati
clack *n. & v. i* klopotati
claim *n* potraživanje
claim *v. t* zahtevati
claimant *n* tužilac
clamber *v. i.* pentrati se
clamour *n* galama
clamour *v. i.* galamiti
clamp *n* stega
clandestine *adj.* tajan
clap *v. i.* pljeskati
clap *n* pljeskanje
clarify *v. t.* razjasniti
clarification *n.* razjašnjenje
clarion *n.* zvuk trube
clarity *n.* jasnoća
clash *n.* sudar
clash *v. t.* sudariti se
clasp *n* kopča
class *n* klasa
classic *a* klasičan
classic *n* klasik
classical *a* klasičan
classification *n* klasifikacija
classify *v. t* razvrstati
clause *n* klauzula
claw *n* kandža
clay *n* glina
clean *adj.* čist
clean *v. t* čistiti
cleanliness *n* čistoća
cleanse *v. t* očistiti
clear *a* jasno
clear *v. t.* razjasniti

clearance *n.* čišćenje
clearly *adv.* očigledno
cleft *n.* rascep
clergy *n.* sveštenstvo
clerical *a.* sveštenički
clerk *n* službenik
clever *a.* pametan
clew *n.* klupko
click *n.* škljocaj
client *n..* klijent
cliff *n.* litica
climate *n.* klima
climax *n.* vrhunac
climb1 *n.* penjanje
climb *v.i.* penjati se
cling *v. i.* prilepiti se
clinic *n.* klinika
clink *n.* zveket
cloak *n.* ogrtač
clock *n.* sat
clod *n.* gruda
cloister *n.* samostan
close *n.* ograda
close *a.* zatvoren
close *v. t* zatvoriti
closet *n.* plakar
closure *n.* zatvaranje
clot *n.* ugrušak
clot *v. t.* zgrušati
cloth *n.* tkanina
clothe *v. t* obući
clothes *n.* odeća
clothing *n* odeća
cloud *n.* oblak
cloudy *a* oblačno
clove *n* češanj
clown *n* klovn
club *n* klub
clue *n* indicija
clumsy *a* nespretan

cluster *n* skupina
cluster *v. i.* nagomilati
clutch *n.* kvačilo
clutter *v. t.* zakrčiti
coach *n.* kočija, trener
coachman *n* kočijaš
coal *n* ugalj
coalition *n* koalicija
coarse *a* grub
coast *n* obala
coat *n* kaput
coating *n* oblaganje
coax *v. t* navesti
cobalt *n* kobalt
cobbler *n* obućar
cobra *n* kobra
cobweb *n* paučina
cocaine *n* kokain
cock *n* petao
cocker *v. t* maziti
cockle *v. i* kukolj
cock-pit *n.* kokpit
cockroach *n* bubašvaba
coconut *n* kokos
code *n* kod
co-education *n.* koedukacija
coefficient *n.* koeficijent
co-exist *v. i* koegzistirati
co-existence *n* koegzistencija
coffee *n* kafa
coffin *n* mrtvački sanduk
cog *n* zubac
cogent *adj.* ubedljiv
cognate *adj* krvni srodnik
cognizance *n* spoznaja
cohabit *v. t* zajedno živeti
coherent *a* dosledan
cohesive *adj.* priljubljen
coif *n* kapa
coin *n* novčić

coinage *n* kovanica
coincide *v. i* podudarati
coir *n* kokosovo vlakno
coke *v. t* koks
cold *a* hladan
cold *n* hladnoća
collaborate *v. i* sarađivati
collaboration *n* saradnja
collapse *v. i* kolabirati
collar *n* okovratnik
colleague *n* kolega
collect *v. t* prikupiti
collection *n* kolekcija
collective *a* kolektivno
collector *n* kolekcionar
college *n* koledž
collide *v. i.* sudariti se
collision *n* sudar
collusion *n* tajni sporazum
colon *n* debelo crevo
colon *n* dvotačka
colonel *n.* pukovnik
colonial *a* kolonijalan
colony *n* kolonija
colour *n* boja
colour *v. t* bojiti
colter *n.* nož pluga
column *n* kolona
coma *n.* koma
comb *n* češalj
combat1 *n* borba
combat *v. t.* boriti se
combatant1 *n* borac
combatant *a.* pobornik
combination *n* kombinacija
combine *v. t* kombinovati
come *v. i.* doći
comedian *n.* komičar
comedy *n.* komedija
comet *n* kometa

comfit *n.* poslastica
comfort *n.* uteha
comfort *v. t.* utešiti
comfortable *a.* udoban
comic *a* komičan
comic *n* komičar
comical *a* šaljiv
comma *n* zarez
command *n* naredba
command *v. t* narediti
commandant *n* zapovednik
commander *n* komandant
commemorate *v. t.* pomen
commemoration *n.* komemoracija
commence *v. t* početi
commencement *n* početak
commend *v. t* pohvaliti
commendable *a.* uzoran
commendation *n* pohvala
comment *v. i* komentarisati
comment *n* komentar
commentary *n* komentar
commentator *n* komentator
commerce *n* trgovina
commercial *a* trgovački
commiserate *v. t* saosećati
commission *n.* provizija
commissioner *n.* poverenik
commit *v. t.* obavezati se
committee *n* odbor
commodity *n.* roba
common *a.* zajednički
commoner *n.* prost čovek
commonplace *a.* svakidašnji
commonwealth *n.* komonvelt
commotion *n* metež
commove *v. t* uznemiriti
communal *a.* komunalan
commune *v. t* komuna
communicate *v. t* komunicirati

communication *n.* komunikacija
communiqué *n.* saopštenje
communism *n* komunizam
community *n.* zajednica
commute *v. t* zameniti
compact *a.* kompaktan
compact *n.* sporazum
companion *n.* saradnik
company *n.* kompanija
comparative *a* komparativno
compare *v. t* uporediti
comparison *n* poređenje
compartment *n.* odeljenje
compass *n* kompas
compassion *n* saosećanje
compel *v. t* prisiliti
compensate *v.t* nadoknaditi
compensation *n* kompenzacija
compete *v. i.* takmičiti se
competence *n* sposobnost
competent *a.* sposoban
competition *n.* takmičenje
competitive *a* konkurentan
compile *v. t.* sastaviti
complacent *adj.* samozadovoljan
complain *v. i.* žaliti se
complaint *n* žalba
complaisance *n.* uslužnost
complaisant *adj.* uslužan
complement *n* dopuna
complementary *a* dopunski
complete *a* kompletan
complete *v. t* kompletirati
completion *n.* završetak
complex *a* složen
complex *n.* kompleks
complexion *n.* ten
compliance *n.* udovoljavanje
compliant *adj.* popustljiv
complicate *v. t* komplikovati

complication *n.* komplikacija
compliment *n.* kompliment
compliment *v. t.* dati kompliment
comply *v. i.* udovoljiti
component *adj.* sastavni
compose *v. t* sastaviti
composition *n* sastav
compositor *n.* kompozitor
compost *n.* đubrivo
composure *n.* pribranost
compound *n* sastav
compound *a.* složen
compound *n* mešavina
compound *v. i* sastaviti
compounder *n.* sastavljač
comprehend *v. t.* obuhvatiti
comprehension *n.* obuhvatanje
comprehensive *a* sveobuhvatan
compress *v. t.* sažeti
compromise *n* nagodba
compromise *v. t.* nagoditi se
compulsion *n* prinuda
compulsory *a* obavezan
compunction *n.* griža savesti
computation *n.* računanje
compute *v.t.* računati
comrade *n.* drug
conation *n.* aspekt ponašanja
concave *adj.* udubljen
conceal *v. t.* prikriti
concede *v.t.* ustupiti
conceit *n* uobraženost
conceive *v. t* začeti
concentrate *v. t* usredsrediti
concentration *n.* usredsređenost
concept *n* koncept
conception *n.* koncepcija
concern *v. t* brinuti
concern *n* briga
concert *n.* koncert

concert *v. t.* dogovoriti se
concession *n.* olakšica
conch *n.* školjka
conciliate *v.t.* pomiriti se
concise *a* koncizan
conclude *v. t* zaključiti
conclusion *n.* zaključak
conclusive *a* zaključni
concoct *v. t* izmisliti
concoction *n.* izmišljotina
concord *n.* sloga
concrescence *n.* srastanje
concrete *n* beton
concrete *a* konkretan
concrete *v. t* betonirati
concubinage *n.* konkubinat
concubine *n* konkubina
conculcate *v.t.* gaziti
condemn *v. t.* osuditi
condemnation *n* osuda
condense *v. t* kondenzovati
condite *v.t.* vrsta ponošanja
condition *n.* uslov, stanje
conditional *a* uslovni
condole *v. i.* izjaviti saučešće
condolence *n* saučešće
condonation *n.* oproštenje
conduct *n* upravljanje
conduct *v. t* upravljati
conductor *n* kondukter
cone *n.* šišarka
confectioner *n* poslastičar
confectionery *n* poslastičarnica
confer *v. i* dodeliti
conference *n* konferencija
confess *v. t.* priznati
confession *n* priznanje
confidant *n* poverenik
confide *v. i* poveriti
confidence *n* poverenje

confident *a.* samouveren
confidential *a.* poverljiv
confine *v. t* ograničiti
confinement *n.* ograničenje
confirm *v. t* potvrditi
confirmation *n* potvrda
confiscate *v. t* konfiskovati
confiscation *n* konfiskacija
conflict *n.* konflikt
conflict *v. i.* sukobiti se
confluence *n* ušće
confluent *adj.* koji se sastavlja
conformity *n.* saglasnost
conformity *n.* sklad
confraternity *n.* bratstvo
confrontation *n.* suočenje
confuse *v. t* zbunjenost
confusion *n* zabuna
confute *v.t.* opovrgnuti
conge *n.* otpust
congenial *a* srodan
conglutinate *v.t.* slepiti
congratulate *v. t* čestitati
congratulation *n* čestitanje
congress *n* kongres
conjecture *n* pretpostavka
conjecture *v. t* pretpostavljati
conjugal *a* bračni
conjugate *v.t. & i.* sjediniti
conjunct *adj.* združeno
conjunctiva *n.* sluznica
conjuncture *n.* konjukcija
conjure *v.t.* prizivati
conjure *v.i.* bajati
connect *v. t.* povezati
connection *n* veza
connivance *n.* popustljivost
conquer *v. t* osvojiti
conquest *n* osvajanje
conscience *n* savest

conscious *a* svestan
consecrate *v.t.* posvetiti
consecutive *adj.* uzastopni
consecutively *adv* uzastopno
consensus *n.* konsenzus
consent *n.* pristanak
consent *v. i* pristati
consent3 *v.t.* privoleti
consequence *n* posledica
consequent *a* dosledan
conservative *a* konzervativan
conservative *n* konzervativanost
conserve *v. t* očuvati
consider *v. t* razmotriti
considerable *a* važan
considerate *a.* promišljen
consideration *n* razmatranje
considering *prep.* uzimajući u obzir
consign *v.t.* izručiti
consign *v. t.* poveriti
consignment *n.* pošiljka
consist *v. i.* sastojati se
consistence,-cy *n.* doslednost
consistent *a* dosledan
consolation *n* uteha
console *v. t* konzola
consolidate *v. t.* konsolidovati
consolidation *n* konsolidacija
consonance *n.* sklad
consonant *n.* suglasnik
consort *n.* bračni drug
conspectus *n.* pregled
conspicuous *a.* upadljiv
conspiracy *n.* zavera
conspirator *n.* zaverenik
conspire *v. i.* kovati zaveru
constable *n* policajac
constant *a* stalan
constellation *n.* sazvežđe
constipation *n.* zatvor

constituency *n* izborna jedinica
constituent *n.* birač
constituent *adj.* sastavni
constitute *v. t* ustanoviti
constitution *n* ustav
constrict *v.t.* stegnuti
construct *v. t.* konstruisati
construction *n* konstrukcija
consult *v. t* konsultovati
consultation *n* konsultacije
consume *v. t* trošiti
consumption *n* potrošnja
consumption *n* konzumacija
contact *n.* kontakt
contact *v. t* kontaktirati
contagious *a* zarazan
contain *v.t.* sadržati
contaminate *v.t.* kontaminirati
contemplate *v. t* razmišljati
contemplation *n* razmišljanje
contemporary *a* savremen
contempt *n* prezir
contemptuous *a* prezriv
contend *v. i.* boriti se
content *a.* zadovoljan
content *v. t* zadovoljiti
content *n.* sadržaj
content *n.* zadovoljstvo
contention *n* tvrdnja
contentment *n* zadovoljstvo
contest *v. t.* takmičiti se
contest *n.* takmičenje
context *n* kontekst
continent *n* kontinent
continental *a* kontinentalni
contingency *n.* slučajnost
continual *adj.* neprestan
continuation *n.* nastavljanje
continue *v. i.* nastaviti
continuity *n* kontinuitet

continuous *a* neprekidan
contour *n* kontura
contra *pref.* protiv
contraception *n.* kontracepcija
contract *n* ugovor
contract *v. t* ugovoriti
contrapose *v.t.* suprotstaviti
contractor *n.* izvođač radova
contradict *v. t* protivrečiti
contradiction *n* kontradikcija
contrary *a* suprotno
contrast *v. t* suprotstaviti
contrast *n* kontrast
contribute *v. t* doprineti
contribution *n* doprinos
control *n* kontrola
control *v. t* kontrolisati
controller *n.* kontrolor
controversy *n* polemika
contuse *v.t.* kontuzovati
conundrum *n.* pitalica
convene *v. t* sazvati
convener *n* sazivač
convenience *n.* pogodnost
convenient *a* pogodan
convent *n* ženski manastir
convention *n.* konvencija
conversant *a* upoznat
conversant *adj.* upućen
conversation *n* razgovor
converse *v.t.* razgovarati
conversion *n* konverzija
convert *v. t* pretvoriti
convert *n* preobraćenik
convey *v. t.* prenositi
conveyance *n* prenos
convict *v. t.* osuditi
convict *n* osuđenik
conviction *n* osuda
convince *v. t* ubediti

convivial *adj.* druželjubiv
convocation *n.* sazivanje
convoke *v.t.* sazivati
convolve *v.t.* namotati
coo *n* gukanje
coo *v. i* gukati
cook *v. t* kuvati
cook *n* kuvar
cooker *n* šporet
cool *a* hladan
cool *v. i.* hladiti
cooler *n* hladnjak
coolie *n* nosač
co-operate *v. i* sarađivati
co-operation *n* saradnja
co-operative *a* zadružni
co-ordinate *a.* usklađen
co-ordinate *v. t* rasporediti
co-ordination *n* koordinacija
coot *n.* glupan
co-partner *n* partner
cope *v. i* dorasti.
coper *n. trgovac* konjima
copper *n* bakar
coppice *n.* šumarak
coprology *n.* koprologija
copulate *v.i.* pariti se
copy *n* kopija
copy *v. t* kopirati
coral *n* koral
cord *n* kabl
cordial *a* srdačan
corbel *n.* podupirač
cordate *adj.* srcolik
core *n.* jezgro
coriander *n.* korijander
Corinth *n.* Korint
cork *n.* pluta
cormorant *n.* kormoran
corn *n* kukuruz

cornea *n* rožnjača
corner *n* ugao
cornet *n.* kornet
cornicle *n.* vrsta organa
coronation *n* krunisanje
coronet *n.* venac
corporal *a* telesni
corporate *adj.* preduzeća
corporation *n* korporacija
corps *n* korpus
corpse *n* leš
correct *a* tačan
correct *v. t* ispraviti
correction *n* korekcija
correlate *v.t.* poklapati se
correlation *n.* korelacija
correspond *v. i* odgovarati
correspondence *n.* prepiska
correspondent *n.* dopisnik
corridor *n.* koridor
corroborate *v.t.* potkrepiti
corrosive *adj.* korozivan
corrupt *v. t.* korumpirati
corrupt *a.* korumpiran
corruption *n.* korupcija
cosier *n.* vrsta krojača
cosmetic *a.* kozmetički
cosmetic *n.* kozmetika
cosmic *adj.* kosmički
cost *v.t.* koštati
cost *n.* cena
costal *adj.* rebreni
cote *n.* staja
costly *a.* skupo
costume *n.* kostim
cosy *a.* udoban
cot *n.* krevetac
cottage *n* koliba
cotton *n.* pamuk
couch *n.* kauč

**cough** *n.* kašalj
**cough** *v. i.* kašljati
**council** *n.* savet
**councillor** *n.* odbornik
**counsel** *n.* savet
**counsel** *v. t.* savetovati
**counsellor** *n.* savetnik
**count** *n.* račun
**count** *v. t.* računati
**countenance** *n.* izraz lica
**counter** *n.* brojilac
**counter** *v. t* uzvratiti
**counteract** *v.t.* suprotstaviti
**countercharge** *n.* protivtužba
**counterfeit** *a.* falsifikovan
**counterfeiter** *n.* falsifikator
**countermand** *v.t.* opozvati
**counterpart** *n.* duplikat
**countersign** *v. t.* lozinka
**countess** *n.* grofica
**countless** *a.* bezbrojan
**country** *n.* zemlja
**county** *n.* okrug
**coup** *n.* udar
**couple** *n* par
**couple** *v. t* spojiti
**couplet** *n.* kuplet
**coupon** *n.* kupon
**courage** *n.* hrabrost
**courageous** *a.* hrabar
**courier** *n.* kurir
**course** *n.* kurs
**court** *n.* sud
**court** *v. t.* udvarati se
**courteous** *a.* uljudan
**courtesan** *n.* kurtizana
**courtesy** *n.* učtivost
**courtier** *n.* dvoranin
**courtship** *n.* udvaranje
**courtyard** *n.* dvorište

**cousin** *n.* rođak
**covenant** *n.* ugovor
**cover** *v. t.* pokriti
**cover** *n.* poklopac
**coverlet** *n.* prekrivač
**covet** *v.t.* žudeti
**cow** *n.* krava
**cow** *v. t.* zastrašiti
**coward** *n.* kukavica
**cowardice** *n.* kukavičluk
**cower** *v.i.* sakriti se
**cozy** *adj.* udoban
**crab** *n* kraba
**crack** *n* prasak
**crack** *v. i* pucketati
**cracker** *n* kreker
**crackle** *v.t.* pucketati
**cradle** *n* kolevka
**craft** *n* zanat
**craftsman** *n* zanatlija
**crafty** *a* lukav
**cram** *v. t* natrpati
**crambo** *n.* igra stihovima
**crane** *n* dizalica
**crankle** *v.t.* savijati
**crash** *v. i* sudariti se
**crash** *n* sudar
**crass** *adj.* potpun
**crate** *n.* sanduk
**crave** *v.t.* žudeti
**craw** *n.* guša
**crawl** *v. t* puziti
**crawl** *n* puzanje
**craze** *n* pomama
**crazy** *a* lud
**creak** *v. i* škripati
**creak** *n* škripanje
**cream** *n* krema
**crease** *n* brazda
**create** *v. t* kreirati

creation *n* stvaranje
creative *adj.* kreativan
creator *n* tvorac
creature *n* stvorenje
credible *a* verodostojan
credit *n* kredit
creditable *a* zaslužan
creditor *n* poverilac
credulity *adj.* lakovernost
creed *n.* vera
creed *n* kredo
creek *n.* potok
creep *v. i* puzati
creeper *n* puzavac
cremate *v. t* kremirati
cremation *n* kremiranje
crest *n* grb
crevet *n.* retorta
crew *n.* posada
crib *n.* krevetac
cricket *n* cvrčak
crime *n* zločin
crimp *n* vrbovnik
crimple *v.t.* naborati
criminal *n* kriminal
criminal *a* krivično
crimson *n* tamno-crven
cringe *v. i.* puzati
cripple *n* bogalj
crisis *n* kriza
crisp *a* hrskav
criterion *n* kriterijum
critic *n* kritičar
critical *a* kritičan
criticism *n* kritika
criticize *v. t* kritikovati
croak *n.* graktanje
crockery *n.* zemljano posuđe
crocodile *n* krokodil
croesus *n.* krez

crook *a* prevarantski
crop *n* usev
cross *v. t* prekrstiti
cross *n* krst
cross *a* ukršten
crossing *n.* prelaz
crotchet *n.* kuka
crouch *v. i.* čučnuti
crow *n* vrana
crow *v. i* graktati
crowd *n* gomila
crown *n* kruna
crown *v. t* krunisati
crucial *adj.* presudan
crude *a* sirov
cruel *a* okrutan
cruelty *n* okrutnost
cruise *v.i.* krstariti
cruiser *n* krstarica
crumb *n* mrvica
crumble *v. t* izmrviti
crump *adj.* hrskav
crusade *n* krstaški pohod
crush *v. t* gnječiti
crust *n.* kora
crutch *n* štaka
cry *n* uzvik
cry *v. i* vikati
cryptography *n.* kriptografija
crystal *n* kristal
cub *n* mladunče
cube *n* kocka
cubical *a* kockast
cubiform *adj.* cilindričnog oblika
cuckold *n.* rogonja
cuckoo *n* kukavica
cucumber *n* krastavac
cudgel *n* toljaga
cue *n* tak
cuff *n* manžetna

cuff v. t ćušnuti
cuisine n. kuhinja
cullet n. otpaci stakla
culminate v.i. kulminirati
culpable a kriv
culprit n krivac
cult n kult
cultivate v. t obrađivati
cultrate adj. šiljat
cultural a kulturni
culture n kultura
culvert n. odvodni kanal
cunning a lukav
cunning n lukavost
cup n. šolja
cupboard n orman
Cupid n kupidon
cupidity n pohlepa
curable a izlečiv
curative a lekovit
curb n ivičnjak
curb v. t obuzdatu
curcuma n. egzotična biljka
curd n surutka
cure n lek
cure v. t. lečiti
curfew n policijski čas
curiosity n radoznalost
curious a radoznao
curl n. uvojak
currant n. ribizla
currency n valuta
current n struja
current a trenutni
curriculum n nastavni plan
curse n kletva
curse v. t prokleti
cursory a površan
curt a odsečan
curtail v. t skratiti

curtain n zavesa
curve n krivina
curve v. t kriva
cushion n jastuk
cushion v. t obložiti jastucima
custard n fil
custodian n staratelj
custody v starateljstvo
custom n. običaj
customary a uobičajen
customer n kupac
cut v. t rezati
cut n rez
cutis n. koža
cuvette n. laboratorijska posuda
cycle n krug
cyclic a kružni
cyclist n biciklista
cyclone n. ciklon
cyclostyle n ciklostil
cyclostyle v. t umnožavati na ciklostilu
cylinder n cilindar
cynic n cinik
cypher n cifra
cypress čempres

# D

dabble v. i. umakati
dacoit n. razbojnik
dacoity n. razbojništvo
dad, daddy n tata
daffodil n. zelenkada
daft adj. lud
dagger n. bodež
daily a dnevni
daily adv. dnevno
daily n. dnevnik
dainty a. nežan

**dainty** n. poslastica
**dairy** n mlekara
**dais** n. podijum
**daisy** n krasuljak
**dale** n dolina
**dam** n brana
**damage** n. šteta
**damage** v. t. oštetiti
**dame** n. dama
**damn** v. t. prokleti
**damnation** n. prokletstvo
**damp** a vlažan
**damp** n vlaga
**damp** v. t. vlažiti
**damsel** n. gospođica
**dance** n ples
**dance** v. t. plesati
**dandelion** n. maslačak
**dandle** v.t. ljuljati
**dandruff** n perut
**dandy** n kicoš
**danger** n. opasnost
**dangerous** a opasan
**dangle** v. t klatiti
**dank** adj. vlažan
**dap** v.i. pecati
**dare** v. i. usuditi se.
**daring** n. smelost
**daring** a smeo
**dark** a taman
**dark** n mrak
**darkle** v.i. sakriti se
**darling** n dragi
**darling** a drag
**dart** n. strelica
**dash** v. i. jurnuti
**dash** n navala
**date** n datum
**date** v. t datirati
**daub** n. mazarija

**daub** v. t. zamazati
**daughter** n ćerka
**daunt** v. t uplašiti
**dauntless** a neustrašiv
**dawdle** v.i. dagubiti
**dawn** n zora
**dawn** v. i. svitati
**day** n dan
**daze** n zapanjenost
**daze** v. t zapanjiti
**dazzle** n blesak
**dazzle** v. t. zaseniti
**deacon** n. đakon
**dead** a mrtav
**deadlock** n ćorsokak
**deadly** a smrtonosan
**deaf** a gluv
**deal** n dogovor
**deal** v. i. dogovoriti se
**dealer** n trgovac
**dealing** n. poslovanje
**dean** n. dekan
**dear** a drag
**dearth** n nestašica
**death** n smrt
**debar** v. t. uskratiti
**debase** v. t. osramotiti
**debate** n. debata
**debate** v. t. debatovati
**debauch** v. t. pijančiti
**debauch** n pijančenje
**debauchee** n razvratnik
**debauchery** n razvrat
**debility** n iznurenost
**debit** n zaduženje
**debit** v. t zadužiti
**debris** n ruševina
**debt** n dug
**debtor** n dužnik
**decade** n decenija**

decadent *a* dekadentan

decamp *v. i.* napustiti logor

decay *n.* raspadanje

decay *v. i* raspadati

decease *n* smrt

decease *v. i* preminuti

deceit *n* prevara

deceive *v. t* obmanuti

december *n* decembar

decency *n* pristojnost

decennary *n.* desetogodišnjica

decent *a* pristojan

deception *n* prevara

decide *v. t* odlučiti

decimal *a* decimal

decimate *v.t.* desetkovati

decision *n* odluka

decisive *a* odlučujući

deck *n* paluba

deck *v. t* ukrasiti

declaration *n* deklaracija

declare *v. t.* proglasiti

decline *n* propadanje

decline *v. t.* propadati

declivous *adj.* strm

decompose *v. t.* razložiti

decomposition *n.* rastavljanje

decontrol *v.t.* ukinuti ograničenje

decorate *v. t* ukrasiti

decoration *n* dekoracija

decorum *n* pristojnost

decrease *v. t* smanjiti

decrease *n* smanjenje

decree *n* dekret

decree *v. i* narediti

decrement *n.* opadanje

dedicate *v. t.* posvetiti

dedication *n* posveta

deduct *v.t.* odbiti

deed *n* delo

deem *v.i.* smatrati

deep *a.* duboko

deer *n* jelen

defamation *n* kleveta

defame *v. t.* klevetati

default *n.* prekršaj

defeat *n* poraz

defeat *v. t.* poraziti

defect *n* nedostatak

defence *n* odbrana

defend *v. t* braniti

defendant *n* optuženi

defensive *adv.* odbrambeno

deference *n* priklanjanje

defiance *n* prkos

deficit *n* deficit

deficient *adj.* nedovoljan

defile *n.* tesnac

define *v. t* definisati

definite *a* određen

definition *n* definicija

deflation *n.* deflacija

deflect *v.t. & i.* odvratiti

deft *adj.* spretan

degrade *v. t* degradirati

degree *n* stepen

dehort *v.i.* obeshrabriti

deist *n.* deist

deity *n.* božanstvo

deject *v. t* oneraspoložiti

dejection *n* utučenost

delay *v.t. & i.* odložiti

delibate *v.t.* gucnuti

deligate1 *n* vezivanje

delegate *v. t* delegat

delegation *n* delegacija

delete *v. t* izbrisati

deliberate *v. i* razmatrati

deliberate *a* nameran

deliberation *n* razmatranje

delicate *a* delikatan
delicious *a* ukusan
delight *n* uživanje
delight *v. t.* uživati
deliver *v. t* dostaviti
delivery *n* isporuka
delta *n* delta
delude *n.t.* obmanuti
delusion *n.* obmana
demand *n* zahtev
demand *v. t* zahtevati
demarcation *n.* razgraničenje
dement *v.t* izludeti
demerit *n* nedostatak
democracy *n* demokratija
democratic *a* demokratski
demolish *v. t.* demolirati
demon *n.* demon
demonetize *v.t.* demonetizirati
demonstrate *v. t* pokazati
demonstration *n.* pokazivanje
demoralize *v. t.* demoralisati
demur *n* oklevanje
demur *v. t* oklevati
demurrage *n.* prekoračenje
den *n* jazbina
dengue *n.* denga
denial *n* poricanje
denote *v. i* označavati
denounce *v. t* oglasiti
dense *a* gust
density *n* gustina
dentist *n* stomatolog
denude *v.t.* ogoliti
denunciation *n.* potkazivanje
deny *v. t.* poricati
depart *v. i.* otići
department *n* odeljenje
departure *n* odlazak
depauperate *v.t.* nedovoljno razviti

depend *v. i.* zavisiti
dependant *n* zavisnik
dependence *n* zavisnost
dependent *a* zavisan
depict *v. t.* prikazivati
deplorable *a* jadan
deploy *v.t.* pregrupisati
deponent *n.* svedok
deport *v.t.* deportovati
depose *v. t* svrgnuti
deposit *n.* depozit
deposit *v. t* založiti
depot *n* stovarište
depreciate *v.t.i.* obezvrediti
depredate *v.t.* opljačkati
depress *v. t* pritisnuti
depression *n* depresija
deprive *v. t* lišiti
depth *n* dubina
deputation *n* ovlašćenje
depute *v. t* ovlastiti
deputy *n* zamenik
derail *v. t.* izbaciti iz koloseka
derive *v. t.* izvesti
descend *v. i.* spuštati se
descendant *n* potomak
descent *n.* silazak
describe *v. t* opisati
description *n* opis
descriptive *a* opisni
desert *v. t.* napustiti
desert *n* pustinja
deserve *v. t.* zaslužiti
design *v. t.* dizajnirati
design *n.* dizajn
desirable *a* poželjan
desire *n* želja
desire *v.t* želeti
desirous *a* željan
desk *n radni* sto

despair *n* očajanje
despair *v. i* očajavati
desperate *a* očajan
despicable *a* dostojan prezira
despise *v. t* prezirati
despot *n* despot
destination *n* destinacija
destiny *n* sudbina
destroy *v. t* uništiti
destruction *n* razaranje
detach *v. t* odvojiti
detachment *n* odvajanje
detail *n* detalj
detail *v. t* detaljisati
detain *v. t* zadržati
detect *v. t* otkriti
detective *a* detektivski
detective *n.* detektiv
determination *n.* odlučnost
determine *v. t* odrediti
dethrone *v. t* zbaciti
develop *v. t.* razviti
development *n.* razvoj
deviate *v. i* odstupati
deviation *n* odstupanje
device *n* uređaj
devil *n* đavo
devise *v. t* izmisliti
devoid *a* lišen
devote *v. t* posvetiti
devotee *n* privrženik
devotion *n* privrženost
devour *v. t* proždirati
dew *n.* rosa
diabetes *n* dijabetes
diagnose *v. t* postaviti dijagnozu
diagnosis *n* dijagnoza
diagram *n* dijagram
dial *n.* brojčanik
dialect *n* dijalekt

dialogue *n* dijalog
diameter *n* prečnik
diamond *n* dijamant
diarrhoea *n* dijareja
diary *n* dnevnik
dice *n.* kocke
dice *v. i.* kockati se
dictate *v. t* diktirati
dictation *n* diktiranje
dictator *n* diktator
diction *n* dikcija
dictionary *n* rečnik
dictum *n* izreka
didactic *a* didaktički
die *v. i* umreti
die *n* umiranje
diet *n* dijeta
differ *v. i* razlikovati se
difference *n* razlika
different *a* različit
difficult *a* težak
difficulty *n* teškoća
dig *n* kopanje
dig *v.t.* kopati
digest *v. t.* svariti
digest *n.* pregled
digestion *n* varenje
digit *n* cifra
dignify *v.t* udostojiti
dignity *n* dostojanstvo
dilemma *n* dilema
diligence *n* marljivost
diligent *a* marljiv
dilute *v. t* razvodniti
dilute *a* razvodnjen
dim *a* nejasan
dim *v. t* potamneti
dimension *n* dimenzija
diminish *v. t* smanjiti
din *n* buka

dine *v. t.* večerati
dinner *n* večera
dip *n.* umakanje
dip *v. t* umočiti
diploma *n* diploma
diplomacy *n* diplomatija
diplomat *n* diplomata
diplomatic *a* diplomatski
dire *a* strašan
direct *a* direktan
direct *v. t* usmeriti
direction *n* pravac
director *n.* direktor
directory *n* direktorijum
dirt *n* nečistoća
dirty *a* prljav
disability *n* nesposobnost
disable *v. t* onesposobiti
disabled *a* nesposoban
disadvantage *n* nedostatak
disagree *v. i.* ne slagati se
disagreeable *a.* neprijatan
disagreement *n.* nesporazum
disappear *v. i* nestati
disappearance *n* nestanak
disappoint *v. t.* razočarati
disapproval *n* neodobravanje
disapprove *v. t* neodobravati
disarm *v. t* razoružati
disarmament *n.* razoružanje
disaster *n* katastrofa
disastrous *a* katastrofalan
disc *n.* disk
discard *v. t* odbaciti
discharge *v. t* prazniti
discharge *n.* pražnjenje
disciple *n* učenik
discipline *n* disciplina
disclose *v. t* otkriti
discomfort *n* nelagodnost

disconnect *v. t* isključiti
discontent *n* nezadovoljstvo
discontinue *v. t* prekinuti
discord *n* nesloga
discount *n* popust
discourage *v. t.* obeshrabriti
discourse *n* diskurs
discourteous *a* neučtiv
discover *v. t* otkriti
discovery *n.* otkriće
discretion *n* diskrecija
discriminate *v. t.* razlikovati
discrimination *n* diskriminacija
discuss *v. t.* diskutovati
disdain *n* prezir
disdain *v. t.* prezirati
disease *n* bolest
disguise *n* prerušen
disguise *v. t* prerušiti se
dish *n* jelo
dishearten *v. t* obeshrabriti
dishonest *a* nepošten
dishonesty *n.* nepoštenje
dishonour *v. t* osramotiti
dishonour *n* sramota
dislike *v. t.* ne voleti
dislike *n* antipatija
disloyal *a* nelojalan
dismiss *v. t.* odbaciti
dismissal *n.* otpuštanje
disobey *v. t.* biti neposlušan
disorder *n* poremećaj
disparity *n* nejednakost
dispensary *n* ambulanta
disperse *v. t* rasuti
displace *v. t* pomeriti
display *v. t* pokazati
display *n* pokazivanje
displease *v. t* ne sviđati se
displeasure *n* nezadovoljstvo

disposal *n* raspolaganje
dispose *v. t* raspolagati
disprove *v. t* opovrgnuti
dispute *n* spor
dispute *v. i* prepirati se
disqualification *n* diskvalifikacija
disqualify *v. t.* diskvalifikovati
disquiet *n* uznemirenost
disregard *n* potcenjivanje
disregard *v. t* potcenjivati
disrepute *n* ozloglašenost
disrespect *n* nepoštovanje
disrupt *v. t* prekinuti
dissatisfaction *n* nezadovoljstvo
dissatisfy *v. t.* ne zadovoljiti
dissect *v. t* secirati
dissection *n* seciranje
dissimilar *a* različit
dissolve *v. t* rastvoriti
dissuade *v. t* odvratiti
distance *n* rastojanje
distant *a* udaljen
distil *v. t* destilovati
distillery *n* destilerija
distinct *a* poseban
distinction *n* razlika
distinguish *v. i* razlikovati
distort *v. t* izobličiti
distress *n* bol
distress *v. t* ožalostiti
distribute *v. t* distribuirati
distribution *n* distribucija
district *n* okrug
distrust *n* nepoverenje
distrust *v. t.* sumnjati
disturb *v. t* uznemiravati
ditch *n* jarak
ditto *n.* isto
dive *v. i* roniti
dive *n* ronjenje

diverse *a* različit
divert *v. t* skrenuti
divide *v. t* podeliti
divine *a* božanski
divinity *n* božanstvenost
division *n* podela
divorce *n* razvod
divorce *v. t* razvesti
divulge *v. t* otkriti
do *v. t* činiti
docile *a* poslušan
dock *n.* pristanište
doctor *n* lekar
doctorate *n* doktorat
doctrine *n* doktrina
document *n* dokument
dodge *n* izmicanje
dodge *v. t* izmicati
doe *n* srna
dog *n* pas
dog *v. t* pratiti
dogma *n* dogma
dogmatic *a* dogmatski
doll *n* lutka
dollar *n* dolar
domain *n* domen
dome *n* kupola
domestic *a* domaći
domestic *n* posluga
domicile *n* prebivalište
dominant *a* dominantan
dominate *v. t* dominirati
domination *n* dominacija
dominion *n* vlast
donate *v. t* pokloniti
donation *n.* donacija
donkey *n* magarac
donor *n* davalac
doom *n* propast
doom *v. t.* osuditi

| | |
|---|---|
| **door** *n* vrata | **draught** *n* nacrt |
| **dose** *n* doza | **draw** *v.t* vući |
| **dot** *n* tačka | **draw** *n* izvlačenje |
| **dot** *v. t* istačkati | **drawback** *n* smetnja |
| **double** *a* dvostruko | **drawer** *n* fioka |
| **double** *v. t.* udvostručiti | **drawing** *n* crtanje |
| **double** *n* dvostrukost | **drawing-room** *n* salon |
| **doubt** *v. i* sumnjati | **dread** *n* strah |
| **doubt** *n* sumnja | **dread** *v.t* strahovati |
| **dough** *n* testo | **dread** *a* strašan |
| **dove** *n* golub | **dream** *n* san |
| **down** *adv* dole | **dream** *v. i.* sanjati |
| **down** *prep* niz | **drench** *v. t* pokvasiti |
| **down** *v. t* baciti | **dress** *n* haljina |
| **downfall** *n* slom | **dress** *v. t* oblačiti |
| **downpour** *n* pljusak | **dressing** *n* oblačenje |
| **downright** *adv* potpuno | **drill** *n* bušilica |
| **downright** *a* potpun | **drill** *v. t.* bušenje |
| **downward** *a* nagnut | **drink** *n* piće |
| **downward** *adv* nadole | **drink** *v. t* piti |
| **downwards** *adv* dole | **drip** *n* kapanje |
| **dowry** *n* miraz | **drip** *v. i* kapati |
| **doze** *n.* dremanje | **drive** *v. t* voziti |
| **doze** *v. i* dremati | **drive** *n* vožnja |
| **dozen** *n* tuce | **driver** *n* vozač |
| **draft** *v. t* skicirati | **drizzle** *n* izmaglica |
| **draft** *n* skica | **drizzle** *v. i* rominjati |
| **draftsman** *a* crtač | **drop** *n* kap |
| **drag** *n* povlačenje | **drop** *v. i* kapati |
| **drag** *v. t* povlačiti | **drought** *n* suša |
| **dragon** *n* zmaj | **drown** *v.i* utopiti |
| **drain** *n* odvod | **drug** *n* lek |
| **drain** *v. t* odvoditi | **druggist** *n* apotekar |
| **drainage** *n* drenaža | **drum** *n* bubanj |
| **dram** *n* gutljaj | **drum** *v.i.* udarati u bubanj |
| **drama** *n* drama | **drunkard** *n* pijanica |
| **dramatic** *a* dramatičan | **dry** *a* suvo |
| **dramatist** *n* dramaturg | **dry** *v. i.* osušiti |
| **draper** *n* suknar | **dual** *a* dvostruk |
| **drastic** *a* drastičan | **duck** *n.* patka |

duck *v.i.* zaroniti
due *a* dužan
due *n* dug
due *adv* tačno
duel *n* dvoboj
duel *v. i.* boriti se
duke *n* vojvoda
dull *a* tup
dull *v. t.* tupiti
duly *adv* propisno
dumb *a* glup
dunce *n* glupan
dung *n* đubre
duplicate *a* dvostruk
duplicate *n* duplikat
duplicate *v. t* udvostručiti
duplicity *n* dvoličnost
durable *a* izdržljiv
duration *n* trajanje
during *prep za* vreme
dusk *n* suton
dust *n* prašina
dust *v.t.* zaprašiti
duster *n* pajalica
dutiful *a* savestan
duty *n* dužnost
dwarf *n* patuljak
dwell *v. i* stanovati
dwelling *n* prebivalište
dwindle *v. t* nestajati
dye *v. t* bojiti
dye *n* boja
dynamic *a* dinamičan
dynamics *n.* dinamika
dynamite *n* dinamit
dynamo *n* generator
dynasty *n* dinastija
dysentery *n* dizenterija

# E

each *a* svaki
each *pron.* svaki
eager *a* željan
eagle *n* orao
ear *n* uvo
early *adv* ran
early *a* rano
earn *v. t* zaslužiti
earnest *a* ozbiljan
earth *n* zemlja
earthen *a* zemljan
earthly *a* zemaljski
earthquake *n* zemljotres
ease *n* jednostavnost
ease *v. t* pojednostaviti
east *n* istok
east *adv* istočno
east *a* istočni
easter *n* uskrs
eastern *a* istočni
easy *a* lako
eat *v. t* jesti
eatable *n.* jestivost
eatable *a* jestiv
ebb *n* oseka
ebb *v. i* opadati
ebony *n* abonos
echo *n* odjek
echo *v. t* odjekivati
eclipse *n* pomračenje
economic *a* ekonomski
economical *a* ekonomičan
economics *n.* ekonomija
economy *n* ekonomija
edge *n* ivica
edible *a* jestivo

edifice *n* građevina
edit *v. t* urediti
edition *n* izdanje
editor *n* urednik
editorial *a* urednički
editorial *n* uvodnik
educate *v. t* obrazovati
education *n* obrazovanje
efface *v. t* izbrisati
effect *n* efekat
effect *v. t* delovanje
effective *a* efikasan
effeminate *a* ženstven
efficacy *n* delotvornost
efficiency *n* efikasnost
efficient *a* efikasan
effigy *n* slika
effort *n* napor
egg *n* jaje
ego *n* ego
egotism *n* egoizam
eight *n* osam
eighteen *a* osamnaest
eighty *n* osamdeset
either *a.* oba
either *adv.* niti
eject *v. t.* izbaciti
elaborate *v. t* razraditi
elaborate *a* razrađen
elapse *v. t* prolaziti
elastic *a* elastičan
elbow *n* lakat
elder *a* stariji
elder *n* starešina
elderly *a* starije
elect *v. t* izabrati
election *n* izbor
electorate *n* biračko telo
electric *a* električni
electricity *n* elektricitet

electrify *v. t* naelektrisati
elegance *n* elegancija
elegant *adj* elegantan
elegy *n* elegija
element *n* element
elementary *a* elementarni
elephant *n* slon
elevate *v. t* podići
elevation *n* uzdignuće
eleven *n* jedanaest
elf *n* patuljak
eligible *a* poželjan
eliminate *v. t* eliminisati
elimination *n* eliminacija
elope *v. i* pobeći
eloquence *n* rečitost
eloquent *a* rečit
else *a* drugi
else *adv* drugo
elucidate *v. t* objasniti
elude *v. t* izbegavati
elusion *n* izbegavanje
elusive *a* nedostižan
emancipation *n.* emancipacija
embalm *v. t* balsamovati
embankment *n* nasip
embark *v. t* ukrcati
embarrass *v. t* posramiti
embassy *n* ambasada
embitter *v. t* zagorčati
emblem *n* amblem
embodiment *n* otelovljenje
embody *v. t.* otelotvoriti
embolden *v. t.* ohrabriti
embrace *v. t.* zagrliti
embrace *n* zagrljaj
embroidery *n* vez
embryo *n* embrion
emerald *n* smaragd
emerge *v. i* pojaviti se

emergency *n* hitan slučaj
eminence *n* eminencija
eminent *a* eminentni
emissary *n* izaslanik
emit *v. t* emitovati
emolument *n* prihod
emotion *n* emocija
emotional *a* emotivan
emperor *n* imperator
emphasis *n* naglasak
emphasize *v. t* naglasiti
emphatic *a* izrazit
empire *n* carstvo
employ *v. t* zaposliti
employee *n* službenik
employer *n* poslodavac
employment *n* zaposlenje
empower *v. t* osposobiti
empress *n* carica
empty *a* prazan
empty *v* prazniti
emulate *v. t* takmičiti se
enable *v. t* omogućiti
enact *v. t* ozakoniti
enamel *n* emajl
enamour *v. t* zaljubiti se
encase *v. t* spakovati
enchant *v. t* opčiniti
encircle *v. t.* okružiti
enclose *v. t* priložiti
enclosure *n.* prilog
encompass *v. t* opkoliti
encounter *n.* susret
encounter *v. t* susresti
encourage *v. t* ohrabriti
encroach *v. i* zadirati
encumber *v. t.* opteretiti
encyclopaedia *n.* enciklopedija
end *v. t* završiti
end *n.* kraj

endanger *v. t.* ugroziti
endear *v.t učiniti* dragim
endearment *n.* nežnost
endeavour *n* nastojanje
endeavour *v.i* nastojati
endorse *v. t.* odobriti
endow *v. t* obdariti
endurable *a* izdržljiv
endurance *n.* izdržljivost
endure *v.t.* izdržati
enemy *n* neprijatelj
energetic *a* energičan
energy *n.* energija
enfeeble *v. t.* oslabiti
enforce *v. t.* primeniti
enfranchise *v.t.* dati pravo glasa
engage *v. t* angažovati
engagement *n.* angažovanje
engine *n* motor
engineer *n* inženjer
English *n* engleski jezik, Englez
engrave *v. t* ugravirati
engross *v.t* zaokupiti
engulf *v.t* progutati
enigma *n* enigma
enjoy *v. t* uživati
enjoyment *n* uživanje
enlarge *v. t* uvećanje
enlighten *v. t.* prosvetliti
enlist *v. t* regrutovati
enliven *v. t.* oživeti
enmity *n* neprijateljstvo
ennoble *v. t.* oplemeniti
enormous *a* ogroman
enough *a* dovoljan
enough *adv* dovoljno
enrage *v. t* razbesneti
enrapture *v. t* ushititi
enrich *v. t* obogatiti
enrol *v. t* upisati

enshrine *v. t* zatvoriti u svetilište

enslave *v.t.* zarobiti

ensue *v.i* proizilaziti

ensure *v. t* obezbediti

entangle *v. t* upetljati

enter *v. t* ulaziti

enterprise *n* preduzeće

entertain *v. t* zabaviti

entertainment *n.* zabava

enthrone *v. t* ustoličiti

enthusiasm *n* entuzijazam

enthusiastic *a* oduševljen

entice *v. t.* namamiti

entire *a* čitav

entirely *adv* potpuno

entitle *v. t.* ovlastiti

entity *n* entitet

entomology *n.* entomologija

entrails *n.* utroba

entrance *n* ulaz

entrap *v. t.* zarobiti

entreat *v. t.* preklinjati

entreaty *n.* preklinjanje

entrust *v. t* poveriti

entry *n* ulazak

enumerate *v. t.* nabrajati

envelop *v. t* zamotati

envelope *n* koverat

enviable *a* zavidan

envious *a* zavidljiv

environment *n.* okruženje

envy *v* biti zavidan

envy *v. t* zavideti

epic *n* ep

epidemic *n* epidemija

epigram *n* epigram

epilepsy *n* epilepsija

epilogue *n* epilog

episode *n* epizoda

epitaph *n* epitaf

epoch *n* epoha

equal *a* jednako

equal *v. t* izjednačiti

equal *n* ravnopravnost

equality *n* jednakost

equalize *v. t.* izjednačiti

equate *v. t* uskladiti

equation *n* jednačina

equator *n* ekvator

equilateral *a* jednakostranični

equip *v. t* opremiti

equipment *n* oprema

equitable *a* pravedan

equivalent *a* ekvivalent

equivocal *a* dvosmislen

era *n* doba

eradicate *v. t* iskoreniti

erase *v. t* brisati

erect *v. t* uspraviti

erect *a* uspravljen

erection *n* erekcija

erode *v. t* erodirati

erosion *n* erozija

erotic *a* erotski

err *v. i* pogrešiti

errand *n* zadatak

erroneous *a* pogrešan

error *n* greška

erupt *v. i* buknuti

eruption *n* erupcija

escape *n* bekstvo

escape *v.i* pobeći

escort *n* pratnja

escort *v. t* pratiti

especial *a* poseban

essay *n.* esej

essay *v. t.* ustanoviti

essayist *n* esejista

essence *n* suština

essential *a* suštinski

establish *v. t.* uspostaviti
establishment *n* osnivanje
estate *n* imanje
esteem *n* poštovanje
esteem *v. t* poštovati
estimate *n.* procena
estimate *v. t* proceniti
estimation *n* procena
etcetera i tako dalje
eternal *adj.* večan
eternity *n* večnost
ether *n* etar
ethica *a* etički
ethics *i.* etika
etiquette *n* etiketa
etymology *n.* etimologija
eunuch *n* evnuh
evacuate *v. t* evakuisati
evacuation *n* evakuacija
evade *v. t* izbeći
evaluate *v. t* oceniti
evaporate *v. i* ispariti
evasion *n* izbegavanje
even *a* ravan
even *v. t* izravnati
even *adv* čak
evening *n* veče
event *n* događaj
eventually *adv.* konačno
ever *adv* ikad
evergreen *a* zimzelen
evergreen *n* evergrin
everlasting *a.* večan
every *a* svaki
evict *v. t* proterati
eviction *n* proterivanje
evidence *n* dokaz
evident *a.* očigledan
evil *n* zlo
evil *a* zao

evoke *v. t* evocirati
evolution *n* evolucija
evolve *v.t* evoluirati
ewe *n* ovca
exact *a* tačan
exaggerate *v. t.* preuveličavati
exaggeration *n.* preuveličavanje
exalt *v. t* veličati
examination *n.* ispitivanje
examine *v. t* ispitati
examinee *n* ispitanik
examiner *n* ispitivač
example *n* primer
excavate *v. t.* iskopavati
excavation *n.* iskopavanje
exceed *v.t* prekoračiti
excel *v.i* nadmašiti
excellence *n.* izvrsnost
excellency *n* ekselencija
excellent *a.* odličan
except *v. t* izuzeti
except *prep* osim
exception *n* izuzetak
excess *n* višak
excess *a* suvišan
exchange *n* razmena
exchange *v. t* razmeniti
excise *n* akciza
excite *v. t* uzbuditi
exclaim *v.i* uzviknuti
exclamation *n* uzvik
exclude *v. t* isključiti
exclusive *a* isključiv
excommunicate *v. t.* ekskomunicirati
excursion *n.* ekskurzija
excuse *v.t* opravdati
excuse *n* izgovor
execute *v. t* izvršiti
execution *n* izvršenje
executioner *n.* izvršilac

exempt *v. t.* osloboditi
exempt *adj.* oslobođen
exercise *n.* vežba
exercise *v. t* vežbati
exhaust *v. t.* izduvati
exhibit *n.* eksponat
exhibit *v. t* izložiti
exhibition *n.* Izložba
exile *n.* progonstvo
exile *v. t* prognati
exist *v.i* postojati
existence *n* postojanje
exit *n.* izlaz
expand *v.t.* proširiti
expansion *n.* proširenje
ex-parte *a* jednostran
ex-parte *adv* jednostrano
expect *v. t* očekivati
expectation *n.* očekivanje
expedient *a* prikladan
expedite *v. t.* požuriti
expedition *n* ekspedicija
expel *v. t.* isključiti
expend *v. t* potrošiti
expenditure *n* rashod
expense *n.* trošak
expensive *a* skup
experience *n* iskustvo
experience *v. t.* iskusiti
experiment *n* eksperiment
expert *a* stručan
expert *n* stručnjak
expire *v.i.* isteći
expiry *n* istek
explain *v. t.* objasniti
explanation *n* objašnjenje
explicit *a.* eksplicitan
explode *v. t.* eksplodirati
exploit *n* eksploatacija
exploit *v. t* eksploatisati

exploration *n* istraživanje
explore *v.t* istražiti
explosion *n.* eksplozija
explosive *n.* eksploziv
explosive *a* eksplozivan
exponent *n* tumač
export *n* izvoz
export *v. t.* izvoziti
expose *v. t* izložiti
express *v. t.* izraziti
express *a* određen
express *n* ekspres
expression *n.* izraz
expressive *a.* izražajan
expulsion *n.* isključenje
extend *v. t* proširiti
extent *n.* obim
external *a* spoljni
extinct *a* izumro
extinguish *v.t* ugasiti
extol *v. t.* veličati
extra *a* dodatni
extra *adv* ekstra
extract *n* ekstrakt
extract *v. t* izdvojiti
extraordinary *a.* izvanredan
extravagance *n* ekstravagancija
extravagant *a* ekstravagantan
extreme *a* ekstreman
extreme *n* ekstrem
extremist *n* ekstremista
exult *v. i* likovati
eye *n* oko
eyeball *n* očna jabučica
eyelash *n* trepavica
eyelet *n* rupica
eyewash *n* prevara

# F

fable  n.  basna
fabric  n  tkanina
fabricate  v.t  proizvoditi
fabrication  n  proizvodnja
fabulous  a  neverovatan
facade  n  fasada
face  n  lice
face  v.t  suočiti se
facet  n  aspekt
facial  a  lični
facile  a  lak
facilitate  v.t  olakšati
facility  n  postrojenje
facsimile  n  faksimil
fact  n  činjenica
faction  n  frakcija
factious  a  stranački
factor  n  faktor
factory  n  fabrika
faculty  n  fakultet
fad  n  hir
fade  v.i  izbledeti
faggot  n  naramak pruća
fail  v.i ne  uspeti
failure  n  neuspeh
faint  a  slab
faint  v.i  onesvestiti se
fair  a  lep
fair  n.  sajam
fairly  adv.  pošteno
fairy  n  vila
faith  n  vera
faithful  a  veran
falcon  n  soko
fall  v.i.  pasti
fall  n  jesen

fallacy  n  zabluda
fallow  n  ugar
false  a  lažan
falter  v.i  posrnuti
fame  n  slava
familiar  a  poznat
family  n  porodica
famine  n  glad
famous  a  poznat
fan  n  blag vetar
fanatic  a  fanatičan
fanatic  n  fanatik
fancy  n  mašta
fancy  v.t  zamisliti
fantastic  a  fantastičan
far  adv.  daleko
far  a  dalek
far  n  daljina
farce  n  farsa
fare n  karta
farewell  n  oproštaj
farewell  interj.  zbogom
farm  n  farma
farmer  n  poljoprivrednik
fascinate  v.t  fascinirati
fascination  n.  fascinacija
fashion  n  moda
fashionable  a  moderan
fast  a  brz
fast  adv  brzo
fast  n  post
fast  v.i  postiti
fasten v.t  pričvrstiti
fat  a  gojazan
fat  n  mast
fatal  a  fatalan
fate  n  sudbina
father  n  otac
fathom  v.t  proniknuti
fathom  n  hvat

fatigue *n* umor
fatigue *v.t* umarati
fault *n* greška
faulty *a* neispravan
fauna *n* fauna
favour1 *n* naklonost
favour *v.t* pomagati
favourable *a* povoljan
favourite *a* omiljen
favourite *n* favorit
fear *n* strah
fear *v.i.* plašiti se
fearful *a.* strašno
feasible *a* izvodljiv
feast *n* gozba
feast *v.i* gostiti se
feat *n* podvig
feather *n* pero
feature *n* odlika
February *n* februar
federal *a* federalni
federation *n* federacija
fee *n* honorar
feeble *a* slab
feed *v.t* hraniti
feed *n* hranjenje
feel *v.t* osećati
feeling *n* osećaj
feign *v.t* pretvarati se
felicitate *v.t* čestitati
felicity *n* blaženstvo
fell *v.t* pasti
fellow *n* kolega
female *a* ženski
female *n* žena
feminine *a.* ženskog roda
fence *n* ograda
fence *v.t* ograditi
fend *v.t braniti* se
ferment *n* kvasac

ferment *v.t* ključati
fermentation *n* fermentacija
ferocious *a* svirep
ferry *n* trajekt
ferry *v.t* prevoziti
fertile *a* plodan
fertility *n* plodnost
fertilize *v.t* oploditi
fertilizer *n* đubrivo
fervent *a* vatren
fervour *n* žestina
festival *n* festival
festive *a* svečan
festivity *n* svečanost
festoon *n* venac
fetch *v.t* doneti
fetter *n* karika
fetter *v.t* sputati
feud *n.* zavada
feudal *a* feudalni
fever *n* groznica
few *a* malo
fiasco *n* fijasko
fibre *n* vlakno
fickle *a* promenljiv
fiction *n* fikcija
fictitious *a* fiktivan
fiddle *n* violina
fiddle *v.i* guditi
fidelity *n* vernost
fie *interj* fuj
field *n* polje
fiend *n* đavo
fierce *a* žestok
fiery *a* užaren
fifteen *n* petnaest
fifty *n.* pedeset
fig *n* smokva
fight *n* borba
fight *v.t* boriti se

**figment** *n* izmišljotina
**figurative** *a* figurativan
**figure** *n* figura
**figure** *v.t* uobličiti
**file** *n* arhiva
**file** *v.t* arhivirati
**file** *n* fascikla
**file** *v.t* ubeležiti
**file** *n* dosije
**file** *v.i.* nizati
**fill** *v.t* popuniti
**film** *n* film
**film** *v.t* snimati
**filter** *n* filter
**filter** *v.t* čistiti
**filth** *n* nečistoća
**filthy** *a* prljav
**fin** *n* peraje
**final** *a* konačan
**finance** *n* finansije
**finance** *v.t* finansirati
**financial** *a* finansijski
**financier** *n* finansijer
**find** *v.t* kazniti
**fine** *n* kazna
**fine** *v.t* čistiti
**fine** *a* dobar
**finger** *n* prst
**finger** *v.t* dodirivati
**finish** *v.t* završiti
**finish** *n* završetak
**finite** *a* konačan
**fir** *n* jela
**fire** *n* vatra
**fire** *v.t* zapaliti
**firm** *a* čvrst
**firm** *n.* firma
**first** *a* prvi
**first** *n* prvi
**first** *adv* prvo

**fiscal** *a* fiskalni
**fish** *n* riba
**fish** *v.i* pecati
**fisherman** *n* ribar
**fissure** *n* pukotina
**fist** *n* pesnica
**fistula** *n* fistula
**fit** *v.t* podesiti
**fit** prikladan
**fit** *n* napad
**fitful** *a* grčevit
**fitter** *n* monter
**five** *n* pet
**fix** *v.t* popraviti
**fix** *n* neprilika
**flabby** *a* mlitav
**flag** *n* zastava
**flagrant** *a* sramotan
**flame** *n* plamen
**flame** *v.i* plamteti
**flannel** *n* flanel
**flare** *v.i* planuti
**flare** *n* blesak
**flash** *n* blic
**flash** *v.t* zasijati
**flask** *n* pljoska
**flat** *a* ravan
**flat** *n* ravnina
**flatter** *v.t* laskati
**flattery** *n* laskanje
**flavour** *n* ukus
**flaw** *n* mana
**flea** *n.* buva
**flee** *v.i* pobeći
**fleece** *n* runo
**fleece** *v.t* ošišati
**fleet** *n* flota
**flesh** *n* meso
**flexible** *a* fleksibilan
**flicker** *n* treperenje

flicker *v.t* treperiti
flight *n* let
flimsy *a* tanak
fling *v.t* baciti
flippancy *n* lakomislenost
flirt *n* flertovanje
flirt *v.i* flertovati
float *v.i* ploviti
flock *n* stado
flock *v.i* gomilati
flog *v.t* šibati
flood *n* poplava
flood *v.t* poplaviti
floor *n* pod
floor *v.t* popločati
flora *n* flora
florist *n* cvećar
flour *n* brašno
flourish *v.i* cvetati
flow *n* protok
flow *v.i* teći
flower *n* cvet
flowery *a* cvetni
fluent *a* tečan
fluid *a* tekući
fluid *n* tečnost
flush *v.i* sprati
flush *n* rumenilo
flute *n* flauta
flute *v.i* svirati flautu
flutter *n* lepršanje
flutter *v.t* lepršati
fly *n* muva
fly *v.i* leteti
foam *n* pena
foam *v.t* peniti se
focal *a* žarišni
focus *n* fokus
focus *v.t* izoštriti
fodder *n* stočna hrana

foe *n* neprijatelj
fog *n* magla
foil *v.t* folija
fold *n* nabor
fold *v.t* saviti
foliage *n* lišće
follow *v.t* pratiti
follower *n* sledbenik
folly *n* glupost
foment *v.t* izazivati
fond *a* naklonjen
fondle *v.t* milovati
food *n* hrana
fool *n* budala
foolish *a* budalast
foolscap *n* tabak za pisanje
foot *n* stopalo
for *prep* za
for *conj.* jer
forbid *v.t* zabraniti
force *n* sila
force *v.t* siliti
forceful *a* snažan
forcible *a* prisilan
forearm *n* podlaktica
forearm *v.t* unapred oružati
forecast *n* predviđanje
forecast *v.t* predviđati
forefather *n* praotac
forefinger *n* kažiprst
forehead *n* čelo
foreign *a* strani
foreigner *n* stranac
foreknowledge *n.* predviđanje
foreleg *n* prednja noga
forelock *n* uvojak
foreman *n* nadzornik
foremost *a* prednji
forenoon *n* pre podne
forerunner *n* prethodnik

**foresee** *v.t* predvideti
**foresight** *n* predviđanje
**forest** *n* šuma
**forestall** *v.t* preduhitriti
**forester** *n* šumar
**forestry** *n* šumarstvo
**foretell** *v.t* proreći
**forethought** *n* promišljenost
**forever** *adv* zauvek
**forewarn** *v.t* upozoriti
**foreword** *n* predgovor
**forfeit** *v.t* izgubiti
**forfeit** *n* gubitak
**forfeiture** *n* gubitak prava
**forge** *n* kovačnica
**forge** *v.t* falsifikovati
**forgery** *n* falsifikat
**forget** *v.t* zaboraviti
**forgetful** *a* zaboravan
**forgive** *v.t* oprostiti
**forgo** *v.t* odreći se
**forlorn** *a* usamljen
**form** *n* forma
**form** *v.t.* formirati
**formal** *a* formalan
**format** *n* format
**formation** *n.* formacija
**former** *a* prethodni
**former** *pron* bivši
**formerly** *adv* ranije
**formidable** *a* znatan
**formula** *n* formula
**formulate** *v.t* formulisati
**forsake** *v.t.* napustiti
**forswear** *v.t.* prekršiti zakletvu
**fort** *n.* utvrđenje
**forte** *n. jaka* tačka
**forth** *adv.* napred
**forthcoming** *a.* predstojeći
**forthwith** *adv.* odmah

**fortify** *v.t.* utvrditi
**fortitude** *n.* hrabrost
**fort-night** *n.* dve nedelje
**fortress** *n.* tvrđava
**fortunate** *a.* srećan
**fortune** *n.* sreća
**forty** *n.* četrdeset
**forum** *n.* forum
**forward** *a.* prednji
**forward** *adv* napred
**forward** *v.t* poslati
**fossil** *n.* fosil
**foster** *v.t.* odgajati
**foul** *a.* prekršaj
**found** *v.t.* utemeljiti
**foundation** *n.* utemeljenje
**founder** *n.* osnivač
**foundry** *n.* livnica
**fountain** *n.* fontana
**four** *n.* četiri
**fourteen** *n.* četrnaest
**fowl** *n.* živina
**fowler** *n.* ptičar
**fox** *n.* lisica
**fraction** *n.* frakcija
**fracture** *n.* prelom
**fracture** *v.t* polomiti
**fragile** *a.* krhak
**fragment** *n.* fragment
**fragrance** *n.* miris
**fragrant** *a.* mirisan
**frail** *a.* slab
**frame** *v.t.* uramiti
**frame** *n* okvir
**frachise** *n.* franšiza
**frank** *a.* iskren
**frantic** *a.* pomaman
**fraternal** *a.* bratski
**fraternity** *n.* bratstvo
**fratricide** *n.* bratoubistvo

fraud *n.* prevara
fraudulent *a.* nepošten
fraught *a.* ispunjen
fray *n* tuča
free *a.* slobodan
free *v.t* osloboditi
freedom *n.* sloboda
freeze *v.i.* zamrznuti
freight *n.* tovar
French *a.* francuski
French *n.* francuski jezik, Francuz
frenzy *n.* pomama
frequency *n.* frekvencija
frequent *n.* učestalost
fresh *a.* svež
fret *n.* uzrujanost
fret *v.t.* uzrujati se
friction *n.* trenje
Friday *n.* petak
fridge *n.* frižider
friend *n.* prijatelj
fright *n.* strah
frighten *v.t.* uplašiti
frigid *a.* frigidan
frill *n.* nabor
fringe *n.* resa
fringe *v.t* obrubiti
frivolous *a.* neozbiljan
frock *n.* haljina
frog *n.* žaba
frolic *n.* zabava
frolic *v.i.* veseliti se
from *prep.* od
front *n.* front
front *a* prednji
front *v.t* gledati
frontier *n.* granica
frost *n.* mraz
frown *n.* mrštenje
frown *v.i.* mrštiti se

frugal *a.* štedljiv
fruit *n.* voće
fruitful *a.* plodan
frustrate *v.t.* frustrirati
frustration *n.* frustracija
fry *v.t.* pržiti
fry *n* ikra
fuel *n.* gorivo
fugitive *a.* odbegao
fugitive *n.* begunac
fulfil *v.t.* ispuniti
fulfilment *n.* ispunjenje
full *a.* pun
full *adv.* puno
fullness *n.* punoća
fully *adv.* potpuno
fumble *v.i.* preturati
fun *n.* zabava
function *n.* funkcija
function *v.i* funkcionisati
functionary *n.* funkcioner
fund *n.* fond
fundamental *a.* osnovni
funeral *n.* sahrana
fungus *n.* gljiva
funny *n.* smešan
fur *n.* krzno
furious *a.* besan
furl *v.t.* smotati
furlong *n.* osmina milje
furnace *n.* peć
furnish *v.t.* opremiti
furniture *n.* nameštaj
furrow *n.* brazda
further *adv.* dalje
further *a* dalji
further *v.t* unaprediti
fury *n.* bes
fuse *v.t.* rastopiti
fuse *n* osigurač

fusion *n.* fuzija
fuss *n.* komešanje
fuss *v.i.* uznemiriti se
futile *a.* uzaludan
futility *n.* uzaludnost
future *a.* budući
future *n* budućnost

# G

gabble *v.i.* blebetati
gadfly *n.* obad
gag *v.t. geg,* čep
gag *n.* začepiti
gaiety *n.* veselost
gain *v.t.* dobiti
gain *n* dobit
gainsay *v.t.* poricati
gait *n.* hod
galaxy *n.* galaksija
gale *n.* oluja
gallant *a.* galantan
gallant *n* kavaljer
gallantry *n.* hrabrost
gallery *n.* galerija
gallon *n.* galon
gallop *n.* galop
gallop *v.t.* galopirati
gallows *n.* . vešala
galore *adv.* u izobilju
galvanize *v.t.* podstaći
gamble *v.i.* kockati se
gamble *n* kockanje
gambler *n.* kockar
game *n.* igra
game *v.i* igrati
gander *n.* glupan
gang *n.* banda
gangster *n.* gangster

gap *n* pukotina
gape *v.i.* zevati
garage *n.* garaža
garb *n.* odeća
garb *v.t* obući
garbage *n.* smeće
garden *n.* bašta
gardener *n.* baštovan
gargle *v.i.* ispirati grlo
garland *n.* venac
garland *v.t.* ovenčati
garlic *n. beli* luk
garment *n.* odeća
garter *n.* podvezica
gas *n.* gas
gasket *n.* zaptivač
gasp *n.* dahtanje
gasp *v.i* dahtati
gassy *a.* gasni
gastric *a.* želudačni
gate *n.* kapija
gather *v.t.* okupiti
gaudy *a.* kitnjast
gauge *n.* kolosek
gauntlet *n.* oklopna rukavica
gay *a.* veseo
gaze *v.t.* zuriti
gaze *n* zurenje
gazette *n.* novine
gear *n.* oprema
geld *v.t.* kastrirati
gem *n* dragulj
gender *n.* pol
general *a.* opšti
generally *adv.* uglavnom
generate *v.t.* generisati
generation *n.* generacija
generator *n.* generator
generosity *n.* velikodušnost
generous *a.* velikodušan

**genius** *n.* genije
**gentle** *a.* nežno
**gentleman** *n.* gospodin
**gentry** *n.* *niže* plemstvo
**genuine** *a.* pravi
**geographer** *n.* geograf
**geographical** *a.* geografski
**geography** *n.* geografija
**geological** *a.* geološki
**geologist** *n.* geolog
**geology** *n.* geologija
**geometrical** *a.* geometrijski
**geometry** *n.* geometrija
**germ** *n.* klica
**germicide** *n.* germicid
**germinate** *v.i.* klijati
**germination** *n.* klijanje
**gerund** *n.* gerund
**gesture** *n.* gest
**get** *v.t.* dobiti
**ghastly** *a.* jeziv
**ghost** *n.* duh
**giant** *n.* džin
**gibbon** *n.* gibon
**gibe** *v.i.* rugati se
**gibe** *n* ruganje
**giddy** *a.* vrtoglav
**gift** *n.* poklon
**gifted** *a.* nadaren
**gigantic** *a.* gigantski
**giggle** *v.i.* kikotati se
**gild** *v.t.* pozlatiti
**gilt** *a.* pozlata
**ginger** *n.* đumbir
**giraffe** *n.* žirafa
**gird** *v.t.* opasati
**girder** *n.* nosač
**girdle** *n.* pojas
**girdle** *v.t* opasivati
**girl** *n.* devojka

**girlish** *a.* devojački
**gist** *n.* suština
**give** *v.t.* dati
**glacier** *n.* glečer
**glad** *a.* radostan
**gladden** *v.t.* obradovati
**glamour** *n.* blistavost
**glance** *n.* pogled
**glance** *v.i.* pogledati
**gland** *n.* žlezda
**glare** *n.* bleštanje
**glare** *v.i* bleštati
**glass** *n.* staklo
**glaucoma** *n.* glaukom
**glaze** *v.t.* glačati
**glaze** *n* glazura
**glazier** *n.* staklorezac
**glee** *n.* radost
**glide** *v.t.* kliziti
**glider** *n.* jedrilica
**glimpse** *n.* letimičan pogled
**glitter** *v.i.* sijati
**glitter** *n* sjaj
**global** *a.* globalni
**globe** *n.* svet
**gloom** *n.* sumornost
**gloomy** *a.* sumoran
**glorification** *n.* slavljenje
**glorify** *v.t.* veličati
**glorious** *a.* slavan
**glory** *n.* slava
**gloss** *n.* sjaj
**glossary** *n.* glosar
**glossy** *a.* sjajan
**glove** *n.* rukavica
**glow** *v.i.* sijati
**glow** *n* sjaj
**glucose** *n.* glukoza
**glue** *n.* lepak
**glut** *v.t.* prezasititi

**glut** *n* prezasićenost
**glutton** *n*. proždrljivac
**gluttony** *n*. proždrljivost
**glycerine** *n*. glicerin
**go** *v.i.* ići
**goad** *n*. podsticaj
**goad** *v.t* podsticati
**goal** *n*. cilj
**goat** *n*. koza
**gobble** *n*. uterivanje u rupu
**goblet** *n*. pehar
**god** *n*. Bog
**goddess** *n*. boginja
**godhead** *n*. božanstvo
**godly** *a*. božji
**godown** *n*. skladište
**godsend** *n*. neočekivana sreća
**goggles** *n*. zaštitne naočare
**gold** *n*. zlato
**golden** *a*. zlatan
**goldsmith** *n*. zlatar
**golf** *n*. *golf,* zaliv
**gong** *n*. gong
**good** *a*. dobar
**good** *n* valjanost
**good-bye** *interj.* zbogom
**goodness** *n*. dobrota
**goodwill** *n*. dobra volja
**goose** *n*. guska
**gooseberry** *n*. ogrozd
**gorgeous** *a*. divan
**gorilla** *n*. gorila
**gospel** *n*. jevanđelje
**gossip** *n*. ogovaranje
**gourd** *n*. tikva
**gout** *n*. giht
**govern** *v.t.* upravljati
**governance** *n*. uprava
**governess** *n*. guvernanta
**government** *n*. Vlada

**governor** *n*. guverner
**gown** *n*. haljina
**grab** *v.t.* zgrabiti
**grace** *n*. milost
**grace** *v.t.* ukrasiti
**gracious** *a*. milostiv
**gradation** *n*. gradacija
**grade** *n*. razred
**grade** *v.t* oceniti
**gradual** *a*. postepen
**graduate** *v.i.* diplomirati
**graduate** *n* diplomirani đak/student
**graft** *n*. kalem
**graft** *v.t* kalemiti
**grain** *n*. zrno
**grammar** *n*. gramatika
**grammarian** *n*. gramatičar
**gramme** *n*. gram
**gramophone** *n*. gramofon
**granary** *n*. ambar
**grand** *a*. velik
**grandeur** *n*. veličanstvenost
**grant** *v.t.* odobriti
**grant** *n* odobrenje
**grape** *n*. grožđe
**graph** *n*. grafikon
**graphic** *a*. grafički
**grapple** *n*. rvanje
**grapple** *v.i.* rvati se
**grasp** *v.t.* sčepati
**grasp** *n* zahvat
**grass** *n* trava
**grate** *n*. rešetka
**grate** *v.t* strugati
**grateful** *a*. zahvalan
**gratification** *n*. zadovoljstvo
**gratis** *adv*. besplatno
**gratitude** *n*. zahvalnost
**gratuity** *n*. napojnica
**grave** *n*. grob

grave *a.* ozbiljan
gravitate *v.i.* težiti ka
gravitation *n.* gravitacija
gravity *n.* ozbiljnost
graze *v.i.* pasti
graze *n lagan* dodir
grease *n* mast
grease *v.t* podmazati
greasy *a.* mastan
great *a* velik
greed *n.* pohlepa
greedy *a.* pohlepan
Greek *n.* grčki jezik, Grk
Greek *a* grčki
green *a.* zelen
green *n* zelena boja
greenery *n.* zelenilo
greet *v.t.* pozdraviti
grenade *n.* granata
grey *a.* siva
greyhound *n.* hrt
grief *n.* žalost
grievance *n.* tuga
grieve *v.t.* tugovati
grievous *a.* žalostan
grind *v.i.* mleti
grinder *n.* mlin
grip *v.t.* stisnuti
grip *n* stisak
groan *v.i.* stenjanje
groan *n* stenjati
grocer *n.* bakalin
grocery *n.* bakalnica
groom *n.* mladoženja
groom *v.t* timariti
groove *n.* žleb
groove *v.t* užlebiti
grope *v.t.* pipati
gross *n.* bruto
gross *a* težak

grotesque *a.* groteskan
ground *n.* tlo
group *n.* grupa
group *v.t.* grupisati
grow *v.t.* rasti
grower *n.* uzgajivač
growl *v.i.* režati
growl *n* režanje
growth *n.* rast
grudge *v.t.* gunđati
grudge *n* zavidnik
grumble *v.i.* zanovetati
grunt *n.* roktati
grunt *v.i.* roktanje
guarantee *n.* garancija
guarantee *v.t* garantovati
guard *v.i.* čuvati
guard *n.* stražar
guardian *n.* čuvar
guerilla *n.* gerila
guess *n.* pretpostavka
guess *v.i* pretpostaviti
guest *n.* gost
guidance *n.* vođstvo
guide *v.t.* voditi
guide *n.* vodič
guild *n.* esnaf
guile *n.* lukavstvo
guilt *n.* krivica
guilty *a.* kriv
guise *n.* izgled
guitar *n.* gitara
gulf *n.* zaliv
gull *n.* galeb
gull *n* glupan
gull *v.t* nadmudriti
gulp *n.* gutljaj
gum *n.* guma
gun *n.* vatreno oružje
gust *n.* nalet

gutter *n.* oluk
guttural *a.* grlen
gymnasium *n.* gimnazija
gymnast *n.* gimnastičar
gymnastic *a.* gimnastički
gymnastics *n.* gimnastika

# H

habit *n.* navika
habitable *a.* pogodan za stanovanje
habitat *n.* stanište
habitation *n.* stanovanje
habituate *v. t.* naviknuti
hack *v.t.* pijuk
hag *n.* veštica
haggard *a.* unezveren
haggle *v.i.* iseckati
hail *n.* grad
hail *v.i* padati
hail *v.t* pozdraviti
hair *n* kosa
hale *a.* čio
half *n.* polovina
half *a* pola
hall *n.* hol
hallmark *n.* žig
hallow *v.t.* posvetiti
halt *v. t.* oklevati
halt *n* zastoj
halve *v.t.* prepoloviti
hamlet *n.* seoce
hammer *n.* čekić
hammer *v.t* čekićati
hand *n* šaka
hand *v.t* uručiti
handbill *n.* oglas
handbook *n.* priručnik
handcuff *n.* lisice

handcuff *v.t* staviti lisice
handful *n.* pregršt
handicap *v.t.* hendikepirati
handicap *n* hendikep
handicraft *n.* rukotvorina
handiwork *n.* ručni rad
handkerchief *n.* maramica
handle *n.* ručka
handle *v.t* rukovati
handsome *a.* zgodan
handy *a.* pogodan
hang *v.t.* obesiti
hanker *v.i.* žudeti
haphazard *a.* slučajan
happen *v.t.* desiti
happening *n.* događaj
happiness *n.* sreća
happy *a.* srećan
harass *v.t.* uznemiravati
harassment *n.* uznemiravanje
harbour *n.* luka
harbour *v.t* pružiti utočište
hard *a.* težak
harden *v.t.* stvrdnuti
hardihood *n.* hrabrost
hardly *adv.* jedva
hardship *n.* teškoća
hardy *adj.* izdržljiv
hare *n.* zec
harm *n.* šteta
harm *v.t* oštetiti
harmonious *a.* harmoničan
harmonium *n.* harmonijum
harmony *n.* harmonija
harness *n.* am
harness *v.t* upregnuti
harp *n.* harfa
harsh *a.* grub
harvest *n.* žetva
haverster *n.* žetelac

haste *n.* žurba
hasten *v.i.* ubrzati
hasty *a.* užurban
hat *n.* šešir
hatchet *n.* sekira
hate *n.* mržnja
hate *v.t.* mrzeti
haughty *a.* ohol
haunt *v.t.* progoniti
haunt *n* utočište
have *v.t.* imati
haven *n.* luka
havoc *n.* pustoš
hawk *n* jastreb
hawker *n* sokolar
hawthorn *n.* glog
hay *n.* seno
hazard *n.* rizik
hazard *v.t* rizikovati
haze *n.* izmaglica
hazy *a.* maglovit
he *pron.* on
head *n.* glava
head *v.t* voditi
headache *n.* glavobolja
heading *n.* naslov
headlong *adv.* strmoglav
headstrong *a.* tvrdoglav
heal *v.i.* lečiti
health *n.* zdravlje
healthy *a.* zdrav
heap *n.* gomila
heap *v.t* gomilati
hear *v.t.* čuti
hearsay *n.* rekla-kazala
heart *n.* srce
hearth *n.* ognjište
heartily *adv.* srdačno
heat *n.* toplota
heat *v.t* zagrejati

heave *v.i.* dignuti
heaven *n.* nebo
heavenly *a.* nebeski
hedge *n.* živa ograda
hedge *v.t* ograditi
heed *v.t.* paziti
heed *n* pažnja
heel *n.* peta
hefty *a.* snažan
height *n.* visina
heighten *v.t.* povisiti
heinous *a.* gnusan
heir *n.* naslednik
hell *a.* pakao
helm *n.* kormilo
helmet *n.* kaciga
help *v.t.* pomoći
help *n* pomoć
helpful *a.* koristan
helpless *a.* bespomoćan
helpmate *n.* pomoćnik
hemisphere *n.* hemisfera
hemp *n.* konoplja
hen *n.* kokoška
hence *adv.* otud
henceforth *adv.* od sada
henceforward *adv.* ubuduće
henchman *n.* sledbenik
henpecked *a.* papučar
her *pron.* njoj
her *a* njen
herald *n.* glasnik
herald *v.t* najaviti
herb *n.* biljka
herculean *a.* herkulski
herd *n.* stado
herdsman *n.* pastir
here *adv.* ovde
hereabouts *adv.* ovde u okolini
hereafter *adv.* od sada

| | |
|---|---|
| **hereditary** *n.* nasleđenost | **his** *pron.* njegov |
| **heredity** *n.* naslednost | **hiss** *n* siktanje |
| **heritable** *a.* nasledan | **hiss** *v.i* siktati |
| **heritage** *n.* nasleđe | **historian** *n.* istoričar |
| **hermit** *n.* pustinjak | **historic** *a.* istorijski |
| **hermitage** *n.* pustinjačka ćelija | **historical** *a.* istorijski |
| **hernia** *n.* hernija | **history** *n.* istorija |
| **hero** *n.* heroj | **hit** *v.t.* pogoditi |
| **heroic** *a.* herojski | **hit** *n* pogodak |
| **heroine** *n.* heroina | **hitch** *n.* zapreka |
| **heroism** *n.* junaštvo | **hither** *adv.* ovamo |
| **herring** *n.* haringa | **hitherto** *adv.* do sada |
| **hesitant** *a.* neodlučan | **hive** *n.* košnica |
| **hesitate** *v.i.* oklevati | **hoarse** *a.* promukao |
| **hesitation** *n.* oklevanje | **hoax** *n.* podvala |
| **hew** *v.t.* tesati | **hoax** *v.t* podvaliti |
| **heyday** *n.* vrhunac | **hobby** *n.* hobi |
| **hibernation** *n.* hibernacija | **hobby-horse** *n.* drveni konjić |
| **hiccup** *n.* štucanje | **hockey** *n.* hokej |
| **hide** *n.* sakrivanje | **hoist** *v.t.* dizati |
| **hide** *v.t* sakriti | **hold** *n.* držanje |
| **hideous** *a.* odvratan | **hold** *v.t* držati |
| **hierarchy** *n.* hijerarhija | **hole** *n* rupa |
| **high** *a.* visok | **hole** *v.t* probušiti |
| **highly** *adv.* visoko | **holiday** *n.* odmor |
| **Highness** *n.* Visost | **hollow** *a.* šupalj |
| **highway** *n.* autoput | **hollow** *n.* šupljina |
| **hilarious** *a.* smešan | **hollow** *v.t* izdupsti |
| **hilarity** *n.* veselje | **holocaust** *n.* holokaust |
| **hill** *n.* brdo | **holy** *a.* sveti |
| **hillock** *n.* breg | **homage** *n.* omaž |
| **him** *pron.* njega | **home** *n.* dom |
| **hinder** *v.t.* ometati | **homicide** *n.* ubistvo |
| **hindrance** *n.* prepreka | **homoeopath** *n.* homeopata |
| **hint** *n.* nagoveštaj | **homeopathy** *n.* homeopatija |
| **hint** *v.i* nagovestiti | **homogeneous** *a.* homogen |
| **hip** *n* kuk | **honest** *a.* pošten |
| **hire** *n.* najam | **honesty** *n.* poštenje |
| **hire** *v.t* zaposliti | **honey** *n.* med |
| **hireling** *n.* najamnik | **honeycomb** *n.* saće |

honeymoon *n.* medeni mesec
honorarium *n.* honorar
honorary *a.* počasni
honour *n.* čast
honour *v. t* poštovati
honourable *a.* častan
hood *n.* hauba
hoodwink *v.t.* prevariti
hoof *n.* kopito
hook *n.* kuka
hooligan *n.* huligan
hoot *n.* trubljenje
hoot *v.i* trubiti
hop *v. i* skočiti
hop *n* skakanje
hope *v.t.* nadati se
hope *n* nada
hopeful *a.* pun nade
hopeless *a.* beznadežan
horde *n.* horda
horizon *n.* horizont
horn *n.* rog
hornet *n.* stršljen
horrible *a.* strašan
horrify *v.t.* zaprepastiti
horror *n.* užas
horse *n.* konj
horticulture *n.* hortikultura
hose *n.* crevo
hosiery *n.* čarape
hospitable *a.* gostoprimljiv
hospital *n.* bolnica
hospitality *n.* gostoprimstvo
host *n.* domaćin
hostage *n.* talac
hostel *n.* hostel
hostile *a.* neprijateljski
hostility *n.* neprijateljstvo
hot *a.* vreo
hotchpotch *n.* papazjanija

hotel *n.* hotel
hound *n.* lovački pas
hour *n.* sat
house *n* kuća
house *v.t* smestiti
how *adv.* kako
however *adv.* ma kako
however *conj* ipak
howl *v.t.* zavijati
howl *n* zavijanje
hub *n.* čvor
hubbub *n.* graja
huge *a.* ogroman
hum *v. i* zujati
hum *n* zujanje
human *a.* čovek
humane *a.* human
humanitarian *a* humanitarno
humanity *n.* čovečanstvo
humanize *v.t.* počovečiti
humble *a.* skroman
humdrum *a.* jednoličan
humid *a.* vlažan
humidity *n.* vlažnost
humiliate *v.t.* poniziti
humiliation *n.* ponižavanje
humility *n.* poniznost
humorist *n.* humorista
humorous *a.* humorističan
humour *n.* humor
hunch *n.* slutnja
hundred *n.* sto
hunger *n* glad
hungry *a.* gladan
hunt *v.t.* loviti
hunt *n* lov
hunter *n.* lovac
huntsman *n.* lovac
hurdle1 *n.* ograda
hurdle2 *v.t* ograditi

**hurl** *v.t.* baciti

**hurrah** *interj.* ura

**hurricane** *n.* uragan

**hurry** *v.t.* žuriti

**hurry** *n* žurba

**hurt** *v.t.* povrediti

**hurt** *n* povreda

**husband** *n* muž

**husbandry** *n.* ratarstvo

**hush** *n* tišina

**hush** *v.i* utišati

**husk** *n.* ljuska

**husky** *a.* hrapav

**hut** *n.* koliba

**hyaena, hyena** *n.* hijena

**hybrid** *a.* hibridan

**hybrid** *n* hibrid

**hydrogen** *n.* vodonik

**hygiene** *n.* higijena

**hygienic** *a.* higijenski

**hymn** *n.* himna

**hyperbole** *n.* hiperbola

**hypnotism** *n.* hipnotizam

**hypnotize** *v.t.* hipnotisati

**hypocrisy** *n.* licemerje

**hypocrite** *n.* licemer

**hypocritical** *a.* licemeran

**hypothesis** *n.* hipoteza

**hypothetical** *a.* hipotetički

**hysteria** *n.* histerija

**hysterical** *a.* histeričan

# I

**I** *pron.* ja

**ice** *n.* led

**iceberg** *n.* santa leda

**icicle** *n.* ledenica

**icy** *a.* leden

**idea** *n.* ideja

**ideal** *a.* idealan

**ideal** *n* ideal

**idealism** *n.* idealizam

**idealist** *n.* idealista

**idealistic** *a.* idealistički

**idealize** *v.t.* idealizovati

**identical** *a.* identičan

**indentification** *n.* identifikacija

**identify** *v.t.* identifikovati

**identity** *n.* identitet

**ideocy** *n.* idiotizam

**idiom** *n.* idiom

**idiomatic** *a.* idiomatski

**idiot** *n.* idiot

**idiotic** *a.* idiotski

**idle** *a.* besposlen

**idleness** *n.* besposlica

**idler** *n.* besposličar

**idol** *n.* idol

**idolater** *n.* obožavalac

**if** *conj.* ako

**ignoble** *a.* koji nije plemenit

**ignorance** *n.* neznanje

**ignorant** *a.* neobrazovan

**ignore** *v.t.* ignorisati

**ill** *a.* bolestan

**ill** *adv.* loše

**ill** *n* nevolja

**illegal** *a.* nezakonit

**illegibility** *n.* nečitkost

**illegible** *a.* nečitak

**illegitimate** *a.* nezakonit

**illicit** *a.* protivzakonit

**illiteracy** *n.* nepismenost

**illiterate** *a.* nepismen

**illness** *n.* bolest

**illogical** *a.* nelogičan

**illuminate** *v.t.* osvetliti

**illumination** *n.* osvetljenje

illusion *n.* iluzija
illustrate *v.t.* ilustrovati
illustration *n.* ilustracija
image *n.* slika
imagery *n.* slikovito izlaganje
imaginary *a.* izmišljen
imagination *n.* mašta
imaginative *a.* maštovit
imagine *v.t.* zamisliti
imitate *v.t.* imitirati
imitation *n.* imitacija
imitator *n.* imitator
immaterial *a.* nematerijalni
immature *a.* nezreo
immaturity *n.* nezrelost
immeasurable *a.* nemerljiv
immediate *a* neposredan
immemorial *a.* prastari
immense *a.* ogroman
immensity *n.* beskrajnost
immerse *v.t.* utonuti
immersion *n.* potapanje
immigrant *n.* imigrant
immigrate *v.i.* imigrirati
immigration *n.* imigracija
imminent *a.* predstojeći
immodest *a.* neskroman
immodesty *n.* neskromnost
immoral *a.* nemoralan
immorality *n.* nemoralnost
immortal *a.* besmrtan
immortality *n.* besmrtnost
immortalize *v.t.* obesmrtiti
immovable *a.* nepokretan
immune *a.* imun
immunity *n.* imunitet
immunize *v.t.* učiniti imunim
impact *n.* udar
impart *v.t.* saopštiti
impartial *a.* nepristrasan

impartiality *n.* nepristrasnost
impassable *a.* neprohodan
impasse *n.* ćorsokak
impatience *n.* nestrpljenje
impatient *a.* nestrpljiv
impeach *v.t.* okriviti
impeachment *n.* optužba
impede *v.t.* ometati
impediment *n.* prepreka
impenetrable *a.* neprobojan
imperative *a.* imperativ
imperfect *a.* nesavršen
imperfection *n.* nesavršenost
imperial *a.* carski
imperialism *n.* imperijalizam
imperil *v.t.* ugroziti
imperishable *a.* neprolazan
impersonal *a.* bezličan
impersonate *v.t.* oličavati
impersonation *n.* predstavljanje
impertinence *n.* drskost
impertinent *a.* drzak
impetuosity *n.* plahovitost
impetuous *a.* nagao
implement *n.* implementacija
implement *v.t.* implementirati
implicate *v.t.* obuhvatati
implication *n.* implikacija
implicit *a.* indirektan
implore *v.t.* preklinjati
imply *v.t.* podrazumevati
impolite *a.* neljubazan
import *v.t.* uvoziti
import *n.* uvoz
importance *n.* značaj
important *a.* važno
impose *v.t.* nametati
imposing *a.* impozantan
imposition *n.* nametanje
impossibility *n.* nemogućnost

| | |
|---|---|
| **impossible** *a.* nemoguć | **incalculable** *a.* neizračunljiv |
| **impostor** *n.* varalica | **incapable** *a.* nesposoban |
| **imposture** *n.* podvala | **incapacity** *n.* nesposobnost |
| **impotence** *n.* impotencija | **incarnate** *a.* utelovljen |
| **impotent** *a.* impotentan | **incarnate** *v.t.* ovaplotiti |
| **impoverish** *v.t.* osiromašiti | **incarnation** *n.* ovaploćenje |
| **impracticability** *n.* neizvodljivost | **incense** *v.t.* kaditi tamjanom |
| **impracticable** *a.* neizvršiv | **incense** *n.* tamjan |
| **impress** *v.t.* impresionirati | **incentive** *n.* podsticaj |
| **impression** *n.* utisak | **inception** *n.* početak |
| **impressive** *a.* impresivan | **inch** *n.* inč |
| **imprint** *v.t.* utisnuti | **incident** *n.* incident |
| **imprint** *n.* otisak | **incidental** *a.* slučajan |
| **imprison** *v.t.* uhapsiti | **incite** *v.t.* huškati |
| **improper** *a.* nepristojan | **inclination** *n.* sklonost |
| **impropriety** *n.* nepristojnost | **incline** *v.i.* nagnuti se |
| **improve** *v.t.* poboljšati | **include** *v.t.* uključivati |
| **improvement** *n.* poboljšanje | **inclusion** *n.* uključivanje |
| **imprudence** *n.* nesmotrenost | **inclusive** *a.* uključivo |
| **imprudent** *a.* nepromišljen | **incoherent** *a.* nepovezan |
| **impulse** *n.* impuls | **income** *n.* prihod |
| **impulsive** *a.* impulsivan | **incomparable** *a.* neuporediv |
| **impunity** *n.* nekažnjivost | **incompetent** *a.* nesposoban |
| **impure** *a.* nečist | **incomplete** *a.* nepotpun |
| **impurity** *n.* nečistoća | **inconsiderate** *a.* nepromišljen |
| **impute** *v.t.* pripisati | **inconvenient** *a.* neprikladan |
| **in** *prep.* u | **incorporate** *v.t.* priključiti |
| **inability** *n.* nesposobnost | **incorporate** *a.* uključen |
| **inaccurate** *a.* netačan | **incorporation** *n.* priključenje |
| **inaction** *n.* neaktivnost | **incorrect** *a.* netačan |
| **inactive** *a.* neaktivan | **incorrigible** *a.* nepopravljiv |
| **inadmissible** *a.* nedopustiv | **incorruptible** *a.* nepodmitljiv |
| **inanimate** *a.* neživ | **increase** *v.t.* porasti |
| **inapplicable** *a.* neprimenljiv | **increase** *n* porast |
| **inattentive** *a.* nepažljiv | **incredible** *a.* neverovatan |
| **inaudible** *a.* nečujan | **increment** *n.* priraštaj |
| **inaugural** *a.* uvodni | **incriminate** *v.t.* okriviti |
| **inauguration** *n.* inauguracija | **incubate** *v.i.* izleći |
| **inauspicious** *a.* zlokoban | **inculcate** *v.t.* utuviti |
| **inborn** *a.* urođen | **incumbent** *n.* koji je obavezan |

incumbent *a* obavezan
incur *v.t.* natovariti
incurable *a.* neizlečiv
indebted *a.* zadužen
indecency *n.* nepristojnost
indecent *a.* nepristojan
indecision *n.* neodlučnost
indeed *adv.* zaista
indefensible *a.* neodbranjiv
indefinite *a.* neodređen
indemnity *n.* odšteta
independence *n.* nezavisnost
independent *a.* nezavisan
indescribable *a.* neopisiv
index *n.* indeks
Indian *a.* indijski
indicate *v.t.* ukazati
indication *n.* indikacija
indicative *a.* indikativan
indicator *n.* indikator
indict *v.t.* optužiti
indictment *n.* optužnica
indifference *n.* ravnodušnost
indifferent *a.* ravnodušan
indigenous *a.* urođenički
indigestible *a.* nesvarljiv
indigestion *n.* loše varenje
indignant *a.* ozlojeđen
indignation *n.* ozlojeđenost
indigo *n.* indigo
indirect *a.* indirektan
indiscipline *n.* nedisciplina
indiscreet *a.* indiskretan
indiscretion *n.* indiskrecija
indiscriminate *a.* nekritički
indispensable *a.* neophodan
indisposed *a.* neraspoložen
indisputable *a.* neosporan
indistinct *a.* nejasan
individual *a.* pojedinačni

individualism *n.* individualizam
individuality *n.* individualnost
indivisible *a.* nedeljiv
indolent *a.* lenj
indomitable *a.* nesavladiv
indoor *a.* unutrašnji
indoors *adv.* unutra
induce *v.t.* navesti
inducement *n.* navođenje
induct *v.t.* uvesti
induction *n.* uvođenje
indulge *v.t.* ugađati
indulgence *n.* ugađanje
indulgent *a.* popustljiv
industrial *a.* industrijski
industrious *a.* vredan
industry *n.* industrija
ineffective *a.* neefikasan
inert *a.* inertan
inertia *n.* inercija
inevitable *a.* neizbežan
inexact *a.* netačan
inexorable *a.* neumoljiv
inexpensive *a.* jeftin
inexperience *n.* neiskustvo
inexplicable *a.* neobjašnjiv
infallible *a.* nepogrešiv
infamous *a.* ozloglašen
infamy *n.* sramota
infancy *n.* rano detinjstvo
infant *n.* odojče
infanticide *n.* čedomorstvo
infantile *a.* infantilan
infantry *n.* pešadija
infatuate *v.t.* zaluđivati
infatuation *n.* zaslepljenost
infect *v.t.* inficirati
infection *n.* infekcija
infectious *a.* zarazan
infer *v.t.* zaključiti

inference *n.* zaključivanje
inferior *a.* inferioran
inferiority *n.* inferiornost
infernal *a.* paklen
infinite *a.* beskonačan
infinity *n.* beskonačnost
infirm *a.* slab
infirmity *n.* nemoć
inflame *v.t.* raspaliti
inflammable *a.* zapaljiv
inflammation *n.* zapaljenje
inflammatory *a.* raspaljiv
inflation *n.* inflacija
inflexible *a.* nefleksibilan
inflict *v.t.* naneti
influence *n.* uticaj
influence *v.t.* uticati
influential *a.* uticajan
influenza *n.* grip
influx *n.* priliv
inform *v.t.* obavestiti
informal *a.* neformalan
information *n.* informacija
informative *a.* informativan
informer *n.* izvestilac
infringe *v.t.* narušiti
infringement *n.* narušivanje
infuriate *v.t.* razbesneti
infuse *v.t.* uliti
infusion *n.* infuzija
ingrained *a.* ukorenjen
ingratitude *n.* nezahvalnost
ingredient *n.* sastojak
inhabit *v.t.* nastaniti
inhabitable *a.* useljiv
inhabitant *n.* stanovnik
inhale *v.i.* udisati
inherent *a.* inherentan
inherit *v.t.* naslediti
inheritance *n.* nasleđe

inhibit *v.t.* inhibirati
inhibition *n.* inhibicija
inhospitable *a.* negostoljubiv
inhuman *a.* nehuman
inimical *a.* neprijateljski
inimitable *a.* jedinstven
initial *a.* početni
initial *n.* inicijal
initial *v.t* obeležiti inicijalima
initiate *v.t.* započeti
initiative *n.* inicijativa
inject *v.t.* ubrizgati
injection *n.* ubrizgavanje
injudicious *a.* nerazborit
injunction *n.* sudski nalog
injure *v.t.* povrediti
injurious *a.* štetan
injury *n.* povreda
injustice *n.* nepravda
ink *n.* mastilo
inkling *n.* nagoveštaj
inland *a. u* unutrašnjosti
inland *adv.* unutrašnji
in-laws *n.* srodnik
inmate *n.* stanar
inmost *a.* najskriveniji
inn *n.* krčma
innate *a.* urođen
inner *a.* unutrašnji
innermost *a.* u samoj unutrašnjosti
innings *n.* razdoblje
innocence *n.* nevinost
innocent *a.* nevin
innovate *v.t.* inovirati
innovation *n.* inovacija
innovator *n.* inovator
innumerable *a.* bezbrojan
inoculate *v.t.* kalemiti
inoculation *n.* kalemljenje
inoperative *a.* nedelotvoran

inopportune *a.* u krivi čas
input *n.* ulazni
inquest *n.* istraga
inquire *v.t.* raspitati se
inquiry *n.* ispitivanje
inquisition *n.* inkvizicija
inquisitive *a.* radoznao
insane *a.* lud
insanity *n.* ludilo
insatiable *a.* nezasit
inscribe *v.t.* upisati
inscription *n.* natpis
insect *n.* insekt
insecticide *n.* insekticid
insecure *a.* nesiguran
insecurity *n.* nesigurnost
insensibility *n.* neosetljivost
insensible *a.* neosetljiv
inseparable *a.* neodvojiv
insert *v.t.* umetnuti
insertion *n.* umetanje
inside *n.* unutrašnjost
inside *prep.* unutar
inside *a* unutrašnji
inside *adv.* unutra
insight *n.* uvid
insignificance *n.* beznačajnost
insignificant *a.* beznačajan
insincere *a.* neiskren
insincerity *n.* neiskrenost
insinuate *v.t.* insinuirati
insinuation *n.* insinuacija
insipid *a.* bljutav
insipidity *n.* bljutavost
insist *v.t.* insistirati
insistence *n.* insistiranje
insistent *a.* uporan
insolence *n.* bezobrazluk
insolent *a.* drzak
insoluble *n.* nerastvoriv

insolvency *n.* insolventnost
insolvent *a.* insolventan
inspect *v.t.* pregledati
inspection *n.* inspekcija
inspector *n.* inspektor
inspiration *n.* inspiracija
inspire *v.t.* inspirisati
instability *n.* nestabilnost
install *v.t.* instalirati
installation *n.* instalacija
instalment *n.* otplata
instance *n.* primer
instant *n.* trenutak
instant *a.* trenutni
instantaneous *a.* istovremen
instantly *adv.* odmah
instigate *v.t.* podstaći
instigation *n.* podstrekivanje
instil *v.t.* ulivati
instinct *n.* instinkt
instinctive *a.* instinktivan
institute *n.* institut
institution *n.* institucija
instruct *v.t.* narediti
instruction *n.* instrukcija
instructor *n.* instruktor
instrument *n.* instrument
instrumental *a.* instrumentalni
instrumentalist *n.* instrumentalista
insubordinate *a.* neposlušan
insubordination *n.* neposlušnost
insufficient *a.* nedovoljan
insular *a.* ostrvski
insularity *n.* ograničenost
insulate *v.t.* izolovati
insulation *n.* izolacija
insulator *n.* izolator
insult *n.* uvreda
insult *v.t.* uvrediti
insupportable *a.* nesnosan

insurance *n.* osiguranje
insure *v.t.* osigurati
insurgent *a.* buntovnički
insurgent *n.* buntovnik
insurmountable *a.* nepremostiv
insurrection *n.* pobuna
intact *a.* netaknut
intangible *a.* neopipljiv
integral *a.* integralan
integrity *n.* integritet
intellect *n.* intelekt
intellectual *a.* intelektualni
intellectual *n.* intelektualac
intelligence *n.* inteligencija
intelligent *a.* inteligentan
intelligentsia *n.* inteligencija
intelligible *a.* shvatljiv
intend *v.t.* nameravati
intense *a.* napregnut
intensify *v.t.* pojačati
intensity *n.* intenzitet
intensive *a.* intenzivan
intent *n.* napet
intent *a.* namerni
intention *n.* namera
intentional *a.* nameran
intercept *v.t.* presresti
interception *n.* presretanje
interchange *n.* razmena
interchange *v.* razmeniti
intercourse *n.* odnos
interdependence *n.* međuzavisnost
interdependent *a.* međuzavisan
interest *n.* interes
interested *a.* zainteresovan
interesting *a.* zanimljiv
interfere *v.i.* uplitati se
interference *n.* uplitanje
interim *n.* međuvreme
interior *a.* unutrašnji

interior *n.* unutrašnjost
interjection *n.* uzvik
interlock *v.t.* spojiti se
interlude *n.* Interludijum
intermediary *n.* posrednik
intermediate *a.* srednji
interminable *a.* beskrajan
intermingle *v.t.* pomešati
intern *v.t.* stažirati
internal *a.* interni
international *a.* internacionalni
interplay *n.* uzajamno dejstvo
interpret *v.t.* protumačiti
interpreter *n.* prevodilac
interrogate *v.t.* saslušavati
interrogation *n.* saslušavanje
interrogative *a.* upitni
interrogative *n* upitnik
interrupt *v.t.* prekinuti
interruption *n.* prekid
intersect *v.t.* seći
intersection *n.* raskrsnica
interval *n.* interval
intervene *v.i.* intervenisati
intervention *n.* intervencija
interview *n.* intervju
interview *v.t.* intervjuisati
intestinal *a.* crevni
intestine *n.* crevo
intimacy *n.* intimnost
intimate *a.* intiman
intimate *v.t.* nagovestiti
intimation *n.* nagoveštaj
intimidate *v.t.* zastrašiti
intimidation *n.* zastrašivanje
into *prep.* u
intolerable *a.* nepodnošljiv
intolerance *n.* nepodnošljivost
intolerant *a.* netolerantan
intoxicant *n.* opojno sredstvo

intoxicate *v.t.* otrovati
intoxication *n.* intoksikacija
intransitive *a.* neprelazni
interpid *a.* neustrašiv
intrepidity *n.* neustrašivost
intricate *a.* zapetljan
intrigue *v.t.* intrigirati
intrigue *n* intriga
intrinsic *a.* unutrašnji
introduce *v.t.* uvesti
introduction *n.* uvod
introductory *a.* uvodni
introspect *v.i.* preispitivati se
introspection *n.* samoispitivanje
intrude *v.t.* upasti
intrusion *n.* upad
intuition *n.* intuicija
intuitive *a.* intuitivan
invade *v.t.* napasti
invalid *a.* nevažeći
invalid *a.* onesposobljen
invalid *n* invalid
invalidate *v.t.* poništiti
invaluable *a.* neprocenjiv
invasion *n.* invazija
invective *n.* grdnja
invent *v.t.* izumeti
invention *n.* pronalazak
inventive *a.* pronalazački
inventor *n.* pronalazač
invert *v.t.* obrnuti
invest *v.t.* investirati
investigate *v.t.* istražiti
investigation *n.* istraga
investment *n.* investicija
invigilate *v.t.* nadzirati
invigilation *n.* nadgledanje
invigilator *n.* nadzornik
invincible *a.* nepobediv
inviolable *a.* neprikosnoven

invisible *a.* nevidljiv
invitation *v.* poziv
invite *v.t.* pozvati
invocation *n.* prizivanje
invoice *n.* faktura
invoke *v.t.* prizivati
involve *v.t.* uključiti
inward *a.* unutrašnji
inwards *adv.* unutra
irate *a.* srdit
ire *n.* ljutnja
Irish *a.* Irski
Irish *n.* irski jezik, Irac
irksome *a.* zamoran
iron *n.* gvožđe
iron *v.t.* okovati
ironical *a.* ironičan
irony *n.* ironija
irradiate *v.i.* ozračiti
irrational *a.* iracionalan
irreconcilable *a.* nepomirljiv
irrecoverable *a.* nepovrativ
irrefutable *a.* nepobitan
irregular *a.* nepravilan
irregularity *n.* nepravilnost
irrelevant *a.* nebitan
irrespective *a.* bez obzira na
irresponsible *a.* neodgovoran
irrigate *v.t.* navodnjavati
irrigation *n.* navodnjavanje
irritable *a.* razdražljiv
irritant *a.* koji draži
irritant *n.* iritiranje
irritate *v.t.* dražiti
irritation *n.* iritacija
irruption *n.* provala
island *n.* ostrvo
isle *n.* ostrvo
isobar *n.* izobara
isolate *v.t.* izolovati

**isolation** *n.* izolacija
**issue** *v.i.* izadati
**issue** *n.* pitanje
**it** *pron.* to
**Italian** *a.* Italijanski
**Italian** *n.* italijanski jezik, Italijan
**italic** *a.* kurzivan
**italics** *n.* kurziv
**itch** *n.* svrab
**itch** *v.i.* svrbeti
**item** *n.* stavka
**ivory** *n.* slonovača
**ivy** *n* bršljan

# J

**jab** *v.t.* probosti
**jabber** *v.t.* blebetati
**jack** *n.* utičnica
**jack** *v.t.* utaknuti
**jackal** *n.* šakal
**jacket** *n.* jakna
**jade** *n.* žad
**jail** *n.* zatvor
**jailer** *n.* tamničar
**jam** *n.* džem
**jam** *v.t.* zakucati
**jar** *n.* tegla
**jargon** *n.* žargon
**jasmine, jessamine** *n.* jasmin
**jaundice** *n.* žutica
**jaundice** *v.t.* izazvati žuticu
**javelin** *n.* koplje
**jaw** *n.* vilica
**jay** *n.* sojka
**jealous** *a.* ljubomoran
**jealousy** *n.* ljubomora
**jean** *n.* jaka pamučna tkanina
**jeer** *v.i.* rugati se

**jelly** *n.* žele
**jeopardize** *v.t.* ugroziti
**jeopardy** *n.* opasnost
**jerk** *n.* trzaj
**jerkin** *n.* kožuh
**jerky** *a.* grčevit
**jersey** *n.* dres
**jest** *n.* šala
**jest** *v.i.* šaliti se
**jet** *n.* mlaznjak
**Jew** *n.* Jevrejin
**jewel** *n.* dragulj
**jewel** *v.t.* ukrasiti draguljima
**jeweller** *n.* juvelir
**jewellery** *n.* nakit
**jingle** *n.* zveckanje
**jingle** *v.i.* zveckati
**job** *n.* posao
**jobber** *n.* nadničar
**jobbery** *n.* korupcija
**jocular** *a.* šaljiv
**jog** *v.t.* džogirati
**join** *v.t.* pridružiti
**joiner** *n.* stolar
**joint** *n.* članak
**jointly** *adv.* zajedničko
**joke** *n.* vic
**joke** *v.i.* zbijati šalu
**joker** *n.* džoker
**jollity** *n.* veselje
**jolly** *a.* radostan
**jolt** *n.* drmusanje
**jolt** *v.t.* drmati
**jostle** *n.* udarac
**jostle** *v.t.* udariti o
**jot** *n.* sitnica
**jot** *v.t.* zabeležiti
**journal** *n.* časopis
**journalism** *n.* novinarstvo
**journalist** *n.* novinar

journey *n.* putovanje
journey *v.i.* putovati
jovial *a.* veseo
joviality *n.* veselost
joy *n.* radost
joyful, joyous *n.* radostan
jubilant *a.* ushićen
jubilation *n.* slavlje
jubilee *n.* jubilej
judge *n.* sudija
judge *v.i.* suditi
judgement *n.* presuda
judicature *n.* pravosuđe
judicial *a.* sudski
judiciary *n.* sudstvo
judicious *a.* razborit
jug *n.* krčag
juggle *v.t.* žonglirati
juggler *n.* žongler
juice *n* sok
juicy *a.* sočan
jumble *n.* zbrka
jumble *v.t.* zbrkati
jump *n.* skok
jump *v.i* skočiti
junction *n.* raskrsnica
juncture *n.* spoj
jungle *n.* džungla
junior *a.* mlađi
junior *n.* junior
junk *n.* đubre
jupiter *n.* jupiter
jurisdiction *n.* nadležnost
jurisprudence *n.* jurisprudencija
jurist *n.* pravnik
juror *n.* porotnik
jury *n.* porota
juryman *n.* porotnik
just *a.* pravedan
just *adv.* upravo

justice *n.* pravda
justifiable *a.* opravdan
justification *n.* opravdanje
justify *v.t.* opravdati
justly *adv.* pravedno
jute *n.* juta
juvenile *a.* maloletnik

# K

keen *a.* bodar
keenness *n.* bodrost
keep *v.t.* držati
keeper *n.* čuvar
keepsake *n.* uspomena
kennel *n.* štenara
kerchief *n.* marama
kernel *n.* koštica
kerosene *n.* kerozin
ketchup *n.* kečap
kettle *n.* čajnik
key *n.* ključ
key *v.t* pričvrstiti
kick *n.* šut
kick *v.t.* šutirati
kid *n.* dete
kidnap *v.t.* kidnapovati
kidney *n.* bubreg
kill *v.t.* ubiti
kill *n.* ubijanje
kiln *n.* sušara
kin *n.* rodbina
kind *n.* vrsta
kind *a* prijatan
kindergarten *n.* obdanište
kindle *v.t.* potpaliti
kindly *adv.* ljubazno
king *n.* kralj
kingdom *n.* kraljevina

kinship *n.* srodstvo
kiss *n.* poljubac
kiss *v.t.* poljubiti
kit *n.* oprema
kitchen *n.* kuhinja
kite *n.* zmaj
kith *n.* poznanici
kitten *n.* mače
knave *n.* podlac
knavery *n.* podlost
knee *n.* koleno
kneel *v.i.* klečati
knife *n.* nož
knight *n.* vitez
knight *v.t.* učiniti vitezom
knit *v.t.* plesti
knock *v.t.* kucati
knot *n.* čvor
knot *v.t.* vezati
know *v.t.* znati
knowledge *n.* znanje

# L

label *n.* etiketa
label *v.t.* etiketirati
labial *a.* labijalni
laboratory *n.* laboratorija
laborious *a.* mučan
labour *n.* rad
labour *v.i.* raditi
laboured *a.* naporan
labourer *n.* radnik
labyrinth *n.* lavirint
lac, lakh *n* lak
lace *n.* čipka
lace *v.t.* vezati
lacerate *v.t.* rastrgnuti
lachrymose *a.* plačljiv

lack *n.* nedostatak
lack *v.t.* nedostajati
lackey *n.* lakej
lacklustre *a.* mutan
laconic *a.* lakonski
lactate *v.i.* dojiti
lactometer *n.* mlekomer
lactose *n.* laktoza
lacuna *n.* praznina
lacy *a.* čipkast
lad *n.* momak
ladder *n.* merdevine
lade *v.t.* natovariti
ladle *n.* kutlača
ladle *v.t.* crpsti
lady *n.* dama
lag *v.i.* uhapsiti
laggard *n.* trom
lagoon *n.* laguna
lair *n.* jazbina
lake *n.* jezero
lama *n.* lama
lamb *n.* jagnje
lambaste *v.t.* izgrditi
lame *a.* hrom
lame *v.t.* osakatiti
lament *v.i.* oplakivati
lament *n* oplakivanje
lamentable *a.* žalostan
lamentation *n.* naricanje
lambkin *n.* jagnješce
laminate *v.t.* spljoštiti
lamp *n.* lampa
lampoon *n.* satira
lampoon *v.t.* izrugivati se
lance *n.* koplje
lance *v.t.* ubosti
lancer *n.* kopljanik
lancet *a.* lanceta
land *n.* zemljište

land *v.i.* iskrcati
landing *n.* pristajanje
landscape *n.* pejzaž
lane *n.* sokak
language *n.* jezik
languish *v.i.* čeznuti
lank *a.* mršav
lantern *n.* fenjer
lap *n.* skut
lapse *v.i.* propustiti
lapse *n* propust
lard *n.* salo
large *a.* velik
largesse *n.* darežljivost
lark *n.* ševa
lascivious *a.* lascivan
lash *a.* bičevan
lash *n.* udarac bičem
lass *n.* draga
last1 *a.* poslednji
last *adv.* najzad
last *v.i.* trajati
last *n* izdržljivost
lastly *adv.* na kraju
lasting *a.* trajan
latch *n.* kvaka
late *a.* kasno
late *adv.* nedavno
lately *adv.* u poslednje vreme
latent *a.* prikriven
lath *n.* letva
lathe *n.* strug
lathe *n.* čekrk
lather *n.* pena
latitude *n.* širina
latrine *n.* nužnik
latter *a.* kasniji
lattice *n.* rešetka
laud *v.t.* pohvaliti
laud *n* pohvala

laudable *a.* pohvalan
laugh *n.* smejanje
laugh *v.i* smejati se
laughable *a.* smešan
laughter *n.* smeh
launch *v.t.* lansirati
launch *n.* lansiranje
launder *v.t.* oprati
laundress *n.* pralja
laundry *n.* rublje
laurel *n.* lovor
laureate *a.* ovenčan lovorom
laureate *n* laureat
lava *n.* lava
lavatory *n.* toalet
lavender *n.* lavanda
lavish *a.* raskošan
lavish *v.t.* obasipati
law *n.* zakon
lawful *a.* zakonit
lawless *a.* nezakonit
lawn *n.* travnjak
lawyer *n.* advokat
lax *a.* labav
laxative *n.* laksativ
laxative *a* pročišćavajući
laxity *n.* labavost
lay *v.t.* položiti
lay *a.* nestručan
lay *n* smer
layer *n.* sloj
layman *n.* laik
laze *v.i.* dangubiti
laziness *n.* lenjost
lazy *n.* lenj
lea *n.* ledina
leach *v.t.* navlažiti
lead *n.* olovo
lead *v.t.* plombirati
lead *n.* visak

leaden a. olovni
leader n. vođa
leadership n. vođstvo
leaf n. list
leaflet n. letak
leafy a. lisnat
league n. liga
leak n. curenje
leak v.i. curiti
leakage n. curenje
lean n. mršavo
lean v.i. nasloniti
leap v.i. skočiti
leap n skok
learn v.i. naučiti
learned a. učen
learner n. učenik
learning n. učenje
lease n. zakup
lease v.t. zakupiti
least a. najmanji
least adv. najmanje
leather n. koža
leave n. dopuštenje
leave v.t. ostaviti
lecture n. predavanje
lecture v predavati
lecturer n. predavač
ledger n. glavna knjiga
lee n. zaklon
leech n. pijavica
leek n. praziluk
left a. levo
left n. levica
leftist n levičar
leg n. noga
legacy n. nasleđe
legal a. pravni
legality n. zakonitost
legalize v.t. legalizovati

legend n. legenda
legendary a. legendaran
legible a. čitljiv
legibly adv. čitko
legion n. legija
legionary n. legionar
legislate v.i. donositi zakon
legislation n. donošenje zakona
legislative a. zakonodavan
legislator n. zakonodavac
legislature n. zakonodavstvo
legitimacy n. legitimitet
legitimate a. legitiman
leisure n. slobodno vreme
leisure a slobodan
leisurely a. ležerno
leisurely adv. lagano
lemon n. limun
lemonade n. limunada
lend v.t. pozajmiti
length n. dužina
lengthen v.t. produžiti
lengthy a. podugačak
lenience, leniency n. popustljivost
lenient a. popustljiv
lens n. objektiv
lentil n. sočivo
Leo n. lav
leonine a lavovski
leopard n. leopard
leper n. gubavac
leprosy n. lepra
leprous a. gubav
less a. manji
less n ono što je manje
less adv. manje
less prep. manje
lessee n. zakupac
lessen v.t smanjiti
lesser a. manji

lesson *n.* lekcija
lest *conj.* da ne bi
let *v.t.* dozvoliti
lethal *a.* smrtonosan
lethargic *a.* letargičan
lethargy *n.* letargija
letter *n* pismo
level *n.* nivo
level *a* izjednačen
level *v.t.* izjednačiti
lever *n.* poluga
lever *v.t.* služiti se polugom
leverage *n.* moć
levity *n.* lakomislenost
levy *v.t.* nametnuti
levy *n.* nametanje
lewd *a.* razvratan
lexicography *n.* leksikografija
lexicon *n.* leksikon
liability *n.* odgovornost
liable *a.* odgovoran
liaison *n.* veza
liar *n.* lažov
libel *n.* kleveta
libel *v.t.* oklevetati
liberal *a.* liberalan
liberalism *n.* liberalizam
liberality *n.* velikodušnost
liberate *v.t.* osloboditi
liberation *n.* oslobođenje
liberator *n.* oslobodilac
libertine *n.* slobodoumnik
liberty *n.* sloboda
librarian *n.* bibliotekar
library *n.* biblioteka
licence *n.* dozvola
license *v.t.* dozvoliti
licensee *n.* onaj koji ima licencu
licentious *a.* raspojasan
lick *v.t.* lizati

lick *n* lizanje
lid *n.* poklopac
lie *v.i.* lagati
lie *v.i* ležati
lie *n* laž
lien *n.* pravo zaloge
lieu *n.* umesto
lieutenant *n.* poručnik
life *n* život
lifeless *a.* beživotan
lifelong *a.* doživotni
lift *n.* podizanje
lift *v.t.* podizati
light *n.* svetlo
light *a* lako
light *v.t.* osvetliti
lighten *v.i.* olakšati
lighter *n.* upaljač
lightly *adv.* olako
lightening *n.* munja
lignite *n.* lignit
like *a.* sličan
like *n.* naklonost
like *v.t.* kao što
like *prep* poput
likelihood *n.* verovatnoća
likely *a.* verovatno
liken *v.t.* porediti
likeness *n.* sličnost
likewise *adv.* takođe
liking *n.* dopadanje
lilac *n.* jorgovan
lily *n.* ljiljan
limb *n.* ud
limber *v.t.* pričvrstiti
limber *n* prednjak
lime *n.* limeta
lime *v.t* namazati
lime *n.* kreč
limelight *n.* centar pažnje

limit *n.* granica
limit *v.t.* ograničiti
limitation *n.* ograničenje
limited *a.* ograničen
limitless *a.* neograničen
line *n.* linija
line *v.t.* iscrtati
line *v.t.* poređati
lineage *n.* loza
linen *n.* platno
linger *v.i.* odugovlačiti
lingo *n.* žargon
lingua franca *n.* mešovit žargon
lingual *a.* jezični
linguist *n.* lingvista
linguistic *a.* jezički
linguistics *n.* lingvistika
lining *n* postava
link *n.* spona
link *v.t* spojiti
linseed *n.* laneno seme
lintel *n.* nadvratink
lion *n* lav
lioness *n.* lavica
lip *n.* usna
liquefy *v.t.* rastopiti
liquid *a.* tečan
liquid *n* tečnost
liquidate *v.t.* likvidirati
liquidation *n.* likvidacija
liquor *n.* alkoholno piće
lisp *v.t.* šuškati
lisp *n* šuškanje
list *n.* rub
list *v.t.* obrubiti
listen *v.i.* slušati
listener *n.* slušalac
listless *a.* trom
lists *n.* borilište
literacy *n.* pismenost

literal *a.* doslovan
literary *a.* književni
literate *a.* pismen
literature *n.* književnost
litigant *n.* parničar
litigate *v.t.* parničiti
litigation *n.* parničenje
litre *n.* litar
litter *n.* slama
litter *v.t.* pokriti slamom
litterateur *n.* literatura
little *a.* malen
little *adv.* malo
little *n.* ono što je malo
littoral *a.* primorski
liturgical *a.* liturgijski
live *v.i.* živeti
live *a.* živ
livelihood *n.* izdržavanje
lively *a.* živo
liver *n.* jetra
livery *n.* livreja
living *a.* živahan
living *n* život
lizard *n.* gušter
load *n.* teret
load *v.t.* natovariti
loadstar *n.* zvezda vodilja
loadstone *n.* magnet
loaf *n.* vekna
loaf *v.i.* dangubiti
loafer *n.* danguba
loan *n.* zajam
loan *v.t.* pozajmiti
loath *a.* nesklon
loathe *v.t.* prezirati
loathsome *a.* gnusan
lobby *n.* predsoblje
lobe *n.* ušna resa
lobster *n.* jastog

| | |
|---|---|
| **local** *a.* lokalno | **look** *v.i* gledati |
| **locale** *n.* poprište | **look** *a koji* izgleda |
| **locality** *n.* položaj | **loom** *n* razboj |
| **localize** *v.t.* lokalizovati | **loom** *v.i.* nazirati se |
| **locate** *v.t.* locirati | **loop** *n.* petlja |
| **location** *n.* lokacija | **loop-hole** *n.* puškarnica |
| **lock** *n.* brava | **loose** *a.* labav |
| **lock** *v.t* zaključati | **loose** *v.t.* odrešiti |
| **lock** *n* uvojak | **loosen** *v.t.* olabaviti |
| **locker** *n.* ormar | **loot** *n.* pljačka |
| **locket** *n.* medaljon | **loot** *v.i.* pljačkati |
| **locomotive** *n.* lokomotiva | **lop** *v.t.* rezati |
| **locus** *n.* mesto | **lop** *n.* obrezivanje |
| **locust** *n.* skakavac | **lord** *n.* gospodar |
| **locution** *n.* izraz | **lordly** *a.* oholo |
| **lodge** *n.* kućica | **lordship** *n.* gospodstvo |
| **lodge** *v.t.* ukonačiti | **lore** *n.* znanje |
| **lodging** *n.* konačište | **lorry** *n.* kamion |
| **loft** *n.* potkrovlje | **lose** *v.t.* izgubiti |
| **lofty** *a.* uzvišen | **loss** *n.* gubitak |
| **log** *n.* zabeležiti | **lot** *n.* mnoštvo |
| **logarithim** *n.* logaritam | **lot** *n* gradilište |
| **loggerhead** *n.* tikvan | **lotion** *n.* losion |
| **logic** *n.* logika | **lottery** *n.* lutrija |
| **logical** *a.* logičan | **lotus** *n.* lotos |
| **logician** *n.* logičar | **loud** *a.* glasno |
| **loin** *n.* slabina | **lounge** *v.i.* šetkati se |
| **loiter** *v.i.* tumarati | **lounge** *n.* predvorje |
| **loll** *v.i.* zavaliti se | **louse** *n.* vaška |
| **lollipop** *n.* lizalica | **lovable** *a.* simpatičan |
| **lone** *a.* usamljen | **love** *n* ljubav |
| **loneliness** *n.* usamljenost | **love** *v.t.* voleti |
| **lonely** *a.* usamljen | **lovely** *a.* divan |
| **lonesome** *a.* usamljen | **lover** *n.* ljubavnik |
| **long** *a.* dug | **loving** *a.* voljen |
| **long** *adv* dugo | **low** *a.* nizak |
| **long** *v.i* čeznuti | **low** *adv.* nisko |
| **longevity** *n.* dugovečnost | **low** *v.i.* mukati |
| **longing** *n.* čežnja | **low** *n.* nizak položaj |
| **longitude** *n.* dužina | **lower** *v.t.* niže |

**lowliness** *n.* skromnost
**lowly** *a.* ponizan
**loyal** *a.* lojalan
**loyalist** *n.* privrženik
**loyalty** *n.* lojalnost
**lubricant** *n.* mazivo
**lubricate** *v.t.* podmazati
**lubrication** *n.* podmazivanje
**lucent** *a.* svetao
**lucerne** *n.* detelina
**lucid** *a.* bistar
**lucidity** *n.* lucidnost
**luck** *n.* sreća
**luckily** *adv.* srećom
**luckless** *a.* nesrećan
**lucky** *a.* srećan
**lucrative** *a.* unosan
**lucre** *n.* novac
**luggage** *n.* prtljag
**lukewarm** *a.* mlak
**lull** *v.t.* utišati
**lull** *n.* zatišje
**lullaby** *n.* uspavanka
**luminary** *n.* prosvetitelj
**luminous** *a.* svetleći
**lump** *n.* gruda
**lump** *v.t.* nagomilati
**lunacy** *n.* ludilo
**lunar** *a.* mesečev
**lunatic** *n.* ludak
**lunatic** *a.* lud
**lunch** *n.* ručak
**lunch** *v.i.* ručati
**lung** *n* pluća
**lunge** *n.* zamah
**lunge** *v.i* baciti se
**lurch** *n.* trzaj
**lurch** *v.i.* zateturati se
**lure** *n.* mamac
**lure** *v.t.* namamiti

**lurk** *v.i.* vrebati
**luscious** *a.* sočan
**lush** *a.* bujan
**lust** *n.* požuda
**lustful** *a.* pohotan
**lustre** *n.* sjaj
**lustrous** *a.* sjajan
**lusty** *a.* sočan
**lute** *n.* lauta
**luxuriance** *n.* raskoš
**luxuriant** *a.* raskošan
**luxurious** *a.* luksuzan
**luxury** *n.* luksuz
**lynch** *v.t.* linč
**lyre** *n.* lira
**lyric** *a.* lirski
**lyric** *n.* lirika
**lyrical** *a.* lirski
**lyricist** *n.* liričar

# M

**magical** *a.* magijski
**magician** *n.* mađioničar
**magisterial** *a.* merodavan
**magistracy** *n.* magistrat
**magistrate** *n.* sudija za prekršaje
**magnanimity** *n.* velikodušnost
**magnanimous** *a.* velikodušan
**magnate** *n.* magnat
**magnet** *n.* magnet
**magnetic** *a.* magnetni
**magnetism** *n.* magnetizam
**magnificent** *a.* veličanstven
**magnify** *v.t.* uveličati
**magnitude** *n.* veličina
**magpie** *n.* svraka
**mahogany** *n.* mahagoni
**mahout** *n.* čuvar slonova u Indiji

maid *n.* služavka
maiden *n.* devojka
maiden *a* čedan
mail *n.* pošta
mail *v.t.* poslati poštom
mail *n* oklop
main *a* glavni
main *n* snaga
mainly *adv.* uglavnom
mainstay *n.* glavna potpora
maintain *v.t.* održavati
maintenance *n.* održavanje
maize *n.* kukuruz
majestic *a.* veličanstven
majesty *n.* veličanstvo
major *a.* glavni
major *n* major
majority *n.* većina
make *v.t.* napraviti
make *n* tvorevina
maker *n.* tvorac
maladjustment *n.* neprilagodljivost
maladministration *n.* loše poslovanje
malady *n.* bolest
malaria *n.* malarija
maladroit *a.* nespretan
malaise *n.* slabost
malcontent *a.* nezadovoljan
malcontent *n* nezadovoljstvo
male *a.* muški
male *n* muški rod
malediction *n.* prokletstvo
malefactor *n.* zločinac
maleficent *a.* škodljiv
malice *n.* zloba
malicious *a.* zlonameran
malign *v.t.* klevetati
malign *a* poguban
malignancy *n.* opakost
malignant *a.* zao

malignity *n.* malignitet
malleable *a.* prilagodljiv
malmsey *n.* malvazija
malnutrition *n.* neuhranjenost
malpractice *n.* pogrešno lečenje
malt *n.* slad
mal-treatment *n.* zlostavljanje
mamma *n.* vime
mammal *n.* sisar
mammary *a.* mlečni
mammon *n.* mamon
mammoth *n.* mamut
mammoth *a* ogroman
man *n.* čovek
man *v.t.* osokoliti
manage *v.t.* upravljati
manageable *a.* izvediv
management *n.* upravljanje
manager *n.* menadžer
managerial *a.* menadžerski
mandate *n.* mandat
mandatory *a.* obavezan
mane *n.* griva
manes *n.* *duše* pokojnika
manful *a.* hrabar
manganese *n.* mangan
manger *n.* jasle
mangle *v.t.* valjati rublje
mango *n* mango
manhandle *v.t.* maltertirati
manhole *n.* šaht
manhood *n.* muškost
mania *n* manija
maniac *n.* manijak
manicure *n.* manikir
manifest *a.* očevidan
manifest *v.t.* manifestovati
manifestation *n.* manifestacija
manifesto *n.* manifest
manifold *a.* mnogostruk

**manipulate** *v.t.* manipulisati
**manipulation** *n.* manipulacija
**mankind** *n.* čovečanstvo
**manlike** *a.* muževan
**manliness** *n* muškost
**manly** *a.* muški
**manna** *n.* mana
**mannequin** *n.* maneken
**manner** *n.* način
**mannerism** *n.* manirizam
**mannerly** *a.* učtiv
**manoeuvre** *n.* manevar
**manoeuvre** *v.i.* manevrisati
**manor** *n.* vlastelinstvo
**manorial** *a.* vlastelinski
**mansion** *n.* palata
**mantel** *n. okvir* kamina
**mantle** *n* omotač
**mantle** *v.t* pokriti
**manual** *a.* ručno
**manual** *n* priručnik
**manufacture** *v.t.* proizvoditi
**manufacture** *n* proizvodnja
**manufacturer** *n* proizvođač
**manumission** *n.* oslobađanje roba
**manumit** *v.t.* osloboditi ropstva
**manure** *n.* đubrivo
**manure** *v.t.* đubriti
**manuscript** *n.* rukopis
**many** *a.* mnogo
**map** *n* mapa
**map** *v.t.* ucrtati
**mar** *v.t.* pokvariti
**marathon** *n.* maraton
**maraud** *v.i.* pljačkati
**marauder** *n.* pljačkaš
**marble** *n.* mermer
**march** *n* mart
**march** *n.* marš
**march** *v.i* marširati

**mare** *n.* kobila
**margarine** *n.* margarin
**margin** *n.* margina
**marginal** *a.* marginalni
**marigold** *n.* neven
**marine** *a.* morski
**mariner** *n.* mornar
**marionette** *n.* marioneta
**marital** *a.* bračni
**maritime** *a.* pomorski
**mark** *n.* znak
**mark** *v.t* označiti
**marker** *n.* marker
**market** *n* tržište
**market** *v.t* trgovati
**marketable** *a.* koji se može prodati
**marksman** *n.* strelac
**marl** *n.* lapor
**marmalade** *n.* marmelada
**maroon** *n.* kestenjasta boja
**maroon** *a* kestenjast
**maroon** *v.t* lutati
**marriage** *n.* brak
**marriageable** *a.* sposoban za brak
**marry** *v.t.* udati
**Mars** *n* mars
**marsh** *n.* močvara
**marshal** *n* maršal
**marshal** *v.t* postrojiti
**marshy** *a.* močvaran
**marsupial** *n.* torbar
**mart** *n.* pijaca
**marten** *n.* kuna
**martial** *a.* vojni
**martinet** *n.* starešina
**martyr** *n.* mučenik
**martyrdom** *n.* mučeništvo
**marvel** *n.* čudo
**marvel** *v.i* čuditi se
**marvellous** *a.* veličanstven

**mascot** *n.* maskota
**masculine** *a.* muški
**mash** *n.* kaša
**mash** *v.t* gnječiti
**mask** *n.* maska
**mask** *v.t.* maskirati
**mason** *n.* zidar
**masonry** *n.* zidarstvo
**masquerade** *n.* maskarada
**mass** *n.* masa
**mass** *v.i* gomilati
**massacre** *n.* masakr
**massacre** *v.t.* masakrirati
**massage** *n.* masaža
**massage** *v.t.* masirati
**masseur** *n.* maser
**massive** *a.* masivan
**massy** *a.* krupan
**mast** *n.* jarbol
**master** *n.* gospodar
**master** *v.t.* savladati
**masterly** *a.* majstorski
**masterpiece** *n.* remek-delo
**mastery** *n.* majstorstvo
**masticate** *v.t.* žvakati
**masturbate** *v.i.* masturbirati
**mat** *n.* otirač
**matador** *n.* matador
**match** *n.* meč
**match** *v.i.* odgovarati
**match** *n* šibica
**matchless** *a.* bez premca
**mate** *n.* prijatelj
**mate** *v.t.* pariti
**mate** *n* bračni drug
**mate** *v.t.* matirati
**material** *a.* materijalan
**material** *n* materijal
**materialism** *n.* materijalizam
**materialize** *v.t.* materijalizovati

**maternal** *a.* materinski
**maternity** *n.* materinstvo
**mathematical** *a.* matematički
**mathematician** *n.* matematičar
**mathematics** *n* matematika
**matinee** *n.* matine
**matriarch** *n.* matrijarh
**matricidal** *a.* materoubilački
**matricide** *n.* materoubistvo
**matriculate** *v.t.* upisati visoku školu
**matriculation** *n.* matura
**matrimonial** *a.* bračni
**matrimony** *n.* brak
**matrix** *n* matrica
**matron** *n.* matrona
**matter** *n.* stvar
**matter** *v.i.* mariti
**mattock** *n.* pijuk
**mattress** *n.* dušek
**mature** *a.* zreo
**mature** *v.i* zreo
**maturity** *n.* zrelost
**maudlin** *a* preosetljiv
**maul** *n.* malj
**maul** *v.t* izmlatiti
**maulstick** *n.* slikarev potporni štap
**maunder** *v.t.* tromo se kretati
**mausoleum** *n.* mauzolej
**mawkish** *a.* sladunjav
**maxilla** *n.* gornja vilica
**maxim** *n.* maksima
**maximize** *v.t.* maksimalno povećati
**maximum** *a.* maksimalan
**maximum** *n* maksimum
**May** *n.* maj
**may** *v* moći
**mayor** *n.* gradonačelnik
**maze** *n.* lavirint
**me** *pron.* mene
**mead** *n.* medovina

meadow *n.* livada
meagre *a.* oskudan
meal *n.* obrok
mealy *a.* brašnjav
mean *a.* značiti
mean *n.* sredina
mean *v.t* značiti
meander *v.i.* meander
meaning *n.* značenje
meaningful *a.* značajan
meaningless *a.* beznačajan
meanness *n.* pakost
means *n* sredstvo
meanwhile *adv.* u međuvremenu
measles *n* male boginje
measurable *a.* merljiv
measure *n.* mera
measure *v.t* meriti
measureless *a.* neizmeran
measurement *n.* mera
meat *n.* meso
mechanic *n.* mehaničar
mechanic *a* mehanički
mechanical *a.* mašinski
mechanics *n.* mehanika
mechanism *n.* mehanizam
medal *n.* medalja
medallist *n.* nosilac medalje
meddle *v.i.* mešati se
medieval *a.* srednjevekovni
medieval *a.* sredovečan
median *a.* srednji
mediate *v.i.* posredovati
mediation *n.* posredovanje
mediator *n.* posrednik
medical *a.* medicinski
medicament *n.* lek
medicinal *a.* medicinski
medicine *n.* medicina
medico *n.* student medicine

mediocre *a.* osrednji
mediocrity *n.* osrednjost
meditate *v.t.* meditirati
mediation *n.* posredovanje
meditative *a.* refleksivan
medium *n* medijum
medium *a* srednji
meek *a.* krotak
meet *n.* utakmica
meet *v.t.* sresti
meeting *n.* sastanak
megalith *n.* golem kamen
megalithic *a.* megalitski
megaphone *n.* megafon
melancholia *n.* melanholija
melancholic *a.* melanholičan
melancholy *n.* tuga
melancholy *adj* tužan
melee *n.* opšta tuča
meliorate *v.t.* poboljšati
mellow *a.* pripit
melodious *a.* melodičan
melodrama *n.* melodrama
melodramatic *a.* melodramatičan
melody *n.* melodija
melon *n.* dinja
melt *v.i.* rastopiti
member *n.* član
membership *n.* članstvo
membrane *n.* membrana
memento *n.* uspomena
memoir *n.* memoari
memorable *a.* nezaboravan
memorandum *n* memorandum
memorial *n.* komemoracija
memorial *a* komemorativan
memory *n.* memorija
menace *n* pretnja
menace *v.t* pretiti
mend *v.t.* popraviti

mendacious *a.* lažljiv
menial *a.* servilan
menial *n* sluga
meningitis *n.* meningitis
menopause *n.* menopauza
menses *n.* menzis
menstrual *a.* menstrualni
menstruation *n.* menstruacija
mental *a.* mentalni
mentality *n.* mentalitet
mention *n.* spominjanje
mention *v.t.* spominjati
mentor *n.* mentor
menu *n.* jelovnik
mercantile *a.* trgovački
mercenary *a.* plaćenički
mercerise *v.t.* mercerizirati
merchandise *n.* roba
merchant *n.* trgovac
merciful *a.* milostiv
merciless *adj.* nemilosrdan
mercurial *a.* živin
mercury *n.* merkur
mercy *n.* milost
mere *a.* puki
merge *v.t.* spojiti
merger *n.* udruživanje
meridian *a.* meridijan
merit *n.* zasluga
merit *v.t* zaslužiti
meritorious *a.* zaslužan
mermaid *n.* sirena
merman *n.* triton
merriment *n.* veselje
merry *a* veseo
mesh *n.* mreža
mesh *v.t* uhvatiti u mrežu
mesmerism *n.* hipnotizam
mesmerize *v.t.* hipnotisati
mess *n.* nered

mess *v.i* pobrkati
message *n.* poruka
messenger *n.* kurir
messiah *n.* mesija
Messrs *n.* gospoda
metabolism *n.* metabolizam
metal *n.* metal
metallic *a.* metalni
metallurgy *n.* metalurgija
metamorphosis *n.* metamorfoza
metaphor *n.* metafora
metaphysical *a.* metafizički
metaphysics *n.* metafizika
mete *v.t* odmeriti
meteor *n.* meteor
meteoric *a.* meteorski
meteorologist *n.* meteorolog
meteorology *n.* meteorologija
meter *n.* metar
method *n.* metod
methodical *a.* metodičan
metre *n.* metar
metric *a.* metrički
metrical *a.* metarski
metropolis *n.* metropola
metropolitan *a.* metropolitski
metropolitan *n.* metropolit
mettle *n.* temperament
mettlesome *a.* odvažan
mew *v.i.* mjaukati
mew *n.* galeb
mezzanine *n.* mezanin
mica *n.* liskun
microfilm *n.* mikrofilm
micrology *n.* mikrologija
micrometer *n.* mikrometar
microphone *n.* mikrofon
microscope *n.* mikroskop
microscopic *a.* mikroskopski
microwave *n.* mikrotalasna peć

mid *a.* srednji
midday *n.* podne
middle *a.* srednji
middle *n* sredina
middleman *n.* posrednik
middling *a.* osrednji
midget *n.* patuljak
midland *n.* unutrašnjost
midnight *n.* ponoć
mid-off *n.* pozicija u kriketu
mid-on *n.* pozicija u kriketu
midriff *n.* dijafragma
midst *n.* sredina
midsummer *n.* sredina leta
midwife *n.* babica
might *n.* moć
mighty *adj.* moćan
migraine *n.* migrena
migrant *n.* migrant
migrate *v.i.* migrirati
migration *n.* migracija
milch *a.* mlečni
mild *a.* blag
mildew *n.* buđ
mile *n.* milja
mileage *n.* miljaža
milestone *n.* prekretnica
milieu *n.* ambijent
militant *a.* ratoboran
militant *n* militant
military *a.* vojni
military *n* vojska
militate *v.i.* ratovati
militia *n.* milicija
milk *n.* mleko
milk *v.t.* musti
milky *a.* mlečan
mill *n.* mlin
mill *v.t.* mleti
millennium *n.* milenijum

miller *n.* mlinar
millet *n.* proso
milliner *n.* modiskinja
milliner *n.* modist
millinery *n.* radnja modistkinje
million *n.* milion
millionaire *n.* milioner
millipede *n.* stonoga
mime *n.* mimika
mime *v.i* izraziti mimikom
mimesis *n.* mimikrija
mimic *a.* imitirati
mimic *n* mimičar
mimic *v.t* imitirati
mimicry *n* mimikrija
minaret *n.* minaret
mince *v.t.* ublažiti
mind *n.* um
mind *v.t.* mariti
mindful *a.* pažljiv
mindless *a.* nepromišljen
mine *pron.* moj
mine *n* rudnik
miner *n.* rudar
mineral *n.* mineral
mineral *a* mineralni
mineralogist *n.* mineralog
mineralogy *n.* mineralogija
mingle *v.t.* mešati
miniature *n.* minijaturan
miniature *a.* minijatura
minim *n.* kapljica
minimal *a.* minimalan
minimize *v.t.* umanjivati
minimum *n.* minimum
minimum *a* minimalan
minion *n.* ljubimac
minister *n.* ministar
minister *v.i.* pomagati
ministrant *a.* ministrant

ministry *n.* ministarstvo
mink *n.* kanadska kuna
minor *a.* manji
minor *n* maloletnik
minority *n.* manjina
minster *n.* katedrala
mint *n.* metvica
mint *n* kovnica
mint *v.t.* kovati
minus *prep.* manje
minus *a* negativan
minus *n* minus
minuscule *a.* beznačajan
minute *a.* minut
minute *n.* uneti u zapisnik
minutely *adv.* svaki čas
minx *n.* namiguša
miracle *n.* čudo
miraculous *a.* čudesan
mirage *n.* fatamorgana
mire *n.* blato
mire *v.t.* blatiti
mirror *n* ogledalo
mirror *v.t.* odražavati
mirth *n.* razdraganost
mirthful *a.* razdragan
misadventure *n.* nezgoda
misalliance *n.* mezalijansa
misanthrope *n.* mizantrop
misapplication *n.* zloupotreba
misapprehend *v.* pogrešno razumeti
misapprehension *n* nesporazum
misappropriate *v.t.* proneveriti
misappropriation *n.* pronevera
misbehave *v.* nedolično se ponašati
misbehaviour *n.* nedolično ponašanje
misbelief *n.* pogrešno verovanje
miscalculate *v.t.* loše proceniti
miscalculation *n.* loša procena
miscall *v.t.* pogrešno nazvati

miscarriage *n.* pobačaj
miscarry *v.i.* pobaciti
miscellaneous *a.* mešovit
miscellany *n.* zbirka
mischance *n.* nesrećan slučaj
mischief *n* nestašluk
mischievous *a.* vragolast
misconceive *v.t.* pogrešno razumeti
misconception *n.* pogrešno shvatanje
misconduct *n.* loše vladanje
misconstrue *v.t.* pogrešno razumeti
miscreant *n.* nitkov
misdeed *n.* nedelo
misdemeanour *n.* prekršaj
misdirect *v.t.* pogrešno uputiti
misdirection *n.* pogrešno upućivanje
miser *n.* tvrdica
miserable *a.* nesrećan
miserly *a.* cicijaški
misery *n.* beda
misfire *v.i.* zatajiti
misfit *n.* loše pristajati
misfortune *n.* nesreća
misgive *v.t.* slutiti
misgiving *n.* slutnja
misguide *v.t.* obmanjivati
mishap *n.* nesrećan slučaj
misjudge *v.t.* pogrešno proceniti
mislead *v.t.* pogrešno voditi
mismanagement *n.* loše upravljanje
mismatch *v.t.* loše spojiti
misnomer *n.* pogrešan naziv
misplace *v.t.* zagubiti
misprint *n.* štamparska greška
misprint *v.t.* pogrešno odštampati
misrepresent *v.* pogrešno predstaviti
misrule *n.* bezakonje
miss *n.* promašaj
miss *v.t.* promašiti
missile *n.* projektil

mission *n.* misija
missionary *n.* misionar
missis, *missus n.* gospođa, supruga
missive *n.* poslanica
mist *n.* izmaglica
mistake *n.* greška
mistake *v.t.* pogrešiti
mister *n.* gospodin
mistletoe *n.* imela
mistreat *v.t.* maltretirati
mistress *n.* gospodarica, ljubavnica
mistrust *n.* nepoverenje
mistrust *v.t.* *biti* nepoverljiv
misty *a.* maglovit
misunderstand *v.t.* pogrešno razumeti
misunderstanding *n.* nesporazum
misuse *n.* zloupotreba
misuse *v.t.* zloupotrebiti
mite *n.* novčić
mite *n* crv
mithridate *n.* protivotrov
mitigate *v.t.* ublažiti
mitigation *n.* ublažavanje
mitre *n.* mitra
mitten *n.* rukavica bez prstiju
mix *v.i* mešati
mixture *n.* mešavina
moan *v.i.* stenjati
moan *n.* stenjanje
moat *n.* šanac
moat *v.t.* opasati šancem
mob *n.* gomila
mob *v.t.* nasrnuti
mobile *a.* pokretan
mobility *n.* pokretnost
mobilize *v.t.* mobilisati
mock *v.i.* ismevati
mock *adj* ismevanje
mockery *n.* izrugivanje
modality *n.* modalitet

mode *n.* način
model *n.* model
model *v.t.* oblikovati
moderate *a.* umeren
moderate *v.t.* ublažiti
moderation *n.* umerenost
modern *a.* moderan
modernity *n.* modernost
modernize *v.t.* modernizovati
modest *a.* skroman
modesty *n* skromnost
modicum *n.* malenkost
modification *n.* modifikacija
modify *v.t.* modifikovati
modulate *v.t.* modulirati
moil *v.i.* mučiti se
moist *a.* vlažan
moisten *v.t.* vlažiti
moisture *n.* vlaga
molar *n.* kutnjak
molar *a* masivan
molasses *n* melasa
mole *n.* krtica
molecular *a.* molekularni
molecule *n.* molekul
molest *v.t.* zlostavljati
molestation *n.* zlostavljanje
molten *a.* izliven
moment *n.* trenutak
momentary *a.* trenutan
momentous *a.* značajan
momentum *n.* impuls
monarch *n.* monarh
monarchy *n.* monarhija
monastery *n.* manastir
monasticism *n* monaštvo
Monday *n.* ponedeljak
monetary *a.* monetarni
money *n.* novac
monger *n.* prodavac

mongoose *n.* mungos
mongrel *a* melez
monitor *n.* monitor
monitory *a.* koji opominje
monk *n.* monah
monkey *n.* majmun
monochromatic *a.* monohromatski
monocle *n.* monokl
monocular *a.* jednook
monody *n.* monodija
monogamy *n.* monogamija
monogram *n.* monogram
monograph *n.* monografija
monolith *n.* monolit
monologue *n.* monolog
monopolist *n.* monopolist
monopolize *v.t.* monopolizovati
monopoly *n.* monopol
monosyllable *n.* jedan slog
monosyllabic *a.* jednosložan
monotheism *n.* monoteizam
monotheist *n.* monoteist
monotonous *a.* monoton
monotony *n* monotonija
monsoon *n.* monsun
monster *n.* čudovište
monstrous *a.* monstruozan
monstrous *n.* monstrum
month *n.* mesec
monthly *a.* mesečni
monthly *adv* mesečno
monthly *n* mesečnik
monument *n.* spomenik
monumental *a.* monumentalan
moo *v.i* mukanje
mood *n.* raspoloženje
moody *a.* ćudljiv
moon *n.* mesec
moor *n.* vresište
moor *v.t* usidriti brod

moorings *n.* sidrište
moot *n.* sporan
mop *n.* metla
mop *v.t.* brisati
mope *v.i.* biti snužden
moral *a.* moralan
moral *n.* pouka
morale *n.* moral
moralist *n.* moralist
morality *n.* moralnost
moralize *v.t.* moralisati
morbid *a.* morbidan
morbidity *n* morbidnost
more *a.* još
more *adv* više
moreover *adv.* štaviše
morganatic *a.* morgantski
morgue *n.* mrtvačnica
moribund *a.* na umoru
morning *n.* jutro
moron *n.* imbecil
morose *a.* mrzovoljan
morphia *n.* morfijum
morrow *n.* jutro
morsel *n.* zalogaj
mortal *a.* smrtan
mortal *n* smrtnik
mortality *n.* mortalitet
mortar *v.t.* malter
mortgage *n.* hipoteka
mortgage *v.t.* založiti
mortagagee *n.* založni verovnik
mortgagor *n.* založni dužnik
mortify *v.t.* poniziti
mortuary *n.* mrtvačnica
mosaic *n.* mozaik
mosque *n.* džamija
mosquito *n.* komarac
moss *n.* mahovina
most *a.* većinom

**most** *adv.* najviše
**most** *n* većina
**mote** *n.* trunčica
**motel** *n.* motel
**moth** *n.* moljac
**mother** *n* majka
**mother** *v.t.* odgajati
**motherhood** *n.* materinstvo
**motherlike** *a.* majčinski
**motherly** *a.* materinski
**motif** *n.* motiv
**motion** *n.* kretanje
**motion** *v.i.* uputiti
**motionless** *a.* nepokretan
**motivate** *v* motivisati
**motivation** *n.* motivacija
**motive** *n.* motiv
**motley** *a.* šarolik
**motor** *n.* motor
**motor** *v.i.* voziti se
**motorist** *n.* vozač
**mottle** *n.* šara
**motto** *n.* moto
**mould** *n.* kalup
**mould** *v.t.* oblikovati
**mould** *n* humus
**mould** *n* plesan
**mouldy** *a.* ustajao
**moult** *v.i.* mitariti se
**mound** *n.* humka
**mount** *n.* postolje
**mount** *v.t.* postaviti
**mount** *n* brdo
**mountain** *n.* planina
**mountaineer** *n.* planinar
**mountainous** *a.* planinski
**mourn** *v.i.* tugovati
**mourner** *n.* ožalošćeni
**mournful** *n.* žalostan
**mourning** *n.* oplakivanje

**mouse** *n.* miš
**moustache** *n.* brkovi
**mouth** *n.* usta
**mouth** *v.t.* izustiti
**mouthful** *n.* zalogaj
**movable** *a.* pokretan
**movables** *n.* pokretna imovina
**move** *n.* potez
**move** *v.t.* pomeriti
**movement** *n.* pokret
**mover** *n.* pokretač
**movies** *n.* bioskop
**mow** *v.t.* kositi
**much** *a* mnogo
**much** *adv* veoma
**mucilage** *n.* biljni lepak
**muck** *n.* blato
**mucous** *a.* sluzav
**mucus** *n.* sluz
**mud** *n.* blato
**muddle** *n.* zbrka
**muddle** *v.t.* zbrkati
**muffle** *v.t.* prigušiti
**muffler** *n.* prigušivač
**mug** *n.* krigla
**muggy** *a.* sparan
**mulatto** *n.* mulat
**mulberry** *n.* dud
**mule** *n.* mazga
**mulish** *a.* tvrdoglav
**mull** *n.* greben
**mull** *v.t.* zabrljati
**mullah** *n.* mula
**mullion** *n.* drveni stub usred prozora
**multifarious** *a.* raznolik
**multiform** *n.* raznolik
**multilateral** *a.* multilateralan
**multiparous** *a.* multiparan
**multiple** *a.* mnogostruk
**multiple** *n* sadržitelj

multiped *n.* mnogonog
multiplex *a.* višestruk
multiplicand *n.* množenik
multiplication *n.* množenje
multiplicity *n.* mnogostrukost
multiply *v.t.* umnožiti
multitude *n.* mnoštvo
mum *a.* miran
mum *n* mama
mumble *v.i.* mrmljati
mummer *n.* pantomimičar
mummy *n.* mumija
mummy *n* mamica
mumps *n.* zauške
munch *v.t.* žvakati
mundane *a.* svetovni
municipal *a.* opštinski
municipality *n.* opština
munificent *a.* darežljiv
muniment *n.* povelja
munitions *n.* municija
mural *a.* zidni
mural *n.* mural
murder *n.* ubistvo
murder *v.t.* ubiti
murderer *n.* ubica
murderous *a.* ubilački
murmur *n.* žamor
murmur *v.t.* mrmljati
muscle *n.* mišić
muscovite *n.* moskovljanin
muscular *a.* mišićav
muse *v.i.* razmišljati
muse *n* muza
museum *n.* muzej
mush *n.* kaša
mushroom *n.* gljiva
music *n.* muzika
musical *a.* muzički
musician *n.* muzičar

musk *n.* mošus
musket *n.* musketa
musketeer *n.* musketar
muslin *n.* muslin
must *v.* morati
must *n.* obaveza
must *n* mošt
mustache *n.* brkovi
mustang *n.* mustang
mustard *n.* senf
muster *v.t.* prikupiti
muster *n* smotra
musty *a.* buđav
mutation *n.* mutacija
mutative *a.* mutativan
mute *a.* nem
mute *n.* nema osoba
mutilate *v.t.* sakatiti
mutilation *n.* sakaćenje
mutinous *a.* buntovan
mutiny *n.* pobuna
mutiny *v. i.* pobuniti se
mutter *v.i.* promrmljati
mutton *n.* ovčetina
mutual *a.* zajednički
muzzle *n.* njuška
muzzle *v.t* ućutkati
my *a.* moj
myalgia *n.* mijalgija
myopia *n.* kratkovidost
myopic *a.* kratkovid
myosis *n.* mijoza
myriad *n.* bezbroj
myriad *a* bezbrojan
myrrh *n.* mirisna smola
myrtle *n.* mirta
myself *pron.* sebe
mysterious *a.* misteriozan
mystery *n.* misterija
mystic *a.* mističan

**mystic** *n* mistik
**mysticism** *n.* misticizam
**mystify** *v.t.* mistifikovati
**myth** *n.* mit
**mythical** *a.* mitski
**mythological** *a.* mitološki
**mythology** *n.* mitologija

# N

**nab** *v.t.* ščepati
**nabob** *n.* nabob
**nadir** *n.* nadir
**nag** *n.* zanovetanje
**nag** *v.t.* zanovetalo
**nail** *n.* ekser
**nail** *v.t.* zabiti
**naive** *a.* naivan
**naivete** *n.* naivnost
**naivety** *n.* naivnost
**naked** *a.* nag
**name** *n.* ime
**name** *v.t.* imenovati
**namely** *adv.* naime
**namesake** *n.* imenjak
**nap** *v.i.* dremati
**nap** *n.* dremež
**nap** *n* rizikovanje
**nape** *n.* potiljak
**napkin** *n.* salveta
**narcissism** *n.* narcisizam
**narcissus** *n* narcis
**narcosis** *n.* narkoza
**narcotic** *n.* narkotik
**narrate** *v.t.* pripovedati
**narration** *n.* naracija
**narrative** *n.* pripovest
**narrative** *a.* pripovedački
**narrator** *n.* pripovedač

**narrow** *a.* uzak
**narrow** *v.t.* suziti
**nasal** *a.* nazalni
**nasal** *n* nazal
**nascent** *a.* koji se rađa
**nasty** *a.* gadan
**natal** *a.* rodni
**natant** *a.* plivajući
**nation** *n.* nacija
**national** *a.* nacionalni
**nationalism** *n.* nacionalizam
**nationalist** *n.* nacionalista
**nationality** *n.* državljanstvo
**nationalization** *n.* nacionalizacija
**nationalize** *v.t.* nacionalizovati
**native** *a.* maternji
**native** *n* urođenik
**nativity** *n.* rađanje
**natural** *a.* prirodni
**naturalist** *n.* prirodnjak
**naturalize** *v.t.* odomaćiti
**naturally** *adv.* prirodno
**nature** *n.* priroda
**naughty** *a.* nevaljao
**nausea** *n.* mučnina
**nautic(al)** *a.* nautički
**naval** *a.* pomorski
**nave** *n.* brod
**navigable** *a.* plovan
**navigate** *v.i.* upravljati
**navigation** *n.* navigacija
**navigator** *n.* navigator
**navy** *n.* mornarica
**nay** *adv.* čak
**neap** *a.* najniža plima
**near** *a.* blizak
**near** *prep.* blizu
**near** *adv.* u blizini
**near** *v.i.* blizu
**nearly** *adv.* skoro

neat *a.* uredan
nebula *n.* maglina
necessary *n.* potreba
necessary *a* potreban
necessitate *v.t.* zahtevati
necessity *n.* nužda
neck *n.* vrat
necklace *n.* ogrlica
necklet *n.* ukras za vrat
necromancer *n.* prizivač duhova
necropolis *n.* groblje
nectar *n.* nektar
need *n.* nevolja
need *v.t.* trebati
needful *a.* potreban
needle *n.* igla
needless *a.* nepotreban
needs *adv.* svakako
needy *a.* siromašan
nefandous *a.* neopisiv
nefarious *a.* zao
negation *n.* negacija
negative *a.* negativan
negative *n.* negativ
negative *v.t.* odbiti
neglect *v.t.* zanemariti
neglect *n* zanemarivanje
negligence *n.* nemar
negligent *a.* nemaran
negligible *a.* zanemarljiv
negotiable *a.* premostiv
negotiate *v.t.* pregovarati
negotiation *n.* pregovaranje
negotiator *n.* pregovarač
negress *n.* crnkinja
negro *n.* crnac
neigh *v.i.* rzati
neigh *n.* rzanje
neighbour *n.* komšija
neighbourhood *n.* komšiluk

neighbourly *a.* susedski
neither *conj.* ni
nemesis *n.* osvetnik
neolithic *a.* neolitski
neon *n.* neon
nephew *n.* nećak
nepotism *n.* nepotizam
Neptune *n.* neptun
Nerve *n.* živac
nerveless *a.* hladnokrvan
nervous *a.* nervozan
nescience *n.* neznanje
nest *n.* gnezdo
nest *v.t.* ugnezditi
nether *a.* niži
nestle *v.i.* gnijezditi se
nestling *n.* goluždravac
net *n.* mreža
net *v.t.* hvatati mrežom
net *a* neto
net *v.t.* zaraditi
nettle *n.* kopriva
nettle *v.t.* opeći koprivom
network *n.* mreža
neurologist *n.* neurolog
neurology *n.* neurologija
neurosis *n.* neuroza
neuter *a.* srednjeg roda
neuter *n* srednji rod
neutral *a.* neutralan
neutralize *v.t.* neutralisati
neutron *n.* neutron
never *adv.* nikada
nevertheless *conj.* ipak
new *a.* nov
news *n.* vesti
next *a.* sledeći
next *adv.* potom
nib *n.* pero
nibble *v.t.* grickati

**nibble** *n* grickanje
**nice** *a.* lep
**nicety** *n.* uglađenost
**niche** *n.* niša
**nick** *n.* zerez
**nickel** *n.* nikl
**nickname** *n.* nadimak
**nickname** *v.t.* dati nadimak
**nicotine** *n.* nikotin
**niece** *n.* nećaka
**niggard** *n.* škrtica
**niggardly** *a.* škrt
**nigger** *n.* crnac
**nigh** *adv.* blisko
**nigh** *prep.* blizu
**night** *n.* noć
**nightingale** *n.* slavuj
**nightly** *adv.* noću
**nightmare** *n.* noćna mora
**nightie** *n.* spavaćica
**nihilism** *n.* nihilizam
**nil** *n.* nula
**nimble** *a.* okretan
**nimbus** *n.* oreol
**nine** *n.* devet
**nineteen** *n.* devetnaest
**nineteenth** *a.* devetnaesti
**ninetieth** *a.* devedeseti
**ninth** *a.* deveti
**ninety** *n.* devedeset
**nip** *v.t* uštinuti
**nipple** *n.* bradavica
**nitrogen** *n.* azot
**no** *a.* ni jedan
**no** *adv.* nikako
**no** *n* ne
**nobility** *n.* plemstvo
**noble** *a.* plemenit
**noble** *n.* plemenit
**nobleman** *n.* plemić

**nobody** *pron.* niko
**nocturnal** *a.* noćni
**nod** *v.i.* klimati glavom
**node** *n.* čvor
**noise** *n.* buka
**noisy** *a.* bučan
**nomad** *n.* nomad
**nomadic** *a.* nomadski
**nomenclature** *n.* nomenklatura
**nominal** *a.* nominalan
**nominate** *v.t.* nominovati
**nomination** *n.* imenovanje
**nominee** *n* kandidat
**non-alignment** *n.* nesvrstanost
**nonchalance** *n.* nonšalantnost
**nonchalant** *a.* nonšalantan
**none** *pron.* niko
**none** *adv.* nikako
**nonentity** *n.* nepostojanje
**nonetheless** *adv.* pored toga
**nonpareil** *a.* neuporediv
**nonpareil** *n.* nonparel
**nonplus** *v.t.* zbuniti
**nonsense** *n.* besmislica
**nonsensical** *a.* besmislen
**nook** *n.* kutak
**noon** *n.* podne
**noose** *n.* zamka
**noose** *v.t.* uhvatiti u zamku
**nor** *conj* niti
**norm** *n.* norma
**norm** *n.* obrazac
**normal** *a.* normalan
**normalcy** *n.* normalnost
**normalize** *v.t.* normalizovati
**north** *n.* sever
**north** *a* severni
**north** *adv.* severno
**northerly** *a.* severni
**northerly** *adv.* severno

| | |
|---|---|
| **northern** *a.* severni | **november** *n.* novembar |
| **nose** *n.* nos | **novice** *n.* početnik |
| **nose** *v.t* njušiti | **now** *adv.* sada |
| **nosegay** *n.* kita cveća | **now** *conj.* sada |
| **nosey** *a.* nosat | **nowhere** *adv.* nigde |
| **nosy** *a.* njuškalo | **noxious** *a.* štetan |
| **nostalgia** *n.* nostalgija | **nozzle** *n.* mlaznica |
| **nostril** *n.* nozdrva | **nuance** *n.* nijansa |
| **nostrum** *n.* nadrilek | **nubile** *a.* stasala za udaju |
| **not** *adv.* ne | **nuclear** *a.* nuklearna |
| **notability** *n.* značajnost | **nucleus** *n.* jezgro |
| **notable** *a.* značajan | **nude** *a.* akt |
| **notary** *n.* beležnik | **nude** *n* nagost |
| **notation** *n.* notacija | **nudity** *n.* golotinja |
| **notch** *n.* zarez | **nudge** *v.t.* gurkati |
| **note** *n.* napomena | **nugget** *n.* grudva |
| **note** *v.t.* zapisati | **nuisance** *n.* neprilika |
| **noteworthy** *a.* vredan pažnje | **null** *a.* nula |
| **nothing** *n.* ništa | **nullification** *n.* poništenje |
| **nothing** *adv.* ništa | **nullify** *v.t.* poništiti |
| **notice** *a.* primećen | **numb** *a.* ukočen |
| **notice** *v.t.* primetiti | **number** *n.* broj |
| **notification** *n.* obaveštenje | **number** *v.t.* brojati |
| **notify** *v.t.* obavestiti | **numberless** *a.* bezbrojan |
| **notion** *n.* pojam | **numeral** *a.* brojčani |
| **notional** *a.* pojmovni | **numerator** *n.* brojač |
| **notoriety** *n.* ozloglašenost | **numerical** *a.* numerički |
| **notorious** *a.* ozloglašen | **numerous** *a.* brojni |
| **notwithstanding** *prep.* uprkos | **nun** *n.* kaluđerica |
| **notwithstanding** *adv.* ipak | **nunnery** *n.* samostan |
| **notwithstanding** *conj.* premda | **nuptial** *a.* svadbeni |
| **nought** *n.* ništa | **nuptials** *n.* svadba |
| **noun** *n.* imenica | **nurse** *n.* medicinska sestra |
| **nourish** *v.t.* hraniti | **nurse** *v.t* negovati |
| **nourishment** *n.* ishrana | **nursery** *n.* jaslice |
| **novel** *a.* nov | **nurture** *n.* odgoj |
| **novel** *n* roman | **nurture** *v.t.* negovati |
| **novelette** *n.* novela | **nut** *n* orah |
| **novelist** *n.* romanopisac | **nutrition** *n.* ishrana |
| **novelty** *n.* novost | **nutritious** *a.* hranljiv |

nutritive *a.* nutritivan
nuzzle *v.* njuškati
nylon *n.* najlon
nymph *n.* nimfa

oak *n.* hrast
oar *n.* veslo
oarsman *n.* veslač
oasis *n.* oaza
oat *n.* zob
oath *n.* zakletva
obduracy *n.* bezdušnost
obdurate *a.* tvrdokoran
obedience *n.* poslušnost
obedient *a.* poslušan
obeisance *n.* naklon
obesity *n.* gojaznost
obey *v.t.* pokoravati se
obituary *a.* posmrtni
object *n.* objekat
object *v.t.* prigovoriti
objection *n.* prigovor
objective *n.* cilj
objective *a.* objektivan
oblation *n.* žrtva
obligation *n.* obaveza
obligatory *a.* obavezan
oblige *v.t.* obavezati
oblique *a.* posredan
obliterate *v.t.* uništiti
obliteration *n.* brisanje
oblivion *n.* zaborav
oblivious *a.* nesvestan
oblong *a.* duguljast
oblong *n.* duguljasta figura
obnoxious *a.* odvratan
obnoxiously *adv.* odvratano

obscene *a.* opscen
obscenity *n.* razvratnost
obscure *a.* nejasan
obscure *v.t.* potamneti
obscurity *n.* nejasnost
observance *n.* pridržavanje
observant *a.* posmatrački
observation *n.* posmatranje
observatory *n.* opservatorija
observe *v.t.* posmatrati
obsess *v.t.* opsednuti
obsession *n.* opsesija
obsolete *a.* zastareo
obstacle *n.* prepreka
obstinacy *n.* tvrdoglavost
obstinate *a.* tvrdoglav
obstruct *v.t.* ometati
obstruction *n.* opstrukcija
obstructive *a.* opstruktivan
obtain *v.t.* dobiti
obtainable *a.* koji se može dobiti
obtuse *a.* tup
obvious *a.* očigledan
occasion *n.* prilika
occasion *v.t* prouzrokovati
occasional *a.* povremen
occasionally *adv.* povremeno
occident *n.* zapad
occidental *a.* zapadnjački
occult *a.* okultan
occupancy *n.* stanovanje
occupant *n.* stanar
occupation *n.* zanimanje
occupier *n.* okupator
occupy *v.t.* zauzeti
occur *v.i.* desiti se
occurrence *n.* događaj
ocean *n.* okean
oceanic *a.* okeanski
octagon *n.* osmougao

octangular *a.* osmougli
octave *n.* oktava
October *n.* oktobar
octogenarian *a.* osamdesetogodišnji
octogenarian *a* osamdesetogodišnje
octroi *n.* porez na uvezenu robu
ocular *a.* očni
oculist *n.* okular
odd *a.* neparan
oddity *n.* nastranost
odds *n.* izgledi
ode *n.* oda
odious *a.* mrzak
odium *n.* mrskost
odorous *a.* miomirisan
odour *n.* miris
offence *n.* uvreda
offend *v.t.* uvrediti
offender *n.* prestupnik
offensive *a.* napadački
offensive *n* napad
offer *v.t.* ponuditi
offer *n* ponuda
offering *n.* pružanje
office *n.* kancelarija
officer *n.* oficir
official *a.* službeni
official *n* zvaničnik
officially *adv.* zvanično
officiate *v.i.* službovati
officious *a.* preterano uslužan
offing *n.* pučina
offset *v.t.* izjednačiti
offset *n* izdanak
offshoot *n.* mladica
offspring *n.* potomak
oft *adv.* često
often *adv.* često
ogle *v.t.* očijukati
ogle *n* očijukanje

oil *n.* ulje
oil *v.t* uljiti
oily *a.* mastan
ointment *n.* mast
old *a.* star
oligarchy *n.* oligarhija
olive *n.* maslina
olympiad *n.* olimpijada
omega *n.* omega
omelette *n.* omplet
omen *n.* slutnja
ominous *a.* zloslustan
omission *n.* izostavljanje
omit *v.t.* izostaviti
omnipotence *n.* svemoć
omnipotent *a.* svemoguć
omnipresence *n.* sveprisutnost
omnipresent *a.* sveprisutan
omniscience *n.* sveznanje
omniscient *a.* sveznajući
on *prep.* na
on *adv.* dalje
once *adv.* jednom
one *a.* jedan
one *pron.* neko
oneness *n.* jedinstvo
onerous *a.* tegoban
onion *n.* luk
on-looker *n.* osmatrač
only *a.* jedini
only *adv.* samo
only *conj.* samo što
onomatopoeia *n.* onomatopeja
onrush *n.* nadiranje
onset *n.* početak
onslaught *n.* juriš
onus *n.* teret
onward *a.* napred
onwards *adv.* nadalje
ooze *n.* glib

**ooze** *v.i.* curiti
**opacity** *n.* neprozirnost
**opal** *n.* opal
**opaque** *a.* neproziran
**open** *a.* otvoren
**open** *v.t.* otvoriti
**opening** *n.* otvaranje
**openly** *adv.* otvoreno
**opera** *n.* opera
**operate** *v.t.* raditi
**operation** *n.* operacija
**operative** *a.* operativan
**operator** *n.* operator
**opine** *v.t.* misliti
**opinion** *n.* mišljenje
**opium** *n.* opijum
**opponent** *n.* protivnik
**opportune** *a.* prikladan
**opportunism** *n.* oportunizam
**opportunity** *n.* prilika
**oppose** *v.t.* suprotstaviti
**opposite** *a.* suprotan
**opposition** *n.* opozicija
**oppress** *v.t.* ugnjetavati
**oppression** *n.* ugnjetavanje
**oppressive** *a.* tiranski
**oppressor** *n.* tlačitelj
**opt** *v.i.* odlučiti se
**optic** *a.* optički
**optician** *n.* optičar
**optimism** *n.* optimizam
**optimist** *n.* optimista
**optimistic** *a.* optimistički
**optimum** *n.* optimum
**optimum** *a* optimalan
**option** *n.* opcija
**optional** *a.* neobavezan
**opulence** *n.* bogatstvo
**opulent** *a.* bogat
**oracle** *n.* proročanstvo

**oracular** *a.* proročanski
**oral** *a.* usmen
**orally** *adv.* usmeno
**orange** *n.* pomorandža
**orange** *a* narandžast
**oration** *n.* govor
**orator** *n.* govornik
**oratorical** *a.* govornički
**oratory** *n.* oratorijum
**orb** *n.* nebesko telo
**orbit** *n.* orbita
**orchard** *n.* voćnjak
**orchestra** *n.* orkestar
**orchestral** *a.* orkestarski
**ordeal** *n.* iskušenje
**order** *n.* red
**order** *v.t* naručiti
**orderly** *a.* uredan
**orderly** *n.* uredno
**ordinance** *n.* obred
**ordinarily** *adv.* redovno
**ordinary** *a.* redovan
**ordnance** *n.* borbena tehnika
**ore** *n.* ruda
**organ** *n.* organ
**organic** *a.* organski
**organism** *n.* organizam
**organization** *n.* organizacija
**organize** *v.t.* organizovati
**orient** *n.* Orijent
**orient** *v.t.* orijentisati
**oriental** *a.* orijentalan
**oriental** *n* istočnjak
**orientate** *v.t.* orijentisati
**origin** *n.* poreklo
**original** *a.* originalan
**original** *n* original
**originality** *n.* originalnost
**originate** *v.t.* voditi poreklo
**originator** *n.* tvorac

ornament *n.* ornament
ornament *v.t.* ukrasiti
ornamental *a.* ukrasni
ornamentation *n.* ukrašavanje
orphan *n.* siroče
orphan *v.t* učiniti siročetom
orphanage *n.* sirotište
orthodox *a.* pravoslavan
orthodoxy *n.* pravoslavlje
oscillate *v.i.* oscilovati
oscillation *n.* oscilacija
ossify *v.t.* okoštati
ostracize *v.t.* prognati
ostrich *n.* noj
other *a.* drugi
other *pron.* drugi
otherwise *adv.* inače
otherwise *conj.* inače
otter *n.* vidra
ottoman *n.* otoman
ounce *n.* unca
our *pron.* naš
oust *v.t.* istisnuti
out *adv.* van
out-balance *v.t.* prevagnuti
outbid *v.t.* više ponuditi
outbreak *n.* izbijanje
outburst *n.* izliv
outcast *n.* izgnanik
outcast *a* izgnan
outcome *n.* ishod
outcry *a.* negodovanje
outdated *a.* zastareo
outdo *v.t.* nadmašiti
outdoor *a.* napolju
outer *a.* spoljni
outfit *n.* oprema
outfit *v.t* otpremiti
outgrow *v.t.* prerasti
outhouse *n.* poljski klozet

outing *n.* izlet
outlandish *a.* čudnovat
outlaw *n.* odmetnik
outlaw *v.t* staviti van zakona
outline *n.* skica
outline *v.t.* skicirati
outlive *v.i.* nadživeti
outlook *n.* gledište
outmoded *a.* staromodan
outnumber *v.t.* nadmašiti u brojnosti
outpatient *n.* ambulantni bolesnik
outpost *n.* predstraža
output *n.* izlaz
outrage *n.* nasilje
outrage *v.t.* počiniti nasilje
outright *adv.* izravno
outright *a* izravan
outrun *v.t.* nadmašiti u trčanju
outset *n.* polazak
outshine *v.t.* nadsijati
outside *a.* spoljni
outside *n* spoljašnjost
outside *adv* napolju
outside *prep* izvan
outsider *n.* autsajder
outsize *a.* prevelik
outskirts *n.pl.* periferija
outspoken *a.* otvoren
outstanding *a.* izvanredan
outward *a.* spoljašnji
outward *adv* van
outwards *adv* napolje
outwardly *adv.* napolju
outweigh *v.t.* pretegnuti
outwit *v.t.* nadmudriti
oval *a.* ovalan
oval *n* oval
ovary *n.* jajnik
ovation *n.* ovacija
oven *n.* peć

over *prep.* preko
over *adv* više
over *n* višak
overact *v.t.* preterivati
overall *n.* ogrtač
overall *a* ukupan
overawe *v.t.* preplašiti
overboard *adv.* preko palube
overburden *v.t.* preopteretiti
overcast *a.* oblačan
overcharge *v.t.* preopteretiti
overcharge *n* preopterećenje
overcoat *n.* kaput
overcome *v.t.* prevazići
overdo *v.t.* preterati
overdose *n.* prevelika doza
overdose *v.t.* predozirati
overdraft *n.* prekoračenje računa
overdraw *v.t.* prekoračiti račun
overdue *a.* zakasneo
overhaul *v.t.* pregledati
overhaul *n.* pregled
overhear *v.t.* načuti
overjoyed *a* presrećan
overlap *v.t.* preklapati
overlap *n* preklapanje
overleaf *adv.* na drugoj strani
overload *v.t.* preopteretiti
overload *n* preopterećenje
overlook *v.t.* prevideti
overnight *adv.* preko noći
overnight *a* noćni
overpower *v.t.* nadjačati
overrate *v.t.* preceniti
overrule *v.t.* nadglasati
overrun *v.t* pretrčati
oversee *v.t.* nadgledati
overseer *n.* nadzornik
overshadow *v.t.* zaseniti
oversight *n.* nadzor

overt *a.* otvoren
overtake *v.t.* prestići
overthrow *v.t.* srušiti
overthrow *n* rušenje
overtime *adv.* prekovremeno
overtime *n* prekovremeni rad
overture *n.* uvertira
overwhelm *v.t.* savladati
overwork *v.i.* preopteretiti radom
overwork *n.* prekomeran rad
owe *v.t* dugovati
owl *n.* sova
own *a.* svoje
own *v.t.* posedovati
owner *n.* vlasnik
ownership *n.* vlasništvo
ox *n.* vo
oxygen *n.* kiseonik
oyster *n.* ostriga

# P

pace *n* korak
pace *v.i.* koračati
pacific *a.* miroljubiv
pacify *v.t.* umiriti
pack *n.* paket
pack *v.t.* upakovati
package *n.* paket
packet *n.* zavežljaj
packing *n.* pakovanje
pact *n.* pakt
pad *n.* jastuk
pad *v.t.* obložiti
padding *n.* punjenje
paddle *v.i.* veslati
paddle *n* veslo
paddy *n.* pirinač
page *n.* strana

page v.t. prelomiti
pageant n. parada
svečanost n. velelepnost
pagoda n. pagoda
pail n. kanta
pain n. bol
pain v.t. boleti
painful a. bolan
painstaking a. radan
paint n. boja
paint v.t. bojiti
painter n. slikar
painting n. slika
pair n. par
pair v.t. spariti
pal n. drug
palace n. palata
palanquin n. palankin
palatable a. ukusan
palatal a. nepčan
palate n. nepce
palatial a. veličanstven
pale n. kolac
pale a bled
pale v.i. pobledeti
palette n. paleta
palm n. palma
palm v.t. dodirnuti
palm n. dlan
palmist n. hiromant
palmistry n. hiromantija
palpable a. opipljiv
palpitate v.i. podrhtavati
palpitation n. treperenje
palsy n. paraliza
paltry a. tričav
pamper v.t. razmaziti
pamphlet n. pamflet
pamphleteer n. pamfletista
panacea n. panaceja

pandemonium n. urnebes
pane n. okno
panegyric n. panegirik
panel n. tabla
panel v.t. oblagati
pang n. žiganje
panic n. panika
panorama n. panorama
pant v.i. brektati
pant n. brektanje
pantaloon n. lakrdijaš
pantheism n. panteizam
pantheist n. panteista
panther n. panter
pantomime n. pantomima
pantry n. ostava
papacy n. papstvo
papal a. papski
paper n. papir
par n. jednakost
parable n. parabola
parachute n. padobran
parachutist n. padobranac
parade n. parada
parade v.t. paradirati
paradise n. raj
paradox n. paradoks
paradoxical a. paradoksalan
paraffin n. parafin
paragon n. uzor
paragraph n. paragraf
parallel a. paralelan
parallel v.t. načiniti paralelnim
parallelism n. paralelizam
parallelogram n. paralelogram
paralyse v.t. paralizovati
paralysis n. paraliza
paralytic a. paralitički
paramount n. ono što je glavno
paramour n. ljubavnik

**paraphernalia** *n. pl* pribor
**paraphrase** *n.* parafraza
**paraphrase** *v.t.* parafrazirati
**parasite** *n.* parazit
**parcel** *n.* parcela
**parcel** *v.t.* razdeliti
**parch** *v.t.* sprziti
**pardon** *v.t.* oprostiti
**pardon** *n.* oproštenje
**pardonable** *a.* oprostiv
**parent** *n.* roditelj
**parentage** *n.* roditeljstvo
**parental** *a.* roditeljski
**parenthesis** *n.* umetak
**parish** *n.* parohija
**parity** *n.* paritet
**park** *n.* park
**park** *v.t.* parkirati
**parlance** *n.* način govora
**parley** *n.* pregovaranje
**parley** *v.i* pregovarati
**parliament** *n.* parlament
**parliamentarian** *n.* parlamentarac
**parliamentary** *a.* parlamentaran
**parlour** *n.* soba za posete
**parody** *n.* parodija
**parody** *v.t.* parodirati
**parole** *n.* uslovni otpust
**parole** *v.t.* uslovno otpustiti
**parricide** *n.* roditeljoubistvo
**parrot** *n.* papagaj
**parry** *v.t.* parirati
**parry** *n.* pariranje
**parson** *n.* paroh
**part** *n.* deo
**part** *v.t.* deliti
**partake** *v.i.* učestvovati
**partial** *a.* delimičan
**partiality** *n.* pristrasnost
**participate** *v.i.* učestvovati

**participant** *n.* učesnik
**participation** *n.* učešće
**particle** *a.* poput čestice
**particular** *a.* poseban
**particular** *n.* pojedinost
**partisan** *n.* partizan
**partisan** *a.* partizanski
**partition** *n.* podela
**partition** *v.t.* podeliti
**partner** *n.* partner
**partnership** *n.* partnerstvo
**party** *n.* stranka
**pass** *v.i.* proći
**pass** *n* prolaz
**passage** *n.* pasus
**passenger** *n.* putnik
**passion** *n.* strast
**passionate** *a.* strastven
**passive** *a.* pasivan
**passport** *n.* pasoš
**past** *a.* prošli
**past** *n.* prošlost
**past** *prep.* posle
**paste** *n.* pasta
**paste** *v.t.* lepiti
**pastel** *n.* pastel
**pastime** *n.* razonoda
**pastoral** *a.* pastirski
**pasture** *n.* pašnjak
**pasture** *v.t.* pasti
**pat** *v.t.* tapkati
**pat** *n* tapkanje
**pat** *adv* upravo
**patch** *v.t.* zakrpiti
**patch** *n* zakrpa
**patent** *a.* patentan
**patent** *n* patent
**patent** *v.t.* patentni
**paternal** *a.* očinski
**path** *n.* put

| | |
|---|---|
| **pathetic** *a.* patetičan | **peasant** *n.* seljak |
| **pathos** *n.* patos | **peasantry** *n.* seljaštvo |
| **patience** *n.* strpljenje | **pebble** *n.* šljunak |
| **patient** *a.* strpljiv | **peck** *n.* kljucanje |
| **patient** *n* pacijent | **peck** *v.i.* kljucati |
| **patricide** *n.* oceubistvo | **peculiar** *a.* čudan |
| **patrimony** *n.* očevina | **peculiarity** *n.* svojstvenost |
| **patriot** *n.* patriota | **pecuniary** *a.* novčan |
| **patriotic** *a.* patriotski | **pedagogue** *n.* pedagog |
| **partiotism** *n.* partiotizam | **pedagogy** *n.* pedagogija |
| **patrol** *v.i.* patrolirati | **pedal** *n.* pedala |
| **patrol** *n* patrola | **pedal** *v.t.* voziti bicikl |
| **patron** *n.* pokrovitelj | **pedant** *n.* pedant |
| **patronage** *n.* pokroviteljstvo | **pedantic** *n.* pedantan |
| **patronize** *v.t.* štititi | **pedantry** *n.* pedanterija |
| **pattern** *n.* obrazac | **pedestal** *n.* postolje |
| **paucity** *n.* malobrojnost | **pedestrian** *n.* pešak |
| **pauper** *n.* siromah | **pedigree** *n.* pedigre |
| **pause** *n.* pauza | **peel** *v.t.* oljuštiti |
| **pause** *v.i.* zastati | **peel** *n.* kora |
| **pave** *v.t.* popločati | **peep** *v.i.* viriti |
| **pavement** *n.* pločnik | **peep** *n* virenje |
| **pavilion** *n.* paviljon | **peer** *n.* plemić |
| **paw** *n.* šapa | **peerless** *a.* bez premca |
| **paw** *v.t.* udariti šapom | **peg** *n.* klin |
| **pay** *v.t.* platiti | **peg** *v.t.* prikovati |
| **pay** *n* plata | **pelf** *n.* dobitak |
| **payable** *a.* plativ | **pell-mell** *adv.* zbrkano |
| **payee** *n.* primalac | **pen** *n.* pero |
| **payment** *n.* plaćanje | **pen** *v.t.* pisati |
| **pea** *n.* grašak | **penal** *a.* kazneni |
| **peace** *n.* mir | **penalize** *v.t.* kazniti |
| **peaceable** *a.* miroljubiv | **penalty** *n.* kazna |
| **peaceful** *a.* miran | **pencil** *n.* olovka |
| **peach** *n.* breskva | **pencil** *v.t.* slikati |
| **peacock** *n.* paun | **pending** *prep.* u toku |
| **peahen** *n.* paunica | **pending** *a* neodređen |
| **peak** *n.* vrh | **pendulum** *n.* klatno |
| **pear** *n.* kruška | **penetrate** *v.t.* prodreti |
| **pearl** *n.* biser | **penetration** *n.* penetracija |

**penis** *n.* penis
**penniless** *a.* bez novca
**penny** *n.* peni
**pension** *n.* penzija
**pension** *v.t.* penzionisati
**pensioner** *n.* penzioner
**pensive** *a.* zadubljen u misli
**pentagon** *n.* pentagon
**peon** *n.* nadničar
**people** *n.* narod
**people** *v.t.* naseliti
**pepper** *n.* biber
**pepper** *v.t.* biberiti
**per** *prep.* na, po
**perambulator** *n.* dečija kolica
**perceive** *v.t.* opaziti
**perceptible** *adj* primetan
**per** *cent adv.* odsto
**percentage** *n.* procenat
**perception** *n.* percepcija
**perceptive** *a.* perceptivan
**perch** *n.* grgeč
**perch** *v.i.* spustiti se
**perennial** *a.* višegodišnji
**perennial** *n.* trajnica
**perfect** *a.* savršen
**perfect** *v.t.* usavršiti
**perfection** *n.* savršenstvo
**perfidy** *n.* podmuklost
**perforate** *v.t.* probušiti
**perforce** *adv.* silom
**perform** *v.t.* izvesti
**performance** *n.* izvođenje
**performer** *n.* izvođač
**perfume** *n.* parfem
**perfume** *v.t.* namirisati
**perhaps** *adv.* možda
**peril** *n.* opasnost
**peril** *v.t.* ugroziti
**perilous** *a.* opasan

**period** *n.* period
**periodical** *n.* časopis
**periodical** *a.* periodičan
**periphery** *n.* periferija
**perish** *v.i.* poginuti
**perishable** *a.* kvarljiv
**perjure** *v.i.* lažno se zakleti
**perjury** *n.* krivokletstvo
**permanence** *n.* trajnost
**permanent** *a.* trajan
**permissible** *a.* dopustiv
**permission** *n.* dopuštenje
**permit** *v.t.* dozvoliti
**permit** *n.* dozvola
**permutation** *n.* permutacija
**pernicious** *a.* škodljiv
**perpendicular** *a.* vertikalan
**perpendicular** *n.* vertikala
**perpetual** *a.* večit
**perpetuate** *v.t.* ovekovečiti
**perplex** *v.t.* zbuniti
**perplexity** *n.* zbunjenost
**persecute** *v.t.* progoniti
**persecution** *n.* proganjanje
**perseverance** *n.* istrajnost
**persevere** *v.i.* istrajati
**persist** *v.i.* izdržati
**persistence** *n.* izdržljivost
**persistent** *a.* uporan
**person** *n.* osoba
**personage** *n.* ugledna ličnost
**personal** *a.* lični
**personality** *n.* ličnost
**personification** *n.* personifikacija
**personify** *v.t.* oličavati
**personnel** *n.* osoblje
**perspective** *n.* perspektiva
**perspiration** *n.* znojenje
**perspire** *v.i.* znojiti se
**persuade** *v.t.* ubediti

| | |
|---|---|
| persuasion n. ubeđivanje | philology n. filologija |
| pertain v.i. odnositi se | philosopher n. filozof |
| pertinent a. prigodan | philosophical a. filozofski |
| perturb v.t. poremetiti | philosophy n. filozofija |
| perusal n. pregled | phone n. telefon |
| peruse v.t. pregledati | phonetic a. fonetski |
| pervade v.t. prožimati | phonetics n. fonetika |
| perverse a. perverzan | phosphate n. fosfat |
| perversion n. perverzija | phosphorus n. fosfor |
| perversity n. izopačenost | photo n fotografija |
| pervert v.t. pokvarenjak | photograph v.t. fotografisati |
| pessimism n. pesimizam | photograph n fotografija |
| pessimist n. pesimista | photographer n. fotograf |
| pessimistic a. pesimističan | photographic a. fotografski |
| pest n. štetočina | photography n. fotografija |
| pesticide n. pesticid | phrase n. fraza |
| pestilence n. kuga | phrase v.t. izraziti |
| pet n. ljubimac | phraseology n. frazeologija |
| pet v.t. milovati | physic n. medicina |
| petal n. latica | physic v.t. lečiti |
| petition n. peticija | physical a. fizički |
| petition v.t. moliti | physician n. lekar |
| petitioner n. molilac | physicist n. fizičar |
| petrol n. benzin | physics n. fizika |
| petroleum n. nafta | physiognomy n. fizionomija |
| petticoat n. podsuknja | physique n. stas |
| petty a. sitan | pianist n. pijanista |
| petulance n. nestašnost | piano n. klavir |
| petulant a. mrzovoljan | pick v.t. izabrati |
| phantom n. fantom | pick n. izbor |
| pharmacy n. apoteka | picket n. kolac |
| phase n. faza | picket v.t. ograditi kolcima |
| phenomenal a. fenomenalan | pickle n. turšija |
| phenomenon n. fenomen | pickle v.t ukiseliti |
| phial n. bočica | picnic n. piknik |
| philanthropic a. filantropski | picnic v.i. ići na izlet |
| philanthropist n. filantrop | pictorical a. slikarski |
| philanthropy n. filantropija | picture n. slika |
| philological a. filološki | picture v.t. naslikati |
| philologist n. filolog | picturesque a. slikovit |

piece *n.* komad
piece *v.t.* sastaviti
pierce *v.t.* izbosti
piety *n.* pobožnost
pig *n.* svinja
pigeon *n.* golub
pigmy *n.* pigmej
pile *n.* gomila
pile *v.t.* gomilati
piles *n.* hemoroidi
pilfer *v.t.* ukrasti
pilgrim *n.* hodočasnik
pilgrimage *n.* hodočašće
pill *n.* pilula
pillar *n.* stub
pillow *n* jastuk
pillow *v.t.* položiti
pilot *n.* pilot
pilot *v.t.* pilotirati
pimple *n.* bubuljica
pin *n.* čioda
pin *v.t.* pribosti
pinch *v.t.* uštinuti
pinch *v.* stisnuti
pine *n.* bor
pine *v.i.* čeznuti
pineapple *n.* ananas
pink *n.* karanfil, ružičasta boja
pink *a* ružičast
pinkish *a.* ružičast
pinnacle *n.* vrhunac
pioneer *n.* pionir
pioneer *v.t.* krčiti
pious *a.* pobožan
pipe *n.* cev, lula
pipe *v.i* svirati na fruli
piquant *a.* pikantan
piracy *n.* piratstvo
pirate *n.* gusar
pirate *v.t* izdavati

pistol *n.* pištolj
piston *n.* klip
pit *n.* jama
pit *v.t.* staviti u jamu
pitch *n.* smola
pitch *v.t.* zaliti
pitcher *n.* krčag
piteous *a.* bedan
pitfall *n.* zamka
pitiable *a.* jadan
pitiful *a.* sažaljiv
pitiless *a.* nemilosrdan
pitman *n.* kopač
pittance *n.* mali deo
pity *n.* sažaljenje
pity *v.t.* sažaljevati
pivot *n.* stožer
pivot *v.t.* okretati se
placard *n.* plakat
place *n.* mesto
place *v.t.* smestiti
placid *a.* miran
plague *a.* kuga
plague *v.t.* zaraziti
plain *a.* jednostavan
plain *n.* ravan
plaintiff *n.* tužilac
plan *n.* plana
plan *v.t.* planirati
plane *n.* ravnica
plane *v.t.* izravnati
plane *a.* ravan
plane *n* platan
planet *n.* planeta
planetary *a.* planetarni
plank *n.* daska
plank *v.t.* obložiti daskama
plant *n.* biljka
plant *v.t.* saditi
plantain *n.* bokvice

plantation *n.* plantaža

plaster *n.* flaster

plaster *v.t.* okrečiti

plate *n.* ploča

plate *v.t.* oklopiti

plateau *n.* plato

platform *n.* platforma

platonic *a.* platonski

platoon *n.* vod

play *n.* igra

play *v.i.* igrati se

player *n.* igrač

plea *n.* molba

plead *v.i.* obraćati se

pleader *n.* branilac

pleasant *a.* prijatan

pleasantry *n.* šala

please *v.t.* ugoditi

pleasure *n.* zadovoljstvo

plebiscite *n.* plebiscit

pledge *n.* zaloga

pledge *v.t.* zaloga

plenty *n.* mnogo

plight *n.* stanje

plod *v.i.* teško koračati

plot *n.* zaplet

plot *v.t.* smišljati

plough *n.* plug

plough *v.i* orati

ploughman *n.* orač

pluck *v.t.* otrgnuti

pluck *n* trzanje

plug *n.* utikač

plug *v.t.* začepiti

plum *n.* šljiva

plumber *n.* vodoinstalater

plunder *v.t.* pljačkanje

plunder *n* pljačkati

plunge *v.t.* zaroniti

plunge *n* ronjenje

plural *a.* množina

plurality *n.* pluralitet

plus *a.* dodatni

plus *n* plus

ply *v.t.* upotrebljavati

ply *n* nabor

pneumonia zapaljenje pluća

pocket *n.* džep

pocket *v.t.* staviti u džep

pod *n.* mahuna

poem *n.* pesma

poesy *n.* poezija

poet *n.* pesnik

poetaster *n.* stihoklepac

poetess *n.* pesnikinja

poetic *a.* poetski

poetics *n.* poetika

poetry *n.* poezija

poignancy *n.* oštrina

poignant *a.* oštar

point *n.* tačka

point *v.t.* zaoštriti

poise *v.t.* izbalansirati

poise *n* ravnoteža

poison *n.* otrov

poison *v.t.* otrovati

poisonous *a.* otrovan

poke *v.t.* gurati

poke *n.* vreća

polar *n.* polarni

pole *n.* pol

police *n.* policija

policeman *n.* policajac

policy *n.* politika

polish *v.t.* polirati

polish *n* sjaj

polite *a.* učtiv

politeness *n.* učtivost

politic *a.* lukav

political *a.* politički

politician *n.* političar
politics *n.* politika
polity *n.* državno uređenje
poll *n.* anketa
poll *v.t.* seći
pollen *n.* polen
pollute *v.t.* zagaditi
pollution *n.* zagađenje
polo *n.* polo
polygamous *a.* poligamski
polygamy *n.* poligamija
polyglot1 *n.* poliglota
polyglot2 *a.* poliglotski
polytechnic *a.* politehnički
polytechnic *n.* politehnika
polytheism *n.* politeizam
polytheist *n.* politeista
polytheistic *a.* politeistički
pomp *n.* raskoš
pomposity *n.* pompeznost
pompous *a.* pompezan
pond *n.* ribnjak
ponder *v.t.* razmišljati
pony *n.* poni
poor *a.* jadan
pop *v.i.* pucati
pop *n* prasak
pope *n.* papa
poplar *n.* topola
poplin *n.* puplin
populace *n.* stanovništvo
popular *a.* popularan
popularity *n.* popularnost
popularize *v.t.* popularizovati
populate *v.t.* naseliti
population *n.* stanovništvo
populous *a.* naseljen
porcelain *n.* porcelan
porch *n.* veranda
pore *n.* pora

pork *n.* svinjsko meso
porridge *n.* kaša
port *n.* luka
portable *a.* pokretan
portage *n.* nošenje
portal *n.* portal
portend *v.t.* nagovestiti
porter *n.* vratar
portfolio *n.* portfolio
portico *n.* trem
portion *n* deo
portion *v.t.* deliti
portrait *n.* portret
portraiture *n.* portretisanje
portray *v.t.* oslikati
portrayal *n.* portret
pose *v.i.* pozirati
pose *n.* poza
position *n.* mesto
position *v.t.* staviti
positive *a.* pozitivan
possess *v.t.* posedovati
possession *n.* posedovanje
possibility *n.* mogućnost
possible *a.* moguć
post *n.* sub
post *v.t.* postaviti
post *n* glasnik
post *v.t.* objaviti
post *adv.* posle
postage *n.* poštarina
postal *a.* poštanski
post-date *v.t.* staviti kasniji datum
poster *n.* plakat
posterity *n.* potomstvo
posthumous *a.* posmrtni
postman *n.* poštar
postmaster *n.* upravnik pošte
post-mortem *a.* obdukcioni
post-mortem *n.* obdukcija

post-office *n.* pošta
postpone *v.t.* odložiti
postponement *n.* odlaganje
postscript *n.* *post* skriptum
posture *n.* stav
pot *n.* lonac
pot *v.t.* ostaviti
potash *n.* potaša
potassium *n.* kalijum
potato *n.* krompir
potency *n.* potentnost
potent *a.* potentan
potential *a.* moguć
potential *n.* mogućnost
pontentiality *n.* potencijal
potter *n.* grnčar
pottery *n.* grnčarija
pouch *n.* vrećica
poultry *n.* živina
pounce *v.i.* zaleteti se
pounce *n* zalet
pound *n.* funta
pound *v.t.* zatvoriti
pour *v.i.* sipati
poverty *n.* siromaštvo
powder *n.* prah
powder *v.t.* naprašiti
power *n.* snaga
powerful *a.* moćan
practicability *n.* izvodljivost
practicable *a.* izvodljiv
practical *a.* praktičan
practice *n.* praksa
practise *v.t.* uvežbavati
practitioner *n.* praktičar
pragmatic *a.* pragmatičan
pragmatism *n.* pragmatizam
praise *n.* pohvala
praise *v.t.* hvaliti
praiseworthy *a.* pohvalan

prank *n.* nestašluk
prattle *v.i.* brbljati
prattle *n.* brbljanje
pray *v.i.* moliti
prayer *n.* molitva
preach *v.i.* propovedati
preacher *n.* propovednik
preamble *n.* predgovor
precaution *n.* predostrožnost
precautionary *a.* obazriv
precede *v.* prethoditi
precedence *n.* prednost
precedent *n.* presedan
precept *n.* pravilo
preceptor *n.* učitelj
precious *a.* dragocen
precis *n.* izvod
precise *n.* preciznost
precision *n.* preciznost
precursor *n.* prethodnik
predecessor *n.* prethodnik
predestination *n.* predodređenje
predetermine *v.t.* predodrediti
predicament *n.* neprilika
predicate *n.* predikat
predict *v.t.* predvideti
prediction *n.* predviđanje
predominance *n.* prevlast
predominant *a.* nadmoćan
predominate *v.i.* preovlađivati
pre-eminence *n.* nadmoćnost
pre-eminent *a.* nadmoćan
preface *n.* predgovor
preface *v.t.* snabdeti predgovorom
prefect *n.* prefekt
prefer *v.t.* *više* voleti
preference *n.* sklonost
preferential *a.* povlašćen
prefix *n.* prefiks
prefix *v.t.* dodati prefiks

**pregnancy** *n.* trudnoća
**pregnant** *a.* trudna
**prehistoric** *a.* praistorijski
**prejudice** *n.* predrasuda
**prelate** *n.* prelat
**preliminary** *a.* preliminaran
**preliminary** *n* priprema
**prelude** *n.* uvod
**prelude** *v.t.* uvesti
**premarital** *a.* predbračni
**premature** *a.* prevremen
**premeditate** *v.t.* unapred smisliti
**premeditation** *n.* predumišljaj
**premier** *a.* premijer
**premier** *n* premijer
**premiere** *n.* premijera
**premium** *n.* premija
**premonition** *n.* predosećanje
**preoccupation** *n.* preokupacija
**preoccupy** *v.t.* zaokupiti
**preparation** *n.* priprema
**preparatory** *a.* pripremni
**prepare** *v.t.* pripremiti
**preponderance** *n.* prevaga
**preponderate** *v.i.* premašivati
**preposition** *n.* predlog
**prerequisite** *a.* preduslovan
**prerequisite** *n* preduslov
**prerogative** *n.* privilegija
**prescience** *n.* predosećanje
**prescribe** *v.t.* propisati
**prescription** *n.* recept
**presence** *n.* prisustvo
**present** *a.* prisutan
**present** *n.* poklon
**present** *v.t.* predstaviti
**presentation** *n.* prezentacija
**presently** *adv.* uskoro
**preservation** *n.* čuvanje
**preservative** *n.* prezervativ

**preservative** *a.* zaštitni
**preserve** *v.t.* sačuvati
**preserve** *n.* ukuvano voće
**preside** *v.i.* predsedavati
**president** *n.* predsednik
**presidential** *a.* predsednički
**press** *v.t.* pritisnite
**press** *n* štampa
**pressure** *n.* pritisak
**pressurize** *v.t.* staviti pod pritisak
**prestige** *n.* prestiž
**prestigious** *a.* prestižan
**presume** *v.t.* pretpostaviti
**presumption** *n.* pretpostavka
**presuppose** *v.t.* pretpostaviti
**presupposition** *n.* pretpostavljanje
**pretence** *n.* pretvaranje
**pretend** *v.t.* pretvarati se
**pretension** *n.* pretenzija
**pretentious** *a.* pretenciozan
**pretext** *n* izgovor
**prettiness** *n.* lepota
**pretty** *a* lep
**pretty** *adv.* prilično
**prevail** *v.i.* preovlađivati
**prevalence** *n.* prevlast
**prevalent** *a.* preovlađujući
**prevent** *v.t.* sprečiti
**prevention** *n.* prevencija
**preventive** *a.* preventivan
**previous** *a.* prethodni
**prey** *n.* plen
**prey** *v.i.* vrebati
**price** *n.* cena
**price** *v.t.* ceniti
**prick** *n.* ubod
**prick** *v.t.* ubosti
**pride** *n.* ponos
**pride** *v.t.* ponositi se
**priest** *n.* sveštenik

**priestess** *n.* sveštenica
**priesthood** *n.* sveštenstvo
**prima** *facie adv.* na prvi pogled
**primarily** *adv.* prvenstveno
**primary** *a.* osnovni
**prime** *a.* glavni
**prime** *n.* početak
**primer** *n.* bukvar
**primeval** *a.* prastar
**primitive** *a.* primitivan
**prince** *n.* princ
**princely** *a.* kneževski
**princess** *n.* princeza
**principal** *n.* starešina
**principal** *a* glavni
**principle** *n.* princip
**print** *v.t.* štampati
**print** *n* otisak
**printer** *n.* štampač
**prior** *a.* raniji
**prior** *n* iguman
**prioress** *n.* igumanija
**priority** *n.* prioritet
**prison** *n.* zatvor
**prisoner** *n.* zatvorenik
**privacy** *n.* privatnost
**private** *a.* privatni
**privation** *n.* oskudica
**privilege** *n.* privilegija
**prize** *n.* nagrada
**prize** *v.t.* ceniti
**probability** *n.* verovatnoća
**probable** *a.* verovatan
**probably** *adv.* verovatno
**probation** *n.* proba
**probationer** *n.* pripravnik
**probe** *v.t.* istraživati
**probe** *n* sonda
**problem** *n.* problem
**problematic** *a.* problematičan

**procedure** *n.* procedura
**proceed** *v.i.* nastaviti
**proceeding** *n.* postupak
**proceeds** *n.* dohodak
**process** *n.* proces
**procession** *n.* povorka
**proclaim** *v.t.* proglasiti
**proclamation** *n.* proglas
**proclivity** *n.* sklonost
**procrastinate** *v.i.* odugovlačiti
**procrastination** *n.* odugovlačenje
**proctor** *n.* prokurator
**procure** *v.t.* nabaviti
**procurement** *n.* nabavka
**prodigal** *a.* rasipan
**prodigality** *n.* rasipnost
**produce** *v.t.* proizvoditi
**produce** *n.* proizvod
**product** *n.* produkt
**production** *n.* proizvodnja
**productive** *a.* produktivan
**productivity** *n.* produktivnost
**profane** *a.* svetovan
**profane** *v.t.* poštovati
**profess** *v.t.* ispovedati
**profession** *n.* profesija
**professional** *a.* profesionalan
**professor** *n.* profesor
**proficiency** *n.* veština
**proficient** *a.* vešt
**profile** *n.* profil
**profile** *v.t.* prikazati u profilu
**profit** *n.* profiter
**profit** *v.t.* profitirati
**profitable** *a.* profitabilan
**profiteer** *n.* profiter
**profiteer** *v.i.* nepošteno zarađivati
**profligacy** *n.* raskalašnost
**profligate** *a.* rasipan
**profound** *a.* dubok

profundity *n.* dubina
profuse *a.* obilan
profusion *n.* obilje
progeny *n.* potomstvo
programme *n.* program
programme *v.t.* programirati
progress *n.* napredak
progress *v.i.* napredovati
progressive *a.* progresivan
prohibit *v.t.* zabraniti
prohibition *n.* zabrana
prohibitive *a.* nedopušten
prohibitory *a.* zabranjujući
project *n.* projekat
project *v.t.* projektovati
projectile *n.* projektil
projectile *a.* koji se može baciti
projection *n.* projekcija
projector *n.* projektor
proliferate *v.i.* razmnožiti se
proliferation *n.* razmnožavanje
prolific *a.* plodan
prologue *n.* prolog
prolong *v.t.* produžiti
prolongation *n.* produženje
prominence *n.* istaknutost
prominent *a.* istaknut
promise *n* obećanje
promise *v.t* obećati
promising *a.* obećavajući
promissory *a.* koji sadrži obećanje
promote *v.t.* promovisati
promotion *n.* promocija
prompt *a.* brz
prompt *v.t.* podstaći
prompter *n.* sufler
prone *a.* sklon
pronoun *n.* zamenica
pronounce *v.t.* izgovarati
pronunciation *n.* izgovor

proof *n.* dokaz
proof *a* otporan
prop *n.* podupirač
prop *v.t.* podupirati
propaganda *n.* propaganda
propagandist *n.* propagator
propagate *v.t.* propagirati
propagation *n.* širenje
propel *v.t.* pokrenuti
proper *a.* pravi
property *n.* imovina
prophecy *n.* proročanstvo
prophesy *v.t.* proreći
prophet *n.* prorok
prophetic *a.* proročki
proportion *n.* proporcija
proportion *v.t.* podesiti
proportional *a.* proporcionalan
proportionate *a.* srazmeran
proposal *n.* predlog
propose *v.t.* predložiti
proposition *n.* predlog
propound *v.t.* predložiti
proprietary *a.* vlasnički
proprietor *n.* vlasnik
propriety *n.* ispravnost
prorogue *v.t.* raspustiti
prosaic *a.* prozaičan
prose *n.* proza
prosecute *v.t.* goniti
prosecution *n.* sudski progon
prosecutor *n.* tužilac
prosody *n.* prozodija
prospect *n.* izgled
prospective *a.* potencijalan
prospectus *n.* prospekt
prosper *v.i.* napredovati
prosperity *n.* blagostanje
prosperous *a.* uspešan
prostitute *n.* prostitutka

| | |
|---|---|
| **prostitute** *v.t.* prostituirati | **prune** *v.t.* orezati |
| **prostitution** *n.* prostitucija | **pry** *v.i.* zavirivati |
| **prostrate** *a.* iznuren | **psalm** *n.* psalm |
| **prostrate** *v.t.* oboriti | **pseudonym** *n.* pseudonim |
| **prostration** *n.* iznurenost | **psyche** *n.* psiha |
| **protagonist** *n.* protagonista | **psychiatrist** *n.* psihijatar |
| **protect** *v.t.* zaštititi | **psychiatry** *n.* psihijatrija |
| **protection** *n.* zaštita | **psychic** *a.* psihički |
| **protective** *a.* zaštitni | **psychological** *a.* psihološki |
| **protector** *n.* zaštitnik | **psychologist** *n.* psiholog |
| **protein** *n.* protein | **psychology** *n.* psihologija |
| **protest** *n.* protest | **psychopath** *n.* psihopata |
| **protest** *v.i.* protestovati | **psychosis** *n.* psihoza |
| **protestation** *n.* protest | **psychotherapy** *n.* psihoterapija |
| **prototype** *n.* prototip | **puberty** *n.* pubertet |
| **proud** *a.* ponosan | **public** *a.* javni |
| **prove** *v.t.* dokazati | **public** *n.* javnost |
| **proverb** *n.* poslovica | **publication** *n.* izdanje |
| **proverbial** *a.* poslovičan | **publicity** *n.* publicitet |
| **provide** *v.i.* obezbediti | **publicize** *v.t.* dati publicitet |
| **providence** *n.* proviđenje | **publish** *v.t.* objaviti |
| **provident** *a.* oprezan | **publisher** *n.* izdavač |
| **providential** *a.* povoljan | **pudding** *n.* puding |
| **province** *n.* provincija | **puddle** *n.* bara |
| **provincial** *a.* provincijski | **puddle** *v.t.* gacati |
| **provincialism** *n.* provincijalizam | **puerile** *a.* detinjast |
| **provision** *n.* odredba | **puff** *n.* dašak |
| **provisional** *a.* privremen | **puff** *v.i.* dahtati |
| **proviso** *n.* uslov | **pull** *v.t.* povući |
| **provocation** *n.* provokacija | **pull** *n.* povlačenje |
| **provocative** *a.* provokativan | **pulley** *n.* kotur |
| **provoke** *v.t.* provocirati | **pullover** *n.* pulover |
| **prowess** *n.* junaštvo | **pulp** *n.* pulpa |
| **proximate** *a.* neposredan | **pulp** *v.t.* pretvoriti u kašu |
| **proximity** *n.* blizina | **pulpit** *a.* propovedaonica |
| **proxy** *n.* zastupnik | **pulpy** *a.* mekan |
| **prude** *n.* preterano čedna žena | **pulsate** *v.i.* kucati |
| **prudence** *n.* razboritost | **pulsation** *n.* pulsacija |
| **prudent** *a.* razborit | **pulse** *n.* puls |
| **prudential** *a.* promišljen | **pulse** *v.i.* pulsirati |

**pulse** *n* puls
**pump** *n.* pumpa
**pump** *v.t.* pumpati
**pumpkin** *n.* bundeva
**pun** *n.* igra rečima
**pun** *v.i.* igrati se rečima
**punch** *n.* punč
**punch** *v.t.* udariti
**punctual** *a.* tačan
**punctuality** *n.* tačnost
**punctuate** *v.t.* naglasiti
**punctuation** *n.* interpunkcija
**puncture** *n.* rupa
**puncture** *v.t.* probušiti
**pungency** *n.* oporost
**pungent** *a.* opor
**punish** *v.t.* kazniti
**punishment** *n.* kazna
**punitive** *a.* kazneni
**puny** *a.* slabašan
**pupil** *n.* učenik
**puppet** *n.* marioneta
**puppy** *n.* štene
**purblind** *n.* poluslep
**purchase** *n.* kupovina
**purchase** *v.t.* kupiti
**pure** *a* čist
**purgation** *n.* pročišćenje
**purgative** *n.* purgativ
**purgative** *a* purgativan
**purgatory** *n.* čistilište
**purge** *v.t.* očistiti
**purification** *n.* prečišćavanje
**purify** *v.t.* očistiti
**purist** *n.* purista
**puritan** *n.* puritanac
**puritanical** *a.* puritanski
**purity** *n.* čistoća
**purple** *adj./n.* ljubičast, ljubičasta boja
**purport** *n.* značenje

**purport** *v.t.* značiti
**purpose** *n.* svrha
**purpose** *v.t.* nameravati
**purposely** *adv.* namerno
**purr** *n.* predenje
**purr** *v.i.* presti
**purse** *n.* novčanik
**purse** *v.t.* namrštiti
**pursuance** *n.* izvođenje
**pursue** *v.t.* progoniti
**pursuit** *n.* potera
**purview** *n.* vidokrug
**pus** *n.* gnoj
**push** *v.t.* gurnuti
**push** *n.* guranje
**put** *v.t.* staviti
**puzzle** *n.* slagalica
**puzzle** *v.t.* zbuniti
**pygmy** *n.* pigmejac
**pyorrhoea** *n.* gnojna upala
**pyramid** *n.* piramida
**pyre** *n.* lomača
**python** *n.* piton

# Q

**quack** *v.i.* blebetati
**quack** *n* šarlatan
**quackery** *n.* nadrilekarstvo
**quadrangle** *n.* četvorougaonik
**quadrangular** *a.* četvorougaoni
**quadrilateral** *a. & n.* četvorostran
**quadruped** *n.* četvoronožni
**quadruple** *a.* četvorostruk
**quadruple** *v.t.* učetvorostručiti
**quail** *n.* prepelica
**quaint** *a.* čudan
**quake** *v.i.* tresti se
**quake** *n* potres

| | |
|---|---|
| **qualification** *n.* kvalifikacija | **quintessence** *n.* suština |
| **qualify** *v.i.* kvalifikovati se | **quit** *v.t.* prestati |
| **qualitative** *a.* kvalitativan | **quite** *adv.* sasvim |
| **quality** *n.* kvalitet | **quiver** *n.* tobolac |
| **quandary** *n.* dilema | **quiver** *v.i.* drhtati |
| **quantitative** *a.* kvantitativan | **quixotic** *a.* donkihotski |
| **quantity** *n.* količina | **quiz** *n.* kviz |
| **quantum** *n.* kvant | **quiz** *v.t.* ispitivati |
| **quarrel** *n.* svađa | **quorum** *n.* kvorum |
| **quarrel** *v.i.* svađati se | **quota** *n.* kvota |
| **quarrelsome** *a.* svadljiv | **quotation** *n.* citat |
| **quarry** *n.* kamenolom | **quote** *v.t.* citirati |
| **quarry** *v.i.* iskopavati | **quotient** *n.* količnik |
| **quarter** *n.* četvrtina | |
| **quarter** *v.t.* podeliti na četiri dela | **R** |
| **quarterly** *a.* tromesečni | |
| **queen** *n.* kraljica | |
| **queer** *a.* nastran | **rabbit** *n.* zec |
| **quell** *v.t.* ugušiti | **rabies** *n.* besnilo |
| **quench** *v.t.* ugasiti | **race** *n.* trka |
| **query** *n.* pitanje | **race** *v.i* trkati se |
| **query** *v.t* pitati | **racial** *a.* rasni |
| **quest** *n.* traganje | **racialism** *n.* rasizam |
| **quest** *v.t.* tragati | **rack** *v.t.* mučiti |
| **question** *n.* pitanje | **rack** *n.* propast |
| **question** *v.t.* pitati | **racket** *n.* reket |
| **questionable** *a.* sumnjiv | **radiance** *n.* sjaj |
| **questionnaire** *n.* upitnik | **radiant** *a.* sjajan |
| **queue** *n.* red | **radiate** *v.t.* zračiti |
| **quibble** *n.* dosetka | **radiation** *n.* zračenje |
| **quibble** *v.i.* praviti dosetke | **radical** *a.* radikalan |
| **quick** *a.* brz | **radio** *n.* radio |
| **quick** *n* živac | **radio** *v.t.* javiti putem radija |
| **quicksand** *n.* živi pesak | **radish** *n.* rotkvica |
| **quicksilver** *n.* živa | **radium** *n.* radijum |
| **quiet** *a.* miran | **radius** *n.* poluprečnik |
| **quiet** *n.* mir | **rag** *n.* krpa |
| **quiet** *v.t.* umiriti | **rag** *v.t.* zadirkivati |
| **quilt** *n.* jorgan | **rage** *n.* bes |
| **quinine** *n.* kinin | **rage** *v.i.* besneti |

raid *n.* racija
raid *v.t.* upasti
rail *n.* šina
rail *v.t.* ograditi
raling *n.* ograda
raillery *n.* zadirkivanje
railway *n.* železnica
rain *v.i.* padati
rain *n* kiša
rainy *a.* kišovit
raise *v.t.* dići
raisin *n.* suvo grožđe
rally *v.t.* skupljanje
rally *n* zbor
ram *n.* ovan
ram *v.t.* zakrčiti
ramble *v.t.* skitanje
ramble *n* skitati
rampage *v.i.* divljati
rampage *n.* divljanje
rampant *a.* osion
rampart *n.* bedem
rancour *n.* zloba
random *a.* slučajan
range *v.t.* postrojiti
range *n.* domet
ranger *n.* skitnica
rank *n.* rang
rank *v.t.* rangirati
rank *a* bujan
ransack *v.t.* pretresti
ransom *n.* otkup
ransom *v.t.* otkupiti
rape *n.* silovanje
rape *v.t.* silovati
rapid *a.* hitar
rapidity *n.* hitrina
rapier *n.* rapir
rapport *n.* prisnost
rapt *a.* ushićen

rapture *n.* zanesenost
rare *a.* redak
rascal *n.* nitkov
rash *a.* osip
rat *n.* pacov
rate *v.t.* proceniti
rate *n.* stopa
rather *adv.* radije
ratify *v.t.* ratifikovati
ratio *n.* odnos
ration *n.* obrok
rational *a.* racionalan
rationale *n.* obrazloženje
rationality *n.* racionalnost
rationalize *v.t.* racionalizovati
rattle *v.i.* zveckati
rattle *n* zvečka
ravage *n.* pustošenje
ravage *v.t.* pustošiti
rave *v.i.* buncati
raven *n.* gavran
ravine *n.* tesnac
raw *a.* sirov
ray *n.* zrak
raze *v.t.* razrušiti
razor *n.* brijač
reach *v.t.* dostići
react *v.i.* reagovati
reaction *n.* reakcija
reactionary *a.* reakcionaran
read *v.t.* čitati
reader *n.* čitalac
readily *adv.* spremno
readiness *n.* spremnost
ready *a.* spreman
real *a.* pravi
realism *n.* realizam
realist *n.* realista
realistic *a.* realističan
reality *n.* realnost

realization *n.* realizacija
realize *v.t.* realizovati
really *adv.* stvarno
realm *a.* carstvo
ream *n. ris* papira
reap *v.t.* žeti
reaper *n.* žetelac
rear *n.* pozadina
rear *v.t.* gajiti
reason *n.* razlog
reason *v.i.* misliti
reasonable *a.* razuman
reassure *v.t.* uveravati
rebate *n.* rabat
rebel *v.i.* buniti se
rebel *n.* buntovnik
rebellion *n.* pobuna
rebellious *a.* buntovan
rebirth *n.* preporod
rebound *v.i.* odbiti
rebound *n.* odbijanje
rebuff *n.* odbacivanje
rebuff *v.t.* odbaciti
rebuke *v.t.* koriti
rebuke *n.* ukor
recall *v.t.* opozvati
recall *n.* opoziv
recede *v.i.* uzmaći
receipt *n.* račun
receive *v.t.* dobiti
receiver *n.* prijemnik
recent *a.* nedavni
recently *adv.* nedavno
reception *n.* prijem
receptive *a.* prijemčiv
recess *n.* udubljenje
recession *n.* recesija
recipe *n.* recept
recipient *n.* primalac
reciprocal *a.* recipročan

reciprocate *v.t.* uzvraćati
recital *n.* recital
recitation *n.* recitacija
recite *v.t.* recitovati
reckless *a.* nemaran
reckon *v.t.* računati
reclaim *v.t.* vratiti
reclamation *n* reklamacija
recluse *n.* pustinjak
recognition *n.* prepoznavanje
recognize *v.t.* prepoznati
recoil *v.i.* ustuknuti
recoil *adv.* odbojno
recollect *v.t.* setiti se
recollection *n.* sećanje
recommend *v.t.* preporučiti
recommendation *n.* preporuka
recompense *v.t.* nadoknaditi
recompense *n.* naknada
reconcile *v.t.* pomiriti
reconciliation *n.* izmirenje
record *v.t.* zapisati
record *n.* zapisnik
recorder *n.* zapisničar
recount *v.t.* iznova brojati
recoup *v.t.* nadoknaditi
recourse *n.* regres
recover *v.t.* oporaviti se
recovery *n.* oporavak
recreation *n.* rekreacija
recruit *n.* regrut
recruit *v.t.* regrutovati
rectangle *n.* pravougaonik
rectangular *a.* pravougaoni
rectification *n.* ispravljanje
rectify *v.i.* ispraviti
rectum *n.* rektum
recur *v.i.* ponavljati se
recurrence *n.* vraćanje
recurrent *a.* povratni

red *a.* crven
red *n.* crvena boja
redden *v.t.* porumeneti
reddish *a.* crvenkast
redeem *v.t.* iskupiti se
redemption *n.* iskupljenje
redouble *v.t.* udvostručiti
redress *v.t.* popraviti
redress *n* obeštećenje
reduce *v.t.* smanjiti
reduction *n.* smanjenje
redundance *n.* obilje
redundant *a.* suvišan
reel *n.* kalem
reel *v.i.* namotati
refer *v.t.* uputiti
referee *n.* sudija
reference *n.* referenca
referendum *n.* referendum
refine *v.t.* preraditi
refinement *n.* prečišćavanje
refinery *n.* rafinerija
reflect *v.t.* odraziti
reflection *n.* odraz
reflective *a.* reflektujuće
reflector *n.* reflektor
reflex *n.* refleks
reflex *a* refleksan
reflexive *a* povratni
reform *v.t.* reformisati
reform *n.* reforma
reformation *n.* reformacija
reformatory *n.* popravni dom
reformatory *a* popravni
reformer *n.* reformator
refrain *v.i.* uzdržavati se
refrain *n* refren
refresh *v.t.* osvežiti
refreshment *n.* osveženje
refrigerate *v.t.* rashladiti

refrigeration *n.* hlađenje
refrigerator *n.* frižider
refuge *n.* utočište
refugee *n.* izbeglica
refulgence *n.* sjaj
refulgent *a.* sjajan
refund *v.t.* povratiti
refund *n.* povraćaj
refusal *n.* odbijanje
refuse *v.t.* odbiti
refuse *n.* smeće
refutation *n.* pobijanje
refute *v.t.* pobiti
regal *a.* kraljevski
regard *v.t.* ceniti
regard *n.* poštovanje
regenerate *v.t.* regenerisati
regeneration *n.* regeneracija
regicide *n.* kraljoubistvo
regime *n.* režim
regiment *n.* puk
regiment *v.t.* rasporediti
region *n.* region
regional *a.* regionalni
register *n.* registar
register *v.t.* registrovati
registrar *n.* matičar
registration *n.* registracija
registry *n.* registar
regret *v.i.* žaliti
regret *n* žaljenje
regular *a.* redovan
regularity *n.* pravilnost
regulate *v.t.* regulisati
regulation *n.* propis
regulator *n.* regulator
rehabilitate *v.t.* rehabilitovati
rehabilitation *n.* rehabilitacija
rehearsal *n.* proba
rehearse *v.t.* probati

reign *v.i.* vladati
reign *n* vladavina
reimburse *v.t.* nadoknaditi
rein *n.* uzda
rein *v.t.* zauzdati
reinforce *v.t.* pojačati
reinforcement *n.* pojačanje
reinstate *v.t.* ponovno postavljanje
reinstatement *n.* ponovo postaviti
reiterate *v.t.* neprestano ponavljati
reiteration *n.* neprestano ponavljanje
reject *v.t.* odbiti
rejection *n.* odbijanje
rejoice *v.i.* radovati se
rejoin *v.t.* ponovo pridružiti
rejoinder *n.* odgovor
rejuvenate *v.t.* podmladiti
rejuvenation *n.* podmlađivanje
relapse *v.i.* vratiti se
relapse *n.* povratak
relate *v.t.* odnositi se
relation *n.* odnos
relative *a.* relativan
relative *n.* rođak
relax *v.t.* opustiti
relaxation *n.* opuštanje
relay *n.* relej
relay *v.t.* prenositi
release *v.t.* pustiti
release *n* puštanje
relent *v.i.* popustiti
relentless *a.* nemilosrdan
relevance *n.* relevantnost
relevant *a.* relevantan
reliable *a.* pouzdan
reliance *n.* pouzdanje
relic *n.* relikvija
relief *n.* reljef
relieve *v.t.* olakšati
religion *n.* religija

religious *a.* verski
relinquish *v.t.* odreći se
relish *v.t.* uživati
relish *n* slast
reluctance *n.* opiranje
reluctant *a.* nerad
rely *v.i.* osloniti
remain *v.i.* ostati
remainder *n.* ostatak
remains *n.* ostaci
remand *v.t.* vratiti u pritvor
remand *n* vraćanje u pritvor
remark *n.* napomena
remark *v.t.* napomenuti
remarkable *a.* izvanredan
remedial *a.* popravni
remedy *n.* pravni lek
remedy *v.t* lek
remember *v.t.* zapamtiti
remembrance *n.* sećanje
remind *v.t.* podsetiti
reminder *n.* podsetnik
reminiscence *n.* uspomena
reminiscent *a.* koji podseća
remission *n.* opraštanje
remit *v.t.* oprostiti
remittance *n.* novčana pošiljka
remorse *n.* pokajanje
remote *a.* dalek
removable *a.* prenosiv
removal *n.* uklanjanje
remove *v.t.* ukloniti
remunerate *v.t.* nagraditi
remuneration *n.* plata
remunerative *a.* unosan
renaissance *n.* renesansa
render *v.t.* učiniti
rendezvous *n.* randevu
renew *v.t.* obnoviti
renewal *n.* obnova

renounce *v.t.* odreći se
renovate *v.t.* renovirati
renovation *n.* obnova
renown *n.* renome
renowned *a.* poznat
rent *n.* iznajmljivanje
rent *v.t.* iznajmljivati
renunciation *n.* odricanje
repair *v.t.* popraviti
repair *n.* popravka
repairable *a.* opravljiv
repartee *n. duhovit* odgovor
repatriate *v.t.* vratiti u domovinu
repatriate *n* povratnik
repatriation *n.* povratak u domovinu
repay *v.t.* isplatiti
repayment *n.* otplata
repeal *v.t.* opozvati
repeal *n* opozivanje
repeat *v.t.* ponoviti
repel *v.t.* odbiti
repellent *a.* odvratan
repellent *n* sredstvo protiv insekata
repent *v.i. pokajati* se
repentance *n.* pokajanje
repentant *a.* pokajnički
repercussion *n.* posledica
repetition *n.* ponavljanje
replace *v.t.* zameniti
replacement *n.* zamena
replenish *v.t.* napuniti
replete *a.* napunjen
replica *n.* replika
reply *v.i.* odgovoriti
reply *n* odgovor
report *v.t.* izvestiti
report *n.* izveštaj
reporter *n.* novinar
repose *n.* odmor
repose *v.i.* odmarati se

repository *n.* skladište
represent *v.t.* predstavljati
representation *n.* predstavljanje
representative *n.* predstavnik
representative *a.* reprezentativan
repress *v.t.* potisnuti
repression *n.* suzbijanje
reprimand *n.* ukor
reprimand *v.t.* ukoriti
reprint *v.t.* ponovo štampati
reprint *n.* preštampavanje
reproach *v.t.* prigovarati
reproach *n.* prekor
reproduce *v.t.* reprodukovati
reproduction *n* reprodukcija
reproductive *a.* reproduktivan
reproof *n.* ukor
reptile *n.* reptil
republic *n.* republika
republican *a.* republikanski
republican *n* republikanac
repudiate *v.t.* razvesti se
repudiation *n.* razvod
repugnance *n.* odvratnost
repugnant *a.* odvratan
repulse *v.t.* odbiti
repulse *n.* odbijanje
repulsion *n.* odbojnost
repulsive *a.* odbojan
reputation *n.* ugled
repute *v.t.* smatrati za
repute *n.* ugled
request *v.t.* zahtevati
request *n* zahtev
requiem *n.* rekvijem
require *v.t.* tražiti
requirement *n.* traženje
requisite *a.* potreban
requisite *n* potreba
requisition *n.* trebovanje

| | |
|---|---|
| requisition *v.t.* trebovati | resplendent *a.* sjajan |
| requite *v.t.* vratiti | respond *v.i.* odgovoriti |
| rescue *v.t.* spasiti | respondent *n.* optuženik |
| rescue *n* spasavanje | response *n.* odgovor |
| research *v.i.* istraživati | responsibility *n.* odgovornost |
| research *n* istraživanje | responsible *a.* odgovoran |
| resemblance *n.* sličnost | rest *v.i.* odmoriti se |
| resemble *v.t.* ličiti | rest *n* odmor |
| resent *v.t.* vređati | restaurant *n.* restoran |
| resentment *n.* ozlojeđenost | restive *a.* jogunast |
| reservation *n.* rezervat | restoration *n.* restauracija |
| reserve *v.t.* rezervisati | restore *v.t.* obnoviti |
| reservoir *n.* rezervoar | restrain *v.t.* obuzdati |
| reside *v.i.* boraviti | restrict *v.t.* ograničiti |
| residence *n.* prebivalište | restriction *n.* ograničenje |
| resident *a.* rezidentan | restrictive *a.* restriktivan |
| resident *n* stanovnik | result *v.i.* proizlaziti |
| residual *a.* preostali | result *n.* rezultat |
| residue *n.* ostatak | resume *v.t.* rezimirati |
| resign *v.t.* dati ostavku | resume *n.* rezime |
| resignation *n.* ostavka | resumption *n.* nastavljanje |
| resist *v.t.* odoleti | resurgence *n.* preporod |
| resistance *n.* otpor | resurgent *a.* koji oživljava |
| resistant *a.* otporan | retail *v.t.* prodavati robu na malo |
| resolute *a.* odlučan | retail *n.* maloprodaja |
| resolution *n.* rezolucija | retail *adv.* maloprodajno |
| resolve *v.t.* rešiti | retail *a* maloprodajni |
| resonance *n.* rezonanca | retailer *n.* trgovac na malo |
| resonant *a.* rezonantan | retain *v.t.* zadržati |
| resort *v.i.* pribeći | retaliate *v.i.* osvetiti se |
| resort *n* pribežište | retaliation *n.* odmazda |
| resound *v.i.* odjeknuti | retard *v.t.* usporiti |
| resource *n.* resurs | retardation *n.* retardiranost |
| resourceful *a.* snalažljiv | retention *n.* zadržavanje |
| respect *v.t.* poštovati | retentive *a.* koji zadržava |
| respect *n.* poštovanje | reticence *n.* povučenost |
| respectful *a.* pun poštovanja | reticent *a.* povučen |
| respective *a.* odnosan | retina *n.* mrežnjača |
| respiration *n.* disanje | retinue *n.* pratnja |
| respire *v.i.* disati | retire *v.i.* penzionisati |

**retirement** n. penzija
**retort** v.t. odgovoriti
**retort** n. odgovor
**retouch** v.t. retуширati
**retrace** v.t. vratiti se istim putem
**retread** v.t. protektirati gumu
**retread** n. protektirana guma
**retreat** v.i. povlačiti se
**retrench** v.t. smanjiti izdatke
**retrenchment** n. štednja
**retrieve** v.t. povratiti
**retrospect** n. retrospektiva
**retrospection** n. retrospekcija
**retrospective** a. retrospektivan
**return** v.i. vratiti se
**return** n. povratak
**revel** v.i. pijančiti
**revel** n. pijanka
**revelation** n. otkrovenje
**reveller** n. mangup
**revelry** n. terevenka
**revenge** v.t. osvetiti
**revenge** n. osveta
**revengeful** a. osvetoljubiv
**revenue** n. prihod
**revere** v.t. duboko poštovati
**reverence** n. poštovanje
**reverend** a. častan
**reverent** a. pun poštovanja
**reverential** a. pun poštovanja
**reverie** n. sanjarenje
**reversal** n. preokret
**reverse** a. suprotan
**reverse** n suprotnost
**reverse** v.t. obrnuti
**reversible** a. povratan
**revert** v.i. vratiti se
**review** v.t. pregledati
**review** n pregled
**revise** v.t. prepraviti

**revision** n. revizija
**revival** n. oživljavanje
**revive** v.i. oživeti
**revocable** a. opozivan
**revocation** n. opoziv
**revoke** v.t. opozvati
**revolt** v.i. pobuniti se
**revolt** n. pobuna
**revolution** n. revolucija
**revolutionary** a. revolucionaran
**revolutionary** n revolucionar
**revolve** v.i. obrtati se
**revolver** n. revolver
**reward** n. nagrada
**reward** v.t. nagraditi
**rhetoric** n. retorika
**rhetorical** a. retorički
**rheumatic** a. reumatski
**rheumatism** n. reumatizam
**rhinoceros** n. nosorog
**rhyme** n. rima
**rhyme** v.i. rimovati se
**rhymester** n. stihopisac
**rhythm** n. ritam
**rhythmic** a. ritmičan
**rib** n. rebro
**ribbon** n. traka
**rice** n. pirinač
**rich** a. bogat
**riches** n. izobilje
**richness** n. bogatstvo
**rick** n. plast
**rickets** n. rahitis
**rickety** a. rahitičan
**rickshaw** n. rikša
**rid** v.t. osloboditi
**riddle** n. zagonetka
**riddle** v.i. prosejati
**ride** v.t. voziti
**ride** n vožnja

| | | | |
|---|---|---|---|
| **rider** *n.* | jahač | **river** *n.* | reka |
| **ridge** *n.* | greben | **rivet** *n.* | zakovica |
| **ridicule** *v.t.* | ismejavati | **rivet** *v.t.* | zakovati |
| **ridicule** *n.* | ismejavanje | **rivulet** *n.* | potočić |
| **ridiculous** *a.* | smešan | **road** *n.* | put |
| **rifle** *v.t.* | opljačkati | **roam** *v.i.* | lutati |
| **rifle** *n* | puška | **roar** *n.* | rika |
| **rift** *n.* | pukotina | **roar** *v.i.* | rikati |
| **right** *a.* | pravi | **roast** *v.t.* | peći |
| **right** *adv* | ispravno | **roast** *a* | pečen |
| **right** *n* | pravo | **roast** *n* | pečenje |
| **right** *v.t.* | postaviti | **rob** *v.t.* | opljačkati |
| **righteous** *a.* | pravedan | **robber** *n.* | pljačkaš |
| **rigid** *a.* | rigidan | **robbery** *n.* | pljačka |
| **rigorous** *a.* | rigorozan | **robe** *n.* | haljina |
| **rigour** *n.* | strogost | **robe** *v.t.* | odenuti |
| **rim** *n.* | obod | **robot** *n.* | robot |
| **ring** *n.* | prsten | **robust** *a.* | kršan |
| **ring** *v.t.* | okružiti | **rock** *v.t.* | ljuljati |
| **ringlet** *n.* | prstenčić | **rock** *n.* | stena |
| **ringworm** *n.* | lišaj (oboljenje kože) | **rocket** *n.* | raketa |
| **rinse** *v.t.* | ispirati | **rod** *n.* | štap |
| **riot** *n.* | pobuna | **rodent** *n.* | glodar |
| **riot** *v.t.* | besneti | **roe** *n.* | srna |
| **rip** *v.t.* | cepati | **rogue** *n.* | bitanga |
| **ripe** *a* | zreo | **roguery** *n.* | nevaljalost |
| **ripen** *v.i.* | sazrevati | **roguish** *a.* | lopovski |
| **ripple** *n.* | talasanje | **role** *n.* | uloga |
| **ripple** *v.t.* | talasati | **roll** *n.* | rolna |
| **rise** *v.* | dići se | **roll** *v.i.* | kotrljati |
| **rise** *n.* | dizanje | **roll-call** *n.* | prozivka |
| **risk** *v.t.* | rizikovati | **roller** *n.* | valjak |
| **risk** *n.* | rizik | **romance** *n.* | romantika |
| **risky** *a.* | rizičan | **romantic** *a.* | romantičan |
| **rite** *n.* | obred | **romp** *v.i.* | skakati |
| **ritual** *n.* | ritual | **romp** *n.* | ludiranje |
| **ritual** *a.* | ritualni | **rood** *n.* | raspeće |
| **rival** *n.* | protivnik | **roof** *n.* | krov |
| **rival** *v.t.* | nadmetati se | **roof** *v.t.* | pokriti krovom |
| **rivalry** *n.* | rivalstvo | **rook** *n.* | kula |

| | |
|---|---|
| **rook** *v.t.* varati | **royalist** *n.* rojalistički |
| **room** *n.* soba | **royalty** *n.* kraljevstvo |
| **roomy** *a.* prostran | **rub** *v.t.* trljati |
| **roost** *n.* kokošinjac | **rub** *n* trljanje |
| **roost** *v.i.* prenoćiti | **rubber** *n.* guma |
| **root** *n.* koren | **rubbish** *n.* đubre |
| **root** *v.i.* ukoreniti | **rubble** *n.* krš |
| **rope** *n.* uže | **ruby** *n.* rubin |
| **rope** *v.t.* povezati | **rude** *a.* nepristojan |
| **rosary** *n.* ružičnjak, brojanice | **rudiment** *n.* osnov |
| **rose** *n.* ruža | **rudimentary** *a.* osnovni |
| **roseate** *a.* ružičast | **rue** *v.t.* žaliti |
| **rostrum** *n.* govornica | **rueful** *a.* žalostan |
| **rosy** *a.* rumen | **ruffian** *n.* siledžija |
| **rot** *n.* trulež | **ruffle** *v.t.* nabrati |
| **rot** *v.i.* truliti | **rug** *n.* ćilim |
| **rotary** *a.* rotacioni | **rugged** *a.* neravan |
| **rotate** *v.i.* rotirati | **ruin** *n.* propast |
| **rotation** *n.* rotacija | **ruin** *v.t.* upropastiti |
| **rote** *n.* učenje napamet | **rule** *n.* pravilo |
| **rouble** *n.* rublja | **rule** *v.t.* vladati |
| **rough** *a.* grub | **ruler** *n.* vladar |
| **round** *a.* okrugao | **ruling** *n.* upravljanje |
| **round** *adv.* okolo | **rum** *n.* rum |
| **round** *n.* okruglost | **rum** *a* čudan |
| **round** *v.t.* zaobliti | **rumble** *v.i.* tutnjati |
| **rouse** *v.i.* probuditi se | **rumble** *n.* tutnjava |
| **rout** *v.t.* razbiti | **ruminant** *a.* koji preživa |
| **rout** *n* trupa | **ruminant** *n.* preživar |
| **route** *n.* put | **ruminate** *v.i.* preživati |
| **routine** *n.* rutina | **rumination** *n.* razmišljanje |
| **routine** *a* rutinski | **rummage** *v.i.* preživanje |
| **rove** *v.i.* lunjati | **rummage** *n* preturanje |
| **rover** *n.* lutalica | **rummy** *n.* remi |
| **row** *n.* red | **rumour** *n.* glasina |
| **row** *v.t.* veslati | **rumour** *v.t.* razglasiti |
| **row** *n* veslanje | **run** *v.i.* trčati |
| **row** *n.* svađa | **run** *n.* trčanje |
| **rowdy** *a.* larmadžija | **rung** *n.* pregača |
| **royal** *a.* kraljevski | **runner** *n.* trkač |

rupee *n.* rupija
rupture *n.* raskid
rupture *v.t.* raskinuti
rural *a.* seoski
ruse *n.* prevara
rush *n.* žurba
rush *v.t.* žuriti
rush *n* nalet
rust *n.* rđa
rust *v.i* rđati
rustic *a.* seoski
rustic *n* seljak
rusticate *v.t.* živeti na selu
rustication *n.* slanje u selo
rusticity *n.* neotesanost
rusty *a.* zarđao
rut *n.* kolosek
ruthless *a.* nemilosrdan
rye *n.* raž

# S

sabbath *n.* sabat
sabotage *n.* sabotaža
sabotage *v.t.* sabotirati
sabre *n.* sablja
sabre *v.t.* poseći sabljom
saccharin *n.* saharin
saccharine *a.* šećerni
sack *n.* vreća
sack *v.t.* opljačkati
sacrament *n.* sakrament
sacred *a.* sveti
sacrifice *n.* žrtvovanje
sacrifice *v.t.* žrtvovati
sacrificial *a.* žrtveni
sacrilege *n.* svetogrđe
sacrilegious *a.* svetogrdan
sacrosanct *a.* sveti

sad *a.* tužan
sadden *v.t.* rastužiti
saddle *n.* sedlo
saddle *v.t.* osedlati
sadism *n.* sadizam
sadist *n.* sadista
safe *a.* siguran
safe *n.* sigurnost
safeguard *n.* zaštita
safety *n.* bezbednost
saffron *n.* šafran
saffron *a* žut poput šafrana
sagacious *a.* mudar
sagacity *n.* mudrost
sage *n.* mudrac
sage *a.* razborit
sail *n.* jedro
sail *v.i.* jedriti
sailor *n.* mornar
saint *n.* svetac
saintly *a.* svetački
sake *n.* korist
salable *a.* koji se može prodati
salad *n.* salata
salary *n.* zarada
sale *n.* prodaja
salesman *n.* prodavac
salient *a.* istaknut
saline *a.* slan
salinity *n.* slanoća
saliva *n.* pljuvačka
sally *n.* ispad
sally *v.i.* ispasti
saloon *n.* krčma
salt *n.* so
salt *v.t* soliti
salty *a.* slan
salutary *a.* zdrav
salutation *n.* pozdrav
salute *v.t.* pozdraviti

**salute** *n* pozdrav
**salvage** *n.* spasavanje
**salvage** *v.t.* spasiti
**salvation** *n.* spasenje
**same** *a.* isti
**sample** *n.* uzorak
**sample** *v.t.* uzorkovati
**sanatorium** *n.* sanatorijum
**sanctification** *n.* posvećivanje
**sanctify** *v.t.* osvetiti
**sanction** *n.* sankcija
**sanction** *v.t.* sankcionisati
**sanctity** *n.* svetost
**sanctuary** *n.* svetilište
**sand** *n.* pesak
**sandal** *n.* sandala
**sandalwood** *n.* sandalovina
**sandwich** *n.* sendvič
**sandwich** *v.t.* umetnuti
**sandy** *a.* peskovit
**sane** *a.* razuman
**sanguine** *a.* sangviničan
**sanitary** *a.* sanitarni
**sanity** *n.* razum
**sap** *n.* rov
**sap** *v.t.* potkopavati
**sapling** *n.* mladica
**sapphire** *n.* safir
**sarcasm** *n.* sarkazam
**sarcastic** *a.* sarkastičan
**sardonic** *a.* zloban
**satan** *n.* sotona
**satchel** *n.* torba
**satellite** *n.* satelit
**satiable** *a.* zajažljiv
**satiate** *v.t.* zasititi
**satiety** *n.* sitost
**satire** *n.* satira
**satirical** *a.* satiričan
**satirist** *n.* satiričar

**satirize** *v.t.* satirizovati
**satisfaction** *n.* zadovoljstvo
**satisfactory** *a.* zadovoljavajući
**satisfy** *v.t.* zadovoljiti
**saturate** *v.t.* zasititi
**saturation** *n.* zasićenje
**Saturday** *n.* subota
**sauce** *n.* sos
**saucer** *n.* tanjirić
**saunter** *v.t.* tumarati
**savage** *a.* divlji
**savage** *n* divljak
**savagery** *n.* divljaštvo
**save** *v.t.* sačuvati
**save** *prep* izuzev
**saviour** *n.* spasitelj
**savour** *n.* miris
**savour** *v.t.* mirisati
**saw** *n.* testera
**saw** *v.t.* testerisati
**say** *v.t.* reč
**say** *n.* reći
**scabbard** *n.* korice
**scabies** *n.* šuga
**scaffold** *n.* skele
**scale** *n.* skala
**scale** *v.t.* vagati
**scalp** *n* skalp
**scamper** *v.i* pobeći
**scamper** *n* bežanje
**scan** *v.t.* skenirati
**scandal** *n* skandal
**scandalize** *v.t.* skandalizovati
**scant** *a.* oskudan
**scanty** *a.* oskudan
**scapegoat** *n.* žrtveni jarac
**scar** *n* ožiljak
**scar** *v.t.* zaderati
**scarce** *a.* redak
**scarcely** *adv.* jedva

scarcity *n.* oskudica
scare *n.* strah
scare *v.t.* uplašiti
scarf *n.* šal
scatter *v.t.* rasturiti
scavenger *n.* skupljač trofeja
scene *n.* scena
scenery *n.* pejzaž
scenic *a.* scenski
scent *n.* miris
scent *v.t.* mirisati
sceptic *n.* skeptik
sceptical *a.* skeptičan
scepticism *n.* skepticizam
sceptre *n.* skiptar
schedule *n.* raspored
schedule *v.t.* rasporediti
scheme *n.* šema
scheme *v.i.* spletkariti
schism *n.* raskol
scholar *n.* stipendista
scholarly *a.* naučni
scholarship *n.* stipendija
scholastic *a.* skolastičar
school *n.* škola
science *n.* nauka
scientific *a.* naučni
scientist *n.* naučnik
scintillate *v.i.* svetlucati
scintillation *n.* svetlucanje
scissors *n.* makaze
scoff *n.* ruganje
scoff *v.i.* rugati se
scold *v.t.* grditi
scooter *n.* skuter
scope *n.* obim
scorch *v.t.* oprljiti
score *n.* brazda
score *v.t.* urezati
scorer *n.* zapisničar

scorn *n.* prezir
scorn *v.t.* prezirati
scorpion *n.* škorpija
Scot *n.* Škot
scotch *a.* škotski
scotch *n.* urez
scot-free *a.* nekažnjen
scoundrel *n.* nitkov
scourge *n.* bič
scourge *v.t.* bičevati
scout *n* izviđač
scout *v.i* izviđati
scowl *v.i.* mrko gledati
scowl *n.* mrk pogled
scramble *v.i.* verati se
scramble *n* penjanje
scrap *n.* otpadak
scratch *n.* grebanje
scratch *v.t.* grebati
scrawl *v.t.* škrabati
scrawl *n* škrabotina
scream *v.i.* vrištati
scream *n* vrisak
screen *n.* ekran
screen *v.t.* zaklanjati
screw *n.* šraf
screw *v.t.* zašrafiti
scribble *v.t.* škrabati
scribble *n.* škrabanje
script *n.* skripte
scripture *n.* biblija
scroll *n.* svitak
scrutinize *v.t.* pregledati
scrutiny *n.* ispitivanje
scuffle *n.* kavga
scuffle *v.i.* tući se
sculptor *n.* vajar
sculptural *a.* vajarski
sculpture *n.* skulptura
scythe *n.* kosa

| | |
|---|---|
| **scythe** *v.t.* pokositi | **secure** *v.t.* osigurati |
| **sea** *n.* more | **security** *n.* bezbednosti |
| **seal** *n.* pečat | **sedan** *n.* nosiljka |
| **seal** *n.* foka | **sedate** *a.* staložen |
| **seal** *v.t.* zapečatiti | **sedate** *v.t.* uravnotežiti |
| **seam** *n.* šav | **sedative** *a.* umirujući |
| **seam** *v.t.* šiti | **sedative** *n* sedativ |
| **seamy** *a.* pun šavova | **sedentary** *a.* sedeći |
| **search** *n.* pretraga | **sediment** *n.* talog |
| **search** *v.t.* tražiti | **sedition** *n.* pobuna |
| **season** *n.* sezona | **seditious** *a.* buntovan |
| **season** *v.t.* začiniti | **seduce** *n.* zavoditi |
| **seasonable** *a.* pravovremen | **seduction** *n.* zavođenje |
| **seasonal** *a.* sezonski | **seductive** *a* zavodljiv |
| **seat** *n.* sedište | **see** *v.t.* videti |
| **seat** *v.t.* sesti | **seed** *n.* seme |
| **secede** *v.i.* otcepiti se | **seed** *v.t.* posaditi |
| **secession** *n.* otcepljenje | **seek** *v.t.* tražiti |
| **secessionist** *n.* secesionista | **seem** *v.i.* činiti se |
| **seclude** *v.t.* osamiti | **seemly** *a.* prikladan |
| **secluded** *a.* osamljen | **seep** *v.i.* curiti |
| **seclusion** *n.* osamljenost | **seer** *n.* vidovnjak |
| **second** *a.* drugi | **seethe** *v.i.* kipeti |
| **second** *n* sekunda | **segment** *n.* segment |
| **second** *v.t.* podupirati | **segment** *v.t.* segmentirati |
| **secondary** *a.* sekundaran | **segregate** *v.t.* odvojiti |
| **seconder** *n.* podupirač | **segregation** *n.* segregacija |
| **secrecy** *n.* tajnost | **seismic** *a.* seizmički |
| **secret** *a.* tajni | **seize** *v.t.* zgrabiti |
| **secret** *n.* tajna | **seizure** *n.* napad |
| **secretariat** *(e) n.* sekretarijat | **seldom** *adv.* retko |
| **secretary** *n.* sekretar | **select** *v.t.* izabrati |
| **secrete** *v.t.* lučiti | **select** *a* izabran |
| **secretion** *n.* lučenje | **selection** *n.* izbor |
| **secretive** *a.* tajanstven | **selective** *a.* selektivan |
| **sect** *n.* sekta | **self** *n. svoja* ličnost |
| **sectarian** *a.* sektaški | **selfish** *a.* sebičan |
| **section** *n.* odeljak | **selfless** *a.* nesebičan |
| **sector** *n.* sektor | **sell** *v.t.* prodavati |
| **secure** *a.* siguran | **seller** *n.* prodavac |

semblance *n.* sličnost
semen *n.* seme
semester *n.* semestar
seminal *a.* iskonski
seminar *n.* seminar
senate *n.* senat
senator *n.* senator
senatorial *a.* senatorski
senatorial *a* senatski
send *v.t.* poslati
senile *a.* senilan
senility *n.* senilnost
senior *a.* stariji
senior *n.* senior
seniority *n.* starešinstvo
sensation *n.* senzacija
sensational *a.* senzacionalan
sense *n.* osećaj
sense *v.t.* osetiti
senseless *a.* besmislen
sensibility *n.* osetljivost
sensible *a.* razuman
sensitive *a.* osetljiv
sensual *a.* senzualan
sensualist *n.* čulna osoba
sensuality *n.* čulnost
sensuous *a.* čulni
sentence *n.* rečenica
sentence *v.t.* osuditi
sentience *n.* osećaj
sentient *a.* osećajan
sentiment *n.* osećanje
sentimental *a.* sentimentalan
sentinel *n.* stražar
sentry *n.* straža
separable *a.* separabilan
separate *v.t.* odvojiv
separate *a.* odvojen
separation *n.* razdvajanje
sepsis *n.* sepsa

September *n.* septembar
septic *a.* septičan
sepulchre *n.* grobnica
sepulture *n.* sahrana
sequel *n.* nastavak
sequence *n.* sekvenca
sequester *v.t.* zapleniti
serene *a.* spokojan
serenity *n.* spokoj
serf *n.* kmet
serge *n.* serž
sergeant *n.* narednik
serial *a.* serijski
serial *n.* časopis
series *n.* serija
serious *a* ozbiljan
sermon *n.* propoved
sermonize *v.i.* propovedati
serpent *n.* zmija
serpentine *n.* serpentina
servant *n.* sluga
serve *v.t.* poslužiti
serve *n.* servis
service *n.* služba
service *v.t* servisirati
serviceable *a.* uslužan
servile *a.* servilan
servility *n.* servilnost
session *n.* sednica
set *v.t* postaviti
set *a* određen
set *n* zalazak
settle *v.i.* naseliti
settlement *n.* naselje
settler *n.* naseljenik
seven *n.* sedam
seven *a* sedmo-
seventeen *n., a* sedamnaest
seventeenth *a.* sedamnaesti
seventh *a.* sedmi

**seventieth** *a.* sedamdeseti
**seventy** *n.*, *a* sedamdeset
**sever** *v.t.* prekinuti
**several** *a* više
**severance** *n.* razdvajanje
**severe** *a.* oštar
**severity** *n.* ozbiljnost
**sew** *v.t.* šiti
**sewage** *n.* odvodni sistem
**sewer** *n* odvodni kanal
**sewerage** *n.* kanalizacija
**sex** *n.* pol
**sexual** *a.* seksualan
**sexuality** *n.* seksualnost
**sexy** *n.* privlačan
**shabby** *a.* otrcan
**shackle** *n.* okovi
**shackle** *v.t.* okovati
**shade** *n.* hlad
**shade** *v.t.* zaseniti
**shadow** *n.* senka
**shadow** *v.t* potamneti
**shadowy** *a.* sanjalački
**shaft** *n.* vratilo
**shake** *v.i.* tresti
**shake** *n* potres
**shaky** *a.* drhtav
**shallow** *a.* plitak
**sham** *v.i.* pretvarati se
**sham** *n* varka
**sham** *a* lažan
**shame** *n.* sramota
**shame** *v.t.* sramotiti
**shameful** *a.* sraman
**shameless** *a.* besraman
**shampoo** *n.* šampon
**shampoo** *v.t.* šamponirati
**shanty** *a.* straćara
**shape** *n.* oblik
**shape** *v.t* oblikovati

**shapely** *a.* skladan
**share** *n.* udeo
**share** *v.t.* deliti
**share** *n* deonica
**shark** *n.* ajkula
**sharp** *a.* oštar
**sharp** *adv.* oštro
**sharpen** *v.t.* izoštriti
**sharpener** *n.* rezač
**sharper** *n.* varalica
**shatter** *v.t.* razbiti
**shave** *v.t.* brijati
**shave** *n* brijanje
**shawl** *n.* šal
**she** *pron.* ona
**sheaf** *n.* snop
**shear** *v.t.* ošišati
**shears** *n. pl.* makaze
**shed** *v.t.* ispuštati
**shed** *n* hangar
**sheep** *n.* ovca
**sheepish** *a.* glup
**sheer** *a.* potpun
**sheet** *n.* list
**sheet** *v.t.* umotati
**shelf** *n.* polica
**shell** *n.* školjka
**shell** *v.t.* ljuštiti
**shelter** *n.* sklonište
**shelter** *v.t.* štititi
**shelve** *v.t.* staviti na policu
**shepherd** *n.* pastir
**shield** *n.* štit
**shield** *v.t.* braniti
**shift** *v.t.* menjati
**shift** *n* smena
**shifty** *a.* snalažljiv
**shilling** *n.* šiling
**shilly-shally** *v.i.* kolebati se
**shilly-shally** *n.* kolebljiv

shin *n.* golenica
shine *v.i.* penjati se
shine *n* sjaj
shiny *a.* blistav
ship *n.* brod
ship *v.t.* ukrcati
shipment *n.* pošiljka
shire *n.* grofovija
shirk *v.t.* zabušavati
shirker *n.* zabušant
shirt *n.* košulja
shiver *v.i.* drhtati
shoal *n.* plićak
shoal *n* mnoštvo
shock *n.* šok
shock *v.t.* šokirati
shoe *n.* cipela
shoe *v.t.* obuti
shoot *v.t.* pucati
shoot *n* pucanje
shop *n.* prodavnica
shop *v.i.* kupovati
shore *n.* obala
short *a.* kratak
short *adv.* kratko
shortage *n.* manjak
shortcoming *n.* mana
shorten *v.t.* skratiti
shortly *adv.* uskoro
shorts *n. pl.* šorts
shot *n.* hitac
shoulder *n.* rame
shoulder *v.t.* preuzeti
shout *n.* povik
shout *v.i.* vikati
shove *v.t.* gurati
shove *n.* guranje
shovel *n.* lopata
shovel *v.t.* kopati
show *v.t.* prikazati

show *n.* prikazivanje
shower *n.* tuš
shower *v.t.* tuširati
shrew *n.* oštrokondža
shrewd *a.* lukav
shriek *n.* vrisak
shriek *v.i.* vrištati
shrill *a.* piskav
shrine *n.* svetinja
shrink *v.i* smanjiti se
shrinkage *n.* skupljanje
shroud *n.* pokrov
shroud *v.t.* pokriti plaštom
shrub *n.* žbun
shrug *v.t.* slegnuti ramenima
shrug *n* sleganje ramenima
shudder *v.i.* ježiti se
shudder *n* jeza
shuffle *v.i.* vući noge
shuffle *n.* težak hod
shun *v.t.* izbegavati
shunt *v.t.* skrenuti
shut *v.t.* zatvoriti
shutter *n.* zatvarač
shuttle *n.* čunak
shuttle *v.t.* ići tamo-ovamo
shuttlecock *n.* loptica za badminton
shy *n.* plašenje
shy *v.i.* plašiti se
sick *a.* bolestan
sickle *n.* srp
sickly *a.* bolesno
sickness *n.* bolest
side *n.* strana
side *v.i.* pristati uz jednu stranu
siege *n.* opsada
siesta *n.* popodnevni odmor
sieve *n.* sito
sieve *v.t.* prosejati
sift *v.t.* sejati

| | |
|---|---|
| **sigh** *n.* uzdah | **simultaneous** *a.* istovremen |
| **sigh** *v.i.* uzdahnuti | **sin** *n.* greh |
| **sight** *n.* pogled | **sin** *v.i.* počiniti greh |
| **sight** *v.t.* ugledati | **since** *prep.* od |
| **sightly** *a.* naočit | **since** *conj.* odkad |
| **sign** *n.* znak | **since** *adv.* odonda |
| **sign** *v.t.* obeležiti | **sincere** *a.* iskren |
| **signal** *n.* signal | **sincerity** *n.* iskrenost |
| **signal** *a.* znamenit | **sinful** *a.* grešan |
| **signal** *v.t.* signalizirati | **sing** *v.i.* pevati |
| **signatory** *n.* potpisnik | **singe** *v.t.* oprljiti |
| **signature** *n.* potpis | **singe** *n* opeklina |
| **significance** *n.* značaj | **singer** *n.* pevač |
| **significant** *a.* značajan | **single** *a.* jedini |
| **signification** *n.* značenje | **single** *n.* samac |
| **signify** *v.t.* označavati | **single** *v.t.* singlirati |
| **silence** *n.* tišina | **singular** *a.* pojedinačan |
| **silence** *v.t.* utišati | **singularity** *n.* pojedinačnost |
| **silencer** *n.* prigušivač | **singularly** *adv.* pojedinačno |
| **silent** *a.* tih | **sinister** *a.* zlokoban |
| **silhouette** *n.* silueta | **sink** *v.i.* potonuti |
| **silk** *n.* svila | **sink** *n* sudopera |
| **silken** *a.* svilen | **sinner** *n.* grešnik |
| **silky** *a.* svilenkast | **sinuous** *a.* vijugav |
| **silly** *a.* glup | **sip** *v.t.* gucnuti |
| **silt** *n.* mulj | **sip** *n.* gutljaj |
| **silt** *v.t.* zamuljiti | **sir** *n.* gospodin |
| **silver** *n.* srebro | **siren** *n.* sirena |
| **silver** *a* srebrn | **sister** *n.* sestra |
| **silver** *v.t.* posrebriti | **sisterhood** *n.* sestrinstvo |
| **similar** *a.* slične | **sisterly** *a.* sestrinski |
| **similarity** *n.* sličnost | **sit** *v.i.* sedeti |
| **simile** *n.* poređenje | **site** *n.* gradilište |
| **similitude** *n.* sličnost | **situation** *n.* situacija |
| **simmer** *v.i.* krčkati | **six** *n.* šest |
| **simple** *a.* jednostavan | **sixteen** *n.* šesnaest |
| **simpleton** *n.* glupak | **sixteenth** *a.* šesnaesti |
| **simplicity** *n.* jednostavnost | **sixth** *a.* šesti |
| **simplification** *n.* uprošćavanje | **sixtieth** *a.* šezdeseti |
| **simplify** *v.t.* pojednostaviti | **sixty** *n., a.* šezdeset |

| | |
|---|---|
| **sizable** *a.* povelik | **slant** *v.t.* nagnuti |
| **size** *n.* veličina | **slant** *n* nagib |
| **size** *v.t.* sortirati | **slap** *n.* šamar |
| **sizzle** *v.i.* cvrčati | **slap** *v.t.* ošamariti |
| **sizzle** *n.* cvrčanje | **slash** *v.t.* bičevati |
| **skate** *n.* klizaljka | **slash** *n* udarac bičem |
| **skate** *v.t.* klizati | **slate** *n.* škriljac |
| **skein** *n.* jato divljih ptica | **slattern** *n.* aljkava žena |
| **skeleton** *n.* skelet | **slatternly** *a.* aljkav |
| **sketch** *n.* skica | **slaughter** *n.* pokolj |
| **sketch** *v.t.* skicirati | **slaughter** *v.t.* zaklati |
| **sketchy** *a.* nedovršen | **slave** *n.* rob |
| **skid** *v.i.* nepovoljnost | **slave** *v.i.* robovati |
| **skid** *n* kočnica | **slavery** *n.* ropstvo |
| **skilful** *a.* vešt | **slavish** *a.* ropski |
| **skill** *n.* veština | **slay** *v.t.* ubiti |
| **skin** *n.* koža | **sleek** *a.* uglađen |
| **skin** *v.t* oderati | **sleep** *v.i.* spavati |
| **skip** *v.i.* preskočiti | **sleep** *n.* san |
| **skip** *n* preskakivanje | **sleeper** *n.* spavač |
| **skipper** *n.* kapetan | **sleepy** *a.* pospan |
| **skirmish** *n.* čarka | **sleeve** *n* rukav |
| **skirmish** *v.t.* čarkati se | **sleight** *n.* majstorija |
| **skirt** *n.* suknja | **slender** *n.* vitak |
| **skirt** *v.t.* ići uzduž | **slice** *n.* parče |
| **skit** *n.* skeč | **slice** *v.t.* seći |
| **skull** *n.* lobanja | **slick** *a* klizav |
| **sky** *n.* nebo | **slide** *v.i.* kliziti |
| **sky** *v.t.* udariti da poleti visoko | **slide** *n* slajd |
| **slab** *n.* ploča | **slight** *a.* blag |
| **slack** *a.* nemaran | **slight** *n.* omalovažavanje |
| **slacken** *v.t.* olabaviti | **slight** *v.t.* omalovažavati |
| **slacks** *n.* pantalone | **slim** *a.* vitak |
| **slake** *v.t.* utoliti | **slim** *v.i.* postati vitak |
| **slam** *v.t.* tresnuti | **slime** *n.* mulj |
| **slam** *n* tresak | **slimy** *a.* muljav |
| **slander** *n.* kleveta | **sling** *n.* praćka |
| **slander** *v.t.* klevetati | **slip** *v.i.* okliznuti se |
| **slanderous** *a.* klevetnički | **slip** *n.* okliznuće |
| **slang** *n.* sleng | **slipper** *n.* papuča |

slippery *a.* klizav
slipshod *a.* nemaran
slit *n.* raspor
slit *v.t.* rasporiti
slogan *n.* parola
slope *n.* nagib
slope *v.i.* nagnuti
sloth *n.* lenjost
slothful *n.* lenj
slough *n.* močvara
slough *n.* košuljica zmije
slough *v.t.* svlačiti
slovenly *a.* aljkav
slow *a* spor
slow *v.i.* usporiti
slowly *adv.* polako
slowness *n.* sporost
sluggard *n.* lenjivac
sluggish *a.* lenj
sluice *n.* brana
slum *n.* sirotinjski kraj
slumber *v.i.* dremati
slumber *n.* dremež
slump *n.* kriza
slump *v.i.* pasti u krizu
slur *n.* uprljati
slush *n.* bljuzgavica
slushy *a.* bljuzgav
slut *n.* kurva
sly *a.* lukav
smack *n.* ukus
smack *v.i.* zveknuti
smack *n* šamar
smack *n.* cmok
smack *v.t.* cmoknuti
small *a.* mali
small *n* mali
smallness *adv.* sićušnost
smallpox *n.* velike boginje
smart *a.* pametan

smart *v.i* žacnuti
smart *n* oštar bol
smash *v.t.* razbiti
smash *n* razbijanje
smear *v.t.* zamazati
smear *n.* mrlja
smell *n.* miris
smell *v.t.* mirisati
smelt *v.t.* istopiti
smile *n.* osmeh
smile *v.i.* smešiti se
smith *n.* kovač
smock *n.* radno odelo
smog *n.* smog
smoke *n.* dim
smoke *v.i.* pušiti se
smoky *a.* zadimljen
smooth *a.* gladak
smooth *v.t.* glatiti
smother *v.t.* ugušiti
smoulder *v.i.* tinjati
smug *a.* samozadovoljan
smuggle *v.t.* prokrijumčariti
smuggler *n.* švercer
snack *n.* užina
snag *n.* čvrga
snail *n.* puž
snake *n.* zmija
snake *v.i.* izvijati se
snap *v.t.* sčepati
snap *n* prasak
snap *a* pras
snare *n.* zamka
snare *v.t.* uhvatiti *u* zamku
snarl *n.* režanje
snarl *v.i.* režati
snatch *v.t.* zgrabiti
snatch *n.* hvatanje
sneak *v.i.* šunjati se
sneak *n* doušnik

**sneer** *v.i* podrugivati se
**sneer** *n* podrugivanje
**sneeze** *v.i.* kinuti
**sneeze** *n* kijanje
**sniff** *v.i.* šmrkati
**sniff** *n* šmrkanje
**snob** *n.* snob
**snobbery** *n.* snobizam
**snobbish** *v* snobovski
**snore** *v.i.* hrkati
**snore** *n* hrkanje
**snort** *v.i.* frktati
**snort** *n.* frktanje
**snout** *n.* rilo
**snow** *n.* sneg
**snow** *v.i.* snežiti
**snowy** *a.* snežan
**snub** *v.t.* izgrditi
**snub** *n.* grdnja
**snuff** *n.* burmut
**snug** *n.* udoban
**so** *adv.* tako
**so** *conj.* pa
**soak** *v.t.* potopiti
**soak** *n.* kvašenje
**soap** *n.* sapun
**soap** *v.t.* nasapunjati
**soapy** *a.* sapunast
**soar** *v.i.* vinuti se
**sob** *v.i.* jecati
**sob** *n* jecaj
**sober** *a.* trezan
**sobriety** *n.* trezvenost
**sociability** *n.* društvenost
**sociable** *a.* društven
**social** *n.* skup
**socialism** *n* socijalizam
**socialist** *n,a* socijalistički
**society** *n.* društvo
**sociology** *n.* sociologija

**sock** *n.* čarapa
**socket** *n.* utičnica
**sod** *n.* busen
**sodomite** *n.* sodomit
**sodomy** *n.* sodomija
**sofa** *n.* sofa
**soft** *n.* zvekan
**soften** *v.t.* ublažiti
**soil** *n.* tlo
**soil** *v.t.* kaljati
**sojourn** *v.i.* boraviti
**sojourn** *n* boravak
**solace** *v.t.* utešiti
**solace** *n.* uteha
**solar** *a.* solarni
**solder** *n.* lemljenje
**solder** *v.t.* zalemiti
**soldier** *n.* vojnik
**soldier** *v.i.* služiti vojsku
**sole** *n.* đon
**sole** *v.t* pođoniti
**sole** *a* jedini
**solemn** *a.* svečan
**solemnity** *n.* svečanost
**solemnize** *v.t.* svetkovati
**solicit** *v.t.* izazvati
**solicitation** *n.* pobuđivanje
**solicitor** *n.* advokat
**solicitous** *a.* zabrinut
**solicitude** *n.* zabrinutost
**solid** *a.* čvrst
**solid** *n* čvrsto telo
**solidarity** *n.* solidarnost
**soliloquy** *n.* monolog
**solitary** *a.* usamljen
**solitude** *n.* usamljenost
**solo** *n* solo
**solo** *a.* sam
**solo** *adv.* solo
**soloist** *n.* solista

solubility *n.* rastvorljivost
soluble *a.* rastvorljiv
solution *n.* rešenje
solve *v.t.* rešiti
solvency *n.* solventnost
solvent *a.* solventan
solvent *n* rastvarač
sombre *a.* tmuran
some *a.* neki
some *pron.* nešto
somebody *pron.* neko
somebody *n.* neko
somehow *adv.* nekako
someone *pron.* neko
somersault *n.* salto
somersault *v.i.* napraviti salto
something *pron.* nešto
something *adv.* nešto
sometime *adv.* jednom
sometimes *adv.* ponekad
somewhat *adv.* nešto
somewhere *adv.* negde
somnambulism *n.* mesečarenje
somnambulist *n.* mesečar
somnolence *n.* pospanost
somnolent *n.* pospan
son *n.* sin
song *n.* pesma
songster *n.* pevač
sonic *a.* zvučni
sonnet *n.* sonet
sonority *n.* zvučnost
soon *adv.* uskoro
soot *n.* čađ
soot *v.t.* čađiti
soothe *v.t.* ublažiti
sophism *n.* sofizam
sophist *n.* sofista
sophisticate *v.t.* sofisticirati
sophisticated *a.* sofisticiran

sophistication *n.* prefinjenost
sorcerer *n.* čarobnjak
sorcery *n.* čarobnjaštvo
sordid *a.* prljav
sore *a.* ranjiv
sore *n* rana
sorrow *n.* tuga
sorrow *v.i.* žaliti
sorry *a.* žalostan
sort *n.* vrsta
sort *v.t* sortirati
soul *n.* duša
sound *a.* zdrav
sound *v.i.* zvučati
sound *n* zvuk
soup *n.* supa
sour *a.* kiseo
sour *v.t.* ukiseliti
source *n.* izvor
south *n.* jug
south *n.* južni krajevi
south *adv* južno
southerly *a.* južni
southern *a.* južni
souvenir *n.* suvenir
sovereign *n.* vladar
sovereign *a* suveren
sovereignty *n.* suverenost
sow *v.t.* sejati
sow *n.* krmača
space *n.* prostor
space *v.t.* ostaviti razmak
spacious *a.* prostran
spade *n.* lopata
spade *v.t.* kopati lopatom
span *n.* raspon
span *v.t.* premostiti
Spaniard *n.* Španac
spaniel *n.* španijel
Spanish *a.* španski

Spanish *n.* španski jezik, Španac
spanner *n.* izvijač
spare *v.t.* štedeti
spare *a* rezervni
spare *n.* rezervni deo
spark *n.* varnica
spark *v.i.* varničiti
spark *n.* veseljak
sparkle *v.i.* sjajiti
sparkle *n.* sjaj
sparrow *n.* vrabac
sparse *a.* oskudan
spasm *n.* grč
spasmodic *a.* grčevit
spate *n.* bujica
spatial *a.* prostorni
spawn *n.* mrest
spawn *v.i.* mrestiti se
speak *v.i.* govoriti
speaker *n.* zvučnik, govornik
spear *n.* koplje
spear *v.t.* probosti kopljem
spearhead *n.* vrh koplja
spearhead *v.t.* voditi napad
special *a.* poseban
specialist *n.* specijalista
speciality *n.* specijalitet
specialization *n.* specijalizacija
specialize *v.i.* specijalizovati se
species *n.* vrsta
specific *a.* specifičan
specification *n.* specifikacija
specify *v.t.* navesti
specimen *n.* primerak
speck *n.* čestica
spectacle *n.* spektakl
spectacular *a.* spektakularan
spectator *n.* gledalac
spectre *n.* avet
speculate *v.i.* spekulisati

speculation *n.* spekulacija
speech *n.* govor
speed *n.* brzina
speed *v.i.* ubrzati
speedily *adv.* brzo
speedy *a.* brz
spell *n.* čarolija
spell *v.t.* spelovati
spell *n* opčinjenost
spend *v.t.* provesti
spendthrift *n.* rasipnik
sperm *n.* sperma
sphere *n.* sfera
spherical *a.* sferni
spice *n.* začin
spice *v.t.* začiniti
spicy *a.* ljut
spider *n.* pauk
spike *n.* šiljak
spike *v.t.* zašiljiti
spill *v.i.* prosuti
spill *n* prolivanje
spin *v.i.* zavrteti
spin *n.* okretanje
spinach *n.* spanać
spinal *a.* kičmeni
spindle *n.* vreteno
spine *n.* kičma
spinner *n.* prelja
spinster *n.* usedelica
spiral *n.* spirala
spiral *a.* spiralni
spirit *n.* duh
spirited *a.* živahan
spiritual *a.* duhovni
spiritualism *n.* spiritualizam
spiritualist *n.* spiritista
spirituality *n.* duhovnost
spit *v.i.* pljunuti
spit *n* pljuvačka

spite *n.* inat
spittle *n* ispljuvak
spittoon *n.* pljuvaonica
splash *v.i.* poprskati
splash *n* prskanje
spleen *n.* slezina
splendid *a.* sjajan
splendour *n.* sjaj
splinter *n.* iverica
splinter *v.t.* rascepiti
split *v.i.* rascepiti
split *n* pukotina
spoil *v.t.* pokvariti
spoil *n* plen
spoke *n.* prečka
spokesman *n.* portparol
sponge *n.* sunđer
sponge *v.t.* obrisati sunđerom
sponsor *n.* sponzor
sponsor *v.t.* sponzorisati
spontaneity *n.* spontanost
spontaneous *a.* spontan
spoon *n.* kašika
spoon *v.t.* uzeti kašikom
spoonful *n.* puna kašika
sporadic *a.* sporadičan
sport *n.* sport
sport *v.i.* zabavljati se
sportive *a.* veseo
sportsman *n.* sportista
spot *n.* mesto
spot *v.t.* okaljati
spotless *a.* neokaljan
spousal *n.* svadba
spouse *n.* bračni drug
spout *n.* pisak posude
spout *v.i.* izbacivati
sprain *n.* uganuće
sprain *v.t.* uganuti
spray *n.* sprej

spray *n* grančica
spray *v.t.* prskati
spread *v.i.* širiti
spread *n.* širenje
spree *n.* pijanka
sprig *n.* grančica
sprightly *a.* živahan
spring *v.i.* skočiti
spring *n* proleće
sprinkle *v. t.* posipati
sprint *v.i.* sprintati
sprint *n* sprint
sprout *v.i.* nicati
sprout *n* mladica
spur *n.* mamuza
spur *v.t.* podbosti
spurious *a.* lažan
spurn *v.t.* gurnuti nogom
spurt *v.i.* špricati
spurt *n* mlaz
sputnik *n.* sputnik
sputum *n.* ispljuvak
spy *n.* špijun
spy *v.i.* špijunirati
squad *n.* vod
squadron *n.* eskadrila
squalid *a.* bedan
squalor *n.* beda
squander *v.t.* traćiti
square *n.* kvadrat
square *a* četvrtast
square *v.t.* načiniti četvorouglastim
squash *v.t.* cediti
squash *n* bundeva
squat *v.i.* čučati
squeak *v.i.* cičati
squeak *n* čiča
squeeze *v.t.* iscediti
squint *v.i.* razrokost
squint *n* razrokost

**squire** *n.* vlastelin
**squirrel** *n.* veverica
**stab** *v.t.* ubosti
**stab** *n.* ubod
**stability** *n.* stabilnost
**stabilization** *n.* stabilizacija
**stabilize** *v.t.* stabilizovati
**stable** *a.* stabilan
**stable** *n* štala
**stable** *v.t.* držati u štali
**stadium** *n.* stadion
**staff** *n.* osoblje
**staff** *v.t.* snabdeti osobljem
**stag** *n.* jelen
**stage** *n.* pozornica
**stage** *v.t.* prirediti
**stagger** *v.i.* teturati se
**stagger** *n.* teturanje
**stagnant** *a.* nepokretan
**stagnate** *v.i.* stagnirati
**stagnation** *n.* stagnacija
**staid** *a.* staložen
**stain** *n.* mrlja
**stain** *v.t.* mrljati
**stainless** *a.* neumrljan
**stair** *n.* stepenik
**stake** *n* ulog
**stake** *v.t.* uložiti
**stale** *a.* ustajao
**stale** *v.t.* istrošiti
**stalemate** *n.* pat
**stalk** *n.* stabljika
**stalk** *v.i.* prikradati se
**stalk** *n* kočoperenje
**stall** *n.* štala
**stall** *v.t.* držati u štali
**stallion** *n.* pastuv
**stalwart** *a.* odlučan
**stalwart** *n* odlučan zagovornik
**stamina** *n.* izdržljivost

**stammer** *v.i.* mucati
**stammer** *n* mucanje
**stamp** *n.* pečat
**stamp** *v.i.* zapečatiti
**stampede** *n.* stampedo
**stampede** *v.i* bežati *u* panici
**stand** *v.i.* stajati
**stand** *n.* štand
**standard** *n.* standard
**standard** *a* standardan
**standardization** *n.* standardizacija
**standardize** *v.t.* standardizovati
**standing** *n.* stajanje
**standpoint** *n.* stanovište
**standstill** *n.* zastoj
**stanza** *n.* strofa
**staple** *n.* spajalica
**staple** *a* heftati
**star** *n.* zvezda
**star** *v.t.* ukrasiti zvezdama
**starch** *n.* skrob
**starch** *v.t.* štirkati
**stare** *v.i.* buljiti
**stare** *n.* buljenje
**stark** *n.* potpunost
**stark** *adv.* potpun
**starry** *a.* zvezdan
**start** *v.t.* početi
**start** *n* start
**startle** *v.t.* iznenaditi
**starvation** *n.* gladovanje
**starve** *v.i.* umirati od gladi
**state** *n.* stanje, država
**state** *v.t* navoditi
**stateliness** *n.* dostojanstvenost
**stately** *a.* veličanstven
**statement** *n.* izjava
**statesman** *n.* državnik
**static** *n.* statičnost
**statics** *n.* statika

station *n.* stanica
station *v.t.* stacionirati
stationary *a.* stacionaran
stationer *n.* trgovac pisaćim priborom
stationery *n.* kancelarijski pribor
statistical *a.* statistički
statistician *n.* statističar
statistics *n.* statistika
statue *n.* statua
stature *n.* stas
status *n.* statusa
statute *n.* statut
statutory *a.* statutarne
staunch *a.* odan
stay *v.i.* ostati
stay *n* boravak
steadfast *a.* postojan
steadiness *n.* postojanost
steady *a.* čvrst
steady *v.t.* učvrstiti
steal *v.i.* ukrasti
stealthily *adv.* krišom
steam *n* para
steam *v.i.* pariti
steamer *n.* parobrod
steed *n.* konj
steel *n.* čelik
steep *a.* strm
steep *v.t.* močiti
steeple *n.* zvonik
steer *v.t.* upravljati
stellar *a.* zvezdan
stem *n.* stabla
stem *v.i.* zaustaviti
stench *n.* smrad
stencil *n.* matrica
stencil *v.i.* umnožiti matricom
stenographer *n.* stenograf
stenography *n.* stenografija
step *n.* korak

step *v.i.* koračati
steppe *n.* stepa
stereotype *n.* stereotip
stereotype *v.t.* stereotipizirati
stereotyped *a.* ukalupljen
sterile *a.* sterilan
sterility *n.* sterilitet
sterilization *n.* sterilizacija
sterilize *v.t.* sterilisati
sterling *a.* prvoklasan
sterling *n.* sterling
stern *a.* ozbiljan
stern *n.* krma
stethoscope *n.* stetoskop
stew *n.* paprikaš
stew *v.t.* dinstati
steward *n.* stjuard
stick *n.* štap
stick *v.t.* zabosti
sticker *n.* nalepnica
stickler *n.* pristalica
sticky *n.* lepljiv
stiff *n.* krut
stiffen *v.t.* ukrutiti
stifle *v.t.* ugušiti
stigma *n.* stigma
still *a.* miran
still *adv.* još uvek
still *v.t.* umiriti
still *n.* mir
stillness *n.* tišina
stilt *n.* štula
stimulant *n.* stimulans
stimulate *v.t.* stimulisati
stimulus *n.* podsticaj
sting *v.t.* ubod
sting *n.* žaoka
stingy *a.* škrt
stink *v.i.* smrdeti
stink *n* smrad

**stipend** *n.* plata
**stipulate** *v.t.* ustanoviti
**stipulation** *n.* odredba
**stir** *v.i.* uskomešati se
**stirrup** *n.* uzengija
**stitch** *n.* šav
**stitch** *v.t.* krpiti
**stock** *n.* zaliha
**stock** *v.t.* opskrbiti
**stock** *a.* spreman
**stocking** *n.* čarapa
**stoic** *n.* stoik
**stoke** *v.t.* ložiti
**stoker** *n.* ložač
**stomach** *n.* stomak
**stomach** *v.t.* podnositi
**stone** *n.* kamen
**stone** *v.t.* kamenovati
**stony** *a.* kamenit
**stool** *n.* stolica
**stoop** *v.i.* pognuti se
**stoop** *n* pognutost
**stop** *v.t.* zaustaviti
**stop** *n* obustava
**stoppage** *n* zastoj
**storage** *n.* skladištenje
**store** *n.* prodavnica
**store** *v.t.* skladištiti
**storey** *n.* sprat
**stork** *n.* roda
**storm** *n.* oluja
**storm** *v.i.* jurišati
**stormy** *a.* olujni
**story** *n.* priča
**stout** *a.* krupan
**stove** *n.* peć
**stow** *v.t.* natovariti
**straggle** *v.i.* lutati
**straggler** *n.* lutalica
**straight** *a.* prav

**straight** *adv.* pravo
**straighten** *v.t.* ispraviti
**straightforward** *a.* iskren
**straightway** *adv.* smesta
**strain** *v.t.* naprezati
**strain** *n* naprezanje
**strait** *n.* moreuz
**straiten** *v.t.* suziti
**strand** *v.i.* nasukati
**strand** *n* obala
**strange** *a.* čudan
**stranger** *n.* stranac
**strangle** *v.t.* ugušiti
**strangulation** *n.* gušenje
**strap** *n.* pojas
**strap** *v.t.* opasati
**strategem** *n.* lukavstvo
**strategic** *a.* strateški
**strategist** *n.* strateg
**strategy** *n.* strategija
**stratum** *n.* naslaga
**straw** *n.* slama
**strawberry** *n.* jagoda
**stray** *v.i.* zalutati
**stray** *a* zalutao
**stray** *n* lutalice
**stream** *n.* potok
**stream** *v.i.* teći
**streamer** *n.* traka
**streamlet** *n.* potočić
**street** *n.* ulica
**strength** *n.* snaga
**strengthen** *v.t.* ojačati
**strenuous** *a.* naporan
**stress** *n.* stres
**stress** *v.t* naglašavati
**stretch** *v.t.* rastezati
**stretch** *n* rastezanje
**stretcher** *n.* nosila
**strew** *v.t.* posuti

strict *a.* strog
stricture *n.* zamerka
stride *v.i.* koračati
stride *n* korak
strident *a.* kreštav
strife *n.* sukob
strike *v.t.* udariti
strike *n* štrajk
striker *n.* štrajkač
string *n.* vrpca
string *v.t.* nategnuti
stringency *n.* oskudica
stringent *a.* strog
strip *n.* traka
strip *v.t.* svlačiti
stripe *n.* pruga
stripe *v.t.* isprugati
strive *v.i.* težiti
stroke *n.* udarac
stroke *v.t.* milovati
stroke *n* milovanje
stroll *v.i.* tumarati
stroll *n* tumaranje
strong *a.* jak
stronghold *n.* uporište
structural *a.* strukturni
structure *n.* struktura
struggle *v.i.* boriti se
struggle *n* borba
strumpet *n.* uličarka
strut *v.i.* razmetati se
strut *n* razmetanje
stub *n.* panj
stubble *n.* strnjika
stubborn *a.* tvrdoglav
stud *n.* ergela
stud *v.t.* odbiti
student *n.* student
studio *n.* studio
studious *a.* marljiv

study *v.i.* učiti
study *n.* radna soba
stuff *n.* materijal
stuff 2 *v.t.* napuniti, ispuniti
stuffy *a.* zagušljiv
stumble *v.i.* spotaći se
stumble *n.* spoticanje
stump *n.* panj
stump *v.t* tabati
stun *v.t.* ošamutiti
stunt *v.t.* praviti akrobacije
stunt *n* majstorija
stupefy *v.t.* omamiti
stupendous *a.* čudesan
stupid *a* glup
stupidity *n.* glupost
sturdy *a.* čvrst
sty *n.* svinjac
stye *n.* čmičak
style *n.* stil
subdue *v.t.* obuzdati
subject *n.* subjekat
subject *a* podložan
subject *v.t.* podvrgnuti
subjection *n.* potčinjenje
subjective *a.* subjektivan
subjugate *v.t.* potčiniti
subjugation *n.* pokoravanje
sublet *v.t.* dati u podzakup
sublimate *v.t.* sublimirati
sublime *a.* uzvišen
sublime *n* uzvišenost
sublimity *n.* otmenost
submarine *n.* podmornica
submarine *a* podmorski
submerge *v.i.* potopiti
submission *n.* pokornost
submissive *a.* pokoran
submit *v.t.* podneti
subordinate *a.* podređen

subordinate *n* podređeni
subordinate *v.t.* potčiniti
subordination *n.* podređenost
subscribe *v.t.* potpisati
subscription *n.* pretplata
subsequent *a.* sledeći
subservience *n.* korist
subservient *a.* koristan
subside *v.i.* opasti
subsidiary *a.* podružnica
subsidize *v.t.* subvencionisati
subsidy *n.* subvencija
subsist *v.i.* opstajati
subsistence *n.* opstanak
substance *n.* supstanca
substantial *a.* znatan
substantially *adv.* bitno
substantiate *v.t.* potvrditi
substantiation *n.* potvrđivanje
substitute *n.* zamena
substitute *v.t.* zameniti
substitution *n.* zamena
subterranean *a.* podzemni
subtle *n.* suptilan
subtlety *n.* suptilnost
subtract *v.t.* oduzeti
subtraction *n.* oduzimanje
suburb *n.* predgrađe
suburban *a.* prigradski
subversion *n.* subverzija
subversive *a.* subverzivan
subvert *v.t.* podriti
succeed *v.i.* uspeti
success *n.* uspeh
successful *a* uspešan
succession *n.* nasledstvo
successive *a.* uzastopan
successor *n.* naslednik
succour *n.* pomoć
succour *v.t.* pomoći

succumb *v.i.* podleći
such *a.* ovakav
such *pron.* takav
suck *v.t.* sisati
suck *n.* sisanje
suckle *v.t.* dojiti
sudden *n.* iznenadnost
suddenly *adv.* iznenada
sue *v.t.* tužiti
suffer *v.t.* patiti
suffice *v.i.* zadovoljavati
sufficiency *n.* dovoljnost
sufficient *a.* dovoljan
suffix *n.* sufiks
suffix *v.t.* dodati
suffocate *v.t* ugušiti
suffocation *n.* gušenje
suffrage *n.* pravo glasa
sugar *n.* šećer
sugar *v.t.* zasladiti
suggest *v.t.* predložiti
suggestion *n.* predlog
suggestive *a.* sugestivan
suicidal *a.* samoubilački
suicide *n.* samoubistvo
suit *n.* odelo
suit *v.t.* odgovarati
suitability *n.* podobnost
suitable *a.* pogodan
suite *n.* apartman
suitor *n.* prosilac
sullen *a.* sumoran
sulphur *n.* sumpor
sulphuric *a.* sumporni
sultry *a.* sparan
sum *n.* suma
sum *v.t.* sumirati
summarily *adv.* ukratko
summarize *v.t.* rezimirati
summary *n.* rezime

summary *a* sažet
summer *n.* leto
summit *n.* vrh
summon *v.t.* pozvati
summons *n.* poziv
sumptuous *a.* raskošan
sun *n.* sunce
sun *v.t.* sunčati
Sunday *n.* nedelja
sunder *v.t.* rastaviti
sunny *a.* sunčan
sup *v.i.* gucnuti
superabundance *n.* preobilje
superabundant *a.* preobilan
superb *a.* izvanredan
superficial *a.* površan
superficiality *n.* površnost
superfine *a.* najfiniji
superfluity *n.* višak
superfluous *a.* suvišno
superhuman *a.* nadljudski
superintend *v.t.* rukovoditi
superintendence *n.* vrhovni nadzor
superintendent *n.* nadzornik
superior *a.* nadmoćan
superiority *n.* superiornost
superlative *a.* superlativan
superlative *n.* superlativ
superman *n.* nadčovek
supernatural *a.* natprirodan
supersede *v.t.* zameniti
supersonic *a.* supersoničan
superstition *n.* sujeverje
superstitious *a.* sujeveran
supertax *n.* poseban porez na dohodak
supervise *v.t.* nadgledati
supervision *n.* nadzor
supervisor *n.* nadzornik
supper *n.* večera
supple *a.* savitljiv

supplement *n.* dopuna
supplement *v.t.* dopuniti
supplementary *a.* dopunski
supplier *n.* dobavljač
supply *v.t.* snabdevati
supply *n* snabdevanje
support *v.t.* podržat
support *n.* podrška
suppose *v.t.* pretpostaviti
supposition *n.* pretpostavka
suppress *v.t.* suzbijati
suppression *n.* suzbijanje
supremacy *n.* prevlast
supreme *a.* vrhovni
surcharge *n.* preopterećenje
surcharge *v.t.* preopteretiti
sure *a.* siguran
surely *adv.* sigurno
surety *n.* izvesnost
surf *n.* surf
surface *n.* površina
surface *v.i* poravnati
surfeit *n.* prezasićenost
surge *n.* talas
surge *v.i.* talas
surgeon *n.* hirurg
surgery *n.* hirurgija
surmise *n.* pretpostavka
surmise *v.t.* pretpostaviti
surmount *v.t.* savladati
surname *n.* prezime
surpass *v.t.* nadmašiti
surplus *n.* višak
surprise *n.* iznenađenje
surprise *v.t.* iznenaditi
surrender *v.t.* predati se
surrender *n* predaja
surround *v.t.* okruživati
surroundings *n.* okruženje
surtax *n.* dopunski porez

surveillance *n.* nadzor
survey *n.* pregled
survey *v.t.* pregledati
survival *n.* opstanak
survive *v.i.* opstati
suspect *v.t.* osumnjičiti
suspect *a.* osumnjičen
suspect *n* osumnjičeni
suspend *v.t.* suspendovati
suspense *n.* neizvesnost
suspension *n.* obustava
suspicion *n.* sumnja
suspicious *a.* sumnjiv
sustain *v.t.* održati
sustenance *n.* izdržavanje
swagger *v.i.* šepuriti se
swagger *n* šepurenje
swallow *v.t.* progutati
swallow *n.* gutljaj
swallow *n.* lasta
swamp *n.* močvara
swamp *v.t.* poplaviti
swan *n.* labud
swarm *n.* roj
swarm *v.i.* rojiti se
swarthy *a.* crnpurast
sway *v.i.* njihati
sway *n* njihanje
swear *v.t.* psovati
sweat *n.* znoj
sweat *v.i.* kleti se
sweater *n.* džemper
sweep *v.i.* čistiti
sweep *n.* zamah
sweeper *n.* čistač
sweet *a.* sladak
sweet *n* slatkiš
sweeten *v.t.* zašećeriti
sweetmeat *n.* slatkiš
sweetness *n.* slatkoća

swell *v.i.* nabreknuti
swell *n* oteklina
swift *a.* brz
swim *v.i.* plivati
swim *n* plivanje
swimmer *n.* plivač
swindle *v.t.* prevariti
swindle *n.* prevara
swindler *n.* varalica
swine *n.* svinja
swing *v.i.* ljuljati
swing *n* ljuljaška
swiss *n.* švajcarska
swiss *a* švajcarski
switch *n.* prekidač
switch *v.t.* skrenuti
swoon *n.* nesvest
swoon *v.i* onesvestiti se
swoop *v.i.* kidisati
swoop *n* prepad
sword *n.* mač
sycamore *n.* javor
sycophancy *n.* ulizivanje
sycophant *n.* ulizica
syllabic *n.* slogovni
syllable *n.* slog
syllabus *n.* pregled
sylph *n.* vazdušni duh
sylvan *a.* pošumljen
symbol *n.* simbol
symbolic *a.* simboličan
symbolism *n.* simbolizam
symbolize *v.t.* simbolizovati
symmetrical *a.* simetričan
symmetry *n.* simetrija
sympathetic *a.* saosećajan
sympathize *v.i.* saosećati
sympathy *n.* simpatija
symphony *n.* simfonija
symposium *n.* simpozijum

symptom *n.* simptom
symptomatic *a.* simptomatičan
synonym *n.* sinonim
synonymous *a.* sinoniman
synopsis *n.* sinopsis
syntax *n.* sintaksa
synthesis *n.* sinteza
synthetic *a.* sintetički
synthetic *n* sintetika
syringe *n.* špric
syringe *v.t.* štrcnuti
syrup *n.* sirup
system *n.* sistem
systematic *a.* sistematičan
systematize *v.t.* sistematizovati

# T

table *n.* sto
table *v.t.* izložiti
tablet *n.* tableta
taboo *n.* tabu
taboo *a* zabranjen
taboo *v.t.* zabraniti
tabular *a.* tabelarni
tabulate *v.t.* poređati
tabulation *n.* tabelisanje
tabulator *n.* tabulator
tacit *a.* prećutan
taciturn *a.* uzdržan
tackle *n.* pribor
tackle *v.t.* prionuti
tact *n.* takt
tactful *a.* taktičan
tactician *n.* taktičar
tactics *n.* taktika
tactile *a.* taktilni
tag *n.* oznaka
tag *v.t.* označiti

tail *n.* rep
tailor *n.* krojač
tailor *v.t.* krojiti
taint *n.* mrlja
taint *v.t.* uprljati
take *v.t* uzeti
tale *n.* priča
talent *n.* talenat
talisman *n.* talisman
talk *v.i.* pričati
talk *n* razgovor
talkative *a.* pričljiv
tall *a.* visok
tallow *n.* loj
tally *n.* evidencija
tally *v.t.* podudarati
tamarind *n.* indijska urma
tame *a.* pitom
tame *v.t.* pripitomiti
tamper *v.i.* pokvariti
tan *v.i.* preplanuti
tan *n., a.* preplanulost
tangent *n.* tangenta
tangible *a.* opipljiv
tangle *n.* zaplet
tangle *v.t.* zamrsiti
tank *n.* rezervoar
tanker *n.* tanker
tanner *n.* kožar
tannery *n.* kožara
tantalize *v.t.* mučiti
tantamount *a.* jednake vrednosti
tap *n.* slavina
tap *v.t.* tapkati
tape *n.* traka
tape *v.t svezati* trakom
taper *v.i.* zašiljiti
taper *n* tanka voštana sveća
tapestry *n.* tapiserija
tar *n.* katran

**tar** v.t. premazati katranom
**target** n. cilj
**tariff** n. tarifa
**tarnish** v.t. gubiti boju
**task** n. zadatak
**task** v.t. uposliti
**taste** n. ukus
**taste** v.t. okusiti
**tasteful** a. ukusan
**tasty** a. ukusan
**tatter** n. dronjak
**tatter** v.t pocepati u dronjke
**tattoo** n. tetoviranje
**tattoo** v.i. tetovirati
**taunt** v.t. podrugivati se
**taunt** n podrugivanje
**tavern** n. krčma
**tax** n. porez
**tax** v.t. oporezovati
**taxable** a. oporeziv
**taxation** n. oporezivanje
**taxi** n. taksi
**taxi** v.i. voziti se u taksiju
**tea** n čaj
**teach** v.t. učiti
**teacher** n. učitelj
**teak** n. tik
**team** n. tim
**tear** v.t. poderati
**tear** n. suza
**tear** n. poderotina
**tearful** a. suzan
**tease** v.t. zadirkivati
**teat** n. sisa
**technical** n. tehnički
**technicality** n. formalnost
**technician** n. tehničar
**technique** n. tehnika
**technological** a. tehnološki
**technologist** n. tehnolog

**technology** n. tehnologija
**tedious** a. dosadan
**tedium** n. dosada
**teem** v.i. vrveti
**teenager** n. tinejdžer
**teens** n. pl. omladina
**teethe** v.i. dobiti zube
**teetotal** a. trezvenjački
**teetotaller** n. trezvenjak
**telecast** n. prenos
**telecast** v.t. prenositi
**telegram** n. telegram
**telegraph** n. telegraf
**telegraph** v.t. telegrafisati
**telegraphic** a. telegrafski
**telegraphist** n. telegrafista
**telegraphy** n. telegrafija
**telepathic** a. telepatski
**telepathist** n. telepata
**telepathy** n. telepatija
**telephone** n. telefon
**telephone** v.t. telefonirati
**telescope** n. teleskop
**telescopic** a. teleskopski
**televise** v.t. emitovati preko televizije
**television** n. televizija
**tell** v.t. reći
**teller** n. blagajnik
**temper** n. temperament
**temper** v.t. mešati
**temperament** n. temperament
**temperamental** a. temperamentan
**temperance** n. umerenost
**temperate** a. umeren
**temperature** n. temperatura
**tempest** n. oluja
**tempestuous** a. buran
**temple** n. hram
**temple** n slepoočnica
**temporal** a. vremenski

**temporary** *a.* privremen
**tempt** *v.t.* dovesti u iskušenje
**temptation** *n.* iskušenje
**tempter** *n.* iskušavač
**ten** *n., a* deset
**tenable** *a.* održiv
**tenacious** *a.* uporan
**tenacity** *n.* istrajnost
**tenancy** *n.* zakup
**tenant** *n.* stanar
**tend** *v.i.* biti sklon
**tendency** *n.* tendencija
**tender** *n* ponuda
**tender** *v.t.* ponuditi
**tender** *n* negovatelj
**tender** *a* nežan
**tenet** *n.* načelo
**tennis** *n.* tenis
**tense** *n.* glagolsko vreme
**tense** *a.* napet
**tension** *n.* tenzija
**tent** *n.* šator
**tentative** *a.* probni
**tenure** *n.* mandat
**term** *n.* rok
**term** *v.t.* nazvati
**terminable** *a.* ograničen
**terminal** *a.* konačni
**terminal** *n* terminal
**terminate** *v.t.* okončati
**termination** *n.* završetak
**terminological** *a.* terminološki
**terminology** *n.* terminologija
**terminus** *n.* kraj
**terrace** *n.* terasa
**terrible** *a.* užasan
**terrier** *n.* terijer
**terrific** *a.* strašan
**terrify** *v.t.* prestraviti
**territorial** *a.* teritorijalni

**territory** *n.* teritorija
**terror** *n.* teror
**terrorism** *n.* terotizam
**terrorist** *n.* terorista
**terrorize** *v.t.* terorisati
**terse** *a.* sažet
**test** *v.t.* testirati
**test** *n* test
**testament** *n.* testament
**testicle** *n.* testis
**testify** *v.i.* svedočiti
**testimonial** *n.* uverenje
**testimony** *n.* svedočanstvo
**tete-a-tete** *n.* sastanak u četiri oka
**tether** *n.* lanac
**tether** *v.t.* privezati
**text** *n.* tekst
**textile** *a.* tekstilni
**textile** *n* tekstil
**textual** *n.* tekstualni
**texture** *n.* sastav
**thank** *v.t.* zahvaliti
**thanks** *n.* zahvalnost
**thankful** *a.* zahvalan
**thankless** *a.* nezahvalan
**that** *a.* taj
**that** *dem. pron.* onaj
**that** *rel. pron.* koji
**that** *adv.* tako
**that** *conj.* da
**thatch** *n.* slama
**thatch** *v.t.* pokriti krov
**thaw** *v.i* topiti se
**thaw** *n* topljenje
**theatre** *n.* pozorište
**theatrical** *a.* pozorišni
**theft** *n.* krađa
**their** *a.* njihov
**theirs** *pron.* njihov
**theism** *n.* teizam

theist *n.* teista
them *pron.* njih
thematic *a.* tematski
theme *n.* tema
then *adv.* onda
then *a* tadašnji
thence *adv.* odande
theocracy *n.* teokratija
theologian *n.* teolog
theological *a.* teološki
theology *n.* teologija
theorem *n.* teorema
theoretical *a.* teorijski
theorist *n.* teoretičar
theorize *v.i.* teoretisati
theory *n.* teorija
therapy *n.* terapija
there *adv.* tamo
thereabouts *adv.* otprilike
thereafter *adv.* posle toga
thereby *adv.* time
therefore *adv.* dakle
thermal *a.* termalni
thermometer *n.* termometar
thermos (flask) *n.* termos (boca)
thesis *n.* teza
thick *a.* debeo
thick *n.* najgušći deo
thick *adv.* debelo
thicken *v.i.* zgusnuti
thicket *n.* gustiš
thief *n.* lopov
thigh *n.* bedro
thimble *n.* naprstak
thin *a.* tanak
thin *v.t.* tanjiti
thing *n.* stvar
think *v.t.* misliti
thinker *n.* mislilac
third *a.* treći

third *n.* trećina
thirdly *adv.* treće
thirst *n.* žeđ
thirst *v.i.* biti žedan
thirsty *a.* žedan
thirteen *n.* trinaest
thirteen *a* trinaest
thirteenth *a.* trinaesti
thirtieth *a.* trideseti
thirtieth *n* tridesetina
thirty *n.* trideset
thirty *a* trideset
thistle *n.* čičak
thither *adv.* tamo
thorn *n.* trn
thorny *a.* trnovit
thorough *a* temeljan
thoroughfare *n.* prolaz
though *conj.* premda
though *adv.* ipak
thought *n* misao
thoughtful *a.* pažljiv
thousand *n.* hiljada
thousand *a* hiljadu
thrall *n.* rob
thraldom *n.* ropstvo
thrash *v.t.* mlatiti
thread *n.* nit
thread *v.t* udenuti
threadbare *a.* otrcan
threat *n.* pretnja
threaten *v.t.* pretiti
three *n.* tri
three *a* tri
thresh *v.t.* vršati
thresher *n.* vršalica
threshold *n.* prag
thrice *adv.* triput
thrift *n.* štednja
thrifty *a.* štedljiv

| | |
|---|---|
| **thrill** *n.* uzbuđenje | **tickle** *v.t.* golicati |
| **thrill** *v.t.* uzbuditi | **ticklish** *a.* golicljiv |
| **thrive** *v.i.* napredovati | **tidal** *a.* plimski |
| **throat** *n.* grlo | **tide** *n.* plima |
| **throaty** *a.* grlen | **tidings** *n. pl.* vesti |
| **throb** *v.i.* lupati | **tidiness** *n.* urednost |
| **throb** *n.* lupanje | **tidy** *a.* uredan |
| **throe** *n.* agonija | **tidy** *v.t.* počistiti |
| **throne** *n.* tron | **tie** *v.t.* vezati |
| **throne** *v.t.* posaditi na presto | **tie** *n* kravata |
| **throng** *n.* gomila | **tier** *n.* niz |
| **throng** *v.t.* gomilati se | **tiger** *n.* tigar |
| **throttle** *n.* dušnik | **tight** *a.* čvrst |
| **throttle** *v.t.* gušiti | **tighten** *v.t.* pritegnuti |
| **through** *prep.* kroz | **tigress** *n.* tigrica |
| **through** *adv.* skroz | **tile** *n.* crep |
| **through** *a* izravan | **tile** *v.t.* pokriti crepom |
| **throughout** *adv.* skroz | **till** *prep.* do |
| **throughout** *prep.* širom | **till** *n. conj.* dok |
| **throw** *v.t.* baciti | **till** *v.t.* obrađivati |
| **throw** *n.* bacanje | **tilt** *v.i.* nagnuti se |
| **thrust** *v.t.* gurati | **tilt** *n.* nagib |
| **thrust** *n* potisak | **timber** *n.* greda |
| **thud** *n.* tutnjava | **time** *n.* vreme |
| **thud** *v.i.* tutnjiti | **time** *v.t.* izabrati vreme |
| **thug** *n.* razbojnik | **timely** *a.* na vreme |
| **thumb** *n.* palac | **timid** *a.* stidljiv |
| **thumb** *v.t.* opipati palcem | **timidity** *n.* bojažljivost |
| **thump** *n.* *tup* udarac | **timorous** *a.* plašljiv |
| **thump** *v.t.* lupiti | **tin** *n.* konzerva |
| **thunder** *n.* grom | **tin** *v.t.* kalajisati |
| **thunder** *v.i.* grmeti | **tincture** *n.* boja |
| **thunderous** *a.* gromovit | **tincture** *v.t.* obojiti |
| **Thursday** *n.* četvrtak | **tinge** *n.* nijansa |
| **thus** *adv.* stoga | **tinge** *v.t.* nijansirati |
| **thwart** *v.t.* osujetiti | **tinker** *n.* kotlar |
| **tiara** *n.* tijara | **tinsel** *n.* šljokica |
| **tick** *n.* otkucaj | **tint** *n.* boja |
| **tick** *v.i.* kucati | **tint** *v.t.* obojiti |
| **ticket** *n.* karta | **tiny** *a.* sićušan |

tip *n.* savet
tip *v.t.* savetovati
tip *n.* vrh
tip *v.t.* prevrnuti
tip *n.* kraj
tip *v.t.* okovati
tipsy *a.* pripit
tirade *n.* tirada
tire *v.t.* izmoriti
tiresome *a.* zamoran
tissue *n.* tkivo
titanic *a.* titanski
tithe *n.* desetina
title *n.* naslov
titular *a.* titularni
toad *n.* žaba krastača
toast *n.* zdravica
toast *v.t.* nazdraviti
tobacco *n.* duvan
today *adv.* danas
today *n.* današnjica
toe *n.* nožni prst
toe *v.t.* dodirnuti nožnim prstima
toffee *n.* karamela
toga *n.* toga
together *adv.* zajedno
toil *n.* rintanje
toil *v.i.* rintati
toilet *n.* toalet
toils *n. pl.* mreže
token *n.* znak
tolerable *a.* podnošljiv
tolerance *n.* tolerancija
tolerant *a.* tolerantan
tolerate *v.t.* tolerisati
toleration *n.* tolerancija
toll *n.* taksa
toll *n* zvonjava
toll *v.t.* zvoniti
tomato *n.* paradajz

tomb *n.* grob
tomboy *n.* nestaško
tomcat *n.* mačak
tome *n.* tom
tomorrow *n.* sutrašnji dan
tomorrow *adv.* sutra
ton *n.* tona
tone *n.* zvuk
tone *v.t.* davati ton
tongs *n. pl.* klešta
tongue *n.* jezik
tonic *a.* toničan
tonic *n.* tonik
to-night *n.* ova noć
tonight *adv.* večeras
tonne *n.* tona
tonsil *n.* krajnik
tonsure *n.* tonzura
too *adv.* suviše
tool *n.* alatka
tooth *n.* zub
toothache *n.* zubobolja
toothsome *a.* ukusan
top *n.* vrh
top *v.t.* pokriti
top *n.* čigra
topaz *n.* topaz
topic *n.* tema
topical *a.* tematski
topographer *n.* topograf
topographical *a.* topografski
topography *n.* topografija
topple *v.i.* srušiti se
topsy *turvy a.* pobrkan
topsy *turvy adv* pobrkano
torch *n.* baklja
torment *n.* muka
torment *v.t.* mučiti
tornado *n.* tornado
torpedo *n.* torpedo

| | |
|---|---|
| **torpedo** v.t. torpedovati | **traction** n. vuča |
| **torrent** n. bujica | **tractor** n. traktor |
| **torrential** a. bujan | **trade** n. trgovina |
| **torrid** a. suv | **trade** v.i trgovati |
| **tortoise** n. kornjača | **trader** n. trgovac |
| **tortuous** a. krivični | **tradesman** n. trgovac |
| **torture** n. mučenje | **tradition** n. tradicija |
| **torture** v.t. mučiti | **traditional** a. tradicionalan |
| **toss** v.t. zbaciti | **traffic** n. saobraćaj |
| **toss** n zbacivanje | **traffic** v.i. trgovati |
| **total** a. ukupan | **tragedian** n. tragičar |
| **total** n. celina | **tragedy** n. tragedija |
| **total** v.t. zbrojiti | **tragic** a. tragičan |
| **totality** n. celokupnost | **trail** n. trag |
| **touch** v.t. dodirnuti | **trail** v.t. puzati |
| **touch** n dodir | **trailer** n. prikolica |
| **touchy** a. osetljiv | **train** n. voz |
| **tough** a. težak | **train** v.t. trenirati |
| **toughen** v.t. očvrsnuti | **trainee** n. pripravnik |
| **tour** n. tura | **training** n. obuka |
| **tour** v.i. putovati | **trait** n. osobina |
| **tourism** n. turizam | **traitor** n. izdajnik |
| **tourist** n. turista | **tram** n. tramvaj |
| **tournament** n. turnir | **trample** v.t. pogaziti |
| **towards** prep. ka | **trance** n. trans |
| **towel** n. peškir | **tranquil** a. miran |
| **towel** v.t. brisati peškirom | **tranquility** n. mir |
| **tower** n. toranj | **tranquillize** v.t. stišati |
| **tower** v.i. dizati se | **transact** v.t. obaviti |
| **town** n. grad | **transaction** n. transakcija |
| **township** a. opštinski | **transcend** v.t. prekoračiti |
| **toy** n. igračka | **transcendent** a. nenadmašan |
| **toy** v.i. igrati se | **transcribe** v.t. prepisati |
| **trace** n. trag | **transcription** n. transkripcija |
| **trace** v.t. tragati | **transfer** n. prenos |
| **traceable** a. kome se može naći trag | **transfer** v.t. prenositi |
| **track** n. staza | **transferable** a. prenosiv |
| **track** v.t. slediti | **transfiguration** n. preobraženje |
| **tract** n. trakt | **transfigure** v.t. preobraziti |
| **tract** n traktat | **transform** v. transformisati |

| | |
|---|---|
| **transformation** *n.* transformacija | **trek** *v.i.* seliti se |
| **transgress** *v.t.* prekršiti | **trek** *n.* putovanje |
| **transgression** *n.* prestup | **tremble** *v.i.* drhtati |
| **transit** *n.* tranzit | **tremendous** *a.* ogroman |
| **transition** *n.* prelaz | **tremor** *n.* drhtanje |
| **transitive** *n.* prelazni | **trench** *n.* rov |
| **transitory** *n.* prolazan | **trench** *v.t.* rezati |
| **translate** *v.t.* prevoditi | **trend** *n.* trend |
| **translation** *n.* prevođenje | **trespass** *v.i.* zgrešiti |
| **transmigration** *n.* seoba | **trespass** *n.* prestup |
| **transmission** *n.* transmisija | **trial** *n.* suđenje |
| **transmit** *v.t.* prenositi | **triangle** *n.* trougao |
| **transmitter** *n.* odašiljač | **triangular** *a.* trougaoni |
| **transparent** *a.* transparentan | **tribal** *a.* plemenski |
| **transplant** *v.t.* presađivati | **tribe** *n.* pleme |
| **transport** *v.t.* prevoziti | **tribulation** *n.* stradanje |
| **transport** *n.* prevoz | **tribunal** *n.* sud |
| **transportation** *n.* transport | **tributary** *n.* pritoka |
| **trap** *n.* zamka | **tributary** *a.* dužan da daje danak |
| **trap** *v.t.* uhvatiti u zamku | **trick** *n* trik |
| **trash** *n.* smeće | **trick** *v.t.* prevariti |
| **travel** *v.i.* putovati | **trickery** *n.* varanje |
| **travel** *n* putovanje | **trickle** *v.i.* kapati |
| **traveller** *n.* putnik | **trickster** *n.* varalica |
| **tray** *n.* poslužavnik | **tricky** *a.* lukav |
| **treacherous** *a.* izdajnički | **tricolour** *a.* trobojni |
| **treachery** *n.* izdaja | **tricolour** *n* trobojnica |
| **tread** *v.t.* koračati | **tricycle** *n.* tricikl |
| **tread** *n* hod | **trifle** *n.* sitnica |
| **treason** *n.* izdaja | **trifle** *v.i* igrati se |
| **treasure** *n.* blago | **trigger** *n.* okidač |
| **treasure** *v.t.* čuvati | **trim** *a.* uredan |
| **treasurer** *n.* blagajnik | **trim** *n* red |
| **treasury** *n.* državna blagajna | **trim** *v.t.* urediti |
| **treat** *v.t.* lečiti | **trinity** *n.* trojstvo |
| **treat** *n* čašćenje | **trio** *n.* trio |
| **treatise** *n.* rasprava | **trip** *v.t.* poigravati |
| **treatment** *n.* tretman | **trip** *n.* putovanje |
| **treaty** *n.* pregovor | **tripartite** *a.* trodelan |
| **tree** *n.* drvo | **triple** *a.* trostruk |

**triple** *v.t.* utrostručiti
**triplicate** *a.* trokratan
**triplicate** *n* triplikat
**triplicate** *v.t.* utrostručiti
**triplication** *n.* utrostručenje
**tripod** *n.* tronožac
**triumph** *n.* trijumf
**triumph** *v.i.* trijumfovati
**triumphal** *a.* trijumfalan
**triumphant** *a.* pobednički
**trivial** *a.* trivijalan
**troop** *n.* četa
**troop** *v.i* skupljati se
**trooper** *n.* policajac
**trophy** *n.* trofej
**tropic** *n.* tropski pojas
**tropical** *a.* tropski
**trot** *v.i.* kasati
**trot** *n* kas
**trouble** *n.* nevolja
**trouble** *v.t.* uzburkati
**troublesome** *a.* mučan
**troupe** *n.* glumačka družina
**trousers** *n. pl* pantalone
**trowel** *n.* mistrija
**truce** *n.* primirje
**truck** *n.* kamion
**true** *a.* pravi
**trump** *n.* adut
**trump** *v.t.* nadmudriti
**trumpet** *n.* truba
**trumpet** *v.i.* trubiti
**trunk** *n.* stablo
**trust** *n.* poverenje
**trust** *v.t* verovati
**trustee** *n.* poverenik
**trustful** *a.* poverljiv
**trustworthy** *a.* pouzdan
**trusty** *n.* veran
**truth** *n.* istina

**truthful** *a.* istinoljubiv
**try** *v.i.* pokušati
**try** *n* pokušaj
**trying** *a.* težak
**tryst** *n.* sastanak
**tub** *n.* kada
**tube** *n.* cev
**tuberculosis** *n.* tuberkuloza
**tubular** *a.* cevasti
**tug** *v.t.* trzati
**tuition** *n.* školarina
**tumble** *v.i.* pasti
**tumble** *n.* pad
**tumbler** *n.* akrobata
**tumour** *n.* tumor
**tumult** *n.* metež
**tumultuous** *a.* bučan
**tune** *n.* melodija
**tune** *v.t.* ugađati
**tunnel** *n.* tunel
**tunnel** *v.i.* bušiti tunel
**turban** *n.* turban
**turbine** *n.* turbina
**turbulence** *n.* turbulencije
**turbulent** *a.* turbulentan
**turf** *n.* treset
**turkey** *n.* ćurka
**turmeric** *n.* kurkuma
**turmoil** *n.* nemir
**turn** *v.i.* okrenuti
**turn** *n* okret
**turner** *n.* strugar
**turnip** *n.* repa
**turpentine** *n.* terpentin
**turtle** *n.* kornjača
**tusk** *n.* kljova
**tussle** *n.* borba
**tussle** *v.i.* boriti se
**tutor** *n.* tutor
**tutorial** *a.* učiteljski

tutorial *n.* uputstvo
twelfth *a.* dvanaesti
twelfth *n.* dvanaestina
twelve *n.* dvanaestorica
twelve *n* dvanaest
twentieth *a.* dvadeseti
twentieth *n* dvadesetina
twenty *a.* dvadeset
twenty *n* dvadesetorica
twice *adv.* dvaput
twig *n.* grančica
twilight *n* suton
twin *n.* blizanac
twin *a* dvostruk
twinkle *v.i.* svetlucati
twinkle *n.* svetlucanje
twist *v.t.* uviti
twist *n.* obrt
twitter *n.* cvrkut
twitter *v.i.* cvrkutati
two *n.* dva
two *a.* dvoje
twofold *a.* dvostruk
type *n.* tip
type *v.t.* tipkati
typhoid *n.* tifozan
typhoon *n.* tajfun
typhus *n.* tifus
typical *a.* tipičan
typify *v.t.* predstaviti
typist *n.* daktilograf
tyranny *n.* tiranija
tyrant *n.* tiranin
tyre *n.* guma

# U

udder *n.* vime
uglify *v.t.* poružnjavati

ugliness *n.* ružnoća
ugly *a.* ružan
ulcer *n.* čir
ulcerous *a.* gnojan
ulterior *a.* prikriven
ultimate *a.* krajnji
ultimately *adv.* na kraju
ultimatum *n.* ultimatum
umbrella *n.* kišobran
umpire *n.* sudija
umpire *v.t.,* osuditi
unable *a.* nemoćan
unanimity *n.* jednoglasnost
unanimous *a.* jednoglasan
unaware *a.* nesvestan
unawares *adv.* nehotice
unburden *v.t.* rasteretiti
uncanny *a.* neugodan
uncertain *a.* neizvestan
uncle *n.* stric, teča, ujak
uncouth *a.* nepoznat
under *prep.* ispod
under *adv* niže
under *a* niži
undercurrent *n.* podvodna struja
underdog *n* gubitnik
undergo *v.t.* pretrpeti
undergraduate *n.* student
underhand *a.* nepošten
underline *v.t.* podvući
undermine *v.t.* podriti
underneath *adv.* ispod
underneath *prep.* pod
understand *v.t.* razumeti
undertake *v.t.* preduzeti
undertone *n.* prigušen glas
underwear *n.* donje rublje
underworld *n.* podzemlje
undo *v.t.* poništi
undue *a.* neprikladan

| | |
|---|---|
| **undulate** *v.i.* talasati se | **up** *prep.* prema gore |
| **undulation** *n.* lelujanje | **upbraid** *v.t* kuditi |
| **unearth** *v.t.* iskopati | **upheaval** *n.* preokret |
| **uneasy** *a.* nelagodan | **uphold** *v.t* podržati |
| **unfair** *a* nepravedan | **upkeep** *n* održavanje |
| **unfold** *v.t.* otvoriti | **uplift** *v.t.* podići |
| **unfortunate** *a.* nesrećan | **uplift** *n* uzdignuće |
| **ungainly** *a.* nezgrapan | **upon** *prep* na |
| **unhappy** *a.* nesrećan | **upper** *a.* gornji |
| **unification** *n.* ujedinjenje | **upright** *a.* čestit |
| **union** *n.* unija | **uprising** *n.* ustanak |
| **unionist** *n.* unionista | **uproar** *n.* metež |
| **unique** *a.* jedinstven | **uproarious** *a.* bučan |
| **unison** *n.* jednoglasje | **uproot** *v.t.* iskoreniti |
| **unit** *n.* jedinica | **upset** *v.t.* uznemiriti |
| **unite** *v.t.* ujediniti | **upshot** *n.* ishod |
| **unity** *n.* jedinstvo | **upstart** *n.* skorojević |
| **universal** *a.* univerzalan | **up-to-date** *a.* savremen |
| **universality** *n.* univerzalnost | **upward** *a.* okrenut uvis |
| **universe** *n.* svemir | **upwards** *adv.* nagore |
| **university** *n.* univerzitet | **urban** *a.* urbani |
| **unjust** *a.* nepravedan | **urbane** *a.* učtiv |
| **unless** *conj.* sem ako | **urbanity** *n.* učtivost |
| **unlike** *a* nejednak | **urchin** *n.* derište |
| **unlike** *prep* za razliku od | **urge** *v.t* nagnati |
| **unlikely** *a.* neverovatan | **urge** *n* nagon |
| **unmanned** *a.* bez posade | **urgency** *n.* hitnost |
| **unmannerly** *a* nevaspitan | **urgent** *a.* hitan |
| **unprincipled** *a.* neprincipijelan | **urinal** *n.* pisoar |
| **unreliable** *a.* nepouzdan | **urinary** *a.* urinarni |
| **unrest** *n* nemir | **urinate** *v.i.* urinirati |
| **unruly** *a.* jogunast | **urination** *n.* mokrenje |
| **unsettle** *v.t.* uznemiriti | **urine** *n.* urin |
| **unsheathe** *v.t.* izvaditi iz korica | **urn** *n* urna |
| **until** *prep.* do | **usage** *n.* primena |
| **until** *conj* dok | **use** *n.* upotreba |
| **untoward** *a.* uporan | **use** *v.t.* upotrebiti |
| **unwell** *a.* bolestan | **useful** *a.* koristan |
| **unwittingly** *adv.* nenamerno | **usher** *n.* vratar |
| **up** *adv.* gore | **usher** *v.t.* uvesti |

usual *a.* uobičajen
usually *adv.* obično
usurer *n.* zelenaš
usurp *v.t.* uzurpirati
usurpation *n.* uzurpacija
usury *n.* zelenaštvo
utensil *n.* pribor
uterus *n.* materica
utilitarian *a.* utilitaristički
utility *n.* korisnost
utilization *n.* korišćenje
utilize *v.t.* iskoristiti
utmost *a.* krajnji
utmost *n* krajnost
utopia *n.* utopija
utopian *a.* utopijski
utter *v.t.* izustiti
utter *a* potpun
utterance *n.* iskaz
utterly *adv.* potpuno

# V

vacancy *n.* upražnjeno mesto
vacant *a.* prazan
vacate *v.t.* napustiti
vacation *n.* odmor
vaccinate *v.t.* vakcinisati
vaccination *n.* vakcinacija
vaccinator *n.* lekar koji vakciniše
vaccine *n.* vakcina
vacillate *v.i.* kolebati se
vacuum *n.* vakuum
vagabond *n.* skitnica
vagabond *a* skitalački
vagary *n.* lutanje
vagina *n.* vagina
vague *a.* nejasan
vagueness *n.* neodređenost

vain *a.* uzaludan
vainglorious *a.* hvalisav
vainglory *n.* hvalisavost
vainly *adv.* uzalud
vale *n.* dolina
valiant *a.* hrabar
valid *a.* validan
validate *v.t.* potvrditi
validity *n.* punovažnost
valley *n.* dolina
valour *n.* junaštvo
valuable *a.* vredan
valuation *n.* procena
value *n.* vrednost
value *v.t.* ceniti
valve *n.* ventil
van *n.* kombi
vanish *v.i.* iščeznuti
vanity *n.* sujeta
vanquish *v.t.* pobediti
vaporize *v.t.* isparavati
vaporous *a.* parni
vapour *n.* para
variable *a.* varijabla
variance *n.* promena
variation *n.* varijacija
varied *a.* raznolik
variety *n.* raznovrsnost
various *a.* različit
varnish *n.* lak
varnish *v.t.* lakirati
vary *v.t.* varirati
vasectomy *n.* vazektomija
vaseline *n.* vazelin
vast *a.* ogroman
vault *n.* svod
vault *n.* skok
vault *v.i.* nadsvoditi
vegetable *n.* povrće
vegetable *a.* povrtni

**vegetarian** *n.* vegetarijanac
**vegetarian** *a* vegetarijanski
**vegetation** *n.* vegetacija
**vehemence** *n.* žestina
**vehement** *a.* žestok
**vehicle** *n.* vozilo
**vehicular** *a.* automobilski
**veil** *n.* veo
**veil** *v.t.* prekriti
**vein** *n.* vena
**velocity** *n.* brzina
**velvet** *n.* somot
**velvety** *a.* baršunast
**venal** *a.* podmitljiv
**venality** *n.* podmitljivost
**vendor** *n.* prodavac
**venerable** *a.* prečasni
**venerate** *v.t.* poštovati
**veneration** *n.* strahopoštovanje
**vengeance** *n.* osveta
**venial** *a.* oprostiv
**venom** *n.* otrov
**venomous** *a.* otrovan
**vent** *n.* odušak
**ventilate** *v.t.* ventilirati
**ventilation** *n.* ventilacija
**ventilator** *n.* ventilator
**venture** *n.* poduhvat
**venture** *v.t.* usuditi se
**venturesome** *a.* riskantan
**venturous** *a.* opasan
**venue** *n.* delokrug
**veracity** *n.* istinitost
**verendah** *n.* veranda
**verb** *n.* glagol
**verbal** *a.* verbalni
**verbally** *adv.* usmeno
**verbatim** *a.* doslovan
**verbatim** *adv.* doslovno
**verbose** *a.* preopširan

**verbosity** *n.* preopširnost
**verdant** *a.* zelen
**verdict** *n.* presuda
**verge** *n.* rub
**verification** *n.* verifikacija
**verify** *v.t.* verifikovati
**verisimilitude** *n.* verovatnost
**veritable** *a.* pravi
**vermillion** *n.* cinober
**vermillion** *a.* boje cinobera
**vernacular** *n.* domaći
**vernacular** *a.* narodni
**vernal** *a.* prolećni
**versatile** *a.* svestran
**versatility** *n.* svestranos
**verse** *n.* stih
**versed** *a.* okretan
**versification** *n.* stihotvorstvo
**versify** *v.t.* pretvoriti u stihove
**version** *n.* verzija
**versus** *prep.* protiv
**vertical** *a.* vertikalan
**verve** *n.* elan
**very** *a.* veoma
**vessel** *n.* brod
**vest** *n.* prsluk
**vest** *v.t.* obući
**vestige** *n.* trag
**vestment** *n.* odežda
**veteran** *n.* veteran
**veteran** *a.* veteranski
**veterinary** *a.* veterinarski
**veto** *n.* veto
**veto** *v.t.* staviti veto
**vex** *v.t.* nasekirati
**vexation** *n* sekiracija
**via** *prep.* preko
**viable** *a.* održiv
**vial** *n.* bočica
**vibrate** *v.i.* vibrirati

vibration *n.* vibracija
vicar *n.* vikar
vicarious *a.* namesnički
vice *n.* porok
viceroy *n.* potkralj
vice-versa *adv.* obrnuto
vicinity *n.* blizina
vicious *a.* opak
vicissitude *n.* nestalnost
victim *n.* žrtva
victimize *v.t.* žrtvovati
victor *n.* pobednik
victorious *a.* pobedonosan
victory *n.* pobeda
victuals *n. pl* hrana
vie *v.i.* nadmetati se
view *n.* pogled
view *v.t.* razgledati
vigil *n.* bdenje
vigilance *n.* budnost
vigilant *a.* oprezan
vigorous *a.* energičan
vile *a.* loš
vilify *v.t.* sramotiti
villa *n.* vila
village *n.* selo
villager *n.* seljak
villain *n.* zlikovac
vindicate *v.t.* opravdati
vindication *n.* opravdanje
vine *n.* vinova loza
vinegar *n.* sirće
vintage *n.* berba
violate *v.t.* povrediti
violation *n.* kršenje
violence *n.* nasilje
violent *a.* nasilan
violet *n.* ljubičica
violin *n.* violina
violinist *n.* violinista

virgin *n.* devac
virgin *n* devica
virginity *n.* nevinost
virile *a.* muški
virility *n.* muževnost
virtual *a* virtuelan
virtue *n.* vrlina
virtuous *a.* vrli
virulence *n.* pakost
virulent *a.* pakostan
virus *n.* virus
visage *n.* lice
visibility *n.* vidljivost
visible *a.* vidljiv
vision *n.* vizija
visionary *a.* vizionarski
visionary *n.* vizionar
visit *n.* poseta
visit *v.t.* posetiti
visitor *n.* posetilac
vista *n.* vidik
visual *a.* vizuelni
visualize *v.t.* vizualizovati
vital *a.* vitalan
vitality *n.* vitalnost
vitalize *v.t.* oživljavati
vitamin *n.* vitamin
vitiate *v.t.* pokvariti
vivacious *a.* čio
vivacity *n.* živahnost
viva-voce *adv.* usmeno
viva-voce *a* usmen
viva-voce *n* usmeni ispit
vivid *a.* živ
vixen *n.* lisica
vocabulary *n.* rečnik
vocal *a.* vokalni
vocalist *n.* pevač
vocation *n.* zanimanje
vogue *n.* moda

voice *n.* glas
voice *v.t.* izgovoriti
void *a.* prazan
void *v.t.* poništiti
void *n.* praznina
volcanic *a.* vulkanski
volcano *n.* vulkan
volition *n.* volja
volley *n.* volej
volley *v.t* skresati
volt *n.* volt
voltage *n.* napon
volume *n.* zapremina
voluminous *a.* obiman
voluntarily *adv.* dobrovoljno
voluntary *a.* dobrovoljan
volunteer *n.* volonter
volunteer *v.t.* volontirati
voluptuary *n.* pohotljivac
voluptuous *a.* pohotan
vomit *v.t.* povraćati
vomit *n* povraćanje
voracious *a.* proždrljiv
votary *n.* kaluđer
vote *n.* glasanje
vote *v.i.* glasati
voter *n.* glasač
vouch *v.i.* jamčiti
voucher *n.* vaučer
vouchsafe *v.t.* odobriti
vow *n.* zavet
vow *v.t.* zavetovati
vowel *n.* samoglasnik
voyage *n.* putovanje
voyage *v.i.* putovati
voyager *n.* putnik
vulgar *a.* vulgaran
vulgarity *n.* vulgarnost
vulnerable *a.* ranjiv
vulture *n.* lešinar

# W

wade *v.i.* gaziti
waddle *v.i.* geganje
waft *v.t.* lebdeti
waft *n* dah
wag *v.i.* mahati
wag *n* mahanje
wage *v.t.* voditi
wage *n.* plata
wager *n.* ulog
wager *v.i.* kladiti se
wagon *n.* vagon
wail *v.i.* jadikovati
wail *n* jadikovanje
wain *n.* kola
waist *n.* struk
waistband *n.* opasač
waistcoat *n.* prsluk
wait *v.i.* čekati
wait *n.* čekanje
waiter *n.* konobar
waitress *n.* konobarica
waive *v.t.* odustati
wake *v.t.* probuditi
wake *n* bdenje
wake *n* daća
wakeful *a.* budan
walk *v.i.* šetati
walk *n* šetnja
wall *n.* zid
wall *v.t.* opasati zidom
wallet *n.* novčanik
wallop *v.t.* istući
wallow *v.i.* valjati se
walnut *n.* orah
walrus *n.* morž
wan *a.* bled

**wand** *n.* štapić
**wander** *v.i.* lutati
**wane** *v.i.* opadati
**wane** *n* opadanje
**want** *v.t.* željeti
**want** *n* potreba
**wanton** *a.* raskalašn
**war** *n.* rat
**war** *v.i.* ratovati
**warble** *v.i.* treperiti
**warble** *n* treperenje
**warbler** *n.* ptica pevačica
**ward** *n.* štićenik
**ward** *v.t.* čuvati
**warden** *n.* upravnik zatvora
**warder** *n.* čuvar
**wardrobe** *n.* garderoba
**wardship** *n.* starateljstvo
**ware** *n.* roba
**warehouse** *v.t* magacin
**warfare** *n.* ratovanje
**warlike** *a.* ratoboran
**warm1** *a.* vruć
**warm** *v.t.* topao
**warmth** *n.* toplota
**warn** *v.t.* upozoriti
**warning** *n.* upozorenje
**warrant** *n.* nalog
**warrant** *v.t.* garantovati
**warrantee** *n.* opunomoćenik
**warrantor** *n.* jemac
**warranty** *n.* garancija
**warren** *n.* odgajivačnica zečeva
**warrior** *n.* ratnik
**wart** *n.* bradavica
**wary** *a.* oprezan
**wash** *v.t.* prati
**wash** *n* pranje
**washable** *a.* koji se može prati
**washer** *n.* perač

**wasp** *n.* osa
**waspish** *a.* naprasit
**wassail** *n.* pijanka
**wastage** *n.* rasipanje
**waste** *a.* pust
**waste** *n.* otpad
**waste** *v.t.* pustošiti
**wasteful** *a.* rasipan
**watch** *v.t.* gledati
**watch** *n.* sat
**watchful** *a.* budan
**watchword** *n.* lozinka
**water** *n.* vode
**water** *v.t.* zalivati
**waterfall** *n.* vodopad
**water-melon** *n.* lubenica
**waterproof** *a.* vodootporan
**waterproof** *n* vodootpornost
**waterproof** *v.t.* učiniti nepromočivim
**watertight** *a.* nepromočiv
**watery** *a.* vodeni
**watt** *n.* vat
**wave** *n.* talas
**wave** *v.t.* talas
**waver** *v.i.* mahati
**wax** *n.* vosak
**wax** *v.t.* rasti
**way** *n.* način
**wayfarer** *n.* putnik
**waylay** *v.t.* napasti iz zasede
**wayward** *a.* svojevoljan
**weak** *a.* slab
**weaken** *v.t. & i* oslabiti
**weakling** *n.* slabić
**weakness** *n.* slabost
**weal** *n.* masnica
**wealth** *n.* bogatstvo
**wealthy** *a.* bogat
**wean** *v.t.* odučiti
**weapon** *n.* oružje

wear *v.t.* pohabati
weary *a.* umoran
weary *v.t. & i* umoriti
weary *a.* dosadan
weary *v.t.* dosađivati
weather *n* vreme
weather *v.t.* odoleti
weave *v.t.* tkati
weaver *n.* tkač
web *n.* mreža
webby *a.* koji je kao tkivo
wed *v.t.* venčati
wedding *n.* venčanje
wedge *n.* klin
wedge *v.t.* pričvrstiti klinom
wedlock *n.* brak
Wednesday *n.* sreda
weed *n.* korov
weed *v.t.* pleviti
week *n.* nedelja
weekly *a.* nedeljni
weekly *adv.* nedeljno
weekly *n.* nedeljnik
weep *v.i.* plakati
weevil *n.* žižak
weigh *v.t.* vagati
weight *n.* težina
weighage *n.* pristojba za vaganje
weighty *a.* važan
weir *n.* brana
weird *a.* čudan
welcome *a.* dobrodošao
welcome *n* dobrodošlica
welcome *v.t* pozdraviti
weld *v.t.* zavarivati
weld *n* zavarak
welfare *n.* blagostanje
well *a.* dobar
well *adv.* dobro
well *n.* bunar

well *v.i.* izvirti
wellignton *n.* velignton
well-known *a.* poznat
well-read *a.* načitan
well-timed *a.* blagovremen
well-to-do *a.* imućan
welt *n.* porub
welter *n.* zbrka
wen *n.* izraslina
wench *n.* devojka
west *n.* zapad
west *a.* zapadni
west *adv.* zapadno
westerly *a.* zapadno
westerly *adv.* zapadni
western *a.* vestern
wet *a.* mokar
wet *v.t.* pokvasiti
wetness *n.* vlažnost
whack *v.t.* udariti
whale *n.* kit
wharfage *n.* taksa za vezivanje broda
what *a.* kakav
what *pron.* šta
what *interj.* šta
whatever *pron.* štagod
wheat *n.* pšenica
wheedle *v.t.* iskamčiti
wheel *a.* točak
wheel *v.t.* kotrljati
whelm *v.t.* poplaviti
whelp *n.* štene
when *adv.* kada
when *conj.* kad
whence *adv.* odakle
whenever *adv. conj* kad god
where *adv.* gde
where *conj.* gde
whereabout *adv.* negde
whereas *conj.* pošto

whereat *conj.* gde
wherein *adv.* u kome
whereupon *conj.* posle čega
wherever *adv.* gde god
whet *v.t.* brusiti
whether *conj.* bilo da
which *pron.* koji
which *a* koji
whichever *pron* koji god
whiff *n.* dašak
while *n.* vremenski period
while *conj.* dok
while *v.t.* provesti
whim *n.* kapric
whimper *v.i.* cviljenje
whimsical *a.* kapriciozan
whine *v.i.* prenemagati se
whine *n* prenemaganje
whip *v.t.* bičevati
whip *n.* bič
whipcord *n.* uzica biča
whir *n.* zujanje
whirl *n.i.* kovitlac
whirl *n* vrtlog
whirligig *n.* zvrk
whirlpool *n.* vrtlog
whirlwind *n.* vihor
whisk *v.t.* mahati
whisk *n* zamah
whisker *n.* dlaka
whisky *n.* viski
whisper *v.t.* šaputati
whisper *n* šapat
whistle *v.i.* zviždati
whistle *n* zvižduk
white *a.* beli
white *n* bela boja
whiten *v.t.* beleti
whitewash *n.* belilo
whitewash *v.t.* obeleti

whither *adv.* kuda
whitish *a.* beličast
whittle *v.t.* strugati
whiz *v.i.* zujanje
who *pron.* ko
whoever *pron.* ma ko
whole *a.* ceo
whole *n* celina
whole-hearted *a.* odan
wholesale *n.* veleprodaja
wholesale *a* veleprodajni
wholesale *adv.* veleprodajno
wholesaler *n.* trgovac na veliko
wholesome *a.* zdrav
wholly *adv.* u potpunosti
whom *pron.* koga
whore *n.* prostitutka
whose *pron.* čiji
why *adv.* zašto
wick *n.* fitilj
wicked *a.* zao
wicker *n.* ispleten od pruća
wicket *n.* vratnice
wide *a.* širok
wide *adv.* široko
widen *v.t.* proširiti
widespread *a.* rasprostranjen
widow *n.* udovica
widow *v.t.* *učiniti* udovicom
widower *n.* udovac
width *n.* širina
wield *v.t.* rukovati
wife *n.* supruga
wig *n.* perika
wight *n.* stvor
wigwam *n.* vigvam
wild *a.* divlji
wilderness *n.* divljina
wile *n.* lukavstvo
will *n.* volja

will *v.t.* hteti
willing *a.* voljan
willingness *n.* spremnost
willow *n.* vrba
wily *a.* lukav
wimble *n.* *ručna* burgija
wimple *n.* kaluđerički veo
win *v.t.* pobediti
win *n* pobeda
wince *v.i.* trzati se
winch *n.* čekrk
wind *n.* vetar
wind *v.t.* navijati
wind *v.t.* namotati
windbag *n.* blebetalo
winder *n.* motač
windlass *v.t.* motovilo
windmill *n.* vetrenjača
window *n.* prozor
windy *a.* vetrovit
wine *n.* vino
wing *n.* krilo
wink *v.i.* namigivati
wink *n* mig
winner *n.* pobednik
winnow *v.t.* razbacati
winsome *a.* dopadljiv
winter *n.* zima
winter *v.i* zimovati
wintry *a.* zimski
wipe *v.t.* brisati
wipe *n.* brisanje
wire *n.* žica
wire *v.t.* svezati žicom
wireless *a.* bežični
wireless *n* radio
wiring *n.* spajanje žicom
wisdom *n.* mudrost
wisdom-tooth *n.* mudrost
wise *a.* mudar

wish *n.* želja
wish *v.t.* želeti
wishful *a.* željan
wisp *n.* čuperak
wistful *a.* zamišljen
wit *n.* duhovitost
witch *n.* veštica
witchcraft *n.* vračanje
witchery *n.* čarolija
with *prep.* sa
withal *adv.* sem toga
withdraw *v.t.* povući
withdrawal *n.* povlačenje
withe *n.* prut
wither *v.i.* uvenuti
withhold *v.t.* zadržati
within *prep.* u
within *adv.* u okviru
within *n.* unutrašnjost
without *prep.* bez
without *adv.* izvan
without *n* bez
withstand *v.t.* izdržati
witless *a.* bezuman
witness *n.* svedok
witness *v.i.* svedočiti
witticism *n.* dosetka
witty *a.* duhovit
wizard *n.* čarobnjak
wobble *v.i* klimati
woe *n.* jad
woebegone *a.* nesrećan
woeful *n.* tužan
wolf *n.* vuk
woman *n.* žena
womanhood *n.* ženstvenost
womanish *n.* ženski
womanize *v.t.* trčati za ženama
womb *n.* materica
wonder *n* čudo

**wonder** *v.i.* čuditi se
**wonderful** *a.* predivan
**wondrous** *a.* čudesan
**wont** *a.* naviknut
**wont** *n* navika
**wonted** *a.* uobičajen
**woo** *v.t.* udvarati se
**wood** *n.* drvo
**woods** *n.* šuma
**wooden** *a.* drveni
**woodland** *n.* šumovit kraj
**woof** *n.* potka
**wool** *n.* vuna
**woollen** *a.* vuneni
**woollen** *n* vunena tkanina
**word** *n.* reč
**word** *v.t* reći
**wordy** *a.* izraziti
**work** *n.* rad
**work** *v.t.* raditi
**workable** *a.* obradiv
**workaday** *a.* svakidašnji
**worker** *n.* radnik
**workman** *n.* radnik
**workmanship** *n.* izrada
**workshop** *n.* radionica
**world** *n.* svet
**worldling** *n.* svetski čovek
**worldly** *a.* svetovni
**worm** *n.* crv
**wormwood** *n.* pelen
**worn** *a.* iznošen
**worry** *n.* briga
**worry** *v.i.* brinuti
**worsen** *v.t.* pogoršati
**worship** *n.* obožavanje
**worship** *v.t.* obožavati
**worshipper** *n.* obožavalac
**worst** *n.* ono što je najgore
**worst** *a* najgori

**worst** *v.t.* pobediti
**worsted** *n.* češljana vuna
**worth** *n.* vrednost
**worth** *a* vredan
**worthless** *a.* bezvredan
**worthy** *a.* dostojan
**would-be** *a.* tobožnji
**wound** *n.* rana
**wound** *v.t.* raniti
**wrack** *n.* olupina
**wraith** *n.* utvara
**wrangle** *v.i.* prepirati se
**wrangle** *n.* prepirka
**wrap** *v.t.* zamotati
**wrap** *n* pokrivač
**wrapper** *n.* omotač
**wrath** *n.* gnev
**wreath** *n.* venac
**wreathe** *v.t.* uplesti
**wreck** *n.* olupina
**wreck** *v.t.* uništiti
**wreckage** *n.* olupina
**wrecker** *n.* brod za spasavanje
**wren** *n.* carić
**wrench** *n.* iščašenje
**wrench** *v.t.* iščašiti
**wrest** *v.t.* istrgnuti
**wrestle** *v.i.* rvati se
**wrestler** *n.* rvač
**wretch** *n.* bednik
**wretched** *a.* bedan
**wrick** *n* iščašenje
**wriggle** *v.i.* vijugati
**wriggle** *n* vijuganje
**wring** *v.t* stiskati
**wrinkle** *n.* bora
**wrinkle** *v.t.* izborati
**wrist** *n.* ručni zglob
**writ** *n.* spis
**write** *v.t.* napisati

writer *n.* pisac
writhe *v.i.* grčiti se
wrong *a.* pogrešan
wrong *adv.* pogrešno
wrong *v.t.* naneti štetu
wrongful *a.* nezakonit
wry *a.* iskrivljen

# X

xerox *n.* način fotokopiranja
xerox *v.t.* fotokopirati
Xmas *n.* Božić
x-ray *n.* rendgen
x-ray *a.* rendgenski
x-ray *v.t.* izložiti rendgenskim zracima
xylophagous *a.* koji se hrani drvetom
xylophilous *a.* koji živi na drvetu
xylophone *n.* ksilofon

# Y

yacht *n.* jahta
yacht *v.i* voziti se na jahti
yak *n.* jak
yap *v.i.* lajati
yap *n* lajanje
yard *n.* dvorište
yarn *n.* predivo
yawn *v.i.* zevati
yawn *n.* zevanje
year *n.* godina
yearly *a.* godišnji
yearly *adv.* godišnje
yearn *v.i.* žudeti
yearning *n.* žudnja
yeast *n.* kvasac
yell *v.i.* vikati

yell *n* vikanje
yellow *a.* žut
yellow *n* žuta boja
yellow *v.t.* požuteti
yellowish *a.* žućkast
Yen *n.* jen
yeoman *n.* slobodnjak
yes *adv.* da
yesterday *n.* jučerašnji dan
yesterday *adv.* juče
yet *adv.* još
yet *conj.* ipak
yield *v.t.* doneti
yield *n* prinos
yoke *n.* jaram
yoke *v.t.* ujarmiti
yolk *n.* žumance
yonder *a.* tamošnji
yonder *adv.* tamo
young *a.* mlad
young *n* mladi
youngster *n.* mladić
youth *n.* mladih
youthful *a.* mladalački

# Z

zany *a.* smešan
zeal *n.* revnost
zealot *n.* fanatik
zealous *a.* revnostan
zebra *n.* zebra
zenith *n.* zenit
zephyr *n.* zefir
zero *n.* nula
zest *n.* polet
zigzag *n.* cik-cak
zigzag *a.* vijugav
zigzag *v.i.* vijugati se

**zinc** *n.* cink
**zip** *n.* aktivnost
**zip** *v.t.* oживети
**zodiac** *n* zodijak
**zonal** *a.* zonski
**zone** *n.* zona
**zoo** *n.* zoološki vrt
**zoological** *a.* zoološki
**zoologist** *n.* zoolog
**zoology** *n.* zoologija
**zoom** *n.* zum
**zoom** *v.i.* zumirati

# SERBIAN-ENGLISH

# A

abecedno *a.* alphabetical
abonos *n* ebony
adekvatan *a.* adequate
adekvatnost *n.* adequacy
adhezija *n.* adhesion
administrator *n.* administrator
admiral *n.* admiral
adresa *n.* address
adut *n.* trump
advokat *n* advocate
advokat *n.* lawyer
advokat *n.* solicitor
advokat *n.* barrister
advokatura *n.* advocacy
aerodrom *n* aerodrome
aeronautika *n.pl.* aeronautics
afera *n.* affair
aforizam *n* aphorism
agencija *n.* agency
agent *n* agent
agilan *a.* agile
agilnost *n.* agility
agonija *n.* throe
agonija *n.* agony
agrarni *a.* agrarian
agresija *n* aggression
agresivan *a.* aggressive
agresor *n.* aggressor
agronomija *n.* agronomy
ajkula *n.* shark
akademija *n* academy
akademski *a* academic
akcija *n.* action
akciza *n* excise
ako *conj.* if
akord *n.* chord

akrobata *n.* tumbler
akrobata *n.* acrobat
akt *a.* nude
aktivan *a.* active
aktivirati *v.t.* activate
aktivnost *n.* zip
akumulacija *n* accumulation
akumulirati *v.t.* accumulate
akustično *a* acoustic
akustika *n.* acoustics
akvadukt *n.* aqueduct
akvarijum *n.* aquarium
akvizicija *n.* acquisition
alatka *n.* tool
albion *n* albion
album *n.* album
alegorija *n.* allegory
alegorijski *a.* allegorical
alergija *n.* allergy
alfa *n.* alpha
algebra *n.* algebra
alhemija *n.* alchemy
ali *prep* but
alibi *n.* alibi
aligator *n* alligator
alimentacija *n.* alimony
aliteracija *n.* alliteration
aljkav *a.* slatternly
aljkav *a.* slovenly
aljkava žena *n.* slattern
alkohol *n* alcohol
alkoholno piće *n.* liquor
almanah *n.* almanac
alpinista *n.* alpinist
alt *n* alto
alternativa *n.* alternative
alternativan *a.* alternative
aludirati *v.i.* allude
aluminijum *n.* aluminium
am *n.* harness

amajlija *n.* amulet
amandman *n.* amendment
amater *n.* amateur
ambar *n.* granary
ambar *n.* barn
ambasada *n* embassy
ambasador *n.* ambassador
ambicija *n.* ambition
ambiciozan *a.* ambitious
ambijent *n.* milieu
ambijent *adj.* ambient
amblem *n* emblem
ambulanta *n* dispensary
ambulanta kola *n.* ambulance
amenoreja *n* amenorrhoea
amfibijski *adj* amphibious
amfiteatar *n* amphitheatre
amin *interj.* amen
amnestija *n.* amnesty
amnezija *n* amnesia
amper *n* ampere
anabaptizam *n* anabaptism
anakronizam *n* anachronism
analitičar *n* analyst
analitički *a* analytical
analiza *n.* analysis
analizirati *v.t.* analyse
analni *adj.* anal
analogan *a.* analogous
analogija *n.* analogy
anamneza *n* anamnesis
anamorfan *adj* anamorphous
ananas *n.* pineapple
anarhija *n* anarchy
anarhista *n* anarchist
anarhizam *n.* anarchism
anatema *n* ban
anatomija *n.* anatomy
anđeo *n* angel
anegdota *n.* anecdote

anemometar *n* anemometer
anestetik *n.* anaesthetic
anestezija *n* anaesthesia
angažovanje *n.* engagement
angažovati *v. t* engage
angina *n* angina
animacija *n* animation
anisovo seme *n* aniseed
anketa *n.* poll
anonimnost *n.* anonymity
antacid *adj.* antacid
antarktički *a.* antarctic
antena *n.* aerial
antene *n.* antennae
anti *pref.* anti
antifonija *n.* antiphony
antika *n.* antiquity
antikvar *n* antiquarian
antilopa *n.* antelope
antipatija *n* dislike
antipatija *n.* antipathy
antipodi *n.* antipodes
antiseptički *a.* antiseptic
antiseptik *n.* antiseptic
antiteza *n.* antithesis
antologija *n.* anthology
antonim *n.* antonym
aparat *n.* apparatus
apartman *n.* suite
apatija *n.* apathy
apelant *n.* appellant
apetit *n.* appetite
aplaudirati *v.t.* applaud
aplauz *n.* applause
apostol *n.* apostle
apostrofiranje *n.* apostrophe
apoteka *n.* pharmacy
apotekar *n* druggist
apsces *n* abscess
apstrakcija *n.* abstraction

apstraktan *a* abstract
apsurd *n* absurdity
apsurdan *a* absurd
arbiter *n.* arbitrator
arbitraža *n.* arbitration
arena *n* arena
arhanđeo *n* archangel
arhiepiskop *n.* archbishop
arhitekta *n.* architect
arhitektura *n.* architecture
arhiv *n* chancery
arhiva *n* file
arhive *n.pl.* archives
arhivirati *v.t* file
aristofanski *adj.* aristophanic
aristokrata *n.* aristocrat
aritmetički *a.* arithmetical
aritmetika *n.* arithmetic
Arktik *n* Arctic
armada *n.* armada
armatura *n.* armature
arsen *n* arsenic
arsenal *n.* arsenal
arterija *n.* artery
artičoka *n.* artichoke
artiljerija *n.* artillery
artritis *n* arthritis
as *n* ace
asibilant *v.* assibilate
asistent *n.* assistant
asket *n.* ascetic
asketski *a.* ascetic
aspekt *n* facet
aspekt ponašanja *n.* conation
aspekt *n.* aspect
astma *n.* asthma
astrolog *n.* astrologer
astrologija *n.* astrology
astronaut *n.* astronaut
astronom *n.* astronomer

astronomija *n.* astronomy
ataše *n.* attache
ateist *n* antitheist
ateista *n* atheist
ateizam *n* atheism
atentat *n* assassination
atentator *n.* assassin
atlas *n.* atlas
atletika *n.* athletics
atletski *a.* athletic
atmosfera *n.* atmosphere
atom *n.* atom
atomski *a.* atomic
autentičan *a.* authentic
autobiografija *n.* autobiography
autobus *n* bus
autogram *n.* autograph
autokrata *n* autocrat
autokratija *n* autocracy
autokratski *a* autocratic
automatski *a.* automatic
automobil *n.* automobile
automobil *n.* car
automobilski *a.* vehicular
autonoman *a* autonomous
autoput *n.* highway
autor *n.* author
autsajder *n.* outsider
avaj *interj.* alas
avantura *n* adventure
avenija *n.* avenue
averzija *n.* aversion
avet *n.* spectre
avet *n* bogle
Avgust *n.* August
avgust *n* august
avijacija *n.* aviation
avijatičar *n.* aviator
avion *n.* aeroplane
azbest *n.* asbestos

**azil** *n* asylum
**azot** *n.* nitrogen

# B

**babica** *n.* midwife
**bacanje** *n.* cast
**bacanje** *n* casting
**bacanje** *n.* throw
**baciti** *v. t* down
**baciti** *v.t* fling
**baciti** *v.t.* hurl
**baciti** *v.t.* throw
**baciti** *se v.i* lunge
**baciti** *v. t.* cast
**bačva** *n.* barrel
**badem** *n.* almond
**badminton** *n.* badminton
**bajati** *v.i.* conjure
**bajonet** *n* bayonet
**bakalin** *n.* grocer
**bakalnica** *n.* grocery
**bakar** *n* copper
**baklja** *n.* torch
**bakterija** *n.* bacteria
**bala** *n.* bale
**balada** *n.* ballad
**balaviti** *v. t* beslaver
**baldahin** *n.* canopy
**balet** *n.* ballet
**balkon** *n.* balcony
**balon** *n.* balloon
**balsamovati** *v. t* embalm
**balzam** *n.* balsam
**bambus** *n.* bamboo
**banalan** *a.* banal
**banana** *n.* banana
**banda** *n.* gang
**banka, nasip** *n.* bank

**bankar** *n.* banker
**banket** *n.* banquet
**bankrot** *n.* bankrupt
**bara** *n.* puddle
**baraka** *n.* barrack
**bard** *n.* bard
**barijera** *n.* barrier
**barikada** *n.* barricade
**barka** *n.* barge
**barometar** *n* barometer
**baršunast** *a.* velvety
**bas** *n.* bass
**basna** *n* apologue
**basna** *n.* fable
**bašta** *n.* garden
**baštovan** *n.* gardener
**bataljon** *n* battalion
**baterija** *n* battery
**baza** *n.* alkali
**baza** *n.* base
**bazen** *n.* basin
**bdenje** *n.* vigil
**bdenje** *n* wake
**beba** *n.* baby
**beda** *n.* misery
**beda** *n.* squalor
**bedan** *a.* abject
**bedan** *a.* piteous
**bedan** *a.* squalid
**bedan** *a.* wretched
**bedem** *n.* rampart
**bedem** *n* bulwark
**bednik** *n.* wretch
**bedro** *n.* thigh
**begunac** *n.* fugitive
**bekhend** *n.* backhand
**bekstvo** *n* escape
**bela boja** *n* white
**belančevina** *n* albumen
**beleti** *v.t.* whiten

beležnik *n.* notary
beli *a.* white
beli *luk n.* garlic
beličast *a.* whitish
belilo *n.* whitewash
bendžo *n.* banjo
benzin *n.* petrol
berba *n.* vintage
berberin *n.* barber
bes *n.* fury
bes *n.* rage
bes *n.* anger
besan *a.* furious
beskonačan *a.* infinite
beskonačnost *n.* infinity
beskrajan *a.* interminable
beskrajnost *n.* immensity
besmislen *a.* nonsensical
besmislen *a.* senseless
besmislica *n.* nonsense
besmislica *v. i* blether
besmrtan *a.* immortal
besmrtnost *n.* immortality
besneti *v.i.* rage
besneti *v.t.* riot
besnilo *n.* rabies
besomučno *adv.* amuck
besplatno *adv.* gratis
bespomoćan *a.* helpless
besposlen *a.* idle
besposlica *n.* idleness
besposličar *n.* idler
besraman *a.* shameless
bešika *n* bladder
betel *n* betel
beton *n* concrete
betonirati *v. t* concrete
bez *prep.* without
bez *n* without
bez novca *a.* penniless

bez obzira na a. irrespective
bez posade *a.* unmanned
bez premca *a.* matchless
bez premca *a.* peerless
bezakonje *n.* misrule
bezbednost *n.* safety
bezbednosti *n.* security
bezbojan *adj* achromatic
bezbračnos *n.* celibacy
bezbroj *n.* myriad
bezbrojan *a.* countless
bezbrojan *a.* innumerable
bezbrojan *a* myriad
bezbrojan *a.* numberless
bezdan *n* abyss
bezdušnost *n.* obduracy
bezglav *adj.* acephalous
bezglavi fetus *n.* acephalus
bezimenost *n.* anonymity
bezličan *a.* impersonal
beznačajan *a.* insignificant
beznačajan *a.* meaningless
beznačajan *a.* minuscule
beznačajnost *n.* insignificance
beznadežan *a.* hopeless
bezobrazluk *n.* insolence
bezsredišnji *adj* acentric
bezuman *a.* witless
bezvredan *a.* worthless
bežanje *n* scamper
bežati u panici *v.i* stampede
bežični *a.* wireless
beživotan *a.* lifeless
biber *n.* pepper
biberiti *v.t.* pepper
biblija *n.* scripture
biblija *n* bible
bibliograf *n* bibliographer
bibliografija *n* bibliography
biblioteka *n.* library

**bibliotekar** *n.* librarian
**biceps** *n* biceps
**bicikl** *n.* bicycle
**biciklista** *n* cyclist
**bič** *n.* scourge
**bič** *n.* whip
**bičevan** *a.* lash
**bičevati** *v.t.* scourge
**bičevati** *v.t.* slash
**bičevati** *v.t.* whip
**bigamija** *n* bigamy
**bik** *n* bull
**biliteralan** *adj* biliteral
**biljka** *n.* herb
**biljka** *n.* plant
**biljni lepak** *n.* mucilage
**bilo da** *conj.* whether
**bilten** *n* bulletin
**binarni** *adj* binary
**biograf** *n* biographer
**biografija** *n* biography
**biolog** *n* biologist
**biologija** *n* biology
**bioskop** *n.* cinema
**bioskop** *n.* movies
**birač** *n.* constituent
**biračko telo** *n* electorate
**biro** *n.* bureau
**birokrata** *n* bureaucrat
**birokratija** *n.* Bureacuracy
**biseksualan** *adj.* bisexual
**biser** *n.* pearl
**biskup** *n* bishop
**bistar** *a.* lucid
**bitanga** *n.* rogue
**biti neposlušan** *v. t* disobey
**biti nepoverljiv** *v.t.* mistrust
**biti neprosvetljen** *v. t* benight
**biti odsutan** *v.t* absent
**biti sklon** *v.i.* tend

**biti snužden** *v.i.* mope
**biti zavidan** *v* envy
**biti zavistan** *v.t.* addict
**biti žedan** *v.i.* thirst
**biti** *v.t.* be
**biti** *pref.* be
**bitka** *n* battle
**bitno** *adv.* substantially
**bivši** *pron* former
**bizaran** *adj* bizarre
**biznismen** *n* businessman
**bizon** *n* bison
**bizon** *n.* buffalo
**blag** *adj* benign
**blag** *a.* mild
**blag** *a.* slight
**blag vetar** *n* fan
**blag** *adj.* bland
**blagajnik** *n.* teller
**blagajnik** *n.* treasurer
**blagajnik** *n.* cashier
**blago** *n.* treasure
**blagodat** *n* boon
**blagonaklon** *a* benevolent
**blagonaklonost** *n* benevolence
**blagoslov** *n* benison
**blagosloviti** *v. t* bless
**blagostanje** *n.* prosperity
**blagostanje** *n.* welfare
**blagovremen** *a.* well-timed
**blanširati** *v. t. & i* blanch
**blatiti** *v.t.* mire
**blato** *n.* mire
**blato** *n.* muck
**blato** *n.* mud
**blaženstvo** *n* felicity
**blaženstvo** *n* bliss
**blebetalo** *n.* windbag
**blebetati** *v.i.* gabble
**blebetati** *v.t.* jabber

| | |
|---|---|
| **blebetati** *v.i.* quack | **bodrenje** *n.* cheer |
| **bled** *a* pale | **bodriti** *v. t.* cheer |
| **bled** *a.* wan | **bodrost** *n.* keenness |
| **blefirati** *v. t* bluff | **Bog** *n.* god |
| **blejanje** *n* bleat | **bogalj** *n* cripple |
| **blejati** *v. i* bleat | **bogat** *a.* affluent |
| **blesak** *n* dazzle | **bogat** *a.* opulent |
| **blesak** *n* flare | **bogat** *a.* rich |
| **bleštanje** *n.* glare | **bogat** *a.* wealthy |
| **bleštati** *v.i* glare | **bogatstvo** *n.* opulence |
| **blic** *n* flash | **bogatstvo** *n.* richness |
| **blisko** *adv.* nigh | **bogatstvo** *n.* wealth |
| **blistav** *a* brilliant | **bogatstvo** *n.* affluence |
| **blistav** *a.* shiny | **boginja** *n.* goddeşş |
| **blistavost** *n* brilliance | **boja** *n* colour |
| **blistavost** *n.* glamour | **boja** *n* dye |
| **blizak** *a.* near | **boja** *n.* paint |
| **blizanac** *n.* twin | **boja** *n.* tincture |
| **blizina** *n.* proximity | **boja** *n.* tint |
| **blizina** *n.* vicinity | **bojažljivost** *n.* timidity |
| **blizu** *adv.* anigh | **boje cinobera** *a.* vermillion |
| **blizu** *adv* by | **bojiti** *v. t* colour |
| **blizu** *prep.* near | **bojiti** *v. t* dye |
| **blizu** *v.i.* near | **bojiti** *v.t.* paint |
| **blizu** *prep.* nigh | **bojkot** *n* boycott |
| **bljutav** *a.* insipid | **bojkotovati** *v. t.* boycott |
| **bljutavost** *n.* insipidity | **bojler** *n* boiler |
| **bljuzgav** *a.* slushy | **boks** *n* boxing |
| **bljuzgavica** *n.* slush | **bokvice** *n.* plantain |
| **blok** *n* bloc | **bol** *n* distress |
| **blokada** *n* blockade | **bol** *n.* pain |
| **blokirati** *v.t* block | **bol** *n.* ache |
| **bluza** *n* blouse | **bol** *n.* anguish |
| **boca** *n* bottle | **bolan** *a.* painful |
| **bočica** *n.* phial | **bolesno** *a.* sickly |
| **bočica** *n.* vial | **bolest** *n* disease |
| **bodar** *a.* keen | **bolest** *n.* illness |
| **bodež** *n.* dagger | **bolest** *n.* malady |
| **bodlja** *n.* barb | **bolest** *n.* sickness |
| **bodljikav** *a.* barbed | **bolestan** *a.* ill |

**bolestan** *a.* sick
**bolestan** *a.* unwell
**boleti** *v.t.* pain
**boleti** *v.i.* ache
**bolje** *adv.* better
**bolji** *a* better
**bolnica** *n.* hospital
**bolovati** *v.t.* ail
**bomba** *n* bomb
**bombarder** *n* bomber
**bombardovanje** *n* bombardment
**bombardovati** *v. t* bomb
**bombardovati** *v. t* bombard
**bonus** *n* bonus
**bor** *n.* pine
**bora** *n.* wrinkle
**borac** *n* combatant
**boravak** *n* sojourn
**boravak** *n* stay
**boraviti** *v.i.* reside
**boraviti** *v.i.* sojourn
**borba** *n* combat
**borba** *n* fight
**borba** *n* struggle
**borba** *n.* tussle
**borbena tehnika** *n.* ordnance
**bordel** *n* brothel
**borilište** *n.* lists
**boriti se** *v. i.* battle
**boriti se** *v. t.* combat
**boriti se** *v. i* contend
**boriti se** *v. i* duel
**boriti se** *v.t* fight
**boriti se** *v.i.* struggle
**boriti se** *v.i.* tussle
**bosiljak** *n.* basil
**botanika** *n* botany
**bova** *n* buoy
**božanski** *a* divine
**božanstvenost** *n* divinity

**božanstvo** *n.* deity
**božanstvo** *n.* godhead
**Božić** *n* Christmas
**Božić** *n.* Xmas
**božji** *a.* godly
**bračni** *a* conjugal
**bračni** *a.* marital
**bračni** *a.* matrimonial
**bračni drug** *n.* consort
**bračni drug** *n* mate
**bračni drug** *n.* spouse
**brada** *n.* chin
**brada** *n* beard
**bradavica** *n.* nipple
**bradavica** *n.* wart
**brajeva azbuka** *n* braille
**brak** *n.* marriage
**brak** *n.* matrimony
**brak** *n.* wedlock
**brana** *n* dam
**brana** *n.* sluice
**brana** *n.* weir
**brana** *n.* barrage
**branik** *n.* bumper
**branilac** *n.* pleader
**braniti** *v. t.* champion
**braniti** *v. t* defend
**braniti** *v.t.* shield
**braniti se** *v.t* fend
**braon** *a* brown
**braon boja** *n* brown
**brašnjav** *a.* mealy
**brašno** *n* flour
**brat** *n* brother
**bratoubica** *n* cain
**bratoubistvo** *n.* fratricide
**bratski** *a.* fraternal
**bratstvo** *n.* confraternity
**bratstvo** *n.* fraternity
**bratstvo** *n* brotherhood

brava *n.* lock
brazda *n* crease
brazda *n.* furrow
brazda *n.* score
brbljanje *n.* babble
brbljanje *n.* prattle
brbljati *v.i.* babble
brbljati *v.i.* prattle
brbrljati *v. t.* chatter
brdo *n.* hill
brdo *n* mount
breg *n.* hillock
brektanje *n.* pant
brektati *v.i.* pant
breskva *n.* peach
breza *n.* birch
briga *n* concern
briga *n.* worry
briga *n.* care
brigada *n.* brigade
brigadir *n* brigadier
brijač *n.* razor
brijanje *n* shave
brijati *v.t.* shave
brinuti *v. t* concern
brinuti *v.i.* worry
brinuti *v. i.* care
brisanje *n.* obliteration
brisanje *n.* wipe
brisati *v. t* erase
brisati *v.t.* mop
brisati *v.t.* wipe
brisati peškirom *v.t.* towel
britanski *adj* british
brkovi *n.* moustache
brkovi *n.* mustache
brod *n.* nave
brod *n.* ship
brod *n.* vessel
brod za spasavanje *n.* wrecker

brod *n* boat
broj *n.* number
brojač *n.* numerator
brojati *v.t.* number
brojčani *a.* numeral
brojčanik *n.* dial
brojilac *n.* counter
brojni *a.* numerous
brokat *n* brocade
broker *n* broker
brokoli *n.* broccoli
bronza *n. & adj* bronze
brošura *n* booklet
brošura *n* brochure
bršljan *n* ivy
brusiti *v.t.* whet
brutalan *a* brutal
bruto *n.* gross
brz *a* fast
brz *a.* prompt
brz *a.* quick
brz *a.* speedy
brz *a.* swift
brzina *n.* speed
brzina *n.* velocity
brzo *adv* fast
brzo *adv.* speedily
buba *n* beetle
buba *n.* bug
bubanj *n* drum
bubašvaba *n* cockroach
bubreg *n.* kidney
bubuljica *n.* pimple
bubuljice *n* acne
bučan *a.* noisy
bučan *a.* tumultuous
bučan *a.* uproarious
buđ *n.* mildew
budala *n* fool
budala *n.* sap

| | |
|---|---|
| **budalast** *a* foolish | **burgija** *n.* auger |
| **budan** *a.* wakeful | **burmut** *n.* snuff |
| **budan** *a.* watchful | **busen** *n.* sod |
| **budan** *a* awake | **bušenje** *v. t.* drill |
| **buđav** *a.* musty | **bušilica** *n* drill |
| **budnost** *n.* vigilance | **bušiti** *v. t* bore |
| **budući** *a.* future | **bušiti tunel** *v.i.* tunnel |
| **budućnost** *n* future | **bušotina** *n* bore |
| **budžet** *n* budget | **buva** *n.* flea |
| **bujan** *a.* lush | |
| **bujan** *a* rank | |
| **bujan** *a.* torrential | # C |
| **bujica** *n.* spate | |
| **bujica** *n.* torrent | **carić** *n.* wren |
| **buka** *n.* ado | **carica** *n* empress |
| **buka** *n* din | **carski** *a.* imperial |
| **buka** *n.* noise | **carstvo** *n* empire |
| **buket** *n* bouquet | **carstvo** *a.* realm |
| **buknuti** *v. i* erupt | **cediti** *v.t.* squash |
| **bukva** *n.* beech | **celibat** *n.* celibacy |
| **bukvar** *n.* primer | **celina** *n.* total |
| **buldog** *n* bulldog | **celina** *n* whole |
| **buljenje** *n.* stare | **celokupnost** *n.* totality |
| **buljiti** *v.i.* stare | **cement** *n.* cement |
| **bunar** *n.* well | **cementirati** *v. t.* cement |
| **buncati** *v.i.* rave | **cena** *n.* cost |
| **bundeva** *n.* pumpkin | **cena** *n.* price |
| **bundeva** *n* squash | **ceniti** *v.t.* price |
| **bungalov** *n* bungalow | **ceniti** *v.t.* prize |
| **buniti se** *v.i.* rebel | **ceniti** *v.t.* regard |
| **bunker** *n* blindage | **ceniti** *v.t.* value |
| **bunker** *n* bunker | **ceniti** *v.t.* appreciate |
| **buntovan** *a.* mutinous | **cenkanje** *n.* bargain |
| **buntovan** *a.* rebellious | **cenkati se** *v.t.* bargain |
| **buntovan** *a.* seditious | **cent** *n* cent |
| **buntovnički** *a.* insurgent | **centar** *n* center |
| **buntovnik** *n.* insurgent | **centar** *n* centre |
| **buntovnik** *n.* rebel | **centar pažnje** *n.* limelight |
| **buran** *a.* tempestuous | **centralni** *a.* central |
| **bure** *n* cask | **centrifugalni** *adj.* centrifugal |

**cenzor** *n.* censor
**cenzura** *n.* censorship
**cenzurisati** *v. t.* censor
**cenzus** *n.* census
**ceo** *n.* all
**ceo** *a.* whole
**cepati** *v.t.* rip
**cepidlačiti** *v. t* cavil
**ceremonija** *n.* ceremony
**cev** *n.* tube
**cev, lula** *n.* pipe
**cevasti** *a.* tubular
**cicijaški** *a.* miserly
**ciča** *n* squeak
**cičati** *v.i.* squeak
**cifra** *n.* cipher, cipher
**cifra** *n* cypher
**cifra** *n* digit
**cigara** *n.* cigar
**cigareta** *n.* cigarette
**cigla** *n* brick
**cik-cak** *n.* zigzag
**ciklon** *n.* cyclone
**ciklostil** *n* cyclostyle
**ćilim** *n.* rug
**cilindar** *n* cylinder
**cilindričan** *adj.* cubiform
**cilj** *n.* goal
**cilj** *n.* objective
**cilj** *n.* target
**cilj** *n.* aim
**ciljati** *v.i.* aim
**cimet** *n* cinnamon
**cinik** *n* cynic
**cink** *n.* zinc
**cinober** *n* cinnabar
**cinober** *n.* vermillion
**cipela** *n.* shoe
**cirkulacija** *n* circulation
**cirkular** *n.* circular

**cirkulisati** *v. i.* circulate
**cirkus** *n.* circus
**citat** *n.* quotation
**citirati** *v. t* cite
**citirati** *v.t.* quote
**civil** *n* civilian
**civilizacija** *n.* civilization
**civilizovati** *v. t* civilize
**civilni** *a* civil
**cmok** *n.* smack
**cmoknuti** *v.t.* smack
**crep** *n.* tile
**crevni** *a.* intestinal
**crevo** *n.* hose
**crevo** *n.* intestine
**crevo** *n.* bowel
**crkva** *n.* church
**crnac** *n.* negro
**crnac** *n.* nigger
**crnkinja** *n.* negress
**crno** *a* black
**crnpurast** *a.* swarthy
**crpsti** *v.t.* ladle
**crtač** *a* draftsman
**crtani film** *n.* cartoon
**crtanje** *n* drawing
**crv** *n* mite
**crv** *n.* worm
**crven** *a.* red
**crvena boja** *n.* red
**crvenkast** *a.* reddish
**curenje** *n.* leak
**curenje** *n.* leakage
**curiti** *v.i.* leak
**curiti** *v.i.* ooze
**curiti** *v.i.* seep
**cvećar** *n* florist
**cvet** *n* flower
**cvet** *n* bloom
**cvetati** *v.i.* bloom

cvetati *v.i* flourish
cvetni *a* flowery
cviljenje *v.i.* whimper
cvrčak *n* cricket
cvrčanje *n.* sizzle
cvrčati *v.i.* sizzle
cvrkut *n* chirp
cvrkut *n.* twitter
cvrkutati *v.i.* chirp
cvrkutati *v.i.* twitter

# Č

čađ *n.* soot
čađiti *v.t.* soot
čaj *n* tea
čajnik *n.* kettle
čak *adv* even
čak *adv.* nay
čarapa *n.* sock
čarapa *n.* stocking
čarape *n.* hosiery
čarka *n.* skirmish
čarkati *se v.t.* skirmish
čarobnjak *n.* sorcerer
čarobnjak *n.* wizard
čarobnjaštvo *n.* sorcery
čarolija *n.* spell
čarolija *n.* witchery
časkom *adv.* awhile
časopis *n.* journal
časopis *n.* periodical
časopis *n.* serial
čast *n.* honour
častan *a.* honourable
častan *a.* reverend
čašćenje *n* treat
čaurast *adj* capsular
čavrljanje *n.* chat

čavrljati *v. i.* chat
čedan *a* maiden
čedomorstvo *n.* infanticide
ček *n.* cheque
čekanje *n.* wait
čekati *v.i.* wait
čekati *v.t.* await
čekati *v. t* bide
čekić *n.* hammer
čekićati *v.t* hammer
čekinja *n* bristle
čekrk *n.* lathe
čekrk *n.* winch
čelik *n.* steel
čelo *n* forehead
čempres *n.* cypress
čerpić *n.* adobe
čestica *n.* speck
čestit *a.* upright
čestitanje *n* congratulation
čestitati *v. t* congratulate
čestitati *v.t* felicitate
često *adv.* oft
često *adv.* often
češalj *n* comb
češanj *n* clove
češljana vuna *n.* worsted
četa *n.* troop
četiri *n.* four
četka *n* brush
četrdeset *n.* forty
četrnaest *n.* fourteen
četvoronožni *n.* quadruped
četvorostran *a. & n.* quadrilateral
četvorostruk *a.* quadruple
četvorougaoni *a.* quadrangular
četvorougaonik *n.* quadrangle
četvrtak *n.* Thursday
četvrtast *a* square
četvrtina *n.* quarter

**čeznuti** *v.i.* languish
**čeznuti** *v.i* long
**čeznuti** *v.i.* pine
**čežnja** *n.* longing
**čičak** *n.* thistle
**čigra** *n.* top
**čiji** *pron.* whose
**čili** *n.* chilli
**čin kapetana** *n.* captaincy
**činija** *n* bowl
**činiti** *v. t* do
**činiti** *se v.i.* seem
**činjenica** *n* fact
**čio** *a.* hale
**čio** *a.* vivacious
**čioda** *n.* pin
**čipka** *n.* lace
**čipkast** *a.* lacy
**čir** *n.* ulcer
**čist** *adj.* clean
**čist** *a* pure
**čistač** *n.* sweeper
**čistilište** *n.* purgatory
**čistiti** *v. t* clean
**čistiti** *v.t* filter
**čistiti** *v.t* fine
**čistiti** *v.i.* sweep
**čistoća** *n* cleanliness
**čistoća** *n.* purity
**čišćenje** *n* clearance
**čitalac** *n.* reader
**čitati** *v.t.* read
**čitav** *a* entire
**čitko** *adv.* legibly
**čitljiv** *a.* legible
**čizma** *n* boot
**član** *n.* member
**članak** *n.* ankle
**članak** *n.* joint
**članak** *n* article

**članstvo** *n.* membership
**čmar** *n.* anus
**čmičak** *n.* stye
**čokolada** *n* chocolate
**čovečanstvo** *n.* humanity
**čovečanstvo** *n.* mankind
**čovek** *a.* human
**čovek** *n.* man
**čovekolik** *adj.* anthropoid
**čučati** *v.i.* squat
**čučnuti** *v. i.* crouch
**čudan** *a.* peculiar
**čudan** *a.* quaint
**čudan** *a* rum
**čudan** *a.* strange
**čudan** *a.* weird
**čuđenje** *n.* astonishment
**čudesan** *a.* miraculous
**čudesan** *a.* stupendous
**čudesan** *a.* wondrous
**čuditi** *se v.i* marvel
**čuditi** *se v.i.* wonder
**čudnovat** *a.* outlandish
**čudo** *n.* marvel
**čudo** *n.* miracle
**čudo** *i.* wonder
**čudovište** *n.* monster
**čulna osoba** *n.* sensualist
**čulni** *a.* sensuous
**čulnost** *n.* sensuality
**čunak** *n.* shuttle
**čuperak** *n.* wisp
**čuti** *v.t.* hear
**čuvanje** *n.* preservation
**čuvar** *n.* guardian
**čuvar** *n.* keeper
**čuvar** *n.* warder
**čuvar slonova** *n.* mahout
**čuvati** *v.i.* guard
**čuvati** *v.t.* treasure

čuvati *v.t.* ward
čuvati *se v.i.* beware
čvor *n.* hub
čvor *n.* knot
čvor *n.* node
čvrga *n.* snag
čvrst *a* firm
čvrst *a.* solid
čvrst *a.* steady
čvrst *a.* sturdy
čvrst *a.* tight
čvrsto telo *n* solid

# Ć

ćerka *n* daughter
ćelav *a.* bald
ćelija *n.* cell
ćelijski *adj* cellular
ćilim *n.* rug
ćorsokak *n.* impasse
ćorsokak *n* deadlock
ćudljiv *a.* moody
ćušnuti *v. t* cuff

# D

da *conj.* that
da *adv.* yes
da ne bi *conj.* lest
dabar *n* beaver
daća *n* wake
dah *n* waft
dah *n* breath
dahtanje *n.* gasp
dahtati *v.i* gasp
dahtati *v.i.* puff
dakle *adv.* therefore
daktilograf *n.* typist

dalek *a* far
dalek *a.* remote
daleko *adv.* aloof
daleko *adv.* far
daleko *adv.* away
dalje *adv.* beyond
dalje *adv.* further
dalje *adv.* on
dalji *a* further
daljina *n* far
dama *n.* dame
dama *n.* lady
dan *n* day
danas *adv.* today
današnjica *n.* today
danguba *n.* loafer
dangubiti *v.i.* dawdle
dangubiti *v.i.* laze
dangubiti *v.i.* loaf
danju *adv.* adays
dar *n* benefice
darežljiv *a* bountiful
darežljiv *a.* munificent
darežljivost *n* bounty
darežljivost *n.* largesse
daska *n.* plank
dašak *n.* puff
dašak *n.* whiff
dati *v.t.* give
dati kompliment *v. t* compliment
dati nadimak *v.t.* nickname
dati ostavku *v.t.* resign
dati pravo glasa *v.t.* enfranchise
dati publicitet *v.t.* publicize
dati u podzakup *v.t.* sublet
dati znak *v. t* beckon
datirati *v. t* date
datum *n* date
davalac *n* donor
davati ton *v.t.* tone

debata *n.* debate
debatovati *v. t.* debate
debelo *adv.* thick
debelo crevo *n* colon
debeo *a.* thick
decembar *n* december
decenija *n* decade
decimal *a* decimal
dečak *n* boy
dečaštvo *n* boyhood
dečija kolica *n.* perambulator
deficit *n* deficit
definicija *n* definition
definisati *v. t* define
deflacija *n.* deflation
degradirati *v. t* degrade
deist *n.* deist
dekadentan *a* decadent
dekan *n.* dean
deklaracija *n* declaration
dekoracija *n* decoration
dekret *n* decree
delatnost *n.* activity
delegacija *n* delegation
delegat *v. t* delegate
delikatan *a* delicate
delimičan *a.* partial
deliti *v.t.* part
deliti *v.t.* portion
deliti *v.t.* share
delo *n* deed
delo *n.* act
delokrug *n.* venue
delotvornost *n* efficacy
delovanje *n.* acting
delovanje *v. t* effect
delta *n* delta
demokratija *n* democracy
demokratski *a* democratic
demolirati *v. t.* demolish

demon *n.* demon
demonetizirati *v.t.* demonetize
demoralisati *v. t.* demoralize
denga *n.* dengue
deo *n.* part
deo *n* portion
koren u medicini *n.* asafoetida
deonica *n* share
deportovati *v.t.* deport
depozit *n.* deposit
depresija *n* depression
derište *n.* urchin
deset *n., a* ten
desetina *n.* tithe
desetkovati *v.t.* decimate
desetogodišnjica *n.* decennary
desiti *v.t.* happen
desiti se *v.i.* occur
despot *n* despot
destilerija *n* distillery
destilovati *v. t* distil
destinacija *n* destination
detalj *n* detail
detaljisati *v. t* detail
dete *n.* babe
dete *n* child
dete *n.* kid
dete *n.* bantling
detektiv *n.* detective
detektivski *a* detective
detelina *n.* lucerne
detinjast *a.* childish
detinjast *a.* puerile
detinjstvo *n.* childhood
devac *n.* virgin
devedeset *n.* ninety
devedeseti *a.* ninetieth
devet *n.* nine
deveti *a.* ninth
devetnaest *n.* nineteen

devetnaesti *a.* nineteenth
devica *n* virgin
devojački *a.* girlish
devojka *n.* girl
devojka *n.* maiden
devojka *n.* wench
dići *v.t.* raise
dići se *v.* rise
didaktički *a* didactic
digitron *n* calculator
dignuti *v.i.* heave
dijabetes *n* diabetes
dijafragma *n.* midriff
dijagnoza *n* diagnosis
dijagram *n* diagram
dijalekt *n* dialect
dijalog *n* dialogue
dijamant *n* diamond
dijareja *n* diarrhoea
dijeta *n* diet
dikcija *n* diction
diktator *n* dictator
diktiranje *n* dictation
diktirati *v. t* dictate
dilema *n* dilemma
dilema *n.* quandary
dim *n.* smoke
dimenzija *n* dimension
dimnjak *n.* chimney
dinamičan *a* dynamic
dinamika *n.* dynamics
dinamit *n* dynamite
dinastija *n* dynasty
dinja *n.* melon
dinstati *v.t.* stew
diploma *n* diploma
diplomata *n* diplomat
diplomatija *n* diplomacy
diplomatski *a* diplomatic
diplomirani đak *n* graduate

diplomirati *v.i.* graduate
direktan *a* direct
direktor *n.* director
direktorijum *n* directory
disajne smetnje *n* apnoea
disanje *n.* respiration
disati *v.i.* respire
disati *v. i.* breathe
disciplina *n* discipline
disk *n.* disc
diskrecija *n* discretion
diskriminacija *n* discrimination
diskurs *n* discourse
diskutovati *v. t.* discuss
diskvalifikacija *n* disqualification
diskvalifikovati *v. t.* disqualify
distribucija *n* distribution
distribuirati *v. t* distribute
divan *a.* gorgeous
divan *a.* lovely
diviti se *v.t.* admire
divljački *a.* barbarian
divljak *n* savage
divljak *n.* barbarian
divljanje *n.* rampage
divljaštvo *n.* savagery
divljaštvo *n.* barbarism
divljati *v.i.* rampage
divljenje *n.* admiration
divlji *a.* savage
divlji *a.* wild
divljina *n.* wilderness
dizajn *n.* design
dizajnirati *v. t.* design
dizalica *n* crane
dizanje *n.* rise
dizati *v.t.* hoist
dizati se *v.i.* tower
dizenterija *n* dysentery
dlaka *n.* whisker

dlan *n.* palm
dleto *n* chisel
dnevni *a* daily
dnevni red *n.* agenda
dnevnik *n.* daily
dnevnik *n* diary
dnevno *adv.* daily
dno *n* bottom
do *prep.* till
do *prep.* until
do sada *adv.* hitherto
doba *n.* age
doba *n* era
dobar *a* fine
dobar *a.* good
dobar *a.* well
dobavljač *n.* supplier
dobit *n* gain
dobitak *n.* pelf
dobiti *v.t.* gain
dobiti *v.t.* get
dobiti *v.t.* obtain
dobiti *v.t.* receive
dobiti zube *v.i.* teethe
dobra volja *n.* goodwill
dobro *adv.* well
dobročinstvo *n.* benefaction
dobroćudno *adv* benignly
dobrodošao *a.* welcome
dobrodošlica *n* welcome
dobronamerno *adv* bonafide
dobrota *n.* goodness
dobrotvorno *a.* charitable
dobrovoljan *a.* voluntary
dobrovoljno *adv.* voluntarily
doći *v. i.* come
doći *v.i.* arrive
dodatak *n.* appendage
dodatak *n.* appendix
dodatak *n.* addition

dodatak *n.* adjunct
dodati *v.t.* suffix
dodati prefiks *v.t.* prefix
dodati *v.t.* add
dodati *v.t.* annex
dodati *v.t.* append
dodatni *a* extra
dodatni *a.* plus
dodatni *a.* additional
dodeliti *v. i* confer
dodeliti *v.t.* allocate
dodeliti *v.t.* assign
dodeliti *v.t.* attribute
dodeljivanje *n.* allotment
dodir *n* touch
dodirivati *v.t* finger
dodirnuti *v.t.* palm
dodirnuti *v.t.* touch
dotaći nožnim prstima *v.t.* toe
događaj *n* event
događaj *n.* happening
događaj *n.* occurrence
dogma *n* dogma
dogmatski *a* dogmatic
dogovor *n* deal
dogovoriti se *v. t* concert
dogovoriti se *v. i* deal
dohodak *n.* proceeds
dojiti *v.i.* lactate
dojiti *v.t.* suckle
dok *n. conj.* till
dok *conj* until
dok *conj.* while
dokaz *n* evidence
dokaz *n.* proof
dokazati *v.t.* prove
doktorat *n* doctorate
doktrina *n* doctrine
dokument *n* document
dolar *n* dollar

**dolazak** *n.* arrival
**dole** *adv* below
**dole** *adv* down
**dole** *adv* downwards
**dolina** *n* dale
**dolina** *n.* vale
**dolina** *n.* valley
**dom** *n.* home
**domaći** *a* domestic
**domaćin** *n.* host
**domaći** *n.* vernacular
**domen** *n* domain
**domet** *n.* range
**dominacija** *n* domination
**dominantan** *a* dominant
**dominirati** *v. t* dominate
**donacija** *n.* donation
**doneti** *v.t* fetch
**doneti** *v.t.* yield
**doneti** *v. t* bring
**donje rublje** *n.* underwear
**donkihotski** *a.* quixotic
**donositi zakon** *v.i.* legislate
**donošenje zakona** *n.* legislation
**dopadanje** *n.* liking
**dopadljiv** *a.* winsome
**dopisnik** *n.* correspondent
**doprineti** *v. t* contribute
**doprinos** *n* contribution
**dopuna** *n* complement
**dopuna** *n.* supplement
**dopuniti** *v.t.* supplement
**dopunski** *adj* adscititious
**dopunski** *a* complementary
**dopunski** *a.* supplementary
**dopunski porez** *n.* surtax
**dopustiti** *v.t.* adhibit
**dopustiti** *v.t.* allow
**dopustiv** *a.* permissible
**dopuštenje** *n.* leave

**dopuštenje** *n.* permission
**dorasti** *v. i* cope
**doručak** *n* breakfast
**dosada** *n.* tedium
**dosadan** *a.* tedious
**dosadan** *a.* weary
**dosađivanje** *n* botheration
**dosađivanje** *n.* annoyance
**dosađivati** *v.t.* annoy
**dosađivati** *v. t* bother
**dosađivati** *v.t.* weary
**dosetka** *n.* quibble
**dosetka** *n.* witticism
**dosije** *n* file
**dosledan** *a* coherent
**dosledan** *a* consequent
**dosledan** *a* consistent
**doslednost** *n.* consistence,-cy
**doslovan** *a.* literal
**doslovan** *a.* verbatim
**doslovno** *adv.* verbatim
**dostaviti** *v. t* deliver
**dostići** *v.t.* reach
**dostignuće** *n.* accomplishment
**dostignuće** *n.* attainment
**dostojan** *a.* worthy
**dostojan prezira** *a* despicable
**dostojanstvenost** *n.* stateliness
**dostojanstvo** *n* dignity
**dosuditi** *v.t.* adjudge
**doušnik** *n* sneak
**dovesti u iskušenje** *v.t.* tempt
**dovoljan** *a* enough
**dovoljan** *a.* sufficient
**dovoljno** *adv* enough
**dovoljnost** *n.* sufficiency
**doza** *n* dose
**dozvola** *n.* allowance
**dozvola** *n.* licence
**dozvola** *n.* permit

**dozvoliti** v.t. let
**dozvoliti** v.t. license
**dozvoliti** v.t. permit
**doživotni** a. lifelong
**drag** a beloved
**drag** a darling
**drag** a dear
**draga** n. lass
**dragi** n beloved
**dragi** n darling
**dragocen** a. precious
**dragulj** n gem
**dragulj** n. jewel
**drama** n drama
**dramatičan** a dramatic
**dramaturg** n dramatist
**drastičan** a drastic
**dražiti** v.t. irritate
**dremanje** n. doze
**dremati** v. i doze
**dremati** v.i. nap
**dremati** v.i. slumber
**dremež** n. nap
**dremež** n. slumber
**drenaža** n drainage
**dres** n. jersey
**drevan** a. archaic
**drevni** a. ancient
**drhtanje** n. tremor
**drhtati** v.i. quiver
**drhtati** v.i. shiver
**drhtati** v.i. tremble
**drhtav** a. shaky
**drmati** v.t. jolt
**drmusanje** n. jolt
**dronjak** n. tatter
**drskost** n. impertinence
**drug** n. comrade
**drug** n. pal
**drugi** a else

**drugi** a. other
**drugi** pron. other
**drugi** a. second
**drugi** a another
**drugo** adv else
**društven** a. sociable
**društvenost** n. sociability
**društvo** n. society
**druželjubiv** adj. convivial
**drveni** a. wooden
**drveni konjić** n. hobby-horse
**drveni stub** n. mullion
**drvo** n. tree
**drvo** n. wood
**drzak** a. impertinent
**drzak** a. insolent
**držanje** n. hold
**držati** v.t hold
**držati** v.t. keep
**držati se** v.i. adhere
**držati u štali** v.t. stable
**držati u štali** v.t. stall
**državljanstvo** n citizenship
**državljanstvo** n. nationality
**državna** blagajna n. treasury
**državnik** n. statesman
**državno** uređenje n. polity
**dubina** n depth
**dubina** n. profundity
**dubok** a. profound
**duboko** a. deep
**duboko poštovati** v.t. revere
**dud** n. mulberry
**dug** n debt
**dug** n due
**dug** a. long
**dugme** n button
**dugo** adv long
**dugovati** v.t owe
**dugovečnost** n. longevity

**dugovi** *n.pl.* arrears
**duguljast** *a.* oblong
**duguljasta figura** *n.* oblong
**duh** *n.* ghost
**duh** *n.* spirit
**duhovit** *a.* witty
**duhovit odgovor** *n.* repartee
**duhovitost** *n.* wit
**duhovni** *a.* spiritual
**duhovnost** *n.* spirituality
**duplikat** *n.* counterpart
**duplikat** *n* duplicate
**duplja** *n.* cavity
**duša** *n.* soul
**duše pokojnika** *n.*    manes
**dušek** *n.* mattress
**dušnik** *n.* throttle
**duvan** *n.* tobacco
**duvanje** *n* blow
**duvati** *v.i.* blow
**duž** *prep.* along
**dužan** *a* due
**dužan dati danak** *a.* tributary
**dužina** *n.* length
**dužina** *n.* longitude
**dužnik** *n* debtor
**dužnost** *n* duty
**dva** *n.* two
**dvadeset** *a.* twenty
**dvadeseti** *a.* twentieth
**dvadesetina** *n* twentieth
**dvadesetorica** *n* twenty
**dvanaest** *n* twelve
**dvanaesti** *a.* twelfth
**dvanaestina** *n.* twelfth
**dvanaestorica** *n.* twelve
**dvaput** *adv.* twice
**dve** nedelje *n.* fort-night
**dvestogodišnji** *adj* bicentenary
**dvoboj** *n* duel

**dvogled** *n.* binocular
**dvogodišnji** *adj* biennial
**dvoje** *a.* two
**dvojezični** *a* bilingual
**dvoličnost** *n* duplicity
**dvomesečni** *adj.* bimonthly
**dvonedeljni** *adj* bi-weekly
**dvonožac** *n* biped
**dvoosni** *adj* biaxial
**dvorac** *n.* castle
**dvoranin** *n.* courtier
**dvorište** *n.* courtyard
**dvorište** *n.* yard
**dvosmislen** *a* equivocal
**dvosmislen** *a.* ambiguous
**dvosmislenost** *n.* ambiguity
**dvostruk** *a* dual
**dvostruk** *a* duplicate
**dvostruk** *a* twin
**dvostruk** *a.* twofold
**dvostruko** *a* double
**dvostrukost** *n* double
**dvotačka** *n* colon
**dvougli** *adj.* biangular

# DŽ

**džamija** *n.* mosque
**džem** *n.* jam
**džemper** *n.* sweater
**džep** *n.* pocket
**džin** *n.* giant
**džogirati** *v.t.* jog
**džoker** *n.* joker
**džungla** *n.* jungle

# Đ

đakon *n.* deacon
đavo *n* devil
đavo *n* fiend
đon *n.* sole
đubre *n* dung
đubre *n.* junk
đubre *n.* rubbish
đubriti *v.t.* manure
đubrivo *n* compost
đubrivo *n* fertilizer
đubrivo *n.* manure
đumbir *n.* ginger

# E

efekat *n* effect
efikasan *a* effective
efikasan *a* efficient
efikasnost *n* efficiency
ego *n* ego
egoizam *n* egotism
egzotična biljka *n.* curcuma
ekonomičan *a* economical
ekonomija *n.* economics
ekonomija *n* economy
ekonomski *a* economic
ekpres *n* express
ekran *n.* screen
ekselencija *n* excellency
ekser *n.* nail
ekskluzivan *a.* exclusive
ekskurzija *n.* excursion
ekspedicija *n* expedition
eksperiment *n* experiment
eksplicitan *a.* explicit

eksploatacija *n* exploit
eksploatisati *v. t* exploit
eksplodirati *v. t.* explode
eksplozija *n.* explosion
eksplozija *n* blast
eksploziv *n.* explosive
eksplozivan *a* explosive
eksponat *n.* exhibit
ekstra *adv* extra
ekstrakt *n* extract
ekstravagancija *n* extravagance
ekstravagantan *a* extravagant
ekstrem *n* extreme
ekstreman *a* extreme
ekstremista *n* extremist
ekvator *n* equator
ekvivalent *a* equivalent
elan *n.* verve
elastičan *a* elastic
elegancija *n* elegance
elegantan *adj* elegant
elegija *n* elegy
elektricitet *n* electricity
električni *a* electric
element *n* element
elementarni *a* elementary
eliminacija *n* elimination
eliminisati *v. t* eliminate
emajl *n* enamel
emancipacija *n.* emancipation
embrion *n* embryo
eminencija *n* eminence
eminentni *a* eminent
emisija *n* broadcast
emitovati *v. t* broadcast
emitovati *v. t* emit
emitovan *adj.* emited
emocija *n* emotion
emotivan *a* emotional
enciklopedija *n.* encyclopaedia

energičan *a.* arduous
energičan *a* energetic
energičan *a.* vigorous
energija *n.* energy
engleski jezik, Englez *n* English
enigma *n* enigma
entitet *n* entity
entomologija *n.* entomology
entuzijazam *n* enthusiasm
ep *n* epic
epidemija *n* epidemic
epigram *n* epigram
epilepsija *n* epilepsy
epilog *n* epilogue
epitaf *n* epitaph
epizoda *n* episode
epoha *n* epoch
erekcija *n* erection
ergela *n.* stud
erodirati *v. t* erode
erotski *a* erotic
erozija *n* erosion
erupcija *n* eruption
esej *n.* essay
esejista *n* essayist
eskadrila *n.* squadron
esnaf *n.* guild
estetika *n.pl.* aesthetics
estetski *a.* aesthetic
etar *n* ether
etički *a* ethical
etika *n.* ethics
etiketa *n* etiquette
etiketa *n.* label
etiketirati *v.t.* label
etimologija *n.* etymology
evakuacija *n* evacuation
evakuisati *v. t* evacuate
evergrin *n* evergreen
evidencija *n.* tally

evnuh *n* eunuch
evocirati *v. t* evoke
evolucija *n* evolution
evoluirati *v.t* evolve

# F

fabrika *n* factory
faksimil *n* facsimile
faktor *n* factor
faktura *n.* invoice
fakultet *n* faculty
falsifikat *n* forgery
falsifikator *n.* counterfeiter
falsifikovan *a.* counterfeit
falsifikovati *v.t.* adulterate
falsifikovati *v.t* forge
fanatičan *a* fanatic
fanatik *n* fanatic
fanatik *n.* zealot
fantastičan *a* fantastic
fantom *n.* phantom
farma *n* farm
farsa *n* farce
fasada *n* facade
fascikla *n* file
fascinacija *n.* fascination
fascinirati *v.t* fascinate
fatalan *a* fatal
fatamorgana *n.* mirage
fauna *n* fauna
favorit *n* favourite
faza *n.* phase
februar *n* February
federacija *n* federation
federalni *a* federal
fenjer *n.* lantern
fenomen *n.* phenomenon
fenomenalan *a.* phenomenal

**fermentacija** *n* fermentation
**festival** *n* festival
**feudalni** *a* feudal
**figura** *n* figure
**figurativan** *a* figurative
**fijaker** *n.* barouche
**fijasko** *n* fiasco
**fikcija** *n* fiction
**fiktivan** *a* fictitious
**fil** *n* custard
**filantrop** *n.* philanthropist
**filantropija** *n.* philanthropy
**filantropski** *a.* philanthropic
**film** *n* film
**filolog** *n.* philologist
**filologija** *n.* philology
**filološki** *a.* philological
**filozof** *n.* Philosopher
**filozofija** *n.* philosophy
**filozofski** *a.* philosophical
**filter** *n* filter
**finansije** *n* finance
**finansijer** *n* financier
**finansijski** *a* financial
**finansirati** *v.t* finance
**fioka** *n* drawer
**firma** *n.* firm
**fiskalni** *a* fiscal
**fistula** *n* fistula
**fitilj** *n.* wick
**fizičar** *n.* physicist
**fizički** *a.* physical
**fizika** *n.* physics
**fizionomija** *n.* physiognomy
**flanel** *n* flannel
**flaster** *n.* plaster
**flauta** *n* flute
**fleksibilan** *a* flexible
**flertovanje** *n* flirt
**flertovati** *v.i* flirt

**flora** *n* flora
**flota** *n* fleet
**foka** *n.* seal
**fokus** *n* focus
**folija** *v.t* foil
**fond** *n.* fund
**fonetika** *n.* phonetics
**fonetski** *a.* phonetic
**fontana** *n.* fountain
**forma** *n* form
**formacija** *n* formation
**formalan** *a* formal
**formalnost** *n.* technicality
**format** *n* format
**formirati** *v.t.* form
**formula** *n* formula
**formulisati** *v.t* formulate
**forum** *n.* forum
**fosfat** *n.* phosphate
**fosfor** *n.* phosphorus
**fosil** *n.* fossil
**fotograf** *n.* photographer
**fotografija** *n* photo
**fotografija** *n* photograph
**fotografija** *n.* photography
**fotografisati** *v.t.* photograph
**fotografski** *a.* photographic
**fotokopirati** *v.t.* xerox
**fragment** *n.* fragment
**frakcija** *n* faction
**frakcija** *n.* fraction
**francuski** *a.* French
**francuski jezik** *n* French
**franšiza** *n.* frachise
**fraza** *n.* phrase
**frazeologija** *n.* phraseology
**frekvencija** *n.* frequency
**frigidan** *a.* frigid
**frižider** *n.* fridge
**frižider** *n.* refrigerator

**frktanje** *n.* snort
**frktati** *v.i.* snort
**front** *n.* front
**frustracija** *n.* frustration
**frustrirati** *v.t.* frustrate
**fuj** *interj* fie
**funkcija** *n.* function
**funkcioner** *n.* functionary
**funkcionisati** *v.i* function
**funta** *n.* pound
**fuzija** *n.* fusion

# G

**gacati** *v.t.* puddle
**gadan** *a.* nasty
**gajde** *n.* bagpipe
**gajiti** *v.t.* rear
**galaksija** *n.* galaxy
**galama** *n* clamour
**galamiti** *v. i.* clamour
**galantan** *a.* gallant
**galeb** *n.* gull
**galeb** *n.* mew
**galerija** *n.* gallery
**galon** *n.* gallon
**galop** *n.* gallop
**galopirati** *v.t.* gallop
**gangster** *n.* gangster
**garancija** *n.* guarantee
**garancija** *n.* warranty
**garantovati** *v.t* guarantee
**garantovati** *v.t.* warrant
**garaža** *n.* garage
**garderoba** *n.* wardrobe
**gas** *n.* gas
**gasni** *a.* gassy
**gavran** *n.* raven
**gaziti** *v.t.* conculcate

**gaziti** *v.i.* wade
**gde** *adv.* where
**gde** *conj.* where
**gde** *conj.* whereat
**gde god** *adv.* wherever
**geg, čep** *v.t.* gag
**geganje** *v.i.* waddle
**generacija** *n.* generation
**generator** *n* dynamo
**generator** *n.* generator
**generisati** *v.t.* generate
**genije** *n.* genius
**geograf** *n.* geographer
**geografija** *n.* geography
**geografski** *a.* geographical
**geolog** *n.* geologist
**geologija** *n.* geology
**geološki** *a.* geological
**geometrija** *n.* geometry
**geometrijski** *a.* geometrical
**gerila** *n.* guerilla
**germicid** *n.* germicide
**gerund** *n.* gerund
**gest** *n.* gesture
**gibon** *n.* gibbon
**gigantski** *a.* gigantic
**giht** *n.* gout
**gimnastičar** *n.* gymnast
**gimnastički** *a.* gymnastic
**gimnastika** *n.* gymnastics
**gimnazija** *n.* gymnasium
**gitara** *n.* guitar
**glačati** *v.t.* glaze
**glad** *n* famine
**glad** *n* hunger
**gladak** *a.* smooth
**gladan** *a.* hungry
**gladiti** *v.t.* smooth
**gladovanje** *n.* starvation
**glagol** *n.* verb

glagolsko vreme *n.* tense
glas *n.* voice
glasač *n.* voter
glasački listić *n* ballot
glasan *a* audible
glasanje *n.* vote
glasati *v.i.* ballot
glasati *v.i.* vote
glasina *n* bruit
glasina *n.* rumour
glasnik *n.* herald
glasnik *n* post
glasno *a.* loud
glaukom *n.* glaucoma
glava *n.* head
glavna knjiga *n.* ledger
glavna potpora *n.* mainstay
glavni *a.* chief
glavni *a* main
glavni *a.* major
glavni *a.* prime
glavni *a* principal
glavni *a.* capital
glavobolja *n.* headache
glazura *n* glaze
glečer *n.* glacier
gledalac *n.* spectator
gledalište *n.* auditorium
gledati *v.t* front
gledati *v.i* look
gledati *v.t.* watch
gledište *n.* outlook
glib *n.* ooze
glicerin *n.* glycerine
glina *n* clay
glina *n* argil
gljiva *n.* fungus
gljiva *n.* mushroom
globalni *a.* global
glodar *n.* rodent

glog *n.* hawthorn
glomazan *a* bulky
glosar *n.* glossary
glukoza *n.* glucose
glumac *n.* actor
glumačka družina *n.* troupe
glumica *n.* actress
glup *a* dumb
glup *a.* sheepish
glup *a.* silly
glup *a* stupid
glupak *n.* simpleton
glupan *n* blockhead
glupan *n.* coot
glupan *n* dunce
glupan *n.* gander
glupan *n* gull
glupost *n* folly
glupost *n.* stupidity
gluv *a* deaf
gnev *n.* wrath
gnezdo *n.* nest
gnijezditi se *v.i.* nestle
gnječiti *v. t* crush
gnječiti *v.t* mash
gnoj *n.* pus
gnojan *a.* ulcerous
gnojna upala *n.* pyorrhoea
gnusan *a* abominable
gnusan *a.* heinous
gnusan *a.* loathsome
gnušanje *n.* abhorrence
gnušati se *v.t.* abhor
godina *n.* year
godišnje *adv.* yearly
godišnji *a.* annual
godišnji *a.* yearly
godišnjica *n.* anniversary
gojazan *a* fat
gojaznost *n.* obesity

golem kamen *n.* megalith
golenica *n.* shin
golf, zaliv *n.* golf
golicati *v.t.* tickle
golicljiv *a.* ticklish
golotinja *n.* nudity
golub *n* dove
golub *n.* pigeon
goluždravac *n.* nestling
gomila *n* crowd
gomila *n.* heap
gomila *n.* mob
gomila *n.* pile
gomila *n.* throng
gomilati *v.i* flock
gomilati *v.t* heap
gomilati *v.i* mass
gomilati *v.t.* pile
gomilati se *v.t.* throng
gong *n.* gong
goniti *v.t.* prosecute
gorak *a* bitter
gore *adv.* badly
gore *adv.* up
goreti *v.i* blaze
goreti *v. t* burn
gorila *n.* gorilla
gorivo *n.* fuel
gornja vilica *n.* maxilla
gornji *prep.* above
gornji *a.* upper
goruće *adv.* ablaze
gospoda *n.* Messrs
gospođa, supruga *n.* missis
gospodar *n.* lord
gospodar *n.* master
gospodarica *n.* mistress
gospođica *n.* damsel
gospodin *n.* gentleman
gospodin *n.* mister

gospodin *n.* sir
gospodstvo *n.* lordship
gost *n.* guest
gostiti se *v.i* feast
gostoprimljiv *a.* hospitable
gostoprimstvo *n.* hospitality
gotovina *n.* cash
govedina *n* beef
govor *n.* oration
govor *n.* speech
govoriti *v.i.* speak
govornica *n.* rostrum
govornički *a.* oratorical
govornik *n.* orator
gozba *n* feast
grad *n* city
grad *n.* hail
grad *n.* town
građa *n* build
gradacija *n.* gradation
građanin *n* citizen
građanski *a* civic
građansko pravo *n* civics
građevina *n* edifice
gradilište *n* lot
gradilište *n.* site
graditi *v. t* build
gradonačelnik *n.* mayor
grafički *a.* graphic
grafikon *n.* chart
grafikon *n.* graph
graja *n.* hubbub
graktanje *n.* caw
graktanje *n.* croak
graktati *v. i.* caw
graktati *v. i* crow
gram *n.* gramme
gramatičar *n.* grammarian
gramatika *n.* grammar
gramofon *n.* gramophone

grana *n* bough
grana *n* branch
granata *n.* grenade
grančica *n* spray
grančica *n.* sprig
grančica *n.* twig
granica *n.* frontier
granica *n.* limit
granica *n* border
granica *n.* bound
graničiti se *v.t.* adjoin
graničiti *v.t* border
grašak *n.* bean
grašak *n.* pea
gravitacija *n.* gravitation
grb *n* crest
grč *n.* spasm
grčevit *a* fitful
grčevit *a.* jerky
grčevit *a.* spasmodic
grčiti se *v.i.* writhe
grčki *a Greek*
grčki jezik, Grk *n.* Greek
grditi *v.t.* scold
grdnja *n.* invective
grdnja *n.* snub
grebanje *n.* scratch
grebati *v.t.* scratch
greben *n.* mull
greben *n.* ridge
greda *n.* timber
greh *n.* sin
grešan *a.* sinful
greška *n* error
greška *n* fault
greška *n.* mistake
grešnik *n.* sinner
grgeč *n.* perch
grickanje *n* nibble
grickati *v.t.* nibble

grip *n.* influenza
griva *n.* mane
griža savesti *n.* compunction
grlen *a.* guttural
grlen *a.* throaty
grlo *n.* throat
grm *n* bush
grmeti *v.i.* thunder
grnčar *n.* potter
grnčarija *n.* pottery
grob *n.* grave
grob *n.* tomb
groblje *n.* necropolis
groblje *n.* cemetery
groblje *n.* churchyard
grobnica *n.* sepulchre
grofica *n.* countess
grofovija *n.* shire
grom *n.* thunder
gromovit *a.* thunderous
groteskan *a.* grotesque
groznica *n* fever
grožđe *n.* grape
grub *a* coarse
grub *a.* harsh
grub *a.* rough
grubijan *n* churl
gruda *n.* clod
gruda *n.* lump
grudi *n* chest
grudi *n bosom*
grudi *n* breast
grudva *n.* nugget
grupa *n.* group
grupa *n.* band
grupisati *v.t.* group
gubav *a.* leprous
gubavac *n.* leper
gubitak *n* forfeit
gubitak *n.* loss

gubitak prava *n* forfeiture
gubiti boju *v.t.* tarnish
gubitnik *n* underdog
gucnuti *v.t.* delibate
gucnuti *v.t.* sip
gucnuti *v.i.* sup
guditi *v.i* fiddle
gukanje *n* coo
gukati *v. i* coo
guma *n.* gum
guma *n.* rubber
guma *n.* tyre
gunđati *v.t.* grudge
guranje *n.* push
guranje *n.* shove
gurati *v.t.* poke
gurati *v.t.* shove
gurati *v.t.* thrust
gurkati *v.t.* nudge
gurnuti *v.t.* push
gurnuti nogom *v.t.* spurn
gusar *n.* pirate
gusenica *n* caterpillar
guska *n.* goose
gust *a* dense
gustina *n* density
gustiš *n.* thicket
guša *n.* craw
gušenje *n.* strangulation
gušenje *n.* suffocation
gušiti *v.t.* throttle
gušiti se *v. t.* choke
gušter *n.* lizard
gutljaj *n* dram
gutljaj *n.* gulp
gutljaj *n.* sip
gutljaj *n.* swallow
guvernanta *n.* governess
guverner *n.* governor
gvožđe *n.* iron

# H

haljina *n* dress
haljina *n.* frock
haljina *n.* gown
haljina *n.* robe
hangar *n* shed
haos *n.* chaos
haotičan *adv.* chaotic
hapšenje *n.* arrest
harfa *n.* harp
haringa *n.* herring
harmoničan *a.* harmonious
harmonija *n.* harmony
harmonijum *n.* harmonium
hauba *n.* hood
heftati *a* staple
hemičar *n.* chemist
hemija *n.* chemistry
hemijski *a.* chemical
hemikalija *n.* chemical
hemisfera *n.* hemisphere
hemoroidi *n.* piles
hendikep *n* handicap
hendikepirati *v.t.* handicap
herkulski *a.* herculean
hernija *n.* hernia
heroina *n.* heroine
heroj *n.* hero
herojski *a.* heroic
hibernacija *n.* hibernation
hibrid *n* hybrid
hibridan *a.* hybrid
higijena *n.* hygiene
higijenski *a.* hygienic
hijena *n.* hyaena, hyena
hijerarhija *n.* hierarchy
hiljada *n.* chiliad

hiljada *n.* thousand
hiljadu *a* thousand
himna *n.* hymn
himna *n.* anthem
hiperbola *n.* hyperbole
hipnotisati *v.t.* hypnotize
hipnotisati *v.t.* mesmerize
hipnotizam *n.* hypnotism
hipnotizam *n.* mesmerism
hipoteka *n.* mortgage
hipotetički *a.* hypothetical
hipoteza *n.* hypothesis
hir *n* fad
hir *n.* caprice
hiromant *n.* palmist
hiromantija *n.* palmistry
hirurg *n.* surgeon
hirurgija *n.* surgery
histeričan *a.* hysterical
histerija *n.* hysteria
hitac *n.* shot
hitan *a.* urgent
hitan slučaj *n* emergency
hitar *a.* rapid
hitna *pomoć n.* ambulance
hitnost *n.* urgency
hitrina *n.* rapidity
hitro *adv.* apace
hlad *n.* shade
hladan *a* cold
hladan *a* cool
hlađenje *n.* refrigeration
hladiti *v. i.* cool
hladnjak *n* cooler
hladnoća *n* cold
hladnokrvan *a.* nerveless
hleb *n* bread
hlor *n* chlorine
hloroform *n* chloroform
hobi *n.* hobby

hod *n.* gait
hod *n* tread
hodočasnik *n.* pilgrim
hodočašće *n.* pilgrimage
hokej *n.* hockey
hol *n.* hall
holokaust *n.* holocaust
homeopata *n.* homoeopath
homeopatija *n.* homeopathy
homogen *a.* homogeneous
honorar *n* fee
honorar *n.* honorarium
hor *n* choir
horda *n.* horde
horizont *n.* horizon
hortikultura *n.* horticulture
hostel *n.* hostel
hotel *n.* hotel
hrabar *a.* courageous
hrabar *a.* manful
hrabar *a.* valiant
hrabar *a.* bold
hrabar *a* brave
hrabrost *n.* courage
hrabrost *n.* fortitude
hrabrost *n.* gallantry
hrabrost *n.* hardihood
hrabrost *n* boldness
hrabrost *n* bravery
hram *n.* temple
hrana *n* food
hrana *n. pl* victuals
hraniti *v.t* feed
hraniti *v.t.* nourish
hranjenje *n* feed
hranljiv *a.* nutritious
hrapav *a.* husky
hrast *n.* oak
hrist *n.* Christ
hrišćanin *n* Christian

hrišćanski a. Christian
hrišćanstvo n. Christendom
hrišćanstvo n. Christianity
hrkanje n snore
hrkati v.i. snore
hrom n chrome
hrom a. lame
hroničan a. chronic
hronograf n chronograph
hronologija n. chronology
hrpa n bulk
hrpa n bunch
hrskav a crisp
hrskav adj. crump
hrt n. greyhound
hteti v.t. will
huligan n. hooligan
human a. humane
humanitarno a humanitarian
humka n. mound
humor n. humour
humorista n. humorist
humorističan a. humorous
humus n mould
huškati v.t. incite
hvalisanje n boast
hvalisanje n brag
hvalisati se v. i brag
hvalisav a. vainglorious
hvalisavost n. vainglory
hvaliti v.t. praise
hvaliti se v.i boast
hvat n fathom
hvatanje n. snatch
hvatanje n. capture
hvatati mrežom v.t. net

# I

i conj. and
i tako dalje etcetera
iako conj. albeit
iako conj. although
ići v.i. go
ići na izlet v.i. picnic
ići tamo-ovamo v.t. shuttle
ići uzduž v.t. skirt
ideal n ideal
idealan a. ideal
idealista n. idealist
idealistički a. idealistic
idealizam n. idealism
idealizovati v.t. idealize
ideja n. idea
identičan a. identical
identifikacija n. indentification
identifikovati v.t. identify
identitet n. identity
idiom n. idiom
idiomatski a. idiomatic
idiot n. idiot
idiotizam n. ideocy
idiotski a. idiotic
idol n. idol
igla n. needle
ignorisati v.t. ignore
igra n. game
igra n. play
igra rečima n. pun
igra stihovima n. crambo
igrač n. player
igrač udarač palicom n. batsman
igračka n. toy
igrati v.i game
igrati se v.i. play

**igrati** *se v.i.* toy
**igrati** *se v.i* trifle
**igrati se rečima** *v.i.* pun
**iguman** *n* prior
**igumanija** *n.* prioress
**ikad** *adv* ever
**ikra** *n* fry
**ilustracija** *n.* illustration
**ilustrovati** *v.t.* illustrate
**iluzija** *n.* illusion
**imanje** *n* estate
**imati** *v.t.* have
**imati korist** *v. t.* benefit
**imbecil** *n.* moron
**ime** *n.* name
**imela** *n.* mistletoe
**imenica** *n.* noun
**imenjak** *n.* namesake
**imenovanje** *n.* nomination
**imenovanje** *n.* appointment
**imenovati** *v.t.* name
**imenovati** *v.t.* appoint
**imigracija** *n.* immigration
**imigrant** *n.* immigrant
**imigrirati** *v.i.* immigrate
**imitacija** *n.* imitation
**imitator** *n.* imitator
**imitirati** *v.t.* imitate
**imitirati** *a.* mimic
**imitirati** *v.t* mimic
**imovina** *n.* asset
**imovina** *n.* property
**imperativ** *a.* imperative
**imperator** *n* emperor
**imperijalizam** *n.* imperialism
**implementacija** *n.* implement
**implementirati** *v.t.* implement
**implikacija** *n.* implication
**impotencija** *n.* impotence
**impotentan** *a.* impotent

**impozantan** *a.* imposing
**impresionirati** *v.t.* impress
**impresivan** *a.* impressive
**impuls** *n.* impulse
**impuls** *n.* momentum
**impulsivan** *a.* impulsive
**imućan** *a.* well-to-do
**imun** *a.* immune
**imunitet** *n.* immunity
**inače** *adv.* otherwise
**inače** *conj.* otherwise
**inat** *n.* spite
**inauguracija** *n.* inauguration
**incident** *n.* incident
**inč** *n.* inch
**indeks** *n.* index
**indicija** *n* clue
**indigo** *n.* indigo
**indijska smokva** *n.* banyan
**indijska urma** *n.* tamarind
**indijski** *a.* Indian
**indikacija** *n.* indication
**indikativan** *a.* indicative
**indikator** *n.* indicator
**indirektan** *a.* implicit
**indirektan** *a.* indirect
**indiskrecija** *n.* indiscretion
**indiskretan** *a.* indiscreet
**individualizam** *n.* individualism
**individualnost** *n.* individuality
**industrija** *n.* industry
**industrijski** *a.* industrial
**inercija** *n.* inertia
**inertan** *a.* inert
**infantilan** *a.* infantile
**infekcija** *n.* infection
**inferioran** *a.* inferior
**inferiornost** *n.* inferiority
**inficirati** *v.t.* infect
**inflacija** *n.* inflation

**informacija** *n.* information
**informativan** *a.* informative
**infuzija** *n.* infusion
**inherentan** *a.* inherent
**inhibicija** *n.* inhibition
**inhibirati** *v.t.* inhibit
**inicijal** *n.* initial
**inicijativa** *n.* initiative
**inkvizicija** *n.* inquisition
**inovacija** *n.* innovation
**inovator** *n.* innovator
**inovirati** *v.t.* innovate
**insekt** *n.* insect
**insekticid** *n.* insecticide
**insinuacija** *n.* insinuation
**insinuirati** *v.t.* insinuate
**insistiranje** *n.* insistence
**insistirati** *v.t.* insist
**insolventan** *a.* insolvent
**insolventnost** *n.* insolvency
**inspekcija** *n.* inspection
**inspektor** *n.* inspector
**inspiracija** *n.* inspiration
**inspirisati** *v.t.* inspire
**instalacija** *n.* installation
**instalirati** *v.t.* install
**instinkt** *n.* instinct
**instinktivan** *a.* instinctive
**institucija** *n.* institution
**institut** *n.* institute
**instrukcija** *n.* instruction
**instruktor** *n.* instructor
**instrument** *n.* instrument
**instrumentalista** *n.* instrumentalist
**instrumentalni** *a.* instrumental
**integralan** *a.* integral
**integritet** *n.* integrity
**intelekt** *n.* intellect
**intelektualac** *n.* intellectual
**intelektualni** *a.* intellectual

**inteligencija** *n.* intelligence
**inteligencija** *n.* intelligentsia
**inteligentan** *a.* intelligent
**intenzitet** *n.* intensity
**intenzivan** *a.* intensive
**interes** *n.* interest
**interludijum** *n.* interlude
**internacionalni** *a.* international
**interni** *a.* internal
**interpunkcija** *n.* punctuation
**interval** *n.* interval
**intervencija** *n.* intervention
**intervenisati** *v.i.* intervene
**intervju** *n.* interview
**intervjuisati** *v.t.* interview
**intiman** *a.* intimate
**intimnost** *n.* intimacy
**intoksikacija** *n.* intoxication
**intriga** *n* intrigue
**intrigirati** *v.t.* intrigue
**intuicija** *n.* intuition
**intuitivan** *a.* intuitive
**invalid** *n* invalid
**invazija** *n.* invasion
**investicija** *n.* investment
**investirati** *v.t.* invest
**inženjer** *n* engineer
**ipak** *conj* however
**ipak** *conj.* nevertheless
**ipak** *adv.* notwithstanding
**ipak** *adv.* though
**ipak** *conj.* yet
**iracionalan** *a.* irrational
**iritacija** *n.* irritation
**iritiranje** *n.* irritant
**ironičan** *a.* ironical
**ironija** *n.* irony
**Irski** *a.* Irish
**irski jezik, Irac** *n.* Irish
**iscediti** *v.t.* squeeze

| | |
|---|---|
| **iscrtati** *v.t.* line | **ismevati** *v.i.* mock |
| **iseckati** *v.i.* haggle | **ispad** *n.* sally |
| **ishod** *n.* outcome | **isparavati** *v.t.* aerify |
| **ishod** *n.* upshot | **isparavati** *v.t.* vaporize |
| **ishrana** *n.* nourishment | **ispariti** *v. i* evaporate |
| **ishrana** *n.* nutrition | **ispasti** *v.i.* sally |
| **iskamčiti** *v.t.* wheedle | **ispeći** *v.t.* bake |
| **iskaz** *n.* utterance | **ispirati** *v.t.* rinse |
| **isključenje** *n.* expulsion | **ispirati grlo** *v.i.* gargle |
| **isključiti** *v. t* disconnect | **ispitanik** *n* examinee |
| **isključiti** *v. t* exclude | **ispitati** *v. t* examine |
| **isključiti** *v. t.* expel | **ispitivač** *n* examiner |
| **isključiv** *a* exclusive | **ispitivanje** *n.* examination |
| **iskonski** *a.* seminal | **ispitivanje** *n.* inquiry |
| **iskopati** *v.t.* unearth | **ispitivanje** *n.* scrutiny |
| **iskopavanje** *n.* excavation | **ispitivati** *v.t.* quiz |
| **iskopavati** *v. t.* excavate | **isplatiti** *v.t.* repay |
| **iskopavati** *v.i.* quarry | **ispleten od pruća** *n.* wicker |
| **iskoreniti** *v. t* eradicate | **ispljuvak** *n* spittle |
| **iskoreniti** *v.t.* uproot | **ispljuvak** *n.* sputum |
| **iskoristiti** *v.t.* advantage | **ispod** *prep.* under |
| **iskoristiti** *v.t.* utilize | **ispod** *adv.* underneath |
| **iskrcati** *v.i.* land | **ispod** *prep* below |
| **iskren** *a.* frank | **ispod** *prep* beneath |
| **iskren** *a.* sincere | **isporuka** *n* delivery |
| **iskren** *a.* straightforward | **ispovedati** *v.t.* profess |
| **iskren** *a.* candid | **ispraviti** *v. t* correct |
| **iskrenost** *n.* sincerity | **ispraviti** *v.i.* rectify |
| **iskrenost** *n.* candour | **ispraviti** *v.t.* straighten |
| **iskrivljen** *a.* wry | **ispravljanje** *n.* rectification |
| **iskupiti se** *v.t.* redeem | **ispravno** *adv* right |
| **iskupljenje** *n.* redemption | **ispravnost** *n.* propriety |
| **iskusiti** *v. t.* experience | **ispred** *adv.* ahead |
| **iskustvo** *n* experience | **isprugati** *v.t.* stripe |
| **iskušavač** *n.* tempter | **ispuniti** *v.t.* fulfil |
| **iskušenje** *n.* ordeal | **ispunjen** *a.* fraught |
| **iskušenje** *n.* temptation | **ispunjenje** *n.* fulfilment |
| **ismejavanje** *n.* ridicule | **ispuštati** *v.t.* shed |
| **ismejavati** *v.t.* ridicule | **istačkati** *v. t* dot |
| **ismevanje** *adj* mock | **istaknut** *a.* prominent |

istaknut *a.* salient
istaknutost *n.* prominence
isteći *v.i.* expire
istek *n* expiry
isti *a.* same
istina *n.* truth
istinitost *n.* veracity
istinoljubiv *a.* truthful
istisnuti *v.t.* oust
isto *n.* ditto
istočni *a east*
istočni *a* eastern
istočnjak *n* oriental
istočno *adv* east
istok *n* east
istopiti *v.t.* smelt
istoričar *n.* historian
istorija *n.* history
istorijski *a .* historic
istorijski *a.* historical
istovremen *a.* instantaneous
istovremen *a.* simultaneous
istraga *n.* inquest
istraga *n.* investigation
istrajati *v.i.* persevere
istrajnost *n.* perseverance
istrajnost *n.* tenacity
istražiti *v.t* explore
istražiti *v.t.* investigate
istraživanje *n* exploration
istraživanje *n* research
istraživati *v.t.* probe
istraživati *v.i.* research
istrgnuti *v.t.* wrest
istrošiti *v.t.* stale
istući *v.t.* wallop
iščašenje *n.* wrench
iščašenje *n* wrick
iščašiti *v.t.* wrench
iščeznuti *v.i.* vanish

išta *n.* aught
Italijanski *a.* Italian
italijanski jezik, Italijan *n.* Italian
iverica *n.* splinter
ivica *n* edge
ivičnjak *n* curb
iza *adv* behind
iza *prep* behind
izabran *a* select
izabrati *v. t.* choose
izabrati *v. t* elect
izabrati *v.t.* pick
izabrati *v.t.* select
izabrati vreme *v.t.* time
izadati *v.i.* issue
izaslanik *n* emissary
izazivati *v.t* foment
izazov *n.* challenge
izazvati *v. t.* challenge
izazvati *v.t.* solicit
izazvati žuticu *v.t.* jaundice
izbaciti *v. t.* eject
izbaciti iz koloseka *v. t.* derail
izbacivač *n* bouncer
izbacivati *v.i.* spout
izbalansirati *v.t.* poise
izbeći *v. t* evade
izbegavanje *n* elusion
izbegavanje *n* evasion
izbegavanje *n.* avoidance
izbegavati *v. t* elude
izbegavati *v.t.* shun
izbegavati *v.t.* avoid
izbeglica *n.* refugee
izbeleti *v. t* bleach
izbijanje *n.* outbreak
izbledeti *v.i* fade
izbor *n.* choice
izbor *n* election
izbor *n.* pick

izbor n. selection
izborati v.t. wrinkle
izborna jedinica n constituency
izbosti v.t. pierce
izbrbljati v. t. & i blab
izbrbljati v. t blurt
izbrisati v. t delete
izbrisati v. t efface
izdaja n. treachery
izdaja n. treason
izdaja n betrayal
izdajnički a. treacherous
izdajnik n. traitor
izdaleka adv. afar
izdanak n offset
izdanje n edition
izdanje n. publication
izdati v.t. betray
izdavač n. publisher
izdavati v.t pirate
izdržati v.t. endure
izdržati v.i. persist
izdržati v.t. withstand
izdržavanje n. aliment
izdržavanje n. livelihood
izdržavanje n. sustenance
izdržljiv n cast-iron
izdržljiv a durable
izdržljiv a endurable
izdržljiv adj. hardy
izdržljivost n. endurance
izdržljivost n last
izdržljivost n. persistence
izdržljivost n. stamina
izdupsti v.t hollow
izduvati v. t. exhaust
izdvojiti v. t extract
izgled n. guise
izgled n. prospect
izgled n appearance

izgledi n. odds
izgnan a outcast
izgnanik n. outcast
izgovarati v.t. pronounce
izgovor n excuse
izgovor n pretext
izgovor n. pronunciation
izgovoriti v.t. voice
izgrditi v.t. lambaste
izgrditi v.t. snub
izgubiti v.t forfeit
izgubiti v.t. lose
izjava n. statement
izjaviti saučešće v. i. condole
izjaviti v.t. allege
izjednačavanje n assimilation
izjednačen a level
izjednačiti v. t equal
izjednačiti v. t. equalize
izjednačiti v.t. level
izjednačiti v.t. offset
izjednačiti v. assimilate
izlaz n. exit
izlaz n. output
izleći v.i. incubate
izlečiv a curable
izlet n. outing
izliv n. outburst
izliven a. molten
izložba n. exhibition
izložiti v. t exhibit
izložiti v. t expose
izložiti v.t. table
izložiti rendg. zracima v.t. x-ray
izludeti v.t dement
izlupati v. t belabour
izmaglica n drizzle
izmaglica n. haze
izmaglica n. mist
između prep. amongst

**između** *prep* between
**izmena** *n* alteration
**izmeniti** *v.t.* alter
**izmicanje** *n* dodge
**izmicati** *v. t* dodge
**izmirenje** *n.* reconciliation
**izmisliti** *v. t* concoct
**izmisliti** *v. t devise*
**izmišljen** *a.* imaginary
**izmišljotina** *n.* concoction
**izmišljotina** *n* figment
**izmlatiti** *v.t* maul
**izmoriti** *v.t.* tire
**izmrviti** *v. t* crumble
**iznajmiti pašnjak** *v.t.* agist
**iznajmljivanje** *n.* rent
**iznajmljivati** *v.t.* rent
**iznenada** *adv.* suddenly
**iznenađenje** *n.* surprise
**iznenaditi** *v.t.* startle
**iznenaditi** *v.t.* surprise
**iznenadnost** *n.* sudden
**iznos** *n* amount
**iznos** *v.* amount
**iznositi** *v.i* amount
**iznošen** *a.* worn
**iznova brojati** *v.t.* recount
**iznova** *adv.* anew
**iznuren** *a.* prostrate
**iznurenost** *n* debility
**iznurenost** *n.* prostration
**izobara** *n.* isobar
**izobilje** *n.* riches
**izobličiti** *v. t* distort
**izolacija** *n.* insulation
**izolacija** *n.* isolation
**izolator** *n.* insulator
**izolovati** *v.t.* insulate
**izolovati** *v.t.* isolate
**izopačenost** *n.* perversity

**izostaviti** *v.t.* omit
**izostavljanje** *n.* omission
**izoštriti** *v.t* focus
**izoštriti** *v.t.* sharpen
**izračunati** *v. t.* calculate
**izrada** *n.* workmanship
**izraslina** *n.* wen
**izravan** *a* outright
**izravan** *a* through
**izravnati** *v. t* even
**izravnati** *v.t.* plane
**izravno** *adv.* outright
**izraz** *n.* expression
**izraz** *n.* locution
**izraz lica** *n.* countenance
**izrazit** *a* emphatic
**izraziti** *v. t.* express
**izraziti** *v.t.* phrase
**izraziti** *a.* wordy
**izraziti mimikom** *v.i* mime
**izražajan** *a.* expressive
**izreka** *n* byword
**izreka** *n* dictum
**izručiti** *v.t.* consign
**izrugivanje** *n.* mockery
**izrugivati se** *v.t.* lampoon
**izumeti** *v.t.* invent
**izumro** *a* extinct
**izustiti** *v.t.* mouth
**izustiti** *v.t.* utter
**izuzetak** *n* exception
**izuzeti** *v. t* except
**izuzev** *prep* save
**izvaditi iz korica** *v.t.* unsheathe
**izvan** *prep* outside
**izvan** *adv.* without
**izvan** *prep.* beyond
**izvanredan** *a.* extraordinary
**izvanredan** *a.* outstanding
**izvanredan** *a.* remarkable

**izvanredan** *a.* superb
**izvediv** *a.* manageable
**izvesnost** *n.* certainty
**izvesnost** *n.* surety
**izvesti** *v. t.* derive
**izvesti** *v.t.* perform
**izvestilac** *n.* informer
**izvestiti** *v.t.* account
**izvestiti** *v.t.* report
**izveštaj** *n.* report
**izviđač** *n* scout
**izviđati** *v.i* scout
**izvijač** *n.* spanner
**izvijati** *se v.i.* snake
**izviniti** *se v.i.* apologize
**izvinjenje** *n.* apology
**izvirti** *v.i.* well
**izvlačenje** *n* draw
**izvod** *n.* precis
**izvođač** *n.* performer
**izvođač radova** *n* contractor
**izvođenje** *n.* performance
**izvođenje** *n.* pursuance
**izvodljiv** *a* feasible
**izvodljiv** *a.* practicable
**izvodljivost** *n.* practicability
**izvor** *n.* source
**izvoz** *n* export
**izvoziti** *v. t.* export
**izvrsnost** *n.* excellence
**izvršenje** *n* execution
**izvršilac** *n.* executioner
**izvršiti** *v. t* execute

# J

**ja** *pron.* I
**jabuka** *n.* apple
**jad** *n.* woe

**jadan** *a* deplorable
**jadan** *a.* pitiable
**jadan** *a.* poor
**jadikovanje** *n* wail
**jadikovati** *v.i.* wail
**jagnje** *n* agnus
**jagnje** *n.* lamb
**jagnješce** *n.* lambkin
**jagoda** *n.* strawberry
**jahač** *n.* rider
**jahta** *n.* yacht
**jaje** *n* egg
**jajnik** *n.* ovary
**jak** *a.* strong
**jak** *n.* yak
**jaka pamučna tkanina** *n.* jean
**jaka tačka** *n.* forte
**jakna** *n.* jacket
**jalovo** *adj.* acarpous
**jama** *n.* pit
**jamčiti** *v.i.* vouch
**jarac** *n* Capricorn
**jarak** *n* ditch
**jaram** *n.* yoke
**jarbol** *n.* mast
**jasle** *n.* manger
**jaslice** *n.* nursery
**jasmin** *n.* jasmine, jessamine
**jasno** *a* clear
**jasnoća** *n* clarity
**jastog** *n.* lobster
**jastreb** *n* hawk
**jastuk** *n* cushion
**jastuk** *n.* pad
**jastuk** *n* pillow
**jato divljih ptica** *n.* skein
**javiti putem radija** *v.t.* radio
**javni** *a.* public
**javnost** *n.* public
**javor** *n.* sycamore

jazavac *n.* badger
jazbina *n.* burrow
jazbina *n* den
jazbina *n.* lair
jecaj *n* sob
jecati *v.i.* sob
ječam *n.* barley
jedan *a.* one
jedan slog *n.* monosyllable
jedanaest *n* eleven
jedini *a.* only
jedini *a. single*
jedini *a* sole
jedinica *n. unit*
jedinstven *a.* inimitable
jedinstven *a.* unique
jedinstvo *n.* oneness
jedinstvo *n.* unity
jednačina *n* equation
jednake vrednosti *a.* tantamount
jednako *a* equal
jednako *adv.* alike
jednakost *n* equality
jednakost *n.* par
jednakostranični *a* equilateral
jednoglasan *a.* unanimous
jednoglasje *n.* unison
jednoglasnost *n.* unanimity
jednoličan *a.* humdrum
jednom *adv.* once
jednom *adv.* sometime
jednook *a.* monocular
jednosložan *a.* monosyllabic
jednostavan *a.* plain
jednostavan *a.* simple
jednostavnost *n* ease
jednostavnost *n.* simplicity
jednostran *a* ex-parte
jednostrano *adv e* x-parte
jedrilica *n.* glider

jedriti *v.i.* sail
jedro *n.* sail
jedva *adv.* hardly
jedva *adv.* scarcely
jedva *adv.* barely
jeftin *a* cheap
jeftin *a.* inexpensive
jela *n* fir
jelen *n* deer
jelen *n.* stag
jelo *n* dish
jelovnik *n.* menu
jemac *n.* warrantor
jemčiti *v. t.* bail
jemstvo *n.* bail
jen *n.* Yen
jer *conj.* for
jer *conj.* because
jesen *n* fall
jesen *n.* autumn
jesti *v. t* eat
jestiv *a* eatable
jestivo *a* edible
jestivost *n.* eatable
jetra *n.* liver
jevanđelje *n.* gospel
Jevrejin *n.* Jew
jeza *n.* chill
jeza *n* shudder
jezero *n.* lake
jezgro *n.* core
jezgro *n.* nucleus
jezički *a.* linguistic
jezični *a.* lingual
jezik *n.* language
jezik *n.* tongue
jeziv *a.* ghastly
ježiti se *v.i.* shudder
jogunast *a.* restive
jogunast *a.* unruly

**jorgan** *n.* quilt
**jorgovan** *n.* lilac
**još** *a.* more
**još** *adv.* yet
**još uvek** *adv.* still
**jubilej** *n.* jubilee
**juče** *adv.* yesterday
**jučerašnji dan** *n.* yesterday
**jug** *n.* south
**junaštvo** *n.* heroism
**junaštvo** *n.* prowess
**junaštvo** *n.* valour
**june** *n* bullock
**junior** *n.* junior
**jupiter** *n.* jupiter
**jurisprudencija** *n.* jurisprudence
**juriš** *n.* onslaught
**jurišati** *v.i.* storm
**juriti** *v. t.* chase
**jurnuti** *v. i.* dash
**juta** *n.* jute
**jutro** *n.* morning
**jutro** *n.* morrow
**jutro (površina)** *n.* acre
**juvelir** *n.* jeweller
**južni** *a.* southerly
**južni** *a.* southern
**južni krajevi** *n.* south
**južno** *adv* south

# K

**ka** *prep.* towards
**kabare** *n.* cabaret
**kabel** *n.* cable
**kabina** *n* booth
**kabinet** *n.* cabinet
**kabl** *n* cord
**kaciga** *n.* helmet

**kad** *conj.* when
**kad god** *adv. conj* whenever
**kada** *n.* tub
**kada** *adv.* when
**kadet** *n.* cadet
**kadionica** *n* censer
**kaditi tamjanom** *v.t.* incense
**kaditi** *v. t* cense
**kadmijum** *n* cadmium
**kafa** *n* coffee
**kafić** *n.* cafe
**kajsija** *n.* apricot
**kakav** *a.* what
**kako** *adv.* how
**kaktus** *n.* cactus
**kalajisati** *v.t.* tin
**kalcijum** *n* calcium
**kalem** *n.* graft
**kalem** *n.* reel
**kalemiti** *v.t* graft
**kalemiti** *v.t.* inoculate
**kalemljenje** *n.* inoculation
**kalendar** *n.* calendar
**kaligrafija** *n* calligraphy
**kalijum** *n.* potassium
**kaljati** *v.t.* soil
**kalorija** *n.* calorie
**kaluđer** *n.* votary
**kaluđerica** *n.* nun
**kaluđerički veo** *n.* wimple
**kalup** *n.* mould
**kamelot** *n* camlet
**kamen** *n.* stone
**kamenit** *a.* stony
**kamenolom** *n.* quarry
**kamenovati** *v.t.* stone
**kamera** *n.* camera
**kamfor** *n.* camphor
**kamila** *n.* camel
**kamion** *n.* lorry

kamion *n.* truck
kamp *n.* camp
kampanja *n.* campaign
kampovati *v. i.* camp
kanadska kuna *n.* mink
kanal *n* channel
kanal *n.* canal
kanalizacija *n.* sewerage
kancelar *n.* chancellor
kancelarija *n.* office
kancelarijski pribor *n.* stationery
kandidat *n.* applicant
kandidat *n* nominee
kandidat *n.* candidate
kandža *n* claw
kanister *n.* canister
kanon *n* canon
kanonada *n. v. & t* cannonade
kanta *n.* pail
kanta *n* bucket
kantina *n.* canteen
kanton *n* canton
kao što *v.t.* like
kao *conj.* as
kap *n* drop
kapa *n* bonnet
kapa *n* coif
kapa *n.* cap
kapacitet *n.* capacity
kapanje *n* drip
kapati *v. i* drip
kapati *v. i* drop
kapati *v.i.* trickle
kapela *n.* chapel
kapetan *n.* skipper
kapetan *n.* captain
kapija *n.* gate
kapital *n.* capital
kapitalista *n.* capitalist
kapitulirati *v. t* capitulate

kapljica *n.* minim
kapric *n.* whim
kapriciozan *a.* whimsical
kapriciozan *a.* capricious
kaput *n* coat
kaput *n.* overcoat
karakter *n.* character
karakteristika *n.* attribute
karamela *n.* toffee
karanfil, ružičasta boja *n.* pink
karat *n.* carat
karavan *n.* caravan
karbid *n.* carbide
kardinal *n.* cardinal
kardinalan *a.* cardinal
karfiol *n.* cauliflower
karijera *n.* career
karika *n* fetter
karikatura *n.* caricature
karneval *n* carnival
karta *n* fare
karta *n.* ticket
kartica *n.* card
karton *n.* cardboard
karton *n* carton
kas *n* trot
kasati *v.i.* trot
kaseta *n.* cassette
kaskada *n.* cascade
kasnije *adv.* afterwards
kasniji *a.* latter
kasno *a.* late
kasta *n* caste
kastrirati *v.t.* geld
kaša *n.* mash
kaša *n.* mush
kaša *n.* porridge
kašalj *n.* cough
kašika *n.* spoon
kašljati *v. i.* cough

katalog *n.* catalogue
katarakt *n.* cataract
katastrofa *n* disaster
katastrofalan *a* disastrous
katedrala *n.* minster
katedrala *n.* cathedral
kategoričan *a.* categorical
kategorija *n.* category
katolički *a.* catholic
katran *n.* tar
kauč *n.* couch
kavaljer *n* gallant
kavez za ptice *n.* aviary
kavez *n.* cage
kavga *n* affray
kavga *n.* scuffle
kazna *n* fine
kazna *n.* penalty
kazna *n.* punishment
kazneni *a.* penal
kazneni *a.* punitive
kazniti *v.t* find
kazniti *v.t.* penalize
kazniti *v.t.* punish
kazniti *v. t.* castigate
kažiprst *n* forefinger
kecelja *n.* apron
kečap *n.* ketchup
kedar *n.* cedar
keks *n* biscuit
keramika *n* ceramics
kerozin *n.* kerosene
kesten *n.* chestnut
kestenjast *a* maroon
kestenjasta boja *n.* maroon
kicoš *n* dandy
kičma *n.* spine
kičmeni *a.* spinal
kidisati *v.i.* swoop
kidnapovati *v.t.* kidnap

kijanje *n* sneeze
kikotati se *v.i.* giggle
Kina *n.* china
kinin *n.* quinine
kinuti *v.i.* sneeze
kipeti *v.i.* seethe
kiselina *n* acid
kiselost *n.* acidity
kiseo *a* acid
kiseo *a.* sour
kiseonik *n.* oxygen
kiša *n* rain
kišobran *n.* umbrella
kišovit *a.* rainy
kit *n.* whale
kita cveća *n.* nosegay
kitnjast *a.* gaudy
kitova kost *n.* baleen
kladiti se *v.i* bet
kladiti se *v.i.* wager
klasa *n* class
klasičan *a* classic
klasičan *a* classical
klasifikacija *n* classification
klasik *n* classic
klati *v. t* butcher
klatiti *v. t* dangle
klatno *n.* pendulum
klauzula *n* clause
klavir *n.* piano
klečati *v.i.* kneel
klesati *v. t.* chisel
klešta *n. pl.* tongs
kleti se *v.i.* sweat
kletva *n* curse
kleveta *n* defamation
kleveta *n.* libel
kleveta *n.* slander
klevetati *v. t.* defame
klevetati *v.t.* malign

klevetati *v.t.* slander
klevetati *v. t.* calumniate
klevetnički *a.* slanderous
klica *n.* chit
klica *n.* germ
klicanje *n* acclamation
klijanje *n.* germination
klijati *v.i.* germinate
klijent *n..* client
klima *n.* climate
klimati *v.i* wobble
klimati glavom *v.i.* nod
klin *n.* peg
klin *n.* wedge
klinika *n.* clinic
klip *n.* piston
klizaljka *n.* skate
klizati *v.t.* skate
klizav *a* slick
klizav *a.* slippery
kliziti *v.t.* glide
kliziti *v.i.* slide
kljova *n.* tusk
kljucanje *n.* peck
kljucati *v.i.* peck
ključ *n.* key
ključanje *n* boil
ključati *v.i.* boil
ključati *v.t* ferment
kljun *n* beak
klopotati *n. & v. i* clack
klovn *n* clown
klub *n* club
klupa *n* bench
klupko *n.* clew
kmet *n.* serf
kneževski *a.* princely
knjiga *n* book
knjigovođa *n* book-keeper
knjiški moljac *n* book-worm

knjiški *n.* bookish
književni *a.* literary
književnost *n.* literature
ko *pron.* who
koalicija *n* coalition
kobalt *n* cobalt
kobila *n.* mare
kobra *n* cobra
kocka *n* cube
kockanje *n* gamble
kockar *n.* gambler
kockast *a* cubical
kockati se *v. i.* dice
kockati se *v.i.* gamble
kocke *n.* dice
kočija *n.* carriage
kočija *n* chariot
kočija, trener *n* coach
kočijaš *n* coachman
kočiti *v. t* brake
kočnica *n* skid
kočnica *n* brake
kočoperenje *n* stalk
kod *prep* by
kod *n* code
koedukacija *n.* co-education
koeficijent *n.* coefficient
koegzistencija *n* co-existence
koegzistirati *v. i* co-exist
koga *pron.* whom
koji *pron.* as
koji *rel. pron.* that
koji *pron.* which
koji *a* which
koji draži *a.* irritant
koji god *pron* whichever
koji izgleda *a* look
koji je kao tkivo *a.* webby
koji je obavezan *n.* incumbent
koji nije plemenit *a.* ignoble

koji opominje *a.* monitory
koji oživljava *a.* resurgent
koji podseća *a.* reminiscent
koji preživa *a.* ruminant
koji sadrži obećanje *a.* promissory
koji jede drvo *a.* xylophagous
koji se može baciti *a* projectile
koji se može dobiti *a.* obtainable
koji se može prati *a.* washable
koji se može prodati *a.* marketable
koji se može prodati *a.* salable
koji je monogaman *a.* monogynous
koji se rađa *a.* nascent
koji se sastavlja *adj.* confluent
koji se tiče zapešća *adj* carpal
koji zadržava *a.* retentive
koji živi na drvetu *a.* xylophilous
kokain *n* cocaine
kokodakati *v. i* cackle
kokos *n* coconut
kokosovo vlakno *n* coir
kokoš *n.* chicken
kokošinjac *n.* roost
kokoška *n.* bantam
kokoška *n.* hen
kokpit *n.* cock-pit
koks *v. t* coke
kola *n.* wain
kolabirati *v. i* collapse
kolac *n.* pale
kolac *n.* picket
kolebati se *v.i.* shilly-shally
kolebati se *v.i.* vacillate
kolebljiv *n.* shilly-shally
koledž *n* college
kolega *n* colleague
kolega *n* fellow
kolekcija *n* collection
kolekcionar *n* collector
kolektivno *a* collective

koleno *n.* knee
kolera *n.* cholera
kolevka *n* cradle
koliba *n.* cabin
koliba *n* cottage
koliba *n.* hut
kolica *n.* cart
količina *n.* quantity
količnik *n.* quotient
kolona *n* column
kolonija *n* colony
kolonijalan *a* colonial
kolosek *n.* gauge
kolosek *n.* rut
koma *n.* coma
komad *n.* piece
komadati *v.* tear
komadić *n* bit
komandant *n* commander
komarac *n.* mosquito
kombi *n.* van
kombinacija *n* combination
kombinovati *v. t* combine
kombinovan *a.* combined
komedija *n.* comedy
komemoracija *n.* commemoration
komemoracija *n.* memorial
komemorativan *a* memorial
komentar *n* comment
komentar *n* commentary
komentarisati *v. i* comment
komentator *n* commentator
komešanje *n.* fuss
kometa *n* comet
komičan *a* comic
komičar *n.* comedian
komičar *n* comic
komonvelt *n.* commonwealth
komora *n.* chamber
kompaktan *a.* compact

**kompanija** *n.* company
**komparativno** *a* comparative
**kompas** *n* compass
**kompenzacija** *n* compensation
**kompleks** *n* complex
**kompletan** *a* complete
**kompletirati** *v. t* complete
**komplikacija** *n.* complication
**komplikovati** *v. t* complicate
**kompliment** *n.* compliment
**kompozitor** compositor
**komšija** *n.* neighbour
**komšiluk** *n.* neighbourhood
**komuna** *v. t* commune
**komunalan** *a* communal
**komunicirati** *v. t* communicate
**komunikacija** *n.* communication
**komunizam** *n* communism
**konačan** *a* final
**konačan** *a* finite
**konačište** *n.* lodging
**konačni** *a.* terminal
**konačno** *adv.* eventually
**koncepcija** *n* conception
**koncept** *n* concept
**koncert** *n.* concert
**koncizan** *a* concise
**kondenzovati** *v. t* condense
**kondukter** *n* conductor
**konferencija** *n* conference
**konfiskacija** *n* confiscation
**konfiskovati** *v. t* confiscate
**konflikt** *n.* conflict
**kongres** *n* congress
**konj** *n.* horse
**konj** *n.* steed
**konjanik** *n* chevalier
**konjica** *n.* cavalry
**konjukcija** *n.* conjuncture
**konkretan** *a* concrete

**konkubina** *n* concubine
**konkubinat** *n.* concubinage
**konkurentan** *a* competitive
**konobar** *n.* waiter
**konobarica** *n.* waitress
**konoplja** *n.* hemp
**konsenzus** *n.* consensus
**konsolidacija** *n* consolidation
**konsolidovati** *v. t.* consolidate
**konstruisati** *v. t.* construct
**konstrukcija** *n* construction
**konsultacije** *n* consultation
**konsultovati** *v. t* consult
**kontakt** *n.* contact
**kontaktirati** *v. t* contact
**kontaminirati** *v.t.* contaminate
**kontekst** *n* context
**kontinent** *n* continent
**kontinentalni** *a* continental
**kontinuitet** *n* continuity
**kontracepcija** *n.* contraception
**kontradikcija** *n.* antinomy
**kontradikcija** *n* contradiction
**kontrast** *n* contrast
**kontrola** *n* control
**kontrolisati** *v. t* control
**kontrolor** *n.* controller
**kontura** *n* contour
**kontuzovati** *v.t.* contuse
**konvencija** *n.* convention
**konverzija** *n* conversion
**konzerva** *n.* tin
**konzervativan** *a* conservative
**konzervativanost** *n* conservative
**konzervirati** *v. t.* can
**konzola** *n* ancon
**konzola** *v. t* console
**konzumacija** *n* consumption
**koordinacija** *n* co-ordination
**kopač** *n.* pitman

kopanje *n* dig
kopati *v.t.* dig
kopati *v.t.* shovel
kopati lopatom *v.t.* spade
kopča *n* clasp
kopča *n* buckle
kopija *n* copy
kopile *n.* bastard
kopirati *v. t* copy
kopito *n.* hoof
kopljanik *n.* lancer
koplje *n.* javelin
koplje *n.* lance
koplje *n.* spear
kopriva *n.* nettle
koprologija *n.* coprology
kora *n.* crust
kora *n.* peel
kora *n.* bark
koračati *v.i.* pace
koračati *v.i.* step
koračati *v.i.* stride
koračati *v.t.* tread
korak *n* pace
korak *n.* step
korak *n* stride
koral *n* coral
koralno ostrvo *n.* atoll
korekcija *n* correction
korelacija *n.* correlation
koren *n.* root
korice *n.* scabbard
koridor *n.* corridor
korijander *n.* coriander
Korint *n.* Corinth
korisnost *n.* utility
korist *n.* sake
korist *n.* subservience
korist *n* behalf
korist *n* benefit

koristan *a* beneficial
koristan *a.* helpful
koristan *a.* subservient
koristan *a.* useful
koristiti aliteraciju *v.* alliterate
korišćenje *n.* utilization
koriti *v.t.* rebuke
kormilo *n.* helm
kormoran *n.* cormorant
kornet *n.* cornet
kornjača *n.* tortoise
kornjača *n.* turtle
korov *n.* weed
korozivan *adj.* corrosive
korpa *n.* basket
korporacija *n* corporation
korpus *n* corps
korumpiran *a.* corrupt
korumpirati *v. t.* corrupt
korupcija *n.* corruption
korupcija *n.* jobbery
kosa *n* hair
kosa *n.* scythe
kosina *n* bias
kositi *v.t.* mow
kosmički *adj.* cosmic
kost *n.* bone
kostim *n.* costume
košnica *n.* hive
košnica *n.* beehive
koštati *v.t.* cost
koštica *n.* kernel
košulja *n.* shirt
košuljica zmije *n.* slough
kotlar *n.* tinker
kotrljati *v.i.* roll
kotrljati *v.t.* wheel
kotur *n.* pulley
kovač *n.* smith
kovač *n* blacksmith

kovačnica *n* forge
kovanica *n* coinage
kovati *v.t.* mint
kovati zaveru *v. i.* conspire
kovčeg *n.* ark
kovčeg *n* casket
koverat *n* envelope
kovitlac *n.i.* whirl
kovnica *n* mint
koza *n.* goat
kozmetički *a.* cosmetic
kozmetika *n.* cosmetic
koža *n.* cutis
koža *n.* leather
koža *n.* skin
kožar *n.* tanner
kožara *n.* tannery
kožuh *n.* jerkin
kraba *n* crab
krađa *n.* theft
krađa stoke *n* abaction
kradljivac stoke *n* abactor
kraj *n.* the end
kraj *n.* terminus
kraj *n.* tip
krajnik *n.* tonsil
krajnji *a.* ultimate
krajnji *a.* utmost
krajnost *n* utmost
kralj *n.* king
kraljevina *n.* kingdom
kraljevski *a.* regal
kraljevski *a.* royal
kraljevstvo *n.* royalty
kraljica *n.* queen
kraljoubistvo *n.* regicide
krastavac *n* cucumber
krasuljak *n* daisy
kratak *a.* short
kratak *a.* brief

kratko *adv.* short
kratkoća *n* brevity
kratkovid *a.* myopic
kratkovidost *n.* myopia
krava *n.* cow
kravata *n* tie
krčag *n.* jug
krčag *n.* pitcher
krčkati *v.i.* simmer
krčma *n.* inn
krčma *n.* saloon
krčma *n.* tavern
krćiti *v.t.* pioneer
kreativan *adj.* creative
kreč *n.* lime
kredit *n* credit
kredo *n* creed
kreirati *v. t* create
kreker *n* cracker
krema *n* cream
kremiranje *n* cremation
kremirati *v. t* cremate
kresta *n.* aigrette
kreštav *a.* strident
kretanje *n.* motion
kretati se *v.t* ambulate
krevet *n* bed
krevetac *n.* cot
krevetac *n.* crib
krez *n.* croesus
krhak *a.* fragile
krigla *n.* mug
krilat *adj.* aliferous
krilo *n.* wing
kriminal *n* criminal
kripta *n* cist
kriptografija *n.* cryptography
kristal *n* crystal
krišom *adv.* stealthily
kriterijum *n* criterion

kritičan *adj* censorious
kritičan *a* critical
kritičar *n* critic
kritika *n.* censure
kritika *n* criticism
kritikovati *v. t.* censure
kritikovati *v. t* criticize
kriv *a* culpable
kriv *a.* guilty
kriva *v. t* curve
krivac *n* culprit
krivica *n.* guilt
krivični *a.* tortuous
krivično *a* criminal
krivina *n* curve
kriviti *v. t* blame
krivokletstvo *n.* perjury
krivudav *adj* anfractuous
kriza *n* crisis
kriza *n.* slump
krma *n.* stern
krmača *n.* sow
krojač *n.* tailor
krojiti *v.t.* tailor
krokodil *n* crocodile
krompir *n.* potato
krotak *a.* meek
krov *n.* roof
kroz *prep.* through
krpa *n.* rag
krpiti *v.t.* stitch
krst *n* cross
krstarica *n* cruiser
krstariti *v.i.* cruise
krstaški pohod *n* crusade
krstiti *v.t.* baptize
krš *n.* rubble
kršan *a.* robust
kršenje *n.* violation
krštenje *n.* baptism

krt *a.* brittle
krtica *n.* mole
krug *n.* circle
krug *n* cycle
kruna *n* crown
krunisanje *n* coronation
krunisati *v. t* crown
krupan *a.* massy
krupan *a.* stout
kruška *n.* pear
krut *n.* stiff
kruženje *n.* circuit
kružni *a* circular
kružni *a* cyclic
krv *n* blood
krvariti *v. i* bleed
krvav *a* bloody
krvni srodnik *adj* cognate
krvoproliće *n* bloodshed
krzno *n.* fur
ksilofon *n.* xylophone
kucati *v.t.* knock
kucati *v.i.* pulsate
kucati *v.i.* tick
kuća *n* house
kućica *n.* lodge
kućište *n.* casing
kuda *adv.* whither
kuditi *v.t* upbraid
kuga *n.* pestilence
kuga *a.* plague
kuglati *se v.i* bowl
kuhinja *n.* cuisine
kuhinja *n.* kitchen
kuja *n* bitch
kuk *n* hip
kuka *n.* crotchet
kuka *n.* hook
kukavica *n.* coward
kukavica *n* cuckoo

**kukavičluk** *n.* cowardice
**kukolj** *v. i* cockle
**kukuruz** *n* corn
**kukuruz** *n.* maize
**kula** *n.* rook
**kulminirati** *v.i.* culminate
**kult** *n* cult
**kultura** *n* culture
**kulturni** *a* cultural
**kuna** *n.* marten
**kupac** *n* customer
**kupac** *n.* buyer
**kupanje** *n* bath
**kupati** *se v. t* bathe
**kupidon** *n* Cupid
**kupiti** *v.t.* purchase
**kupiti** *v. t.* buy
**kuplet** *n.* couplet
**kupola** *n* dome
**kupon** *n.* coupon
**kupovati** *v.i.* shop
**kupovina** *n.* purchase
**kupus** *n.* cabbage
**kurir** *n.* courier
**kurir** *n.* messenger
**kurkuma** *n.* turmeric
**kurs** *n.* course
**kurtizana** *n.* courtesan
**kurva** *n.* slut
**kurziv** *n.* italics
**kurzivan** *a.* italic
**kutak** *n.* nook
**kutija** *n* box
**kutlača** *n.* ladle
**kutnjak** *n.* molar
**kuvar** *n* cook
**kuvati** *v. t* cook
**kvačilo** *n* clutch
**kvadrat** *n.* square
**kvaka** *n.* latch

**kvalifikacija** *n.* qualification
**kvalifikovati** *se v.i.* qualify
**kvalitativan** *a.* qualitative
**kvalitet** *n.* quality
**kvant** *n.* quantum
**kvantitativan** *a.* quantitative
**kvarenje** *n.* adulteration
**kvarljiv** *a.* perishable
**kvasac** *n* ferment
**kvasac** *n.* yeast
**kvašenje** *n.* soak
**kviz** *n.* quiz
**kvorum** *n.* quorum
**kvota** *n.* quota

# L

**labav** *a.* lax
**labav** *a.* loose
**labavost** *n.* laxity
**labijalni** *a.* labial
**laboratorija** *n.* laboratory
**laboratorijska posuda** *n.* cuvette
**labud** *n.* swan
**lagan dodir** *n* graze
**lagano** *adv.* leisurely
**lagati** *v.i.* lie
**laguna** *n.* lagoon
**laik** *n.* layman
**lajanje** *n* yap
**lajati** *v.t.* bark
**lajati** *v.i.* yap
**lak** *a* facile
**lak** *n* lac, lakh
**lak** *n.* varnish
**lakat** *n* elbow
**lakej** *n.* lackey
**laki galop** *n* canter
**lakirati** *v.t.* varnish

lako *a* easy
lako *a i*
lakomislenost *n* flippancy
lakomislenost *n.* levity
lakomo *adv* avidly
lakonski *a.* laconic
lakovernost *adj.* credulity
lakrdijaš *n* antic
lakrdijaš *n.* pantaloon
lakrdijaš *n* buffoon
laksativ *n.* laxative
laktoza *n.* lactose
lama *n.* lama
lampa *n.* lamp
lanac *n* chain
lanac *n.* tether
lanceta *a.* lancet
laneno seme *n.* linseed
lansiranje *n.* launch
lansirati *v.t.* launch
lapor *n.* marl
larmadžija *a.* rowdy
lascivan *a.* lascivious
laskanje *n* flattery
laskati *v.t* flatter
lasta *n.* swallow
latica *n.* petal
laureat *n* laureate
lauta *n.* lute
lav *n.* Leo
lav *n* lion
lava *n.* lava
lavanda *n.* lavender
lavica *n.* lioness
lavirint *n.* labyrinth
lavirint *n.* maze
lavovski *a* leonine
laž *n* lie
lažan *a* false
lažan *a* sham

lažan *a.* spurious
lažljiv *a.* mendacious
lažna vest *n* canard
lažno se zakleti *v.i.* perjure
lažov *n.* liar
lebdeti *v.t.* waft
lečiti *v. t.* cure
lečiti *v.i.* heal
lečiti *v.t.* physic
lečiti *v.t.* treat
led *n.* ice
leden *a.* icy
ledenica *n.* icicle
ledina *n.* lea
legalizovati *v.t.* legalize
legenda *n.* legend
legendaran *a.* legendary
legija *n.* legion
legionar *n.* legionary
legitiman *a.* legitimate
legitimitet *n.* legitimacy
leglo *n* brood
legura *žive n* amalgam
legura *n.* alloy
lek *n* cure
lek *n* drug
lek *n.* medicament
lek *v.t* remedy
lekar *n* doctor
lekar *n.* physician
lekar koji vakciniše *n.* vaccinator
lekcija *n.* lesson
lekovit *a* curative
leksikografija *n.* lexicography
leksikon *n.* lexicon
lelujanje *n.* undulation
lemljenje *n.* solder
lenj *a.* indolent
lenj *n.* lazy
lenj *n.* slothful

| | |
|---|---|
| **lenj** *a.* sluggish | **ležaj** *n* bearing |
| **lenjivac** *n.* sluggard | **ležaj** *n* bunk |
| **lenjost** *n.* laziness | **ležati** *v.i* lie |
| **lenjost** *n.* sloth | **ležeran** *a.* casual |
| **leopard** *n.* leopard | **ležerno** *a.* leisurely |
| **lep** *a* fair | **liberalan** *a.* liberal |
| **lep** *a.* nice | **liberalizam** *n.* liberalism |
| **lep** *a* pretty | **lice** *n* face |
| **lep** *a* beautiful | **lice** *n.* visage |
| **lepak** *n.* glue | **licemer** *n.* hypocrite |
| **lepak za ptice** *n* birdlime | **licemeran** *a.* hypocritical |
| **lepiti** *v.t.* paste | **licemerje** *n.* hypocrisy |
| **lepljiv** *n.* sticky | **licitacija** *n* auction |
| **lepljiva materija** *n.* adhesive | **licitirati** *v.t.* auction |
| **lepljiva materija** *a.* adhesive | **ličiti** *v.t.* resemble |
| **lepota** *n.* prettiness | **lični** *a* facial |
| **lepota** *n* beauty | **lični** *a.* personal |
| **lepotica** *n* belle | **ličnost** *n.* personality |
| **lepra** *n.* leprosy | **liga** *n.* league |
| **lepršanje** *n* flutter | **lignit** *n.* lignite |
| **lepršati** *v.t* flutter | **likovati** *v. i* exult |
| **leptir** *n* butterfly | **likvidacija** *n.* liquidation |
| **leš** *n* corpse | **likvidirati** *v.t.* liquidate |
| **lešinar** *n.* vulture | **limenka** *n.* can |
| **let** *n* flight | **limeta** *n.* lime |
| **letak** *n.* leaflet | **limun** *n.* lemon |
| **letargičan** *a.* lethargic | **limunada** *n.* lemonade |
| **letargija** *n.* lethargy | **limunski** *adj.* citric |
| **letelica** *n.* aircraft | **linč** *v.t.* lynch |
| **leteti** *v.i* fly | **lingvista** *n.* linguist |
| **letimičan pogled** *n.* glimpse | **lingvistika** *n.* linguistics |
| **letnji** *adj* aestival | **linija** *n.* line |
| **leto** *n.* summer | **lira** *n.* lyre |
| **letopis** *n.* chronicle | **liričar** *n.* lyricist |
| **letopisac** *n.* annalist | **lirika** *n.* lyric |
| **letopisi** *n.pl.* annals | **lirski** *a.* lyric |
| **letva** *n.* lath | **lirski** *a.* lyrical |
| **levica** *n.* left | **lisica** *n.* fox |
| **levičar** *n* leftist | **lisica** *n.* vixen |
| **levo** *a.* left | **lisice** *n.* handcuff |

**liskun** *n.* mica
**lisnat** *a.* leafy
**list** *n.* leaf
**list** *n.* sheet
**lišaj (oboljenje kože)** *n.* ringworm
**lišće** *n* foliage
**lišen** *a* devoid
**lišiti** *v. t* deprive
**litar** *n.* litre
**literatura** *n.* litterateur
**litica** *n.* cliff
**liturgijski** *a.* liturgical
**livada** *n.* meadow
**livnica** *n.* foundry
**livreja** *n.* livery
**lizalica** *n.* lollipop
**lizanje** *n* lick
**lizati** *v.t.* lick
**lobanja** *n.* skull
**locirati** *v.t.* locate
**logaritam** *n.* logarithim
**logičan** *a.* logical
**logičar** *n.* logician
**logika** *n.* logic
**loj** *n.* tallow
**lojalan** *a.* loyal
**lojalnost** *n.* loyalty
**lokacija** *n.* location
**lokalizovati** *v.t.* localize
**lokalni propis** *n* bylaw, bye-law
**lokalno** *a.* local
**lokomotiva** *n.* locomotive
**lom** *n* breakage
**lomača** *n.* pyre
**lomača** *n* bonfire
**lonac** *n.* pot
**lopata** *n.* shovel
**lopata** *n.* spade
**lopov** *n.* thief
**lopovski** *a.* roguish

**lopta** *n.* ball
**loptica za badminton** *n.* shuttlecock
**losion** *n.* lotion
**loš** *a.* vile
**loša procena** *n.* miscalculation
**loše** *adv.* ill
**loše poslovanje** *n.* maladministration
**loše pristajati** *n.* misfit
**loše proceniti** *v.t.* miscalculate
**loše spojiti** *v.t.* mismatch
**loše upravljanje** *n.* mismanagement
**loše varenje** *n.* indigestion
**loše vladanje** *n.* misconduct
**loše** *adv.* amiss
**loše** *a.* bad
**lotos** *n.* lotus
**lov** *n* hunt
**lovac** *n.* hunter
**lovac** *n.* huntsman
**lovački pas** *n.* hound
**loviti** *v.t.* hunt
**lovor** *n.* laurel
**loza** *n.* lineage
**lozinka** *v. t.* countersign
**lozinka** *n.* watchword
**ložač** *n.* stoker
**ložiti** *v.t.* stoke
**lubenica** *n.* water-melon
**lucidnost** *n.* lucidity
**lučenje** *n.* secretion
**lučiti** *v.t.* secrete
**lud** *a* crazy
**lud** *adj.* daft
**lud** *a.* insane
**lud** *a.* lunatic
**ludak** *n.* lunatic
**ludilo** *n.* insanity
**ludilo** *n.* lunacy
**ludiranje** *n.* romp
**luk** *n.* onion

**luk** *n.* arc
**luk** *n* bow
**luka** *n.* harbour
**luka** *n.* haven
**luka** *n.* port
**lukav** *a* crafty
**lukav** *a* cunning
**lukav** *a.* politic
**lukav** *a.* shrewd
**lukav** *a.* sly
**lukav** *a.* tricky
**lukav** *a.* wily
**lukav** *a.* artful
**lukavost** *n* cunning
**lukavstvo** *n.* guile
**lukavstvo** *n.* strategem
**lukavstvo** *n.* wile
**luksuz** *n.* luxury
**luksuzan** *a.* luxurious
**lunjati** *v.i.* rove
**lupanje** *n.* throb
**lupati** *v.i.* throb
**lupiti** *v.t.* bang
**lupiti** *v.t.* thump
**lutalica** *n.* rover
**lutalica** *n.* straggler
**lutalice** *n* stray
**lutanje** *n.* vagary
**lutati** *v.t* maroon
**lutati** *v.i.* roam
**lutati** *v.i.* straggle
**lutati** *v.i.* wander
**lutka** *n* doll
**lutrija** *n.* lottery

# LJ

**ljiljan** *n.* lily
**ljubav** *n* love

**ljubavna afera** *n* amour
**ljubavni** *adj* amatory
**ljubavnik** *n.* lover
**ljubavnik** *n.* paramour
**ljubazan** *a.* affable
**ljubazan** *a.* amiable
**ljubazno** *adv.* kindly
**ljubaznost** *n.* amiability
**ljubičast, ljubičasta** *adj./n.* purple
**ljubičica** *n.* violet
**ljubimac** *n.* minion
**ljubimac** *n.* pet
**ljubomora** *n.* jealousy
**ljubomoran** *a.* jealous
**ljudožderi** *n.* androphagi
**ljuljaška** *n* swing
**ljuljati** *v.t.* rock
**ljuljati** *v.i.* swing
**ljuljati** *v.t.* dandle
**ljuska** *n.* husk
**ljuštiti** *v.t.* shell
**ljut** *a.* spicy
**ljut** *a.* angry
**ljutina** *n* acrimony
**ljutnja** *n.* ire

# M

**ma kako** *adv.* however
**ma ko** *pron.* whoever
**ma koji** *adv.* any
**mač** *n.* sword
**mačak** *n.* tomcat
**mače** *n.* kitten
**mačka** *n.* cat
**mađioničar** *n.* magician
**magacin** *v.t* warehouse
**magarac** *n* donkey
**magarac** *n.* ass

**magijski** *a.* magical
**magistrat** *n.* magistracy
**magla** *n* fog
**maglina** *n.* nebula
**maglovit** *a.* hazy
**maglovit** *a.* misty
**magnat** *n.* magnate
**magnet** *n.* loadstone
**magnet** *n.* magnet
**magnetizam** *n.* magnetism
**magnetni** *a.* magnetic
**mahagoni** *n.* mahogany
**mahanje** *n* wag
**mahati** *v.i.* wag
**mahati** *v.i.* waver
**mahati** *v.t.* whisk
**mahovina** *n.* moss
**mahuna** *n.* pod
**maj** *n.* May
**majčinski** *a.* motherlike
**majka** *n* mother
**majmun** *n.* monkey
**majmun** *n* ape
**majmunski** *a.* apish
**major** *n* major
**majstorija** *n.* sleight
**majstorija** *n* stunt
**majstorski** *a.* masterly
**majstorstvo** *n.* mastery
**makaze** *n.* scissors
**makaze** *n. pl.* shears
**maksima** *n.* maxim
**maksimalan** *a.* maximum
**maksimalno povećati** *v.t.* maximize
**maksimum** *n* maximum
**malarična groznica** *n.* ague
**malarija** *n.* malaria
**male boginje** *n* measles
**malen** *a.* little
**malenkost** *n.* modicum

**mali** *a.* small
**mali** *n* small
**mali deo** *n.* pittance
**malignitet** *n.* malignity
**malj** *n.* maul
**malo** *a* few
**malo** *adv.* little
**malobrojnost** *n.* paucity
**malokrvnost** *n* anaemia
**maloletnik** *a.* juvenile
**maloletnik** *n* minor
**maloprodaja** *n.* retail
**maloprodajni** *a* retail
**maloprodajno** *adv.* retail
**malter** *v.t.* mortar
**maltertirati** *v.t.* manhandle
**maltretirati** *v.t.* mistreat
**malvazija** *n.* malmsey
**mama** *n* mum
**mamac** *n.* lure
**mamac** *n* bait
**mamica** *n* mummy
**mamon** *n.* mammon
**mamut** *n.* mammoth
**mamuza** *n.* spur
**mana** *n* blemish
**mana** *n i*
**mana** *n.* manna
**mana** *n.* shortcoming
**manastir** *n.* abbey
**manastir** *n.* monastery
**mandat** *n.* mandate
**mandat** *n.* tenure
**maneken** *n.* mannequin
**manevar** *n.* manoeuvre
**manevrisati** *v.i.* manoeuvre
**mangan** *n.* manganese
**mango** *n* mango
**mangup** *n.* reveller
**manifest** *n.* manifesto

| | |
|---|---|
| **manifestacija** *n.* manifestation | **masakr** *n.* massacre |
| **manifestovati** *v.t.* manifest | **masakrirati** *v.t.* massacre |
| **manija** *n* mania | **masaža** *n.* massage |
| **manijak** *n.* maniac | **maser** *n.* masseur |
| **manikir** *n.* manicure | **masirati** *v.t.* massage |
| **manipulacija** *n.* manipulation | **masivan** *a.* massive |
| **manipulisati** *v.t.* manipulate | **masivan** *a* molar |
| **manirizam** *n.* mannerism | **maska** *n.* mask |
| **manjak** *n.* shortage | **maskarada** *n.* masquerade |
| **manje** *adv.* less | **maskirati** *v.t.* mask |
| **manje** *prep.* less | **maskirati** *se v. t* bemask |
| **manje** *prep.* minus | **maskota** *n.* mascot |
| **manji** *a.* less | **maslačak** *n.* dandelion |
| **manji** *a.* lesser | **maslina** *n.* olive |
| **manji** *a.* minor | **masnica** *n.* weal |
| **manjina** *n.* minority | **mast** *n* fat |
| **manžetna** *n* cuff | **mast** *n* grease |
| **mapa** *n* map | **mast** *n.* ointment |
| **marama** *n.* kerchief | **mastan** *a.* greasy |
| **maramica** *n.* handkerchief | **mastan** *a.* oily |
| **maraton** *n.* marathon | **mastilo** *n.* ink |
| **margarin** *n.* margarine | **masturbirati** *v.i.* masturbate |
| **margina** *n.* margin | **mašinski** *a.* mechanical |
| **marginalni** *a.* marginal | **mašta** *n* fancy |
| **marioneta** *n.* marionette | **mašta** *n.* imagination |
| **marioneta** *n.* puppet | **maštovit** *a.* imaginative |
| **mariti** *v.i.* matter | **mat** *n* checkmate |
| **mariti** *v.t.* mind | **matador** *n .* matador |
| **marka** *n* brand | **matematičar** *n.* mathematician |
| **marker** *n.* marker | **matematički** *a.* mathematical |
| **marljiv** *a* diligent | **matematika** *n* mathematics |
| **marljiv** *a.* studious | **materica** *n.* uterus |
| **marljivost** *n* diligence | **materica** *n.* womb |
| **marmelada** *n.* marmalade | **materijal** *n* material |
| **mars** *n* Mars | **materijal** *n.* stuff |
| **marš** *n.* march | **materijalan** *a.* material |
| **maršal** *n* marshal | **materijalizam** *n.* materialism |
| **marširati** *v.i* march | **materijalizovati** *v.t.* materialize |
| **mart** *n* march | **materinski** *a.* maternal |
| **masa** *n.* mass | **materinski** *a.* motherly |

materinstvo *n.* maternity
materinstvo *n.* motherhood
maternji *a.* native
materoubilački *a.* matricidal
materoubistvo *n.* matricide
matičar *n.* registrar
matine *n.* matinee
matirati *v.t.* mate
matrica *n* matrix
matrica *n.* stencil
matrijarh *n.* matriarch
matrona *n.* matron
matura *n.* matriculation
mauzolej *n.* mausoleum
mazarija *n.* daub
mazati *v.t.* anoint
mazga *n.* mule
maziti *v. t* cocker
mazivo *n.* lubricant
meander *v.i.* meander
meč *n.* match
mećava *n* blizzard
med *n.* honey
međa *n* boundary
medalja *n.* medal
medaljon *n.* locket
medeni mesec *n.* honeymoon
medicina *n.* medicine
medicina *n.* physic
medicinska sestra *n.* nurse
medicinski *a.* medical
medicinski *a.* medicinal
medijum *n* medium
meditirati *v.t.* meditate
medovina *n.* mead
među *prep.* amid
među *prep.* among
međuvreme *n.* interim
međuzavisan *a.* interdependent
međuzavisnost *n.* interdependence

medved *n* bear
megafon *n.* megaphone
megalitski *a.* megalithic
meh *n.* bellows
mehaničar *n.* mechanic
mehanički *a* mechanic
mehanika *n.* mechanics
mehanizam *n.* mechanism
mehurić *n* bubble
mekan *a.* pulpy
melanholičan *a.* melancholic
melanholija *n.* melancholia
melasa *n* molasses
melem *n.* balm
melez *a* mongrel
melodičan *a.* melodious
melodija *n.* melody
melodija *n.* tune
melodrama *n.* melodrama
melodramatičan *a.* melodramatic
membrana *n.* membrane
memoari *n.* memoir
memorandum *n* memorandum
memorija *n.* memory
menadžer *n.* manager
menadžerski *a.* managerial
mene *pron.* me
meningitis *n.* meningitis
menjati *v.t.* shift
menopauza *n.* menopause
menstruacija *n.* menstruation
menstrualni *a.* menstrual
mentalitet *n.* mentality
mentalni *a.* mental
mentor *n.* mentor
menzis *n.* menses
mera *n.* measure
mera *n.* measurement
mercerizirati *v.t.* mercerise
merdevine *n.* ladder

**meridijan** *a.* meridian
**meriti** *v.t* measure
**merkur** *n.* mercury
**merljiv** *a.* measurable
**mermer** *n.* marble
**merodavan** *a.* magisterial
**mesar** *n* butcher
**mesec** *n.* month
**mesec** *n.* moon
**mesečar** *n.* somnambulist
**mesečarenje** *n.* somnambulism
**mesečev** *a.* lunar
**mesečni** *a.* monthly
**mesečnik** *n* monthly
**mesečno** *adv* monthly
**mesija** *n.* messiah
**mesing** *n.* brass
**meso** *n* flesh
**meso** *n.* meat
**mesto** *n.* locus
**mesto** *n.* place
**mesto** *n.* position
**mesto** *n.* spot
**mešanje** *n* amalgamation
**mešati** *n* blend
**mešati** *v.t.* mingle
**mešati** *v.i* mix
**mešati** *v.t.* temper
**mešati sa živom** *v.t.* amalgamate
**mešati se** *v.i.* meddle
**mešavina** *n* compound
**mešavina** *n.* mixture
**mešovit** *a.* miscellaneous
**mešovit žargon** *n.* lingua franca
**meta** *n* bull's eye
**metabolizam** *n.* metabolism
**metafizički** *a.* metaphysical
**metafizika** *n.* metaphysics
**metafora** *n.* metaphor
**metak** *n* bullet

**metal** *n.* metal
**metalni** *a.* metallic
**metalurgija** *n.* metallurgy
**metamorfoza** *n.* metamorphosis
**metar** *n.* meter
**metar** *n.* metre
**metarski** *a.* metrical
**meteor** *n.* meteor
**meteorolog** *n.* meteorologist
**meteorologija** *n.* meteorology
**meteorski** *a.* meteoric
**metež** *n* babel
**metež** *n* commotion
**metež** *n.* tumult
**metež** *n.* uproar
**metla** *n.* *mop*
**metla** *n* broom
**metod** *n.* method
**metodičan** *a.* methodical
**metrički** *a.* metric
**metropola** *n.* metropolis
**metropolit** *n.* metropolitan
**metropolitski** *a.* metropolitan
**metvica** *n.* mint
**mezalijansa** *n.* misalliance
**mezanin** *n.* mezzanine
**mig** *n.* beck
**mig** *n* wink
**migracija** *n.* migration
**migrant** *n.* migrant
**migrena** *n.* migraine
**migrirati** *v.i.* migrate
**mijalgija** *n.* myalgia
**mijoza** *n.* myosis
**mikrofilm** *n.* microfilm
**mikrofon** *n.* microphone
**mikrologija** *n.* micrology
**mikrometar** *n.* micrometer
**mikroskop** *n.* microscope
**mikroskopski** *a.* microscopic

mikrotalasna peć *n.* microwave
milenijum *n.* millennium
milicija *n.* militia
milijarda *n* billion
milion *n.* million
milioner *n.* millionaire
militant *n* militant
milja *n.* mile
miljaža *n.* mileage
milosrđe *n.* charity
milost *n.* grace
milost *n.* mercy
milostinja *n.* alms
milostiv *a.* gracious
milostiv *a.* merciful
milovanje *n* stroke
milovati *v.t* fondle
milovati *v.t.* pet
milovati *v.t.* stroke
milovati *v. t.* caress
mimičar *n* mimic
mimika *n.* mime
mimikrija *n.* mimesis
mimikrija *n* mimicry
minaret *n.* minaret
mineral *n.* mineral
mineralni *a* mineral
mineralog *n.* mineralogist
mineralogija *n.* mineralogy
minijatura *a.* miniature
minijaturan *n.* miniature
minimalan *a.* minimal
minimalan *a* minimum
minimum *n.* minimum
ministar *n.* minister
ministarstvo *n.* ministry
ministrant *a.* ministrant
minus *n* minus
minut *a.* minute
miomirisan *a.* odorous

mir *n.* calm
mir *n.* peace
mir *n.* quiet
mir *n.* still
mir *n.* tranquility
miran *a.* mum
miran *a.* peaceful
miran *a.* placid
miran *a.* quiet
miran *a.* still
miran *a.* tranquil
miraz *n* dowry
miris *n.* fragrance
miris *n.* odour
miris *n.* savour
miris *n.* scent
miris *n.* smell
mirisan *a.* fragrant
mirisati *v.t.* savour
mirisati *v.t.* scent
mirisati *v.t.* smell
mirisna smola *n.* myrrh
miroljubiv *a.* pacific
miroljubiv *a.* peaceable
mirta *n.* myrtle
misao *n* thought
misija *n.* mission
misionar *n.* missionary
mislilac *n.* thinker
misliti *v.t.* opine
misliti *v.i.* reason
misliti *v.t.* think
misterija *n.* mystery
misteriozan *a.* mysterious
misticizam *n.* mysticism
mističan *a.* mystic
mistifikovati *v.t.* mystify
mistik *n* mystic
mistrija *n.* trowel
miš *n.* mouse

mišić *n.* muscle
mišićav *a.* muscular
mišljenje *n.* opinion
mit *n.* myth
mitariti se *v.i.* moult
mito *n* bribe
mitologija *n.* mythology
mitološki *a.* mythological
mitra *n.* mitre
mitski *a.* mythical
mizantrop *n.* misanthrope
mjaukati *v.i.* mew
mlad *a.* adolescent
mlad *a.* young
mladalački *a.* youthful
mladi *n* young
mlađi *a.* junior
mladić *n.* youngster
mladica *n.* offshoot
mladica *n.* sapling
mladica *n* sprout
mladih *n.* youth
mladost *n.* adolescence
mladoženja *n.* groom
mladoženja *n.* bridegroom
mladunče *n* cub
mlak *a.* lukewarm
mlatiti *v.t.* thrash
mlaz *n* spurt
mlaznica *n.* nozzle
mlaznjak *n.* jet
mlečan *a.* milky
mlečni *a.* mammary
mlečni *a.* milch
mlekara *n* dairy
mleko *n.* milk
mlekomer *n.* lactometer
mleti *v.i.* grind
mleti *v.t.* mill
mlin *n.* grinder

mlin *n.* mill
mlinar *n.* miller
mlitav *a* flabby
mnogo *a.* many
mnogo *a* much
mnogo *n.* plenty
mnogonog *n.* multiped
mnogostruk *a.* manifold
mnogostruk *a.* multiple
mnogostrukost *n.* multiplicity
mnoštvo *n.* lot
mnoštvo *n.* multitude
mnoštvo *n* shoal
množenik *n.* multiplicand
množenje *n.* multiplication
množina *a.* plural
mobilisati *v.t.* mobilize
moć *n.* leverage
moćan *adj.* mighty
moćan *a.* powerful
močiti *v.t.* steep
močvara *n.* marsh
močvara *n.* slough
močvara *n.* swamp
močvara *n* bog
močvaran *a.* marshy
moć *n.* might
moći *v* may
moći *v.* can
moda *n* fashion
moda *n.* vogue
modalitet *n.* modality
model *n.* model
moderan *a* fashionable
moderan *a.* modern
modernizovati *v.t.* modernize
modernost *n.* modernity
modifikacija *n.* modification
modifikovati *v.t.* modify
modiskinja *n.* milliner

**modist** *n.* milliner
**modrica** *n* bruise
**modulirati** *v.t.* modulate
**moguć** *a.* possible
**mogućnost** *n.* possibility
**moguć** *a* able
**moguć** *a.* potential
**mogućnost** *n.* potential
**moj** *pron.* mine
**moj** *a.* my
**mokar** *a.* wet
**mokrenje** *n.* urination
**molba** *n.* plea
**molekul** *n.* molecule
**molekularni** *a.* molecular
**molilac** *n.* petitioner
**moliti** *v. t.* beg
**moliti** *v.t.* petition
**moliti** *v.i.* pray
**molitva** *n.* prayer
**molitvenik** *n.* breviary
**moljac** *n.* moth
**momak** *n* carl
**momak** *n.* lad
**monah** *n.* monk
**monarh** *n.* monarch
**monarhija** *n.* monarchy
**monaštvo** *n* monasticism
**monetarni** *a.* monetary
**monitor** *n.* monitor
**monodija** *n.* monody
**monogamija** *n.* monogamy
**monografija** *n.* monograph
**monogram** *n.* monogram
**monohromatski** *a.* monochromatic
**monokl** *n.* monocle
**monolit** *n.* monolith
**monolog** *n.* monologue
**monolog** *n.* soliloquy
**monopol** *n.* monopoly

**monopolist** *n.* monopolist
**monopolizovati** *v.t.* monopolize
**monoteist** *n.* monotheist
**monoteizam** *n.* monotheism
**monoton** *a.* monotonous
**monotonija** *n* monotony
**monstrum** *n.* monstrous
**monstruozan** *a.* monstrous
**monsun** *n.* monsoon
**monter** *n* fitter
**monumentalan** *a.* monumental
**moral** *n.* morale
**moralan** *a.* moral
**moralisati** *v.t.* moralize
**moralist** *n.* moralist
**moralnost** *n.* morality
**morati** *v.* must
**morbidan** *a.* morbid
**morbidnost** *n* morbidity
**more** *n.* sea
**moreuz** *n.* strait
**morfijum** *n.* morphia
**morgantski** *a.* morganatic
**mornar** *n.* mariner
**mornar** *n.* sailor
**mornarica** *n.* navy
**morski** *a.* marine
**mortalitet** *n.* mortality
**morž** *n.* walrus
**moskovljanin** *n.* muscovite
**most** *n* bridge
**mošt** *n* must
**mošus** *n.* musk
**motač** *n.* winder
**motel** *n.* motel
**motiv** *n.* motif
**motiv** *n.* motive
**motivacija** *n.* motivation
**motivisati** *v* motivate
**motka** *n* bat

| | |
|---|---|
| **moto** *n.* motto | **mrvica** *n* crumb |
| **motor** *n* engine | **mrzak** *a.* odious |
| **motor** *n.* motor | **mrzeti** *v.t.* hate |
| **motovilo** *v.t.* windlass | **mrzovoljan** *a.* morose |
| **mozaik** *n.* mosaic | **mrzovoljan** *a.* petulant |
| **mozak** *n* brain | **mržnja** *n.* hate |
| **možda** *adv.* perhaps | **mucanje** *n* stammer |
| **moždani** *adj* cerebral | **mucati** *v.i.* stammer |
| **mrak** *n* dark | **mučan** *a.* laborious |
| **mrav** *n* ant | **mučan** *a.* troublesome |
| **mraz** *n.* frost | **mučenik** *n.* martyr |
| **mrdnuti** *v. i. & n* budge | **mučeništvo** *n.* martyrdom |
| **mrest** *n.* spawn | **mučenje** *n.* torture |
| **mrestiti** *se v.i.* spawn | **mučiti** *v.t.* rack |
| **mreža** *n.* mesh | **mučiti** *v.t.* tantalize |
| **mreža** *n.* web | **mučiti** *v.t.* torment |
| **mreža** *n.* net | **mučiti** *v.t.* torture |
| **mreža** *n.* network | **mučiti** *se v.i.* moil |
| **mreže** *n. pl.* toils | **mučiti** *v.t.* agonize |
| **mrežnjača** *n.* retina | **mučnina** *n.* nausea |
| **mrk pogled** *n.* scowl | **mućkalica** *v. t. & i.* churn |
| **mrko gledati** *v.i.* scowl | **mućkati** *n.* churn |
| **mrlja** *n.* smear | **mudar** *a.* sagacious |
| **mrlja** *n.* stain | **mudar** *a.* wise |
| **mrlja** *n.* taint | **mudrac** *n.* sage |
| **mrlja** *n.* blot | **mudrost** *n.* sagacity |
| **mrlja** *n blur* | **mudrost** *n.* wisdom |
| **mrljati** *v.t.* stain | **mudrost** *n.* wisdom-tooth |
| **mrmljati** *v.i.* mumble | **muka** *n.* torment |
| **mrmljati** *v.t.* murmur | **mukanje** *v.i* moo |
| **mrskost** *n.* odium | **mukati** *v.i.* Moo |
| **mršav** *a.* lank | **mula** *n.* mullah |
| **mršavo** *n.* lean | **mulat** *n.* mulatto |
| **mrštenje** *n.* frown | **mulj** *n.* silt |
| **mrštiti** *se v.i* frown | **mulj** *n.* slime |
| **mrtav** *a* dead | **muljav** *a.* slimy |
| **mrtvačka nosila** *n* bier | **multilateralan** *a.* multilateral |
| **mrtvački sanduk** *n* coffin | **multiparan** *a.* multiparous |
| **mrtvačnica** *n.* morgue | **mumija** *n.* mummy |
| **mrtvačnica** *n.* mortuary | **mungos** *n.* mongoose |

municija *n.* munitions
municija *n.* ammunition
munja *n.* lightening
mural *n.* mural
musketa *n.* musket
musketar *n.* musketeer
muslin *n.* muslin
mustang *n.* mustang
musti *v.t.* milk
muški *a.* male
muški *a.* manly
muški *a.* masculine
muški *a.* virile
muški *rod n* male
muškost *n.* manhood
muškost *n* manliness
mutacija *n.* mutation
mutan *a.* lacklustre
mutativan *a.* mutative
muva *n* fly
muza *n* muse
muzej *n.* museum
muzičar *n.* musician
muzički *a.* musical
muzika *n.* music
muž *n* husband
muževan *a.* manlike
muževnost *n.* virility

# N

na *prep.* on
na *prep upon*
na drugoj strani *adv.* overleaf
na kraju *adv.* lastly
na kraju *adv.* ultimately
na obali *adv.* ashore
na prvi pogled *adv.* prima facie
na umoru *a.* moribund

na vreme *a.* timely
na, po *prep.* per
nabaviti *v.t.* procure
nabavka *n.* procurement
nabob *n.* nabob
nabor *n i*
nabor *n.* frill
nabor *n* ply
naborati *v.t.* crimple
nabrajati *v. t.* enumerate
nabrati *v.t.* ruffle
nabreknuti *v.i.* swell
nacija *n.* nation
nacionalista *n.* nationalist
nacionalizacija *n.* nationalization
nacionalizam *n.* nationalism
nacionalizovati *v.t.* nationalize
nacionalni *a.* national
nacrt *n* draught
načelo *n.* tenet
način *n.* manner
način *n.* mode
način *n.* way
način fotokopiranja *n.* xerox
način govora *n.* parlance
načiniti četvorouglastim *v.t.* square
načiniti paralelnim *v.t.* parallel
način *a.* well-read
načuti *v.t.* overhear
naći srednju vrednost *v.t.* average
nada *n* hope
nadalje *adv.* onwards
nadaren *a.* gifted
nadati se *v.t.* hope
nadčovek *n.* superman
nadglasati *v.t.* overrule
nadgledanje *n.* invigilation
nadgledati *v.t.* oversee
nadgledati *v.t.* supervise
nadimak *n.* nickname

nadir *n.* nadir
nadiranje *n.* onrush
nadjačati *v.t.* overpower
nadležan *a* amenable
nadležnost *n.* jurisdiction
nadljudski *a.* superhuman
nadmašiti *v.i* excel
nadmašiti *v.t.* outdo
nadmašiti *v.t.* surpass
nadmašiti u brojnosti *v.t.* outnumber
nadmašiti u trčanju *v.t.* outrun
nadmetati se *v.t.* rival
nadmetati se *v.i.* vie
nadmoćan *a.* pre-eminent
nadmoćnost *n.* pre-eminence
nadmoćan *a.* predominant
nadmoćan *a.* superior
nadmudriti *v.t* gull
nadmudriti *v.t.* outwit
nadmudriti *v.t.* trump
nadničar *n.* jobber
nadničar *n.* peon
nadoknaditi *v.t* compensate
nadoknaditi *v.t.* recompense
nadoknaditi *v.t.* recoup
nadoknaditi *v.t.* reimburse
nadole *adv* downward
nadrilek *n.* nostrum
nadrilekarstvo *n.* quackery
nadsijati *v.t.* outshine
nadsvoditi *v.i.* vault
nadvoje *adv.* asunder
nadvratink *n.* lintel
nadzirati *v.t.* invigilate
nadzor *n.* oversight
nadzor *n.* supervision
nadzor *n.* surveillance
nadzornik *n* foreman
nadzornik *n.* invigilator
nadzornik *n.* overseer

nadzornik *n.* superintendent
nadzornik *n.* supervisor
nadživeti *v.i.* outlive
naelektrisati *v. t* electrify
nafta *n.* petroleum
nag *a.* bare
nag *a.* naked
nagao *a.* impetuous
nagib *n* slant
nagib *n.* slope
nagib *n.* tilt
naginjati ukoso *v. t* bias
naglas *adv.* aloud
naglasak *n* accent
naglasak *n* emphasis
naglasiti *v.t* accent
naglasiti *v. t* emphasize
naglasiti *v.t.* punctuate
naglašavati *v.t* stress
naglo *a* abrupt
nagnati *v.t* urge
nagnut *a* downward
nagnuti *v.t.* slant
nagnuti *v.i.* slope
nagnuti se *v.i.* incline
nagnuti se *v.i.* tilt
nagodba *n* compromise
nagoditi se *v. t* compromise
nagomilati *v.t.* aggregate
nagomilati *v.t.* amass
nagomilati *v.t.* bank
nagomilati *v. i.* cluster
nagomilati *v.t.* lump
nagomilati se *v.i.* accrue
nagon *n.* appetite
nagon *n* urge
nagore *adv.* upwards
nagost *n* nude
nagovaranje *n.* abetment
nagovestiti *v.i* hint

| | |
|---|---|
| **nagovestiti** *v.t.* intimate | **nakon** *prep.* after |
| **nagovestiti** *v.t.* portend | **nakon** *adv* after |
| **nagoveštaj** *n* allusion | **nakovanj** *n.* anvil |
| **nagoveštaj** *n.* hint | **nalepnica** *n.* sticker |
| **nagoveštaj** *n.* inkling | **nalet** *n.* gust |
| **nagoveštaj** *n.* intimation | **nalet** *n* rush |
| **nagovoriti** *v.t.* abet | **nalik** *a.* alike |
| **nagrada** *n.* prize | **nalog** *n.* warrant |
| **nagrada** *n.* reward | **namamiti** *v.t.* bait |
| **nagrada** *n.* award | **namamiti** *v. t.* entice |
| **nagraditi** *v.t.* award | **namamiti** *v.t.* lure |
| **nagraditi** *v.t.* remunerate | **namazati** *v.t* lime |
| **nagraditi** *v.t.* reward | **namazati puterom** *v. t* butter |
| **naime** *adv.* namely | **namera** *n.* intention |
| **naivan** *a.* naive | **nameran** *a* deliberate |
| **naivnost** *n.* naivete | **nameran** *a.* intentional |
| **naivnost** *n.* naivety | **nameravati** *v.t.* intend |
| **naizmenično** *a.* alternate | **nameravati** *v.t.* purpose |
| **najam** *n.* hire | **namerni** *a.* intent |
| **najamnik** *n.* hireling | **namerno** *adv.* purposely |
| **najaviti** *v.t* herald | **namesnički** *a.* vicarious |
| **najfiniji** *a.* superfine | **nameštaj** *n.* furniture |
| **najgori** *a* worst | **nametanje** *n.* imposition |
| **najgušći deo** *n.* thick | **nametanje** *n.* levy |
| **najlon** *n.* nylon | **nametati** *v.t.* impose |
| **najmanje** *adv.* least | **nametnuti** *v.t. levy* |
| **najmanji** *a.* least | **namigivati** *v.i.* wink |
| **najniža plima** *a.* neap | **namignuti** *v.t.* beckon |
| **najskriveniji** *a.* inmost | **namiguša** *n.* minx |
| **najviše** *adv.* most | **namirisati** *v.t.* perfume |
| **najzad** *adv.* last | **namotati** *v.t.* convolve |
| **nakit** *n.* jewellery | **namotati** *v.i.* reel |
| **naklon** *n* bow | **namotati** *v.t.* wind |
| **naklon** *n.* obeisance | **namrštiti** *v.t.* purse |
| **naklonjen** *a* fond | **naneti** *v.t.* inflict |
| **naklonjenost** *n.* affection | **naneti štetu** *v.t.* wrong |
| **naklonost** *n* favour | **naočit** *a.* sightly |
| **naklonost** *n. like* | **naoružanje** *n.* armament |
| **naknada** *n.* recompense | **naoružati** *v.t.* arm |
| **naknadni izbori** *n* by-election | **napad** *n* fit |

napad *n* offensive
napad *n.* seizure
napad *n.* assault
napad *n.* attack
napadački *a.* offensive
napasti *v.t.* invade
napasti iz zasede *v.t.* waylay
napasti *v.t.* assault
napasti *v.t.* attack
napet *n.* intent
napet *a.* tense
napisati *v.t.* write
napitak *n* beverage
napojnica *n.* gratuity
napolje *adv* outwards
napolju *a.* outdoor
napolju *adv* outside
napolju *adv.* outwardly
napolju *adv.* afield
napomena *n.* note
napomena *n.* remark
napomenuti *v.t.* remark
napon *n.* voltage
napor *n* effort
naporan *a.* laboured
naporan *a.* strenuous
naprasit *a.* waspish
naprašiti *v.t.* powder
napraviti *v.t.* make
napraviti od hleba *v. t. & i* breaden
napraviti salto *v.i.* somersault
napred *adv.* forth
napred *adv* forward
napred *a.* onward
napredak *n.* progress
napredovanje *n.* advancement
napredovati *v.i.* progress
napredovati *v.i.* prosper
napredovati *v.i.* thrive
napregnut *a.* intense

naprezanje *n* strain
naprezati *v.t.* strain
naprstak *n.* thimble
napuniti *v.t.* replenish
napuniti, ispuniti 2 *v.t.* stuff
napunjen *a.* replete
napustiti *v.t.* abandon
napustiti *v. t.* desert
napustiti *v.t.* forsake
napustiti *v.t.* vacate
napustiti logor *v. i* decamp
naracija *n.* narration
naramak pruća *n* faggot
narandžast *a* orange
narcis *n* narcissus
narcisizam *n.* narcissism
naredba *n* command
narediti *v. t* command
narediti *v. i* decree
narediti *v.t.* instruct
narednik *n.* sergeant
naricanje *n.* lamentation
narkotik *n.* narcotic
narkoza *n.* narcosis
narod *n.* people
narodni *a.* vernacular
naručiti *v.t* order
narukvica *a.* armlet
narukvica *n.* bangle
narukvica *n* bracelet
narušiti *v.t.* infringe
narušivanje *n.* infringement
nasapunjati *v.t.* soap
nasekirati *v.t.* vex
naseliti *v.t.* people
naseliti *v.t.* populate
naseliti *v.i.* settle
naselje *n.* settlement
naselje od baraka *n.* cantonment
naseljen *a.* populous

naseljenik *n.* settler
nasilan *a.* violent
nasilje *n.* outrage
nasilje *n.* violence
nasilno odvajanje *n.* avulsion
nasip *n* causeway
nasip *n* embankment
naslaga *n.* stratum
naslanjati se *v.* abutted
nasledan *a.* heritable
nasleđe *n.* heritage
nasleđe *n.* inheritance
nasleđe *n.* legacy
nasleđen *a.* ancestral
nasleđenost *n.* hereditary
naslediti *v.t.* inherit
naslednik *n.* heir
naslednik *n.* successor
naslednost *n.* heredity
nasledstvo *n.* succession
naslikati *v.t.* picture
nasloniti *v.i.* lean
naslov *n.* heading
naslov *n.* title
naslov *n.* caption
nasrnuti *v.* assail
nasrnuti *v.t.* mob
nastaniti *v.t.* inhabit
nastavak *n.* sequel
nastaviti *v. i.* continue
nastaviti *v.i.* proceed
nastavljanje *n.* continuation
nastavljanje *n.* resumption
nastavni plan *n* curriculum
nastojanje *n* endeavour
nastojati *v.i* endeavour
nastran *a.* queer
nastranost *n.* oddity
nastup *n* bout
nasukati *v.i.* strand

nasuprot *prep.* against
naš *pron.* our
nateći *v. i.* bag
nategnuti *v.t.* string
natovariti *v. t* burden
natovariti *v.t.* lade
natovariti *v.t.* load
natovariti *v.t.* stow
natovariti *v.t.* incur
natpis *n.* inscription
natprirodan *a.* supernatural
natrpati *v. t* cram
naučiti *v.i.* learn
naučni *a.* scholarly
naučni *a.* scientific
naučnik *n.* scientist
nauka *n.* science
nautički *a.* nautic(al)
navala *n* dash
navesti *v. t* coax
navesti *v.t.* induce
navesti *v.t.* specify
navesti *v.t.* adduce
navigacija *n.* navigation
navigator *n.* navigator
navijati *v.t.* wind
navika *n.* habit
navika *n* wont
naviknut *a.* accustomed
naviknut *a.* wont
naviknuti *v. t.* habituate
navlažiti *v.t.* leach
navod *n.* allegation
navođenje *n.* inducement
navoditi *v.t* state
navodnjavanje *n.* irrigation
navodnjavati *v.t.* irrigate
nazad *n.* back
nazal *n* nasal
nazalni *a.* nasal

nazdraviti *v.t.* toast
nazirati *se v.i.* loom
nazvati *v.t.* term
ne *n* no
ne *adv.* not
ne slagati se *v. i* disagree
ne sviđati se *v. t* displease
ne uspeti *v.i* fail
ne voleti *v. t* dislike
ne zadovoljiti *v. t.* dissatisfy
neaktivan *a.* inactive
neaktivnost *n.* inaction
nebeski *a.* heavenly
nebeski *adj* celestial
nebesko *telo n.* orb
nebitan *a.* irrelevant
nebo *n.* heaven
nebo *n.* sky
nećak *n.* nephew
nečist *a.* impure
nečistoća *n* dirt
nečistoća *n* filth
nečistoća *n.* impurity
nečitak *a.* illegible
nečitkost *n.* illegibility
nečovek *n* brute
nečujan *a.* inaudible
nećaka *n.* niece
nedavni *a.* recent
nedavno *adv.* late
nedavno *adv.* recently
nedelja *n.* Sunday
nedelja *n.* week
nedeljiv *a.* indivisible
nedeljni *a.* weekly
nedeljnik *n.* weekly
nedeljno *adv.* weekly
nedelo *n.* misdeed
nedelotvoran *a.* inoperative
nedisciplina *n.* indiscipline

nedolično ponašanje *n.* misbehaviour
nedolično se ponašati *v.i.* misbehave
nedopustiv *a.* inadmissible
nedopušten *a.* prohibitive
nedostajati *v.t.* lack
nedostatak *n* defect
nedostatak *n* demerit
nedostatak *n* disadvantage
nedostatak *n.* lack
nedostižan *a* elusive
nedovoljan *adj.* deficient
nedovoljan *a.* insufficient
nedovoljno *razviti v.t.* depauperate
nedovršen *a.* sketchy
neefikasan *a.* ineffective
nefleksibilan *a.* inflexible
neformalan *a.* informal
negacija *n.* negation
negativ *n.* negative
negativan *a* minus
negativan *a.* negative
negde *adv.* somewhere
negde *adv.* whereabout
negodovanje *a.* outcry
negostoljubiv *a.* inhospitable
negovatelj *n* tender
negovati *v. t.* cherish
negovati *v.t* nurse
negovati *v.t.* nurture
nehotice *adv.* unawares
nehuman *a.* inhuman
neiskren *a.* insincere
neiskrenost *n.* insincerity
neiskustvo *n.* inexperience
neispravan *a* faulty
neizbežan *a.* inevitable
neizlečiv *a.* incurable
neizmeran *a.* measureless
neizračunljiv *a.* incalculable
neizvesnost *n.* abeyance

**neizvesnost** *n.* suspense
**neizvestan** *a.* uncertain
**neizvodljivost** *n.* impracticability
**neizvršiv** *a.* impracticable
**nejasan** *a* dim
**nejasan** *a.* indistinct
**nejasan** *a.* obscure
**nejasan** *a.* vague
**nejasnost** *n.* obscurity
**nejednak** *a* unlike
**nejednakost** *n* disparity
**nekako** *adv.* somehow
**nekažnjen** *a.* scot-free
**nekažnjivost** *n.* impunity
**neki** *a.* some
**neko** *pron.* one
**neko** *pron.* somebody
**neko** *n.* somebody
**neko** *pron.* someone
**nekritički** *a.* indiscriminate
**nektar** *n.* nectar
**nelagodan** *a.* uneasy
**nelagodnost** *n* discomfort
**neljubazan** *a.* impolite
**nelogičan** *a.* illogical
**nelojalan** *a* disloyal
**nem** *a.* mute
**nema osoba** *n.* mute
**nemar** *n.* negligence
**nemaran** *a.* negligent
**nemaran** *a.* reckless
**nemaran** *a.* slack
**nemaran** *a.* slipshod
**nematerijalni** *a.* immaterial
**nemerljiv** *a.* immeasurable
**nemilosrdan** *adj.* merciless
**nemilosrdan** *a.* pitiless
**nemilosrdan** *a.* relentless
**nemilosrdan** *a.* ruthless
**nemir** *n.* turmoil

**nemir** *n* unrest
**nemoć** *n.* infirmity
**nemoćan** *a.* unable
**nemoguć** *a.* impossible
**nemogućnost** *n.* impossibility
**nemoralan** *a.* immoral
**nemoralan** *a.* amoral
**nemoralnost** *n.* immorality
**nenadmašan** *a.* transcendent
**nenamerno** *adv.* unwittingly
**nenormalan** *a* abnormal
**nenormalnost** *n.* aberrance
**neobavezan** *a.* optional
**neobjašnjiv** *a.* inexplicable
**neobrazovan** *a.* ignorant
**neočekivana sreća** *n.* godsend
**neodbranjiv** *a.* indefensible
**neodgovoran** *a.* irresponsible
**neodlučan** *a.* hesitant
**neodlučnost** *n.* indecision
**neodobravanje** *n* disapproval
**neodobravati** *v. t* disapprove
**neodoljiv** *a.* adorable
**neodređen** *a.* indefinite
**neodređen** *a* pending
**neodređeni** *član art* an
**neodređenost** *n.* vagueness
**neodvojiv** *a.* inseparable
**neograničen** *a.* limitless
**neokaljan** *a.* spotless
**neolitski** *a.* neolithic
**neon** *n.* neon
**neophodan** *a.* indispensable
**neopipljiv** *a.* intangible
**neopisiv** *a.* indescribable
**neopisiv** *a.* nefandous
**neoprezan** *a.* careless
**neosetljiv** *a.* insensible
**neosetljivost** *n.* insensibility
**neosnovan** *a.* baseless

neosporan a. indisputable
neotesanost n. rusticity
neozbiljan a. frivolous
neparan a. odd
nepažljiv a. inattentive
nepce n. palate
nepčan a. palatal
nepismen a. illiterate
nepismenost n. illiteracy
neplodnost n barren
nepobediv a. invincible
nepobitan a. irrefutable
nepodmitljiv a. incorruptible
nepodnošljiv a. intolerable
nepodnošljivost n. intolerance
nepogrešiv a. infallible
nepokretan a. immovable
nepokretan a. motionless
nepokretan a. stagnant
nepomirljiv a. irreconcilable
nepopravljiv a. incorrigible
nepopustljiv a. adamant
neposlušan a. insubordinate
neposlušnost n. insubordination
neposredan a immediate
neposredan a. proximate
nepostojanje n. nonentity
nepošten a dishonest
nepošten a. fraudulent
nepošten a. underhand
nepoštenje n. dishonesty
nepošteno zarađivati v.i. profiteer
nepoštovanje n disrespect
nepotizam n. nepotism
nepotpun a. incomplete
nepotreban a. needless
nepouzdan a. unreliable
nepoverenje n distrust
nepoverenje n. mistrust
nepovezan a. incoherent

nepovoljnost v.i. skid
nepovrativ a. irrecoverable
nepoznat a. anonymous
nepoznat a. uncouth
nepravda n. injustice
nepravedan a unfair
nepravedan a. unjust
nepravilan a anomalous
nepravilan a. irregular
nepravilnost n anomaly
nepravilnost n. irregularity
neprekidan a continuous
neprelazni a. intransitive
nepremostiv a. insurmountable
neprestan a. ceaseless
neprestan adj. continual
neprestano ponavljanje n. reiteration
neprestano ponavljati v.t. reiterate
neprijatan a. disagreeable
neprijatelj n enemy
neprijatelj n foe
neprijateljski a. hostile
neprijateljski a. inimical
neprijateljstvo n enmity
neprijateljstvo n. hostility
neprijateljstvo n animosity
neprikladan a. improper
neprikladan a. inconvenient
neprikladan a. undue
neprikladnost n. impropriety
neprikosnoven a. inviolable
neprilagodljivost n. maladjustment
neprilika n fix
neprilika n. nuisance
neprilika n. predicament
neprimenljiv a. inapplicable
neprincipijelan a. unprincipled
nepristojan a. indecent
nepristojan a. rude
nepristojnost n. indecency

nepristrasan *a.* impartial
nepristrasnost *n.* impartiality
neprobojan *a.* impenetrable
neprocenjiv *a.* invaluable
neprohodan *a.* impassable
neprolazan *a.* imperishable
nepromišljen *a.* imprudent
nepromišljen *a.* inconsiderate
nepromišljen *a.* mindless
nepromočiv *a.* watertight
neproziran *a.* opaque
neprozirnost *n.* opacity
neptun *n.* Neptune
nerad *a.* reluctant
neraspoložen *a.* indisposed
nerastvoriv *n.* insoluble
neravan *a.* rugged
neravan *adj* bumpy
nerazborit *a.* injudicious
nered *n.* mess
nervozan *a.* nervous
nesavladiv *a.* indomitable
nesavršen *a.* imperfect
nesavršenost *n.* imperfection
nesebičan *a.* selfless
nesiguran *a.* insecure
nesigurnost *n.* insecurity
neskladan *adj* absonant
nesklon *a.* loath
neskroman *a.* immodest
neskromnost *n.* immodesty
nesloga *n* discord
nesmotrenost *n.* imprudence
nesnosan *a.* insupportable
nesporazum *n.* disagreement
nesporazum *n* misapprehension
nesporazum *n.* misunderstanding
nesposoban *a* disabled
nesposoban *a.* incapable
nesposoban *a.* incompetent

nesposobnost *n* disability
nesposobnost *n.* inability
nesposobnost *n.* incapacity
nespretan *a* clumsy
nespretan *a.* maladroit
nesreća *n.* misfortune
nesrećan *a.* unfortunate
nesrećan *a.* unhappy
nesrećan slučaj *n.* mischance
nesrećan slučaj *n.* mishap
nesreća *n* accident
nesreća *n.* adversity
nesreća *n.* calamity
nesrećan *a.* luckless
nesrećan *a.* miserable
nesrećan *a.* woebegone
nestabilan *adj.* astatic
nestabilnost *n.* instability
nestajati *v. t* dwindle
nestalnost *n.* vicissitude
nestanak *n* disappearance
nestašica *n* dearth
nestaško *n.* tomboy
nestašluk *n* mischief
nestašluk *n.* prank
nestašnost *n.* petulance
nestati *v. i* disappear
nestrpljenje *n.* impatience
nestrpljiv *a.* impatient
nestrpljiv *adj.* agog
nestručan *a.* lay
nesvarljiv *a.* indigestible
nesvest *n.* swoon
nesvestan *a.* oblivious
nesvestan *a.* unaware
nesvrstanost *n.* non-alignment
nešto *pron.* some
nešto *pron.* something
nešto *adv.* something
nešto *adv.* somewhat

netačan *a.* inaccurate
netačan *a.* incorrect
netačan *a.* inexact
netaknut *a.* intact
neto *a* net
netolerantan *a.* intolerant
neučtiv *a* discourteous
neugodan *a.* uncanny
neuhranjenost *n.* malnutrition
neumetnički *a.* artless
neumoljiv *a.* inexorable
neumrljan *a.* stainless
neuporediv *a.* incomparable
neuporediv *a.* nonpareil
neurolog *n.* neurologist
neurologija *n.* neurology
neuroza *n.* neurosis
neuspeh *n* failure
neuspeo *adv* abortive
neustrašiv *a* dauntless
neustrašiv *a.* interpid
neustrašivost *n.* intrepidity
neutralan *a.* neutral
neutralisati *v.t.* neutralize
neutron *n.* neutron
nevaljalost *n.* roguery
nevaljao *a.* naughty
nevaspitan *a* unmannerly
nevažeći *a.* invalid
neven *n.* marigold
neverovatan *a* fabulous
neverovatan *a.* incredible
neverovatan *a.* unlikely
neveseo *a* cheerless
nevesta *n* bride
nevidljiv *a.* invisible
nevin *a.* chaste
nevin *a.* innocent
nevinost *n.* chastity
nevinost *n.* innocence

nevinost *n.* virginity
nevolja *n* ill
nevolja *n.* need
nevolja *n.* trouble
nezaboravan *a.* memorable
nezadovoljan *a.* malcontent
nezadovoljstvo *n* discontent
nezadovoljstvo *n* displeasure
nezadovoljstvo *n* dissatisfaction
nezadovoljstvo *n* malcontent
nezahvalan *a.* thankless
nezahvalnost *n.* ingratitude
nezakonit *a.* illegal
nezakonit *a.* illegitimate
nezakonit *a.* lawless
nezakonit *a.* wrongful
nezasit *a.* insatiable
nezavisan *a.* independent
nezavisnost *n.* independence
nezgoda *n.* misadventure
nezgodan *a.* awkward
nezgrapan *a.* ungainly
neznanje *n.* ignorance
neznanje *n.* nescience
nezrelost *n.* immaturity
nezreo *a.* immature
nezreo *adj* callow
nežan *a.* dainty
nežan *a* tender
nežan *a.* affectionate
neženja *n* agamist
neženja *n.* bachelor
neživ *a.* inanimate
nežno *a.* gentle
nežnost *n.* endearment
ni *conj.* neither
ni jedan *a.* no
nicati *v.i.* sprout
nigde *adv.* nowhere
nihilizam *n.* nihilism

nijansa *n.* nuance
nijansa *n.* tinge
nijansirati *v.t.* tinge
nikada *adv.* never
nikako *adv.* no
nikako *adv.* none
nikl *n.* nickel
niko *pron.* nobody
niko *pron.* none
nikotin *n.* nicotine
nimfa *n.* nymph
nisko *adv.* low
niša *n.* niche
ništa *n.* nothing
ništa *adv.* nothing
ništa *n.* nought
nit *n.* thread
niti *adv.* either
niti *conj* nor
nitkov *n* cad
nitkov *n.* miscreant
nitkov *n.* rascal
nitkov *n.* scoundrel
nivo *n.* level
niz *prep* down
niz *n.* tier
nizak *a.* low
nizak položaj *n.* low
nizati *v.i.* file
niže *adv* beneath
niže *v.t.* lower
niže *adv* under
niže plemstvo *n.* gentry
niži *a.* nether
niži *a* under
noć *n.* night
noćna mora *n.* nightmare
noćni *a.* nocturnal
noću *adv.* nightly
noćni *a* overnight

noga *n.* leg
noj *n.* ostrich
nomad *n.* nomad
nomadski *a.* nomadic
nomenklatura *n.* nomenclature
nominalan *a.* nominal
nominovati *v.t.* nominate
nonparel *n.* nonpareil
nonšalantan *a.* nonchalant
nonšalantnost *n.* nonchalance
norma *n.* norm
normalan *a.* normal
normalizovati *v.t.* normalize
normalnost *n.* normalcy
nos *n.* nose
nosač *n.* carrier
nosač *n* coolie
nosač *n.* girder
nosat *a.* nosey
nosila *n.* stretcher
nosilac medalje *n.* medallist
nosiljka *n.* sedan
nositi *v.t* bear
nositi *v. t.* carry
nosorog *n.* rhinoceros
nostalgija *n.* nostalgia
nošen *adj.* borne
nošenje *n.* portage
notacija *n.* notation
nov *a.* new
nov *a.* novel
novac *n.* lucre
novac *n.* money
novčan *a.* pecuniary
novčana pošiljka *n.* remittance
novčanik *n.* purse
novčanik *n.* wallet
novčić *n* coin
novčić *n.* mite
novela *n.* novelette

novembar *n.* november
novinar *n.* journalist
novinar *n.* reporter
novinarstvo *n.* journalism
novine *n.* gazette
novost *n.* novelty
nozdrva *n.* nostril
nož *n.* knife
nož pluga *n* colter
nožni prst *n.* toe
nuklearna *a.* nuclear
nula *n.* nil
nula *a.* null
nula *n.* zero
numerički *a.* numerical
nusproizvod *n* by-product
nutritivan *a.* nutritive
nužda *n.* necessity
nužnik *n.* latrine

# NJ

njakanje *n* bray
njakati *v. i* bray
njega *pron.* him
njegov *pron.* his
njen *a* her
njih *pron.* them
njihanje *n* sway
njihati *v.i.* sway
njihov *a.* their
njihov *pron.* theirs
njoj *pron.* her
njušiti *v.t* nose
njuška *n.* muzzle
njuškalo *a.* nosy
njuškati *v.* nuzzle

# O

o *prep* about
oaza *n.* oasis
oba *a.,* either
oba *a* both
oba *pron* both
oba *conj* both
obad *n.* gadfly
obala *n* coast
obala *n.* shore
obala *n* strand
obasipati *v.t.* lavish
obavestiti *v.t.* apprise
obavestiti *v.t.* inform
obavestiti *v.t.* notify
obaveštenje *n.* notification
obaveza *n.* must
obaveza *n.* obligation
obavezan *a* compulsory
obavezan *a* incumbent
obavezan *a.* mandatory
obavezan *a.* obligatory
obavezati *v.t.* oblige
obavezati se *v. t.* commit
obavezujuć *a* binding
obaviti *v.t.* transact
obazriv *adj.* circumspect
obazriv *a.* precautionary
obdanište *n.* kindergarten
obdariti *v. t* endow
obdukcija *n.* post-mortem
obdukcioni *a.* post-mortem
obećanje *n* promise
obećati *v.t* promise
obećavajući *a.* promising
obeleti *v.t.* whitewash
obeleženo mesto *n.* book-mark

obeležiti *v.t.* sign
obeležiti inicijalima *v.t* initial
obeshrabriti *v.i.* dehort
obeshrabriti *v. t.* discourage
obeshrabriti *v. t* dishearten
obesiti *v.t.* hang
obesmrtiti *v.t.* immortalize
obeštećenje *n* redress
obezbediti *v. t* ensure
obezbediti *v.i.* provide
obezvrediti *v.t.i.* depreciate
običaj *n.* custom
obično *adv.* usually
obilan *a* abundant
obilan *a.* profuse
obilje *n* abundance
obilje *n.* profusion
obilje *n.* redundance
obilovati *v.i.* abound
obim *n.* extent
obim *n.* scope
obiman *a.* voluminous
objasniti *v. t* elucidate
objasniti *v. t.* explain
objašnjenje *n* explanation
objava *n.* announcement
objaviti *v.t.* announce
objaviti *v.t.* post
objaviti *v.t.* publish
objekat *n.* object
objektiv *n.* lens
objektivan *a.* objective
oblačan *a.* overcast
oblačenje *n* dressing
oblačiti *v. t* dress
oblačno *a* cloudy
oblaganje *n* coating
oblagati *v.t.* panel
oblak *n.* cloud
oblik *n.* shape

oblikovati *v.t.* model
oblikovati *v.t.* mould
oblikovati *v.t* shape
obložiti *v.t.* pad
obložiti daskama *v.t.* plank
obložiti jastucima *v. t* cushion
obmana *n.* delusion
obmanjivati *v.t.* misguide
obmanuti *v. t* beguile
obmanuti *v. t* deceive
obmanuti *n.t.* delude
obnova *n.* renewal
obnova *n.* renovation
obnoviti *v.t.* renew
obnoviti *v.t.* restore
obod *n.* rim
obod *n* brim
obogatiti *v. t* enrich
obojiti *v.t.* tincture
obojiti *v.t.* tint
oboljenje *n.* ailment
oboriti *v.t.* prostrate
obožavalac *n.* idolater
obožavalac *n.* worshipper
obožavanje *n.* apotheosis
obožavanje *n.* worship
obožavanje *n.* adoration
obožavati *v.t.* worship
obožavati *v.t.* adore
obraćati se *v.i.* plead
obradiv *a.* workable
obradiv *adj.* arable
obrađivati *v. t* cultivate
obrađivati *v.t.* till
obradovati *v.t.* gladden
obratiti se *v.t.* address
obraz *n* cheek
obrazac *n.* norm
obrazac *n.* pattern
obrazloženje *n.* rationale

**obrazovanje** *n* education
**obrazovati** *v. t* educate
**obred** *n.* ordinance
**obred** *n.* rite
**obredni** *a.* ceremonious
**obrezivanje** *n.* lop
**obrisati sunđerom** *v.t.* sponge
**obrnuti** *v.t.* invert
**obrnuti** *v.t.* reverse
**obrnuto** *adv.* vice-versa
**obrok** *n.* meal
**obrok** *n.* ration
**obrt** *n.* twist
**obrtati** *se v.i.* revolve
**obrubiti** *v.t* fringe
**obrubiti** *v.t.* list
**obrva** *n* brow
**obućar** *n* cobbler
**obući** *v.t.* apparel
**obući** *v.t.* attire
**obući** *v. t* clothe
**obući** *v.t* garb
**obući** *v.t.* vest
**obuhvatanje** *n* comprehension
**obuhvatati** *v.t.* implicate
**obuhvatiti** *v. t* comprehend
**obuka** *n.* training
**obustava** *n* stop
**obustava** *n.* suspension
**obuti** *v.t.* shoe
**obuzdati** *v.t.* restrain
**obuzdati** *v.t.* subdue
**obuzdatu** *v. t* curb
**oceniti** *v. t* evaluate
**oceniti** *v.t* grade
**oceubistvo** *n.* patricide
**očajan** *a* desperate
**očajanje** *n* despair
**očajavati** *v. i* despair
**očekivanje** *n.* expectation

**očekivati** *v. t* expect
**očevidan** *a.* manifest
**očevina** *n.* patrimony
**očigledan** *a.* evident
**očigledan** *a.* obvious
**očigledno** *adv* clearly
**očijukanje** *n* ogle
**očijukati** *v.t.* ogle
**očinski** *a.* paternal
**očistiti** *v. t* cleanse
**očistiti** *v.t.* purge
**očistiti** *v.t.* purify
**očna jabučica** *n* eyeball
**očni** *a.* ocular
**očuvati** *v. t* conserve
**očvrsnuti** *v.t.* toughen
**od** *prep.* from
**od** *prep.* since
**od sada** *adv.* henceforth
**od sada** *adv.* hereafter
**oda** *n.* ode
**odakle** *adv.* whence
**odan** *a.* staunch
**odan** *a.* whole-hearted
**odande** *adv.* thence
**odašiljač** *n.* transmitter
**odbaciti** *v. t* discard
**odbaciti** *v. t.* dismiss
**odbaciti** *v.t.* rebuff
**odbacivanje** *n.* rebuff
**odbegao** *a.* fugitive
**odbijanje** *n.* rebound
**odbijanje** *n.* refusal
**odbijanje** *n.* rejection
**odbijanje** *n.* repulse
**odbijanje dojenčeta** *n* ablactation
**odbiti** *v.t.* deduct
**odbiti** *v.t.* negative
**odbiti** *v.i.* rebound
**odbiti** *v.t.* refuse

**odbiti** *v.t.* reject
**odbiti** *v.t.* repel
**odbiti** *v.t.* repulse
**odbiti** *v.t.* stud
**odbiti dojenče** *v. t* ablactate
**odbojan** *a.* repulsive
**odbojno** *adv.* recoil
**odbojnost** *n.* repulsion
**odbor** *n* committee
**odbor** *n* board
**odbornik** *n.* councillor
**odbrambeno** *adv.* defensive
**odbrana** *n* defence
**odeća** *n.* clothes
**odeća** *n* clothing
**odeća** *n.* garb
**odeća** *n.* garment
**odeća** *n.* apparel
**odeća** *n.* attire
**odeljak** *n.* section
**odeljenje** *n.* compartment
**odeljenje** *n* department
**odelo** *n.* suit
**odenuti** *v.t.* robe
**oderati** *v.t* skin
**odežda** *n.* vestment
**odgajati** *v.t.* foster
**odgajati** *v.t.* mother
**odgajivačnica zečeva** *n.* warren
**odgoditi** *v.t.* adjourn
**odgoj** *n.* nurture
**odgovarati** *v. i* correspond
**odgovarati** *v.i.* match
**odgovarati** *v.t.* suit
**odgovor** *n.* rejoinder
**odgovor** *n* reply
**odgovor** *n.* response
**odgovor** *n.* retort
**odgovor** *n* answer
**odgovoran** *a.* liable

**odgovoran** *a.* responsible
**odgovoran** *a* accountable
**odgovoriti** *v.i.* reply
**odgovoriti** *v.i.* respond
**odgovoriti** *v.t.* retort
**odgovoriti** *v.t* answer
**odgovorljiv** *a.* answerable
**odgovornost** *n* blame
**odgovornost** *n.* liability
**odgovornost** *n.* responsibility
**odjek** *n* echo
**odjekivati** *v. t* echo
**odjeknuti** *v.i.* resound
**odkad** *conj.* since
**odlaganje** *n.* postponement
**odlaganje** *n.* adjournment
**odlazak** *n* departure
**odličan** *a.* excellent
**odlika** *n* feature
**odložiti** *v.t. & i.* delay
**odložiti** *v.t.* postpone
**odlučan** *a.* resolute
**odlučan** *a.* stalwart
**odlučan zagovornik** *n* stalwart
**odlučiti** *v. t* decide
**odlučiti** *se v.i.* opt
**odlučnost** *n.* determination
**odlučujući** *a* decisive
**odluka** *n* decision
**odmah** *adv.* forthwith
**odmah** *adv.* instantly
**odmah** *adv.* anon
**odmarati se** *v.i.* repose
**odmazda** *n.* retaliation
**odmeriti** *v.t* mete
**odmetnik** *n.* outlaw
**odmor** *n.* holiday
**odmor** *n.* repose
**odmor** *n* rest
**odmor** *n.* vacation

| | |
|---|---|
| **odmor** *n* break | **odrešiti** *v.t.* loose |
| **odmoriti se** *v.i.* rest | **odricanje** *n* abdication |
| **odnos** *n.* intercourse | **odricanje** *n.* renunciation |
| **odnos** *n.* ratio | **odrubiti glavu** *v. t.* behead |
| **odnos** *n.* relation | **održati** *v.t.* sustain |
| **odnosan** *a.* respective | **održavanje** *n.* maintenance |
| **odnositi se** *v.i.* pertain | **održavanje** *n* upkeep |
| **odnositi se** *v.t.* relate | **održavati** *v.t.* maintain |
| **odobravanje** *n* acclaim | **održiv** *a.* tenable |
| **odobrenje** *n* grant | **održiv** *a.* viable |
| **odobrenje** *n.* approbation | **odsečan** *a* curt |
| **odobrenje** *n.* approval | **odsto** *adv.* per cent |
| **odobriti** *v.t* acclaim | **odstupanje** *n* deviation |
| **odobriti** *v. t.* endorse | **odstupati** *v. i* deviate |
| **odobriti** *v.t.* grant | **odsutan** *a* absent |
| **odobriti** *v.t.* vouchsafe | **odsutnost** *n* absence |
| **odobriti** *v.t* approbate | **odšteta** *n.* indemnity |
| **odobriti** *v.t.* approve | **odšteta** *n.pl.* amends |
| **odojče** *n.* infant | **odučiti** *v.t.* wean |
| **odoleti** *v.t.* resist | **odugovlačenje** *n.* procrastination |
| **odoleti** *v.t.* weather | **odugovlačiti** *v.i.* linger |
| **odomaćiti** *v.t.* naturalize | **odugovlačiti** *v.i.* procrastinate |
| **odonda** *adv.* since | **odustati** *v.t.* waive |
| **odrasla osoba** *n.* adult | **odušak** *n.* vent |
| **odrastao** *a* adult | **oduševljen** *a* enthusiastic |
| **odraz** *n.* reflection | **oduzeti** *v.t.* subtract |
| **odraziti** *v.t.* reflect | **oduzimanje** *n.* subtraction |
| **odražavati** *v.t.* mirror | **odvajanje** *n* detachment |
| **odreći se** *v.t* forgo | **odvažan** *a.* mettlesome |
| **odreći se** *v.t.* relinquish | **odvod** *n* drain |
| **odreći se** *v.t,* abdicate | **odvoditi** *v. t* drain |
| **odreći se** *v.t.* renounce | **odvodni kanal** *n.* culvert |
| **odredba** *n.* provision | **odvodni kanal** *n* sewer |
| **odredba** *n.* stipulation | **odvodni sistem** *n.* sewage |
| **određen** *a* definite | **odvojen** *a.* separate |
| **određen** *a* express | **odvojeno** *adv.* apart |
| **određen** *a* set | **odvojiti** *v. t* detach |
| **određeni** *a* certain | **odvojiti** *v.t.* segregate |
| **odrediti** *v.t.* allot | **odvojiv** *v.t.* separate |
| **odrediti** *v. t* determine | **odvratan** *a.* hideous |

odvratan *a.* obnoxious
odvratan *a.* repellent
odvratan *a.* repugnant
odvratiti *v.t. & i.* deflect
odvratiti *v. t* dissuade
odvratnost *n.* repugnance
oficir *n.* officer
oglas *n.* handbill
oglas *n* advertisement
oglasiti *v. t* denounce
oglašavati *v.t.* advertise
ogledalo *n* mirror
ognjište *n.* hearth
ogoliti *v.t.* denude
ogovaranje *n.* gossip
ogovaranje *v.t.* backbite
ograda *n.* close
ograda *n* fence
ograda *n.* hurdle1
ograda *n.* raling
ograditi *v.t* fence
ograditi *v.t* hedge
ograditi *v.t* hurdle2
ograditi *v.t.* rail
ograditi kolcima *v.t.* picket
ograničen *a.* limited
ograničen *a.* terminable
ograničenje *n.* confinement
ograničenje *n.* limitation
ograničenje *n.* restriction
ograničenost *n.* insularity
ograničiti *v. t* confine
ograničiti *v.t.* limit
ograničiti *v.t.* restrict
ogrlica *n.* necklace
ogroman *a* enormous
ogroman *a.* huge
ogroman *a.* immense
ogroman *a* mammoth
ogroman *a.* tremendous

ogroman *a.* vast
ogrozd *n.* gooseberry
ogrtač *n.* cloak
ogrtač *n.* overall
ohol *a.* arrogant
ohol *a.* haughty
oholo *a.* lordly
oholost *n.* arrogance
ohrabriti *v. t.* embolden
ohrabriti *v. t* encourage
ojačati *v.t.* strengthen
okaljati *v.t.* spot
okean *n.* ocean
okeanski *a.* oceanic
okidač *n.* trigger
oklevanje *n* demur
oklevanje *n.* hesitation
oklevati *v. t* demur
oklevati *v. t.* halt
oklevati *v.i.* hesitate
oklevetati *v.t.* libel
okliznuće *n.* slip
okliznuti se *v.i.* slip
oklop *n* mail
oklop *n.* armour
oklopiti *v.t.* plate
oklopna rukavica *n.* gauntlet
okno *n.* pane
oko *n* eye
oko *prep.* around
okolnost *n* circumstance
okolo *adv.* round
okolo *adv.* around
okončati *v.t.* terminate
okoreo *a.* callous
okoštati *v.t.* ossify
okovati *v.t.* iron
okovati *v.t.* shackle
okovati *v.t.* tip
okovi *n.* shackle

| | |
|---|---|
| **okovratnik** *n* collar | **olakšati** *v.i.* lighten |
| **okrečiti** *v.t.* plaster | **olakšati** *v.t.* relieve |
| **okrenut** *uvis a.* upward | **olakšica** *n* concession |
| **okrenuti** *v.i.* turn | **oličavati** *v.t.* impersonate |
| **okret** *n* turn | **oličavati** *v.t.* personify |
| **okretan** *a.* nimble | **oligarhija** *n.* oligarchy |
| **okretan** *a.* versed | **olimpijada** *n.* olympiad |
| **okretanje** *n.* spin | **oljuštiti** *v.t.* peel |
| **okretati** *se v.t.* pivot | **olovka** *n.* pencil |
| **okriviti** *v.t.* impeach | **olovni** *a.* leaden |
| **okriviti** *v.t.* incriminate | **olovo** *n.* lead |
| **okrug** *n.* county | **oltar** *n.* altar |
| **okrug** *n* district | **oluja** *n.* gale |
| **okrugao** *a.* round | **oluja** *n.* storm |
| **okruglost** *n.* round | **oluja** *n.* tempest |
| **okrutan** *a.* atrocious | **olujni** *a.* stormy |
| **okrutan** *a* cruel | **oluk** *n.* gutter |
| **okrutnost** *n* cruelty | **olupina** *n.* wrack |
| **okruženje** *n.* environment | **olupina** *n.* wreck |
| **okruženje** *n.* surroundings | **olupina** *n.* wreckage |
| **okružiti** *v. t.* encircle | **omalovažavanje** *n.* slight |
| **okružiti** *v.t.* ring | **omalovažavati** *v.t.* slight |
| **okruživati** *v.t.* surround | **omamiti** *v.t.* stupefy |
| **oksidisati** *v.* acetify | **omašiti** *v.i* blunder |
| **oktava** *n.* octave | **omaška** *n* blunder |
| **oktobar** *n.* October | **omaž** *n.* homage |
| **okular** *n.* oculist | **omča** *n* bight |
| **okultan** *a.* occult | **omega** *n.* omega |
| **okupator** *n.* occupier | **ometati** *v.t.* hinder |
| **okupiti** *v.t.* gather | **ometati** *v.t.* impede |
| **okusiti** *v.t.* taste | **ometati** *v.t.* obstruct |
| **okutnost** *n* atrocity | **omiljen** *a* favourite |
| **okvir** *n* frame | **omladina** *n. pl.* teens |
| **okvir kamina** *n.* mantel | **omogućiti** *v. t* enable |
| **olabaviti** *v.t.* loosen | **omotač** *n* mantle |
| **olabaviti** *v.t.* slacken | **omotač** *n.* wrapper |
| **olako** *adv.* lightly | **omplet** *n.* omelette |
| **olakšanje** *n.* alleviation | **on** *pron.* he |
| **olakšati** *v.t.* alleviate | **ona** *pron.* she |
| **olakšati** *v.t* facilitate | **onaj** *dem. pron.* that |

**onaj koji ima licencu** *n.* licensee
**onda** *adv.* then
**oneraspoložiti** *v. t* deject
**onesposobiti** *v. t* disable
**onesposobljen** *a.* invalid
**onesvestiti se** *v.i* faint
**onesvestiti se** *v.i* swoon
**ono što je glavno** *n.* paramount
**ono što je malo** *n.* little
**ono što je manje** *n* less
**ono što je najgore** *n.* worst
**onomatopeja** *n.* onomatopoeia
**opadanje** *n.* decrement
**opadanje** *n* wane
**opadati** *v. i* ebb
**opadati** *v.i.* wane
**opak** *n.* arrant
**opak** *a.* vicious
**opakost** *n.* malignancy
**opal** *n.* opal
**opasač** *n.* waistband
**opasan** *a* dangerous
**opasan** *a.* perilous
**opasan** *a.* venturous
**opasan** *n* breakneck
**opasati** *v.t.* gird
**opasati** *v.t.* strap
**opasati šancem** *v.t.* moat
**opasati zidom** *v.t.* wall
**opasati** *v.t.* begird
**opasivati** *v.t* girdle
**opasnost** *n.* danger
**opasnost** *n.* jeopardy
**opasnost** *n.* peril
**opasti** *v.i.* subside
**opaziti** *v. t* behold
**opaziti** *v.t.* perceive
**opcija** *n.* option
**opčiniti** *v. t* bedevil
**opčiniti** *v. t* enchant

**opčinjenost** *n* spell
**opeći koprivom** *v.t.* nettle
**opeklina** *n* singe
**opekotina** *n.* burn
**opera** *n.* opera
**operacija** *n.* operation
**operativan** *a.* operative
**operator** *n.* operator
**opet** *adv.* again
**opijum** *n.* opium
**opipati palcem** *v.t.* thumb
**opipljiv** *a.* palpable
**opipljiv** *a.* tangible
**opiranje** *n.* reluctance
**opis** *n* description
**opisati** *v. t* describe
**opisni** *a* descriptive
**opklada** *n* bet
**opkoliti** *v. t* encompass
**oplakivanje** *n* lament
**oplakivanje** *n.* mourning
**oplakivati** *v.i.* lament
**oplemeniti** *v. t.* ennoble
**opljačkati** *v.t.* depredate
**opljačkati** *v.t.* rifle
**opljačkati** *v.t.* rob
**opljačkati** *v.t.* sack
**oploditi** *v.t* fertilize
**opojno sredstvo** *n.* intoxicant
**oponašati** *v.t.* ape
**opor** *a.* pungent
**oporavak** *n.* recovery
**oporaviti se** *v.t.* recover
**oporeziv** *a.* taxable
**oporezivanje** *n.* taxation
**oporezovati** *v.t.* tax
**oporost** *n.* pungency
**oportunizam** *n.* opportunism
**opovrgnuti** *v.t.* confute
**opovrgnuti** *v. t* disprove

opozicija *n.* opposition
opoziv *n.* recall
opoziv *n.* revocation
opozivan *a.* revocable
opozivanje *n* repeal
opozvati *v.t.* countermand
opozvati *v.t.* recall
opozvati *v.t.* repeal
opozvati *v.t.* revoke
opraštanje *n.* remission
oprati *v.t.* launder
opravdan *a.* justifiable
opravdanje *n.* justification
opravdanje *n.* vindication
opravdati *v.t* excuse
opravdati *v.t.* justify
opravdati *v.t.* vindicate
opravljiv *a.* repairable
oprema *n* equipment
oprema *n.* gear
oprema *n.* kit
oprema *n.* outfit
opremiti *v. t* equip
opremiti *v.t.* furnish
oprez *n.* caution
oprezan *a.* provident
oprezan *a.* vigilant
oprezan *a.* wary
oprezan *a.* alert
oprezan *a* careful
oprezan *a.* cautious
opreznost *n.* alertness
oprljiti *v.t.* scorch
oprljiti *v.t.* singe
oprostiti *v.t.* assoil
oprostiti *v.t* forgive
oprostiti *v.t.* pardon
oprostiti *v.t.* remit
oprostiv *a.* pardonable
oprostiv *a.* venial

oproštaj *n* farewell
oproštenje *n.* condonation
oproštenje *n.* pardon
opsada *n.* siege
opscen *a.* obscene
opsedati *v. t* besiege
opsednuti *v.t.* obsess
opseg *n.* circumference
opservatorija *n.* observatory
opsesija *n.* obsession
opsežan *a.* ample
opskrbiti *v.t.* stock
opstajati *v.i.* subsist
opstanak *n.* subsistence
opstanak *n.* survival
opstati *v.i.* survive
opstrukcija *n.* obstruction
opstruktivan *a.* obstructive
opšta tuča *n.* melee
opšti *a.* general
opština *n.* municipality
opštinski *a.* municipal
opštinski *a.* township
opteretiti *v. t.* encumber
optičar *n.* optician
optički *a.* optic
optimalan *a* optimum
optimista *n.* optimist
optimistički *a.* optimistic
optimizam *n.* optimism
optimum *n.* optimum
optužba *n.* impeachment
optužba *n* accusation
optuženi *n* defendant
optuženik *n.* respondent
optuženik *n.* accused
optužiti *v.* arraign
optužiti *v.t.* indict
optužiti *v.t.* accuse
optužnica *n.* indictment

opunomoćenik *n.* warrantee
opunomoćiti *v.t.* accredit
opustiti *v.t.* relax
opuštanje *n.* relaxation
orač *n.* ploughman
orah *n* nut
orah *n.* walnut
orao *n* eagle
orati *v.i* plough
oratorijum *n.* oratory
orbita *n.* orbit
oreol *n.* nimbus
orezati *v.t.* prune
organ *n.* organ
organizacija *n.* organization
organizam *n.* organism
organizovati *v.t.* organize
organski *a.* organic
original *n* original
originalan *a.* original
originalnost *n.* originality
Orijent *n.* orient
orijentalan *a.* oriental
orijentisati *v.t.* orient
orijentisati *v.t.* orientate
orkestar *n.* orchestra
orkestarski *a.* orchestral
orman *n* cupboard
ormar *n.* ambry
ormar *n.* locker
ornament *n.* ornament
ornamentni *nož n.* baslard
oružarnica *n.* armoury
oružje *n.* weapon
osa *n.* wasp
osakatiti *v.t.* lame
osam *n* eight
osamdeset *n* eighty
osamdesetogodišnje *a* octogenarian
osamdesetogodišnji *a.* octogenarian

osamiti *v.t.* seclude
osamljen *a.* secluded
osamljenost *n.* seclusion
osamnaest *a* eighteen
oscilacija *n.* oscillation
oscilovati *v.i.* oscillate
osećaj *n* feeling
osećaj *n.* sentience
osećanje *n.* sentiment
osećati *v.t* feel
osećaj *n.* sense
osećajan *a.* sentient
osedlati *v.t.* saddle
oseka *n* ebb
osetiti *v.t.* sense
osetljiv *a.* sensitive
osetljiv *a.* touchy
osetljivost *n.* sensibility
osigurač *n* fuse
osiguranje *n.* insurance
osigurati *v.t.* insure
osigurati *v.t.* secure
osim *prep* except
osim *da conj.* but
osion *a.* rampant
osip *a.* rash
osiromašiti *v.t.* impoverish
oskudan *a.* meagre
oskudan *a.* scant
oskudan *a.* scanty
oskudan *a.* sparse
oskudica *n.* privation
oskudica *n.* scarcity
oskudica *n.* stringency
oslabiti *v. t.* enfeeble
oslabiti *v.t. & i* weaken
oslikati *v.t.* portray
oslobađajuća presuda *n.* acquittal
oslobađanje roba *n.* manumission
oslobođen *adj.* exempt

oslobođenje n. liberation
oslobodilac n. liberator
osloboditi v.t absolve
osloboditi v. t. exempt
osloboditi v.t free
osloboditi v.t. liberate
osloboditi v.t. rid
osloboditi ropstva v.t. manumit
osloboditi v.t. acquit
oslonac n. backbone
osloniti v.i. rely
osmatrač n. on-looker
osmeh n. smile
osmina milje n. furlong
osmougao n. octagon
osmougli a. octangular
osnivač n. founder
osnivanje n establishment
osnov n. rudiment
osnova n. basis
osnovni a. fundamental
osnovni a. primary
osnovni a. rudimentary
osnovni adj. basal
osnovni a. base
osnovni a. basic
osoba n. person
osobina n. trait
osoblje n. personnel
osoblje n. staff
osokoliti v.t. man
osovina n. axis
osovina n. axle
osposobiti v. t empower
osramotiti v.t. attaint
osramotiti v. t. debase
osramotiti v. t dishonour
osrednji a. mediocre
osrednji a. middling
osrednjost n. mediocrity

ostaci n. remains
ostareo a. aged
ostatak n. remainder
ostatak n. residue
ostati v.i. remain
ostati v.i. stay
ostava n. pantry
ostaviti v.t. leave
ostaviti v.t. pot
ostaviti razmak v.t. space
ostavka n. resignation
ostriga n. oyster
ostrvo n. island
ostrvo n. isle
ostrvski a. insular
ostvaren a accomplished
ostvariti v.t. accomplish
osuda n condemnation
osuda n conviction
osuđenik n convict
osuditi v. t. condemn
osuditi v. t. convict
osuditi v. t. doom
osuditi v.t. sentence
osuditi v.t., umpire
osujetiti v.t. thwart
osumnjičen a. suspect
osumnjičeni n suspect
osumnjičiti v.t. suspect
osušiti v. i. dry
osvajanje n conquest
osveta n. revenge
osveta n. vengeance
osvetiti v.t. revenge
osvetiti v.t. sanctify
osvetiti se v.i. retaliate
osvetliti v.t. illuminate
osvetliti v.t. light
osvetljen v.i. alight
osvetljenje n. illumination

**osvetnik** *n.* nemesis
**osvetoljubiv** *a.* revengeful
**osveženje** *n.* refreshment
**osvežiti** *v.t.* refresh
**osvojiti** *v. t* conquer
**ošamariti** *v.t.* slap
**ošamutiti** *v.t.* stun
**ošišati** *v.t* fleece
**ošišati** *v.t.* shear
**oštar** *a.* acute
**oštar** *a.* caustic
**oštar** *a.* poignant
**oštar** *a.* severe
**oštar** *a.* sharp
**oštar bol** *n* smart
**oštetiti** *v. t.* damage
**oštetiti** *v.t* harm
**oštrica** *n.* blade
**oštrina** *n.* poignancy
**oštro** *adv.* sharp
**oštrokondža** *n.* shrew
**oštrouman** *adj.* argute
**otac** *n* father
**otcepiti se** *v.i.* secede
**otcepljenje** *n.* secession
**oteklina** *n* swell
**otelotvoriti** *v. t.* embody
**otelovljenje** *n* embodiment
**oteti** *v.t.* abduct
**otići** *v. i.* depart
**otirač** *n.* mat
**otisak** *n.* imprint
**otisak** *n* print
**otkazati** *v. t.* cancel
**otkazivanje** *n* cancellation
**otkriće** *n.* discovery
**otkriti** *v. t* detect
**otkriti** *v. t* disclose
**otkriti** *v. t* discover
**otkriti** *v. t* divulge

**otkrovenje** *n.* revelation
**otkucaj** *n.* tick
**otkup** *n.* ransom
**otkupiti** *v.t.* ransom
**otmenost** *n.* sublimity
**otmica** *n* abduction
**otoman** *n.* ottoman
**otpaci stakla** *n.* cullet
**otpad** *n.* waste
**otpadak** *n.* scrap
**otplata** *n.* instalment
**otplata** *n.* repayment
**otpor** *n.* resístance
**otporan** *a* proof
**otporan** *a.* resistant
**otpremiti** *v.t* outfit
**otprilike** *adv* about
**otprilike** *adv.* thereabouts
**otpust** *n.* conge
**otpuštanje** *n* dismissal
**otrcan** *a.* shabby
**otrcan** *a.* threadbare
**otrgnuti** *v.t.* pluck
**otrov** *n.* poison
**otrov** *n.* venom
**otrovan** *a.* poisonous
**otrovan** *a.* venomous
**otrovati** *v.t.* intoxicate
**otrovati** *v.t.* poison
**otud** *adv.* hence
**otuđiti** *v.t.* alienate
**otvaranje** *n.* opening
**otvor** *n.* aperture
**otvoren** *a.* open
**otvoren** *a.* outspoken
**otvoren** *a.* overt
**otvoreno** *adv.* openly
**otvoriti** *v.t.* open
**otvoriti** *v.t.* unfold
**ova noć** *n.* to-night

**ovacija** *n.* ovation
**ovakav** *a.* such
**oval** *n* oval
**ovalan** *a.* oval
**ovamo** *adv.* hither
**ovan** *n.* ram
**ovan** *n.* aries
**ovaploćenje** *n.* incarnation
**ovaplotiti** *v.t.* incarnate
**ovca** *n* ewe
**ovca** *n.* sheep
**ovčetina** *n.* mutton
**ovde** *adv.* here
**ovde u okolini** *adv.* hereabouts
**ovekovečiti** *v.t.* perpetuate
**ovenčan lovorom** *a.* laureate
**ovenčati** *v.t.* garland
**ovlastiti** *v. t* depute
**ovlastiti** *v. t.* entitle
**ovlastiti** *v.t.* authorize
**ovlašćenje** *n* deputation
**ozakoniti** *v. t* enact
**ozbiljan** *a* earnest
**ozbiljan** *a.* grave
**ozbiljan** *a* serious
**ozbiljan** *a.* stern
**ozbiljnost** *n.* gravity
**ozbiljnost** *n.* severity
**ozloglašen** *a.* infamous
**ozloglašen** *a.* notorious
**ozloglašenost** *n* disrepute
**ozloglašenost** *n.* notoriety
**ozlojeđen** *a.* indignant
**ozlojeđenost** *n.* indignation
**ozlojeđenost** *n.* resentment
**označavati** *v. i* denote
**označavati** *v.t.* signify
**označiti** *v.t* mark
**označiti** *v.t.* tag
**oznaka** *n.* tag

**ozračiti** *v.i.* irradiate
**ožalostiti** *v. t* distress
**ožalostiti** *v.t.* afflict
**ožalostiti** *v.t.* aggrieve
**ožalošćeni** *n.* mourner
**ožiljak** *n* scar
**oživeti** *v.t.* animate
**oživeti** *v. t.* enliven
**oživeti** *v.i.* revive
**oživeti** *v.t.* zip
**oživljavanje** *n.* revival
**oživljavati** *v.t.* vitalize

# P

**pa** *conj.* so
**pacijent** *n* patient
**pacov** *n.* rat
**pad** *n.* tumble
**padati** *v.i* hail
**padati** *v.i.* rain
**padobran** *n.* parachute
**padobranac** *n.* parachutist
**pagoda** *n.* pagoda
**pajalica** *n* duster
**pakao** *a.* hell
**paket** *n.* pack
**paket** *n.* package
**paklen** *a.* infernal
**pakost** *n.* meanness
**pakost** *n.* virulence
**pakostan** *a.* virulent
**pakovanje** *n.* packing
**pakovati u bale** *v.t.* bale
**pakt** *n.* pact
**palac** *n.* thumb
**palankin** *n.* palanquin
**palata** *n.* mansion
**palata** *n.* palace

paleta *n.* palette
palica *n* baton
palma *n.* palm
paluba *n* deck
pametan *a.* clever
pametan *a.* smart
pamflet *n.* pamphlet
pamfletista *n.* pamphleteer
pamuk *n.* cotton
panaceja *n.* panacea
panegirik *n.* panegyric
panika *n.* panic
panj *n.* stub
panj *n.* stump
panj *n* block
panorama *n.* panorama
pantalone *n.* breeches
pantalone *n.* slacks
pantalone *n. pl* trousers
panteista *n.* pantheist
panteizam *n.* pantheism
panter *n.* panther
pantomima *n.* pantomime
pantomimičar *n.* mummer
papa *n.* pope
papagaj *n.* parrot
papazjanija *n.* hotchpotch
papir *n.* paper
paprika *n* capsicum
paprikaš *n.* stew
papski *a.* papal
papstvo *n.* papacy
papuča *n.* slipper
papučar *a.* henpecked
par *n* couple
par *n.* pair
para *n* steam
para *n.* vapour
parabola *n.* parable
parada *n.* pageant

parada *n.* parade
paradajz *n.* tomato
paradirati *v.t.* parade
paradoks *n.* paradox
paradoksalan *a.* paradoxical
parafin *n.* paraffin
parafraza *n.* paraphrase
parafrazirati *v.t.* paraphrase
paragraf *n.* paragraph
paralelan *a.* parallel
paralelizam *n.* parallelism
paralelogram *n.* parallelogram
paralitički *a.* paralytic
paraliza *n.* palsy
paraliza *n.* paralysis
paralizovati *v.t.* paralyse
parazit *n.* parasite
parcela *n.* parcel
parče *n.* slice
parfem *n.* perfume
pariranje *n.* parry
parirati *v.t.* parry
paritet *n.* parity
pariti *v.t.* mate
pariti *v.i.* steam
pariti se *v.i.* copulate
park *n.* park
parkirati *v.t.* park
parlament *n.* parliament
parlamentarac *n.* parliamentarian
parlamentaran *a.* parliamentary
parni *a.* vaporous
parničar *n.* litigant
parničenje *n.* litigation
parničiti *v.t.* litigate
parobrod *n.* steamer
parodija *n.* parody
parodirati *v.t.* parody
paroh *n.* parson
parohija *n.* parish

parola *n.* slogan
partiotizam *n.* partiotism
partizan *n.* partisan
partizanski *a.* partisan
partner *n* co-partner
partner *n.* partner
partnerstvo *n.* partnership
pas *n* dog
pasit u krizu *v.i.* slump
pasivan *a.* passive
pasmina *n* breed
pasoš *n.* passport
pasta *n.* paste
pastel *n.* pastel
pasti *v.i.* fall
pasti *v.t* fell
pasti *v.i.* graze
pasti *v.t.* pasture
pasti *v.i.* tumble
pastir *n.* herdsman
pastir *n.* shepherd
pastirski *a.* pastoral
pastuv *n.* stallion
pasus *n.* passage
pašnjak *n.* pasture
pat *n.* stalemate
patent *n* patent
patentan *a.* patent
patentni *v.t.* patent
patetičan *a.* pathetic
patiti *v.t.* suffer
patka *n.* duck
patos *n.* pathos
patriota *n.* patriot
patriotski *a.* patriotic
patrola *n* patrol
patrolirati *v.i.* patrol
patrona *n.* cartridge
patuljak *n* dwarf
patuljak *n* elf

patuljak *n.* midget
paučina *n* cobweb
pauk *n.* spider
paun *n.* peacock
paunica *n.* peahen
pauza *n.* pause
pavijan *n.* baboon
paviljon *n.* pavilion
paziti *v.t.* heed
pažljiv *a.* mindful
pažljiv *a.* thoughtful
pažljiv *a.* attentive
pažnja *n.* attention
pažnja *n* heed
pčela *n.* bee
pčelarstvo *n.* apiculture
pčelinjak *n.* apiary
peć *n.* furnace
peć *n.* oven
peć *n.* stove
pecati *v.i.* dap
pecati *v.i* fish
pečat *n.* seal
pečat *n.* stamp
pečat *n* cachet
pečen *a* roast
pečenje *n* roast
peći *v.t.* roast
pećina *n.* cave
pećina *n.* cavern
pedagog *n.* pedagogue
pedagogija *n.* pedagogy
pedala *n.* pedal
pedant *n.* pedant
pedantan *n.* pedantic
pedanterija *n.* pedantry
pedeset *n.* fifty
pedigre *n.* pedigree
pehar *n.* goblet
pehar *n* beaker

**pejzaž** *n.* landscape
**pejzaž** *n.* scenery
**pekar** *n.* baker
**pekara** *n* bakery
**pelen** *n.* wormwood
**pena** *n* foam
**pena** *n.* lather
**penetracija** *n.* penetration
**peni** *n.* penny
**penis** *n.* penis
**peniti se** *v.t* foam
**penjanje** *n.* climb1
**penjanje** *n* scramble
**penjati se** *v.i* climb
**penjati se** *v.i.* shine
**pentagon** *n.* pentagon
**pentrati se** *v. i* clamber
**penzija** *n.* pension
**penzija** *n.* retirement
**penzioner** *n.* pensioner
**penzionisati** *v.t.* pension
**penzionisati** *v.i.* retire
**pepeo** *n.* ash
**perač** *n.* washer
**peraje** *n* fin
**percepcija** *n.* perception
**perceptivan** *a.* perceptive
**periferija** *n.pl.* outskirts
**periferija** *n.* periphery
**perika** *n.* wig
**period** *n.* period
**periodičan** *a.* periodical
**perla** *n* bead
**permutacija** *n.* permutation
**pero** *n* feather
**pero** *n.* nib
**pero** *n.* pen
**personifikacija** *n.* personification
**perspektiva** *n.* perspective
**perut** *n* dandruff

**perverzan** *a.* perverse
**perverzija** *n.* perversion
**pesak** *n.* sand
**pesimista** *n.* pessimist
**pesimističan** *a.* pessimistic
**pesimizam** *n.* pessimism
**peskovit** *a.* sandy
**pesma** *n.* poem
**pesma** *n.* song
**pesma** *n* carol
**pesma** *n* chant
**pesnica** *n* fist
**pesnik** *n.* poet
**pesnikinja** *n.* poetess
**pesticid** *n.* pesticide
**pešadija** *n.* infantry
**pešak** *n.* pedestrian
**pešice** *adv.* afoot
**peškir** *n.* towel
**pet** *n* five
**peta** *n.* heel
**petak** *n.* Friday
**petao** *n* cock
**peticija** *n.* petition
**petlja** *n.* loop
**petljanje** *n* bungle
**petnaest** *n* fifteen
**pevač** *n.* singer
**pevač** *n.* songster
**pevač** *n.* vocalist
**pevati** *v.i.* sing
**piće** *n* drink
**pigmej** *n.* pigmy
**pigmejac** *n.* pygmy
**pijaca** *n.* mart
**pijanac** *n* bibber
**pijančenje** *n* debauch
**pijančiti** *v. t.* debauch
**pijančiti** *v.i.* revel
**pijančiti** *v. i* booze

**pijanica** *n* drunkard
**pijanista** *n.* pianist
**pijanka** *n.* revel
**pijanka** *n.* spree
**pijanka** *n.* wassail
**pijavica** *n.* leech
**pijuk** *v.t.* hack
**pijuk** *n.* mattock
**pijukati** *v. i* cheep
**pikantan** *a.* piquant
**piknik** *n.* picnic
**pilot** *n.* pilot
**pilotirati** *v.t.* pilot
**pilula** *n.* pill
**pionir** *n.* pioneer
**pipati** *v.t.* grope
**piramida** *n.* pyramid
**piratstvo** *n.* piracy
**pirinač** *n.* paddy
**pirinač** *n.* rice
**pisac** *n.* writer
**pisak posude** *n.* spout
**pisati** *v.t.* pen
**piskav** *a.* shrill
**pismen** *a.* literate
**pismena izjava** *n* affidavit
**pismenost** *n.* literacy
**pismo** *n* letter
**pisoar** *n.* urinal
**pištolj** *n.* pistol
**pitalica** *n.* conundrum
**pitanje** *n.* issue
**pitanje** *n.* query
**pitanje** *n.* question
**pitati** *v.t* query
**pitati** *v.t.* question
**pitati** *v.t.* ask
**piti** *v. t* drink
**pitom** *a.* tame
**piton** *n.* python

**pivara** *n* brewery
**pivo** *n* ale
**pivo** *n* beer
**plaćanje** *n.* payment
**plačljiv** *a.* lachrymose
**plaćenički** *a.* mercenary
**plafon** *n.* ceiling
**plahovitost** *n.* impetuosity
**plakar** *n.* closet
**plakat** *n.* placard
**plakat** *n.* poster
**plakati** *v.i.* weep
**plamen** *n* blaze
**plamen** *n* flame
**plamteti** *v.i* flame
**plana** *n.* plan
**planeta** *n.* planet
**planetarni** *a.* planetary
**planina** *n.* mountain
**planinar** *n.* mountaineer
**planinski** *a.* mountainous
**planinski vrh** *n.* alp
**planirati** *v.t.* plan
**plantaža** *n.* plantation
**planuti** *v.i* flare
**plast** *n.* rick
**plašenje** *n.* shy
**plašiti se** *v.i* fear
**plašiti se** *v.i.* shy
**plašljiv** *a.* timorous
**plata** *n* pay
**plata** *n.* remuneration
**plata** *n.* stipend
**plata** *n.* wage
**platan** *n* plane
**platforma** *n.* platform
**platiti** *v.t.* pay
**plativ** *a.* payable
**platno** *n.* linen
**platno** *n.* canvas

plato *n.* plateau
platonski *a.* platonic
plav *a.* blue
plava boja *n.* blue
plaža *n* beach
plebiscit *n.* plebiscite
pleme *n.* tribe
plemenit *a.* noble
plemenit *n.* noble
plemenski *a.* tribal
plemić *n.* nobleman
plemić *n.* peer
plemstvo *n.* nobility
plemstvo *n.* aristocracy
plen *n.* prey
plen *n* spoil
plen *n* booty
ples *n* dance
plesan *n* mould
plesati *v. t.* dance
plesti *v.t.* knit
pleviti *v.t.* weed
plićak *n.* shoal
plik *n* blain
plik *n* bleb
plima *n.* tide
plimski *a.* tidal
plitak *a.* shallow
plivač *n.* swimmer
plivajući *a.* natant
plivanje *n* swim
plivati *v.i.* swim
pljačka *n.* loot
pljačka *n.* robbery
pljačkanje *v.t.* plunder
pljačkaš *n.* marauder
pljačkaš *n.* robber
pljačkati *v.i.* loot
pljačkati *v.i.* maraud
pljačkati *n* plunder

pljeskanje *n* clap
pljeskati *v. i.* clap
pljoska *n* flask
pljunuti *v.i.* spit
pljusak *n* downpour
pljuvačka *n.* saliva
pljuvačka *n* spit
pljuvaonica *n.* spittoon
ploča *n.* plate
ploča *n.* slab
pločnik *n.* pavement
plodan *a* fertile
plodan *a.* fruitful
plodan *a.* prolific
plodnost *n* fertility
plombirati *v.t.* lead
plovan *a.* navigable
ploveći *adv.* afloat
ploviti *v.i* boat
ploviti *v.i* float
pluća *n* lung
plug *n.* plough
pluralitet *n.* plurality
plus *n* plus
pluta *n.* cork
po strani *adv.* aside
pobaciti *v.i.* miscarry
pobačaj *n* abortion
pobačaj *n.* miscarriage
pobeći *v. i* elope
pobeći *v.i* flee
pobeći *v.i* escape
pobeći *v.i* scamper
pobeći od zakona *v.i* abscond
pobeda *n.* victory
pobeda *n* win
pobediti *v.t.* vanquish
pobediti *v.t.* win
pobediti *v.t.* worst
pobednički *a.* triumphant

**pobednik** *n.* victor
**pobednik** *n.* winner
**pobedonosan** *a.* victorious
**pobijanje** *n.* refutation
**pobiti** *v.t.* refute
**pobledeti** *v.i.* pale
**poboljšanje** *n.* improvement
**poboljšanje** *n.* amelioration
**poboljšanje** *n* betterment
**poboljšati** *v. t* better
**poboljšati** *v.t.* improve
**poboljšati** *v.t.* meliorate
**poboljšati** *v.t.* ameliorate
**pobornik** *n* bigot
**pobornik** *a.* combatant
**pobožan** *a.* pious
**pobožnost** *n.* piety
**pobratim** *n* chum
**pobrkan** *a.* topsy turvy
**pobrkano** *adv* topsy turvy
**pobrkati** *v.i* mess
**pobrkati** *v. t* bungle
**pobuditi** *v.t.* arouse
**pobuđivanje** *n.* solicitation
**pobuna** *n.* insurrection
**pobuna** *n.* mutiny
**pobuna** *n.* rebellion
**pobuna** *n.* revolt
**pobuna** *n.* riot
**pobuna** *n.* sedition
**pobuniti se** *v. i* mutiny
**pobuniti se** *v.i.* revolt
**pocepati u dronjke** *v.t* tatter
**pocrvenelo** *adv* ablush
**počasni** *a.* honorary
**početak** *n* commencement
**početak** *n.* inception
**početak** *n.* onset
**početak** *n.* prime
**početak** *n.* beginning

**početi** *v. t* commence
**početi** *v.t.* start
**početi** *n* begin
**početni** *a.* initial
**početnik** *n.* novice
**počiniti greh** *v.i.* sin
**počiniti nasilje** *v.t.* outrage
**počistiti** *v.t.* tidy
**počovečiti** *v.t.* humanize
**pod** *n* floor
**pod** *prep.* underneath
**podbosti** *v.t.* spur
**podela** *n* division
**podela** *n.* partition
**podeliti** *v. t* divide
**podeliti** *v.t.* partition
**podeliti na četiri dela** *v.t.* quarter
**poderati** *v.t.* tear
**poderotina** *n.* tear
**podesiti** *v.t* fit
**podesiti** *v.t.* proportion
**podići** *v. t* elevate
**podići** *v.t.* uplift
**podijum** *n.* dais
**podizanje** *n* boost
**podizanje** *n.* lift
**podizati** *v.t.* lift
**podlac** *n.* knave
**podlaktica** *n* forearm
**podleći** *v.i.* succumb
**podlost** *n.* knavery
**podložan** *a* subject
**podmazati** *v.t* grease
**podmazati** *v.t.* lubricate
**podmazivanje** *n.* lubrication
**podmetanje požara** *n* arson
**podmiti** *v. t.* bribe
**podmitljiv** *a.* venal
**podmitljivost** *n.* venality
**podmladiti** *v.t.* rejuvenate

podmlađivanje *n.* rejuvenation
podmornica *n.* submarine
podmorski *a* submarine
podmuklost *n.* perfidy
podne *n.* midday
podne *n.* noon
podneti *v.t.* submit
podnositi *v.t.* stomach
podnošljiv *a.* tolerable
podobnost *n.* suitability
podoniti *v.t* sole
podrazumevati *v.t.* imply
podređen *a.* subordinate
podređeni *n* subordinate
podređenost *n.* subordination
podrhtavati *v.i.* palpitate
podrigivanje *v. t* belch
podrignuti *n* belch
podriti *v.t.* subvert
podriti *v.t.* undermine
podrška *n.* support
područje *n* area
podrugivanje *n* sneer
podrugivanje *n* taunt
podrugivati *se v.i* sneer
podrugivati *se v.t.* taunt
podrum *n.* basement
podrum *n* cellar
podružnica *a.* subsidiary
podržat *v.t.* support
podržati *v.t* uphold
podsetiti *v.t.* remind
podsetnik *n.* reminder
podstaći *v.t.* galvanize
podstaći *v.t.* instigate
podstaći *v.t.* prompt
podsticaj *n.* goad
podsticaj *n.* incentive
podsticaj *n.* stimulus
podsticati *v.t* goad

podstrekivanje *n.* instigation
podsuknja *n.* petticoat
podudarati *v. i* coincide
podudarati *v.t.* tally
podugačak *a.* lengthy
poduhvat *n.* venture
podupirač *n.* corbel
podupirač *n.* prop
podupirač *n.* seconder
podupirati *v.t.* prop
podupirati *v.t.* second
podvala *n.* hoax
podvala *n.* imposture
podvaliti *v.t* hoax
podvezica *n.* garter
podvig *n* feat
podvodačica *n.* bawd
podvodna struja *n.* undercurrent
podvrgnuti *v.t.* subject
podvući *v.t.* underline
podzemlje *n.* underworld
podzemni *a.* subterranean
poetika *n.* poetics
poetski *a.* poetic
poezija *n.* poesy
poezija *n.* poetry
pogaziti *v.t.* trample
poginuti *v.i.* perish
poglavica *n.* chieftain
poglavlje *n.* chapter
pogled *n.* glance
pogled *n.* sight
pogled *n.* view
pogledati *v.i.* glance
pognuti *se v.i.* stoop
pognutost *n* stoop
pogodak *n* hit
pogodan *a* convenient
pogodan *a.* handy
pogodan *a.* suitable

pogodan za stanovanje *a.* habitable
pogodan za stanovanje *a.* inhabitable
pogoditi *v.t.* hit
pogodnost *n.* convenience
pogoršati *v.t.* worsen
pogoršati *v.t.* aggravate
pogoršavanje *n.* aggravation
pogrešan *a* erroneous
pogrešan *a.* wrong
pogrešan naziv *n.* misnomer
pogrešiti *v. i* err
pogrešiti *v.t.* mistake
pogrešno *adv.* wrong
pogrešno lečenje *n.* malpractice
pogrešno nazvati *v.t.* miscall
pogrešno odštampati *v.t.* misprint
pogrešno predstaviti *v.t.* misrepresent
pogrešno proceniti *v.t.* misjudge
pogrešno razumeti *v.t.* misapprehend
pogrešno razumeti *v.t.* misconceive
pogrešno razumeti *v.t.* misconstrue
pogrešno razumeti *v.t.* misunderstand
pogrešno shvatanje *n.* misconception
pogrešno upućivanje *n.* misdirection
pogrešno uputiti *v.t.* misdirect
pogrešno verovanje *n.* misbelief
pogrešno voditi *v.t.* mislead
poguban *a* malign
pohabati *v.t.* wear
pohađanje *n.* attendance
pohlepa *n* cupidity
pohlepa *n.* greed
pohlepan *adj.* avid
pohlepan *a.* greedy
pohlepno *adv.* avidity
pohotan *a.* lustful
pohotan *a.* voluptuous
pohotljivac *n.* voluptuary
pohvala *n* commendation
pohvala *n* laud

pohvala *n.* praise
pohvalan *a.* laudable
pohvalan *a.* praiseworthy
pohvaliti *v. t* commend
pohvaliti *v.t.* laud
poigravati *v.t.* trip
pojačalo *n* amplifier
pojačanje *n.* reinforcement
pojačanje *n* amplification
pojačati *v.t.* intensify
pojačati *v.t.* reinforce
pojačati *v.t.* amplify
pojačati *v. t* boost
pojam *n.* notion
pojas *n.* girdle
pojas *n.* strap
pojas *n* belt
pojava *n.* advent
pojaviti se *v.i.* appear
pojaviti se *v. i* emerge
pojedinačan *a.* singular
pojedinačni *a.* individual
pojedinačno *adv.* singularly
pojedinačnost *n.* singularity
pojedinost *n.* particular
pojednostaviti *v. t* ease
pojednostaviti *v.t.* simplify
pojeftiniti *v. t.* cheapen
pojmovni *a.* notional
pokajanje *n.* remorse
pokajanje *n.* repentance
pokajanje *n.* atonement
pokajati se *v.i.* repent
pokajnički *a.* repentant
pokazati *v. t* demonstrate
pokazati *v. t* display
pokazivanje *n.* demonstration
pokazivanje *n* display
poklapati se *v.t.* correlate
poklon *n.* gift

**poklon** *n.* present
**pokloniti** *v. t* donate
**pokloniti se** *v. t* bow
**poklopac** *n.* cover
**poklopac** *n.* lid
**poklopiti** *v. t.* cap
**pokolj** *n.* slaughter
**pokolj** *n* carnage
**pokop** *n* burial
**pokoran** *a.* submissive
**pokoravanje** *n.* subjugation
**pokoravati se** *v.t.* obey
**pokornost** *n.* submission
**pokositi** *v.t.* scythe
**pokrenuti** *v.t.* propel
**pokret** *n.* movement
**pokretač** *n.* mover
**pokretan** *a.* mobile
**pokretan** *a.* movable
**pokretan** *a.* portable
**pokretna imovina** *n.* movables
**pokretnost** *n.* mobility
**pokriti** *v. t.* cover
**pokriti** *v.t* mantle
**pokriti** *v.t.* top
**pokriti crepom** *v.t.* tile
**pokriti krov** *v.t.* thatch
**pokriti krovom** *v.t.* roof
**pokriti plaštom** *v.t.* shroud
**pokriti slamom** *v.t.* litter
**pokrivač** *n* blanket
**pokrivač** *n* wrap
**pokrov** *n.* shroud
**pokrovitelj** *n.* patron
**pokroviteljstvo** *n.* patronage
**pokušaj** *n* try
**pokušaj** *n.* attempt
**pokušati** *v.t.* attempt
**pokušati** *v.i.* try
**pokvarenjak** *v.t.* pervert

**pokvareno** *adj.* addle
**pokvariti** *v.t.* mar
**pokvariti** *v.t.* spoil
**pokvariti** *v.i.* tamper
**pokvariti** *v.t.* vitiate
**pokvasiti** *v. t* drench
**pokvasiti** *v.t.* wet
**pol** *n.* gender
**pol** *n.* pole
**pol** *n.* sex
**pola** *a* half
**polako** *adv.* slowly
**polarni** *n.* polar
**polazak** *n.* outset
**polemika** *n* controversy
**polen** *n.* pollen
**polet** *n.* zest
**polica** *n.* shelf
**policajac** *n* constable
**policajac** *n.* policeman
**policajac** *n.* trooper
**policija** *n.* police
**policijski čas** *n* curfew
**poligamija** *n.* polygamy
**poligamski** *a.* polygamous
**poliglota** *n.* polyglot1
**poliglotski** *a.* polyglot2
**polirati** *v.t.* polish
**politehnički** *a.* polytechnic
**politehnika** *n.* polytechnic
**politeista** *n.* polytheist
**politeistički** *a.* polytheistic
**politeizam** *n.* polytheism
**političar** *n.* politician
**politički** *a.* political
**politika** *n.* policy
**politika** *n.* politics
**polje** *n* field
**poljoprivreda** *n.* agriculture
**poljoprivredni** *a.* agricultural

**poljoprivrednik** *n* farmer
**poljoprivrednik** *n.* agriculturist
**poljski klozet** *n.* outhouse
**poljubac** *n.* kiss
**poljubiti** *v.t.* kiss
**polo** *n.* polo
**polomiti** *v.t* fracture
**polovina** *n.* half
**položaj** *n.* locality
**položiti** *v.t.* lay
**položiti** *v.t.* pillow
**poluga** *n.* lever
**poluprečnik** *n.* radius
**poluslep** *n.* purblind
**pomagati** *v.t* aid
**pomagati** *v.t* favour
**pomagati** *v.i.* minister
**pomama** *n* craze
**pomama** *n.* frenzy
**pomaman** *a.* frantic
**pomen** *v. t.* commemorate
**pomeriti** *v. t* displace
**pomeriti** *v.t.* move
**pomešati** *v.t.* intermingle
**pomirenje** *n.* acquiescence
**pomiriti** *v.t.* reconcile
**pomiriti se** *v.t.* conciliate
**pomoć** *n* help
**pomoć** *n.* succour
**pomoći** *v.t.* help
**pomoći** *v.t.* succour
**pomoćnik** *n.* helpmate
**pomoć** *n.* aid
**pomoć** *n.* assistance
**pomoći** *v.t.* assist
**pomoći** *v.t.* avail
**pomoćni** *a.* auxiliary
**pomoćnik** *n.* auxiliary
**pomorandža** *n.* orange
**pomorski** *a.* maritime

**pomorski** *a.* naval
**pompezan** *a.* pompous
**pompeznost** *n.* pomposity
**pomračenje** *n* eclipse
**ponašanje** *n* behaviour
**ponašati se** *v. i.* behave
**ponavljanje** *n.* repetition
**ponavljati se** *v.i.* recur
**ponedeljak** *n.* Monday
**ponekad** *adv.* sometimes
**poni** *n.* pony
**poništenje** *n.* nullification
**poništi** *v.t.* undo
**poništiti** *v. t.* abrogate
**poništiti** *v.t.* invalidate
**poništiti** *v.t.* nullify
**poništiti** *v.t.* void
**poništiti** *v.t.* annul
**ponizan** *a.* lowly
**poniziti** *v.t.* abase
**poniziti** *v.t.* humiliate
**poniziti** *v.t.* mortify
**poniznost** *n.* humility
**ponižavanje** *n.* humiliation
**poniženje** *n* abasement
**ponoć** *n.* midnight
**ponos** *n.* pride
**ponosan** *a.* proud
**ponositi se** *v.t.* pride
**ponoviti** *v.t.* repeat
**ponovno postavljanje** *v.t.* reinstate
**ponovo** *adv.* afresh
**ponovo postaviti** *n.* reinstatement
**ponovo pridružiti** *v.t.* rejoin
**ponovo štampati** *v.t.* reprint
**ponovo zapasti u grieh** *v.i.* backslide
**ponuda** *n* offer
**ponuda** *n* tender
**ponuda** *n* bid
**ponuđač** *n* bidder

| | |
|---|---|
| **ponuditi** *v.t* bid | **poravnati** *v.t.* align |
| **ponuditi** *v.t.* offer | **poravnati** *v.i* surface |
| **ponuditi** *v.t.* tender | **poraz** *n* defeat |
| **poplava** *n* flood | **poraziti** *v. t.* defeat |
| **poplaviti** *v.t* flood | **porcelan** *n* bisque |
| **poplaviti** *v.t.* swamp | **porcelan** *n.* porcelain |
| **poplaviti** *v.t.* whelm | **pored toga** *adv.* nonetheless |
| **popločati** *v.t* floor | **pored** *prep.* beside |
| **popločati** *v.t.* pave | **poređati** *v.t.* line |
| **popodnevni odmor** *n.* siesta | **poređati** *v.t.* tabulate |
| **popraviti** *v.t.* amend | **poređenje** *n* comparison |
| **popraviti** *v.i.* atone | **poređenje** *n.* simile |
| **popraviti** *v.t* fix | **porediti** *v.t.* liken |
| **popraviti** *v.t.* mend | **poreklo** *n.* ancestry |
| **popraviti** *v.t.* redress | **poreklo** *n.* origin |
| **popraviti** *v.t.* repair | **poremećaj** *n* disorder |
| **popravka** *n.* repair | **poremetiti** *v.t.* perturb |
| **popravni** *a* reformatory | **porez** *n.* tax |
| **popravni** *a.* remedial | **porez na uvezenu robu** *n.* octroi |
| **popravni dom** *n.* reformatory | **poricanje** *n* abnegation |
| **popreko** *prep.* athwart | **poricanje** *n* denial |
| **poprište** *n.* locale | **poricati** *v. t* abnegate |
| **poprskati** *v.i.* splash | **poricati** *v. t.* deny |
| **popularan** *a.* popular | **poricati** *v.t.* gainsay |
| **popularizovati** *v.t.* popularize | **porodica** *n* family |
| **popularnost** *n.* popularity | **porok** *n.* vice |
| **popuniti** *v.t* fill | **porota** *n.* jury |
| **popust** *n* discount | **porotnik** *n.* juror |
| **popustiti** *v.i.* relent | **porotnik** *n.* juryman |
| **popustljiv** *adj.* compliant | **portal** *n.* portal |
| **popustljiv** *a.* indulgent | **portfolio** *n.* portfolio |
| **popustljiv** *a.* lenient | **portparol** *n.* spokesman |
| **popustljivost** *n.* connivance | **portret** *n.* portrait |
| **popustljivost** *n.* lenience, leniency | **portret** *n.* portrayal |
| **poput** *prep* like | **portretisanje** *n.* portraiture |
| **poput čestice** *a.* particle | **porub** *n.* welt |
| **pora** *n.* pore | **poručnik** *n.* lieutenant |
| **porast** *n* increase | **poruka** *n.* message |
| **porasti** *v.t.* increase | **porumeneti** *v.i* blush |
| **poravnanje** *n.* alignment | **porumeneti** *v.t.* redden |

**poružnjavati** *v.t.* uglify
**posada** *n.* crew
**posaditi** *v.t.* seed
**posaditi na presto** *v.t.* throne
**posao** *n* business
**posao** *n.* job
**poseban** *a* distinct
**poseban** *a* especial
**poseban** *a.* particular
**poseban** *a.* special
**poseban porez na platu** *n.* supertax
**poseći sabljom** *v.t.* sabre
**posedovanje** *n.* possession
**posedovati** *v.t.* own
**posedovati** *v.t.* possess
**poseta** *n.* visit
**posetilac** *n.* visitor
**posetiti** *v.t.* visit
**posipati** *v. t.* sprinkle
**poslanica** *n.* missive
**poslastica** *n.* comfit
**poslastica** *n.* dainty
**poslastičar** *n* confectioner
**poslastičarnica** *n* confectionery
**poslati** *v.t* forward
**poslati** *v.t.* send
**poslati poštom** *v.t.* mail
**posle** *prep.* past
**posle** *adv.* post
**posle čega conj.** whereupon
**posle toga** *adv.* thereafter
**posledica** *n* consequence
**posledica** *n.* repercussion
**poslednji** *a* after
**poslednji** *a.* last1
**poslodavac** *n* employer
**poslovanje** *n.* dealing
**poslovica** *n.* proverb
**poslovica** *n.* adage
**poslovičan** *a.* proverbial

**posluga** *n* domestic
**poslušan** *a* docile
**poslušan** *a.* obedient
**poslušnost** *n.* obedience
**poslužavnik** *n.* tray
**poslužitelj** *n.* beadle
**poslužiti** *v.t.* serve
**posmatrački** *a.* observant
**posmatranje** *n.* observation
**posmatrati** *v.t.* observe
**posmrtni** *a.* obituary
**posmrtni** *a.* posthumous
**pospan** *a.* sleepy
**pospan** *n.* somnolent
**pospanost** *n.* somnolence
**posramiti** *v. t* embarrass
**posramljen** *a.* ashamed
**posrebriti** *v.t.* silver
**posredan** *a.* oblique
**posrednik** *n.* intermediary
**posrednik** *n.* mediator
**posrednik** *n.* middleman
**posredovanje** *n.* mediation
**posredovanje** *n.* mediation
**posredovati** *v.i.* mediate
**posrnuti** *v.i* falter
**post** *n* fast
**post skriptum** *n.* postscript
**postati vitak** *v.i.* slim
**postati** *v. i* become
**postava** *n* lining
**postaviti** *v.t.* mount
**postaviti** *v.t.* post
**postaviti** *v.t.* right
**postaviti** *v.t* set
**postaviti dijagnozu** *v. t* diagnose
**posteljina** *n.* bedding
**postepen** *a.* gradual
**postići** *v.t.* achieve
**postići** *v.t.* attain

**postideti** *v.t.* abash
**postiti** *v.i* fast
**postizanje** *n.* acquirement
**postojan** *a.* steadfast
**postojanje** *n* existence
**postojanost** *n.* steadiness
**postojati** *v.i* exist
**postojeći** *n* being
**postolje** *n.* mount
**postolje** *n.* pedestal
**postrojenje** *n* facility
**postrojiti** *v.t* marshal
**postrojiti** *v.t.* range
**postupak** *n.* proceeding
**postupati** *v.i.* act
**posuti** *v.t.* strew
**posvećivanje** *n.* sanctification
**posveta** *n* dedication
**posvetiti** *v.t.* consecrate
**posvetiti** *v. t.* dedicate
**posvetiti** *v. t* devote
**posvetiti** *v.t.* hallow
**pošiljka** *n.* consignment
**pošiljka** *n.* shipment
**pošta** *n.* mail
**pošta** *n.* post-office
**poštanski** *a.* postal
**poštar** *n.* postman
**poštarina** *n.* postage
**pošten** *a.* honest
**poštenje** *n.* honesty
**pošteno** *adv.* fairly
**pošto** *conj.* after
**pošto** *conj.* whereas
**poštovanje** *n* esteem
**poštovanje** *n.* regard
**poštovanje** *n.* respect
**poštovanje** *n.* reverence
**poštovati** *v. t* esteem
**poštovati** *v. t* honour

**poštovati** *v.t.* profane
**poštovati** *v.t.* respect
**poštovati** *v.t.* venerate
**pošumiti** *v.t.* afforest
**pošumljen** *a.* sylvan
**potamneti** *v. t* dim
**potamneti** *v.t.* obscure
**potamneti** *v.t* shadow
**potamneti** *v. t.* blacken
**potapanje** *n.* immersion
**potaša** *n.* potash
**potcenjivanje** *n* disregard
**potcenjivati** *v. t* disregard
**potčiniti** *v.t.* subjugate
**potčiniti** *v.t.* subordinate
**potčinjenje** *n.* subjection
**potencijal** *n.* pontentiality
**potencijalan** *a.* prospective
**potentan** *a.* potent
**potentnost** *n.* potency
**potera** *n.* chase2
**potera** *n.* pursuit
**potez** *n.* move
**potiljak** *n.* nape
**potisak** *n.* thrust
**potisak** *n* buoyancy
**potisnuti** *v.t.* repress
**potka** *n.* woof
**potkazivanje** *n.* denunciation
**potkopavati** *v.t.* sap
**potkralj** *n.* viceroy
**potkrepiti** *v.t.* corroborate
**potkrovlje** *n.* loft
**potočić** *n.* rivulet
**potočić** *n.* streamlet
**potok** *n.* creek
**potok** *n.* stream
**potok** *n.* brook
**potom** *adv.* next
**potomak** *n* descendant

potomak *n.* offspring
potomstvo *n.* posterity
potomstvo *n.* progeny
potonuti *v.i.* sink
potopiti *v.t.* soak
potopiti *v.i.* submerge
potpaliti *v.t.* kindle
potpis *n.* signature
potpisati *v.t.* subscribe
potpisnik *n.* signatory
potpun *a* absolute
potpun *adj.* crass
potpun *a* downright
potpun *a.* sheer
potpun *adv.* stark
potpun *a* utter
potpuno *adv* absolutely
potpuno *adv* downright
potpuno *adv* entirely
potpuno *adv.* fully
potpuno *adv.* utterly
potpunost *n.* stark
potraživanje *n* claim
potreba *n.* necessary
potreba *n* requisite
potreba *n* want
potreban *a* necessary
potreban *a.* needful
potreban *a.* requisite
potres *n* quake
potres *n* shake
potrostručiti *v.t.* triplicate
potrošiti *v. t* expend
potrošnja *n* consumption
potvrda *n* affirmation
potvrda *n* confirmation
potvrdan *a* affirmative
potvrditi *v. t.* certify
potvrditi *v. t* confirm
potvrditi *v.t.* substantiate

potvrditi *v.t.* validate
potvrditi *v.t.* affirm
potvrditi *v.t.* attest
potvrđivanje *n.* substantiation
pouka *n.* moral
pouzdan *a.* reliable
pouzdan *a.* trustworthy
pouzdanje *n.* reliance
povećanje *n.* augmentation
povećati *v.t.* augment
povelik *a.* sizable
povelja *n* charter
povelja *n.* muniment
poverenik *n.* commissioner
poverenik *n* confidant
poverenik *n.* trustee
poverenje *n* confidence
poverenje *n.* trust
poverilac *n* creditor
poveriti *v. i* confide
poveriti *v. t.* consign
poveriti *v. t* entrust
poverljiv *a.* confidential
poverljiv *a.* trustful
povetarac *n* breeze
povezati *v. t.* connect
povezati *v.t.* rope
povik *n.* shout
povisiti *v.t.* heighten
povlačenje *n* drag
povlačenje *n.* pull
povlačenje *n.* withdrawal
povlačiti *v. t* drag
povlačiti se *v.i.* retreat
povlašćen *a.* preferential
povoljan *a* favourable
povoljan *a.* providential
povoljan *a.* advantageous
povoljan *a.* auspicious
povorka *n.* procession

| | |
|---|---|
| **povraćaj** *n.* refund | **pozdraviti** *v.t* hail |
| **povraćanje** *n* vomit | **pozdraviti** *v.t.* salute |
| **povraćati** *v.t.* vomit | **pozdraviti** *v.t* welcome |
| **povratak** *n.* relapse | **pozdraviti se** *n.* adieu |
| **povratak** *n.* return | **pozicija u kriketu** *n.* mid-off |
| **povratak u domovinu** *n.* repatriation | **pozicija u kriketu** *n.* mid-on |
| **povratan** *a.* reversible | **pozirati** *v.i.* pose |
| **povratiti** *v.t.* refund | **pozitivan** *a.* positive |
| **povratiti** *v.t.* retrieve | **poziv** *n.* calling |
| **povratni** *a.* recurrent | **poziv** *v.* invitation |
| **povratni** *a* reflexive | **poziv** *n.* summons |
| **povratnik** *n* repatriate | **poziv** *n.* call |
| **povrće** *n.* vegetable | **pozivač** *n* caller |
| **povreda** *n* hurt | **pozlata** *a.* gilt |
| **povreda** *n.* injury | **pozlatiti** *v.t.* gild |
| **povrediti** *v.t.* hurt | **poznanici** *n.* kith |
| **povrediti** *v.t.* injure | **poznanstvo** *n.* acquaintance |
| **povrediti** *v.t.* violate | **poznat** *a* familiar |
| **povremen** *a.* occasional | **poznat** *a* famous |
| **povremeno** *adv.* occasionally | **poznat** *a.* renowned |
| **povrh** *adv* above | **poznat** *a.* well-known |
| **površan** *a* cursory | **pozorišni** *a.* theatrical |
| **površan** *a.* superficial | **pozorište** *n.* theatre |
| **površina** *n.* surface | **pozornica** *n.* stage |
| **površina u jutrima** *n.* acreage | **pozvati** *v.t.* invite |
| **površnost** *n.* superficiality | **pozvati** *v.t.* summon |
| **povrtni** *a.* vegetable | **pozvati** *v. t.* call |
| **povući** *v.t.* pull | **poželjan** *a* desirable |
| **povući** *v.t.* withdraw | **poželjan** *a* eligible |
| **povučen** *a.* reticent | **požuda** *n.* appetence |
| **povučenost** *n.* reticence | **požuda** *n.* lust |
| **poza** *n.* pose | **požuriti** *v. t.* expedite |
| **pozadina** *n.* rear | **požuteti** *v.t.* yellow |
| **pozadina** *n.* background | **praćka** *n.* sling |
| **pozajmiti** *v.t.* lend | **prag** *n.* threshold |
| **pozajmiti** *v.t.* loan | **pragmatičan** *a.* pragmatic |
| **pozajmiti** *v. t* borrow | **pragmatizam** *n.* pragmatism |
| **pozdrav** *n.* salutation | **prah** *n.* powder |
| **pozdrav** *n* salute | **praistorijski** *a.* prehistoric |
| **pozdraviti** *v.t.* greet | **praksa** *n.* practice |

praktičan *a.* practical
praktičar *n.* practitioner
pralja *n.* laundress
pranje *n* ablution
pranje *n* wash
praotac *n* forefather
pras *a* snap
prasak *n* crack
prasak *n* pop
prasak *n* snap
prasak *n.* bang
prasak *n* burst
prasnuti *v. i.* burst
prastar *a.* primeval
prastari *a.* immemorial
prašina *n* dust
prati *v.t.* wash
pratilac *n.* attendant
pratiti *v.t.* accompany
pratiti *v. t* dog
pratiti *v. t* escort
pratiti *v.t* follow
pratnja *n* accompaniment
pratnja *n* escort
pratnja *n.* retinue
prav *a.* straight
pravac *n* direction
pravda *n.* justice
pravedan *a* equitable
pravedan *a.* just
pravedan *a.* righteous
pravedno *adv.* aright
pravedno *adv.* justly
pravi *a.* genuine
pravi *a.* proper
pravi *a.* real
pravi *a.* right
pravi *a.* true
pravi *a.* veritable
pravilno *adv* aright

pravilnost *n.* regularity
pravilo *n.* precept
pravilo *n.* rule
praviti akrobacije *v.t.* stunt
praviti dosetke *v.i.* quibble
pravni *a.* legal
pravni lek *n.* remedy
pravnik *n.* jurist
pravo *n* right
pravo *adv.* straight
pravo glasa *n.* suffrage
pravo zaloge *n.* lien
pravoslavan *a.* orthodox
pravoslavlje *n.* orthodoxy
pravosuđe *n.* judicature
pravougaoni *a.* rectangular
pravougaonik *n.* rectangle
pravovremen *a.* seasonable
prazan *a* empty
prazan *a.* vacant
prazan *a.* void
prazan *a* blank
praziluk *n.* leek
praznina *n* blank
praznina *n.* lacuna
praznina *n.* void
prazniti *v. t* discharge
prazniti *v* empty
pražnjenje *n.* discharge
pre *prep* before
pre nego *conj* before
pre podne *n* forenoon
pre *prep.* afore
pre *adv.* ago
prebivalište *n* abode
prebivalište *n* domicile
prebivalište *n* dwelling
prebivalište *n.* residence
preceniti *v.t.* overrate
preciznost *n.* precise

preciznost *n.* precision
prećutan *a.* tacit
prečasni *a.* venerable
prečišćavanje *n.* purification
prečišćavanje *n.* refinement
prečka *n.* spoke
prečnik *n* diameter
prećutna saglasnost *v.i.* acquiesce
predaja *n* surrender
predak *n.* ancestor
predati se *v.t.* surrender
predavač *n.* lecturer
predavanje *n.* lecture
predavati *v* lecture
predbračni *a.* premarital
predbračni *adj.* antenuptial
predenje *n.* purr
predgovor *n* foreword
predgovor *n.* preamble
predgovor *n.* preface
predgrađe *n.* suburb
predikat *n.* predicate
predivan *a.* wonderful
predivo *n.* yarn
predjelo *n* appetizer
predlog *n.* preposition
predlog *n.* proposal
predlog *n.* proposition
predlog *n.* suggestion
predložiti *v.t.* propose
predložiti *v.t.* propound
predložiti *v.t.* suggest
prednja noga *n* foreleg
prednjak *n* limber
prednji *a* foremost
prednji *a.* forward
prednji *a* front
prednost *n.* precedence
prednost *n.* advantage
predodređenje *n.* predestination

predodrediti *v.t.* predetermine
predosećanje *n.* premonition
predosećanje *n.* prescience
predostrožnost *n.* precaution
predozirati *v.t.* overdose
predrasuda *n.* prejudice
predsedavati *v.i.* preside
predsednički *a.* presidential
predsednik *n* chairman
predsednik *n.* president
predsoblje *n.* lobby
predstaviti *v.t.* present
predstaviti *v.t.* typify
predstavljanje *n.* impersonation
predstavljanje *n.* representation
predstavljati *v.t.* represent
predstavnik *n.* representative
predstojeći *a.* forthcoming
predstojeći *a.* imminent
predstraža *n.* outpost
preduhitriti *v.t* forestall
predujam *n.* advance
predumišljaj *n.* premeditation
preduslov *n* prerequisite
preduslovan *a.* prerequisite
preduzeća *adj.* corporate
preduzeće *n* enterprise
preduzeti *v.t.* undertake
predviđanje *n.* anticipation
predviđanje *n* forecast
predviđanje *n.* foreknowledge
predviđanje *n* foresight
predviđanje *n.* prediction
predviđati *v.t* forecast
predvideti *v.t* foresee
predvideti *v.t.* predict
predvideti *v.t.* anticipate
predvorje *n.* lounge
prefekt *n.* prefect
prefiks *n.* prefix

**prefinjenost** *n.* sophistication
**pregača** *n.* rung
**pregled** *n.* conspectus
**pregled** *n.* digest
**pregled** *n.* overhaul
**pregled** *n.* perusal
**pregled** *n* review
**pregled** *n.* survey
**pregled** *n.* syllabus
**pregledanje** *n* browse
**pregledati** *v.t.* inspect
**pregledati** *v.t.* overhaul
**pregledati** *v.t.* peruse
**pregledati** *v.t.* review
**pregledati** *v.t.* scrutinize
**pregledati** *v.t.* survey
**pregovarač** *n.* negotiator
**pregovaranje** *n.* negotiation
**pregovaranje** *n.* parley
**pregovarati** *v.t.* negotiate
**pregovarati** *v.i* parley
**pregovor** *n.* treaty
**pregršt** *n.* handful
**pregrupisati** *v.t.* deploy
**preispitivati** *se v.i.* introspect
**prekid** *n* abruption
**prekid** *n.* interruption
**prekidač** *n.* switch
**prekinuti** *v.i* abort
**prekinuti** *v. t* break
**prekinuti** *v. t* discontinue
**prekinuti** *v. t* disrupt
**prekinuti** *v.t.* interrupt
**prekinuti** *v.t.* sever
**preklapanje** *n* overlap
**preklapati** *v.t.* overlap
**preklinjanje** *n.* entreaty
**preklinjanje** *n* adjuration
**preklinjati** *v. t.* entreat
**preklinjati** *v.t.* implore

**preko** *prep.* over
**preko** *prep.* via
**preko noći** *adv.* overnight
**preko palube** *adv.* overboard
**preko** *adv.* across
**preko puta** *prep.* across
**prekomeran rad** *n.* overwork
**prekor** *n.* reproach
**prekoračenje** *n.* demurrage
**prekoračenje računa** *n.* overdraft
**prekoračiti** *v.t* exceed
**prekoračiti** *v.t.* transcend
**prekoračiti račun** *v.t.* overdraw
**prekovremeni rad** *n* overtime
**prekovremeno** *adv.* overtime
**prekretnica** *n.* milestone
**prekriti** *v.t.* veil
**prekrivač** *n.* coverlet
**prekrstiti** *v. t* cross
**prekršaj** *n.* default
**prekršaj** *a.* foul
**prekršaj** *n.* misdemeanour
**prekršiti** *v.t.* transgress
**prekršiti zakletvu** *v.t.* forswear
**prelat** *n.* prelate
**prelaz** *n.* crossing
**prelaz** *n.* transition
**prelazni** *n.* transitive
**preliminaran** *a.* preliminary
**prelja** *n.* spinner
**preljuba** *n.* adultery
**prelom** *n.* fracture
**prelomiti** *v.t.* page
**prema gore** *prep.* up
**prema tome** *adv.* accordingly
**premašivati** *v.i.* preponderate
**premazait katranom** *v.t.* tar
**premda** *conj.* notwithstanding
**premda** *conj.* though
**premija** *n.* premium

premijer *a.* premier
premijer *n* premier
premijera *n.* premiere
preminuti *v. i* decease
premostiti *v.t.* span
premostiv *a.* negotiable
prenatalni *adj.* antenatal
prenemaganje *n* whine
prenemaganje *n* affectation
prenemagati se *v.i.* whine
prenoćiti *v.i.* roost
prenos *n* conveyance
prenos *n.* telecast
prenos *n.* transfer
prenositi *v. t.* convey
prenositi *v.t.* relay
prenositi *v.t.* telecast
prenositi *v.t.* transfer
prenositi *v.t.* transmit
prenosiv *a.* removable
prenosiv *a.* transferable
preobilan *a.* superabundant
preobilje *n.* superabundance
preobraćenik *n* convert
preobraziti *v.t.* transfigure
preobraženje *n.* transfiguration
preokret *n.* reversal
preokret *n.* upheaval
preokupacija *n.* preoccupation
preopširan *a.* verbose
preopširnost *n.* verbosity
preopterećenje *n* overload
preopterećenje *n.* surcharge
preopterećenje *n* overcharge
preopteretiti *v.t.* overburden
preopteretiti *v.t.* overcharge
preopteretiti *v.t.* overload
preopteretiti *v.t.* surcharge
preopteretiti radom *v.i.* overwork
preosetljiv *a* maudlin

preostali *a.* residual
preovlađivati *v.i.* predominate
preovlađivati *v.i.* prevail
preovlađujući *a.* prevalent
prepad *n* swoop
prepelica *n.* quail
prepirati se *v. i* dispute
prepirati se *v.i.* wrangle
prepirati se *v. t* bicker
prepirka *n.* altercation
prepirka *v. t* brangle
prepirka *n.* wrangle
prepisati *v.t.* transcribe
prepiska *n.* correspondence
preplanulost *n., a.* tan
preplanuti *v.i.* tan
preplašiti *v.t.* overawe
prepoloviti *v.t.* halve
prepoloviti *v. t* bisect
preporod *n.* rebirth
preporod *n.* resurgence
preporučiti *v.t.* recommend
preporučiv *a.* advisable
preporučivost *n* advisability
preporuka *n.* recommendation
prepoznati *v.t.* recognize
prepoznavanje *n.* recognition
prepraviti *v.t.* revise
prepreden *a* arch
prepreka *n.* hindrance
prepreka *n.* impediment
prepreka *n.* obstacle
preraditi *v.t.* refine
prerasti *v.t.* outgrow
prerušen *n* disguise
prerušiti se *v. t* disguise
presađivati *v.t.* transplant
presedan *n.* precedent
preskakivanje *n* skip
preskočiti *v.i.* skip

presrećan *a* overjoyed
presresti *v.t.* intercept
presretanje *n.* interception
prestati *v.t.* quit
prestati *v. i.* cease
presti *v.i.* purr
prestići *v.t.* overtake
prestiž *n.* prestige
prestižan *a.* prestigious
prestraviti *v.t.* terrify
prestravljen *a.* aghast
prestup *n.* transgression
prestup *n.* trespass
prestupnik *n.* offender
presuda *n.* judgement
presuda *n.* verdict
presudan *adj.* crucial
presuditi *v.t.* arbitrate
preštampavanje *n.* reprint
pretegnuti *v.t.* outweigh
pretenciozan *a.* pretentious
pretendent *n.* aspirant
pretenzija *n.* pretension
preterano čedna žena *n.* prude
preterano laskanje *n* adulation
preterano uslužan *a.* officious
preterati *v.t.* overdo
preterivati *v.t.* overact
prethoditi *v.* precede
prethoditi *v.t.* antecede
prethodni *a.* antecedent
prethodni *a* former
prethodni *a.* previous
prethodnik *n* forerunner
prethodnik *n.* precursor
prethodnik *n.* predecessor
pretiti *v.t* menace
pretiti *v.t.* threaten
pretnja *n* menace
pretnja *n.* threat

pretplata *n.* subscription
pretpostaviti *v.i* guess
pretpostaviti *v.t.* presume
pretpostaviti *v.t.* presuppose
pretpostaviti *v.t.* suppose
pretpostaviti *v.t.* surmise
pretpostaviti *v.t.* assume
pretpostavka *n* conjecture
pretpostavka *n.* guess
pretpostavka *n.* presumption
pretpostavka *n.* supposition
pretpostavka *n.* surmise
pretpostavka *n.* assumption
pretpostavljanje *n.* presupposition
pretpostavljati *v. t* conjecture
pretraga *n.* search
pretrčati *v.t* overrun
pretresti *v.t.* ransack
pretrpeti *v.t.* undergo
preturanje *n* rummage
preturati *v.i.* fumble
pretvaranje *n.* pretence
pretvarati se *v.t* feign
pretvarati se *v.t.* pretend
pretvarati se *v.i.* sham
pretvoriti *v. t* convert
pretvoriti u kašu *v.t.* pulp
pretvoriti u stihove *v.t.* versify
preuveličavanje *n.* exaggeration
preuveličavati *v. t.* exaggerate
preuzeti *v.t.* shoulder
prevaga *n.* preponderance
prevagnuti *v.t.* out-balance
prevara *n* deceit
prevara *n* deception
prevara *n* eyewash
prevara *n.* fraud
prevara *n.* ruse
prevara *n.* swindle
prevara *n.* bam

prevarantski *a* crook
prevariti *v.t.* hoodwink
prevariti *v.t.* swindle
prevariti *v.t.* trick
prevariti *v. t.* bilk
prevazići *v.t.* overcome
prevelik *a.* outsize
prevelika doza *n.* overdose
prevencija *n.* prevention
preventivan *a.* preventive
predideti *v.t.* overlook
prevlast *n.* predominance
prevlast *n.* prevalence
prevlast *n.* supremacy
prevođenje *n.* translation
prevodilac *n.* interpreter
prevoditi *v.t.* translate
prevoz *n.* transport
prevoziti *v.t* ferry
prevoziti *v.t.* transport
prevremen *a.* premature
prevrnuti *v.t.* tip
prevrnuti *v. i.* capsize
prezasićenost *n* glut
prezasićenost *n.* surfeit
prezasititi *v.t.* glut
prezentacija *n.* presentation
prezervativ *n.* preservative
prezime *n.* surname
prezir *n* contempt
prezir *n* disdain
prezir *n.* scorn
prezirati *v. t* despise
prezirati *v. t.* disdain
prezirati *v.t.* loathe
prezirati *v.t.* scorn
prezriv *a* contemptuous
preživanje *v.i.* rummage
preživar *n.* ruminant
preživati *v.i.* ruminate

pribeći *v.i.* resort
pribežište *n* resort
približan *a.* approximate
pribor *n* accessory
pribor *n. pl* paraphernalia
pribor *n.* tackle
pribor *n.* utensil
pribosti *v.t.* pin
pribranost *n.* composure
priča *n.* story
priča *n.* tale
pričati *v.i.* talk
pričljiv *a.* talkative
pričvrstiti *v.t* fasten
pričvrstiti *v.t* key
pričvrstiti *v.t.* limber
pričvrstiti klinom *v.t.* wedge
pričvrstiti *v.t.* affix
pričvrstiti *v.t.* attach
pridev *n.* adjective
pridruženje *n.* affiliation
pridružiti *v.t.* join
pridržavanje *n.* observance
prigodan *a.* pertinent
prigovarati *v.t.* reproach
prigovor *n.* objection
prigovoriti *v.t.* object
prigradski *a.* suburban
prigrušeno se smejati *v. i* chuckle
prigušen glas *n.* undertone
prigušiti *v.t.* muffle
prigušivač *n.* muffler
prigušivač *n.* silencer
prihod *n* emolument
prihod *n.* income
prihod *n.* revenue
prihvatanje *n* acceptance
prihvatiti *&* accept
prihvatljiv *a* acceptable
prihvatljiv *a.* admissible

prijatan *a* kind
prijatan *a*. pleasant
prijatelj *n*. friend
prijatelj *n*. mate
prijateljski *adj.* amicable
prijateljstvo *n*. amity
prijem *n*. reception
prijemčiv *a*. receptive
prijemnik *n*. receiver
prikazati *v.t.* show
prikazati u profilu *v.t.* profile
prikazivanje *n*. show
prikazivati *v. t.* depict
prikladan *a* expedient
prikladan fit
prikladan *a*. opportune
prikladan *a*. seemly
prikladan *adj* apposite
prikladan *a*. appropriate
prikladno *adv* appositely
priklanjanje *n* deference
priključenje *n*. incorporation
priključiti *v.t.* incorporate
prikolica *n*. trailer
prikovati *v.t.* peg
prikradati se *v.i.* stalk
prikriti *v. t.* conceal
prikriven *a*. latent
prikriven *a*. ulterior
prikupiti *v. t* collect
prikupiti *v.t.* muster
prilagođavanje *n*. adaptation
prilagođavanje *n*. adjustment
prilagoditi se *v.t* acclimatise
prilagoditi *v.t.* adapt
prilagoditi *v.t.* adjust
prilagodljiv *a*. malleable
prilepiti se *v. i.* cling
prilično *adv.* pretty
prilika *n*. occasion

prilika *n*. opportunity
priliv *n*. influx
priljubljen *adj* cohesive
prilog *n*. attachment
prilog *n*. enclosure
prilog *n*. adverb
priloški *a*. adverbial
priložiti *v. t* enclose
primalac *n*. payee
primalac *n*. recipient
primalac *n*. addressee
primećen *a*. notice
primena *n*. usage
primena *n*. application
primeniti *v. t.* enforce
primeniti *v.t.* apply
primeniti *v.t.* appropriate
primenljiv *a*. applicable
primer *n* example
primer *n*. instance
primerak *n*. specimen
primeran *a*. apposite
primetan *adj* perceptible
primetan *a*. appreciable
primetiti *v.t.* notice
primirje *n*. truce
primirje *n*. armistice
primitivan *a*. primitive
primorski *a*. littoral
princ *n*. prince
princeza *n*. princess
princip *n*. principle
prinos *n* yield
prinuda *n* compulsion
prionuti *v.t.* tackle
prioritet *n*. priority
pripadanje *n* appurtenance
pripadati *v. i* belong
pripajanje *n* annexation
pripisati *v.t.* impute

pripisati *v.t.* ascribe
pripit *a.* mellow
pripit *a.* tipsy
pripitomiti *v.t.* tame
pripovedač *n.* narrator
pripovedački *a.* narrative
pripovedati *v.t.* narrate
pripovest *n.* narrative
pripravnik *n.* probationer
pripravnik *n.* trainee
priprema *n* preliminary
priprema *n.* preparation
pripremiti *v.t.* prepare
pripremni *a.* preparatory
priraštaj *n.* increment
prirediti *v.t.* stage
priroda *n.* nature
prirodni *a.* natural
prirodnjak *n.* naturalist
prirodno *adv.* naturally
priručnik *n.* handbook
priručnik *n* manual
prisilan *a* forcible
prisiliti *v. t* compel
prisnost *n.* rapport
pristajanje *n.* landing
pristalica *n.* stickler
pristanak *n.* consent
pristanak *n.* assent
pristanište *n.* dock
pristati *v.i.* assent
pristati *v. i* consent
pristati uz jednu stranu *v.i.* side
pristojan *a* becoming
pristojan *a* decent
pristojba za vaganje *n.* weighage
pristojnost *n* decency
pristojnost *n* decorum
pristrasnost *n.* partiality
pristup *n* access

pristup *n.* admission
pristup *n.* approach
pristupanje *n* accession
pristupanje *n.* admittance
pristupiti *v.t.* accede
pristupiti *v.t.* approach
prisustvo *n.* presence
prisustvovati *v.t.* attend
prisutan *a.* present
prisvajanje *n.* appropriation
pritegnuti *v.t.* tighten
pritisak *n.* pressure
pritisnite *v.t.* press
pritisnuti *v. t* depress
pritoka *n.* tributary
pritvoren *adv.* ajar
priuštiti *v.t.* afford
privatni *a.* private
privatnost *n.* privacy
privezati *v.t.* tether
privići se *v.t.* accustom
prividan *a.* apparent
prividan *a* bogus
privilegija *n.* prerogative
privilegija *n.* privilege
privlačan *a.* attractive
privlačan *n.* sexy
privlačiti *v.t.* allure
privlačnost *n* allurement
privlačnost *n.* attraction
privoleti *v.t.* consent3
privremen *a.* provisional
privremen *a.* temporary
privrženik *n* devotee
privrženik *n.* loyalist
privrženost *n.* adherence
privrženost *n* devotion
privući *v.t.* attract
prizivač duhova *n.* necromancer
prizivanje *n.* invocation

prizivati *v.t.* conjure
prizivati *v.t.* invoke
priznanica *n* bill
priznanje *n.* acknowledgement
priznanje *n* confession
priznati *v. t.* confess
priznati *v.* acknowledge
priznati *v.t.* admit
priznati *v.t.* avow
prkos *n* defiance
prljav *a* dirty
prljav *a* filthy
prljav *a.* sordid
proba *n.* probation
proba *n.* rehearsal
probati *v.t.* rehearse
problem *n.* problem
problematičan *a.* problematic
probni *a.* tentative
probosti *v.t.* jab
probosti kopljem *v.t.* spear
probuditi *v.t.* awake
probuditi *v.t.* wake
probuditi se *v.i.* rouse
probušiti *v.t* hole
probušiti *v.t.* perforate
probušiti *v.t.* puncture
procedura *n.* procedure
procena *n.* estimate
procena *n* estimation
procena *n.* valuation
procena *n.* assessment
procenat *n.* percentage
proceniti *v. t* estimate
proceniti *v.t.* rate
proceniti *v.t.* appraise
proceniti *v.t.* assess
proces *n.* process
proći *v.i.* pass
procvat *n* blossom

procvetati *v.i* blossom
pročišćenje *n.* purgation
pročišćavajući *a* laxative
prodaja *n.* sale
prodavac *n.* monger
prodavac *n.* salesman
prodavac *n.* seller
prodavac *n.* vendor
prodavac knjiga *n* book-seller
prodavati *v.t.* sell
prodavati robu na malo *v.t.* retail
prodavnica *n.* shop
prodavnica *n.* store
prodor *n* breach
prodreti *v.t.* penetrate
produkt *n.* product
produktivan *a.* productive
produktivnost *n.* productivity
produženje *n.* prolongation
produžiti *v.t.* lengthen
produžiti *v.t.* prolong
profesija *n.* profession
profesionalan *a.* professional
profesor *n.* professor
profil *n.* profile
profitabilan *a.* profitable
profiter *n.* profit
profiter *n.* profiteer
profitirati *v.t.* profit
proganjanje *n.* persecution
proglas *n.* proclamation
proglasiti *v. t.* declare
proglasiti *v.t.* proclaim
prognati *v. t* exile
prognati *v.t.* ostracize
progoniti *v.t.* haunt
progoniti *v.t.* persecute
progoniti *v.t.* pursue
progonstvo *n.* exile
program *n.* programme

programirati *v.t.* programme
progresivan *a.* progressive
progutati *v.t* engulf
progutati *v.t.* swallow
prohladno *a* chilly
proizilaziti *v.i* ensue
proizlaziti *v.i.* result
proizvod *n.* produce
proizvođač *n* manufacturer
proizvoditi *v.t* fabricate
proizvoditi *v.t.* manufacture
proizvoditi *v.t.* produce
proizvodnja *n* fabrication
proizvodnja *n* manufacture
proizvodnja *n.* production
proizvoljno *a.* arbitrary
projekat *n.* project
projekcija *n.* projection
projektil *n.* missile
projektil *n.* projectile
projektor *n.* projector
projektovati *v.t.* project
proklet *a.* accursed
prokleti *v. t* curse
prokleti *v. t.* damn
prokletstvo *n.* damnation
prokletstvo *n.* malediction
prokrijumčariti *v.t.* smuggle
prokurator *n.* proctor
prolaz *n* pass
prolaz *n.* thoroughfare
prolazan *n.* transitory
prolaziti *v. t* elapse
proleće *n* spring
prolećni *a.* vernal
prolivanje *n* spill
prolog *n.* prologue
promašaj *n.* miss
promašiti *v.t.* miss
promena *n.* change

promena *n.* variance
promeniti *v. t.* change
promenljiv *a* fickle
promišljen *a.* considerate
promišljen *a.* prudential
promišljenost *n* forethought
promocija *n.* promotion
promovisati *v.t.* promote
promrmljati *v.i.* mutter
promukao *a.* hoarse
pronalazač *n.* inventor
pronalazački *a.* inventive
pronalazak *n.* invention
pronevera *n.* misappropriation
proneveriti *v.t.* misappropriate
pronicljiv *a.* apprehensive
proniknuti *v.t* fathom
propadanje *n* decline
propadati *v. t.* decline
propaganda *n.* propaganda
propagator *n.* propagandist
propagirati *v.t.* propagate
propast *n* doom
propast *n.* rack
propast *n.* ruin
propis *n.* regulation
propisati *v.t.* prescribe
propisno *adv* duly
proporcija *n.* proportion
proporcionalan *a.* proportional
propoved *n.* sermon
propovedaonica *a.* pulpit
propovedati *v.i.* preach
propovedati *v.i.* sermonize
propovednik *n.* preacher
propust *n* lapse
propustiti *v.i.* lapse
proračun *n.* calculation
proreći *v.t.* prophesy
proreći *v.t* foretell

proricanje *n.* auspice
proricati *v.t.* auspicate
proročanski *a.* oracular
proročanstvo *n.* oracle
proročanstvo *n.* prophecy
proročki *a.* prophetic
prorok *n.* prophet
prosečan *a.* average
prosejati *v.i.* riddle
prosejati *v.t.* sieve
prosek *n.* average
prosilac *n.* suitor
prositi *v. i* cadge
prosjak *n* beggar
proso *n.* millet
prospekt *n* brochure
prospekt *n.* prospectus
prost čovek *n.* commoner
prostitucija *n.* prostitution
prostituirati *v.t.* prostitute
prostitutka *n.* prostitute
prostitutka *n.* whore
prostor *n.* space
prostorni *a.* spatial
prostran *a.* roomy
prostran *a.* spacious
prostran *a.* capacious
prosuti *v.i.* spill
prosvetitelj *n.* luminary
prosvetliti *v. t.* enlighten
proširenje *n.* expansion
proširiti *v.t.* expand
proširiti *v. t* extend
proširiti *v.t.* widen
prošli *a.* past
prošlost *n.* antecedent
prošlost *n.* past
protagonista *n.* protagonist
protein *n.* protein
protektirana guma *n.* retread

protektirati gumu *v.t.* retread
proterati *v. t* evict
proterati *v.t.* banish
proterivanje *n.* banishment
proterivanje *n* eviction
protest *n.* protest
protest *n.* protestation
protestovati *v.i.* protest
protiv *pref.* contra
protiv *prep.* versus
protivan *a.* averse
protivavionski *a.* anti-aircraft
protiviti se *v.t.* antagonize
protivljenje *n.* antagonism
protivnik *n.* antagonist
protivnik *n.* opponent
protivnik *n.* rival
protivnik *n.* adversary
protivotrov *n.* mithridate
protivotrov *n.* antidote
protivrečiti *v. t* contradict
protivtužba *n.* countercharge
protivzakonit *a.* illicit
protok *n* flow
prototip *n.* prototype
protumačiti *v.t.* interpret
prouzrokovati *v.t* occasion
provala *n.* irruption
provala *n* burglary
provalnik *n* burglar
provera *n* check
proveriti *v. t.* check
provesti *v.t.* spend
provesti *v.t.* while
proviđenje *n.* providence
provincija *n.* province
provincijalizam *n.* provincialism
provincijski *a.* provincial
provizija *n.* commission
provocirati *v.t.* provoke

**provokacija** *n.* provocation
**provokativan** *a.* provocative
**proza** *n.* prose
**prozaičan** *a.* prosaic
**prozivka** *n.* roll-call
**prozodija** *n.* prosody
**prozor** *n.* window
**proždirati** *v. t* devour
**proždrljiv** *a.* voracious
**proždrljivac** *n.* glutton
**proždrljivost** *n.* gluttony
**prožimati** *v.t.* pervade
**prskanje** *n* splash
**prskati** *v.t.* spray
**prsluk** *n.* vest
**prsluk** *n.* waistcoat
**prsluk** *n* bodice
**prst** *n* finger
**prsten** *n.* ring
**prstenčić** *n.* ringlet
**prstenčić** *n* annulet
**prtljag** *n.* luggage
**prtljag** *n.* baggage
**pruga** *n.* stripe
**prut** *n.* withe
**pružanje** *n.* offering
**pružiti utočište** *v.t* harbour
**prvenstveno** *adv.* primarily
**prvi** *a* first
**prvi** *n* first
**prvo** *adv* first
**prvoklasan** *a.* sterling
**pržiti** *v.t.* fry
**psalm** *n.* psalm
**pseudonim** *n.* pseudonym
**pseudonim** *n.* alias
**psiha** *n.* psyche
**psihički** *a.* psychic
**psihijatar** *n.* psychiatrist
**psihijatrija** *n.* psychiatry

**psiholog** *n.* psychologist
**psihologija** *n.* psychology
**psihološki** *a.* psychological
**psihopata** *n.* psychopath
**psihoterapija** *n.* psychotherapy
**psihoza** *n.* psychosis
**psovati** *v. t.* chide
**psovati** *v.t.* swear
**pšenica** *n.* wheat
**ptica pevačica** *n.* warbler
**ptica** *n* bird
**ptičar** *n.* fowler
**pubertet** *n.* puberty
**publicitet** *n.* publicity
**publika** *n.* audience
**pucanje** *n* shoot
**pucati** *v.i.* pop
**pucati** *v.t.* shoot
**pucketati** *v. t* brustle
**pucketati** *v. i* crack
**pucketati** *v.t.* crackle
**pučina** *n.* offing
**puding** *n.* pudding
**puk** *n.* regiment
**puki** *a.* mere
**pukotina** *n* fissure
**pukotina** *n* gap
**pukotina** *n.* rift
**pukotina** *n* split
**pukovnik** *n.* colonel
**pulover** *n.* pullover
**pulpa** *n.* pulp
**puls** *n.* pulse
**puls** *n* pulse
**pulsacija** *n.* pulsation
**pulsirati** *v.i.* pulse
**pumpa** *n.* pump
**pumpati** *v.t.* pump
**pun** *a.* full
**pun nade** *a.* hopeful

pun poštovanja *a.* respectful
pun poštovanja *a.* reverent
pun poštovanja *a.* reverential
pun šavova *a.* seamy
puna kašika *n.* spoonful
punč *n.* punch
punilac flaša *n* bottler
puniti *v. t.* charge
punjenje *n.* charge
punjenje *n.* padding
puno *adv.* full
punoća *n.* fullness
punomoćnik *n.* assignee
punovažnost *n.* validity
puplin *n.* poplin
pupoljak *n* bud
purgativ *n.* purgative
purgativan *a* purgative
purista *n.* purist
puritanac *n.* puritan
puritanski *a.* puritanical
pust *a.* waste
pustinja *n* desert
pustinjačka ćelija *n.* hermitage
pustinjak *n.* hermit
pustinjak *n.* recluse
pustiti *v.t.* release
pustolovan *a.* adventurous
pustoš *n.* havoc
pustošenje *n.* ravage
pustošiti *v.t.* ravage
pustošiti *v.t.* waste
pušiti *se v.i.* smoke
puška *n* rifle
puškarnica *n.* loop-hole
puštanje *n* release
put *n.* path
put *n.* road
put *n.* route
putarina *n.* cartage

puter *n* butter
putnik *n.* passenger
putnik *n.* traveller
putnik *n.* voyager
putnik *n.* wayfarer
putovanje *n.* journey
putovanje *n* travel
putovanje *n.* trek
putovanje *n.* trip
putovanje *n.* voyage
putovati *v.i.* journey
putovati *v.i.* tour
putovati *v.i.* travel
putovati *v.i.* voyage
putujući *adj* ambulant
puzanje *n* crawl
puzati *v. i* creep
puzati *v. i.* cringe
puzati *v.t.* trail
puzavac *n* creeper
puziti *v. t* crawl
puž *n.* snail

# R

rabat *n.* rebate
racija *n.* raid
racionalan *a.* rational
racionalizovati *v.t.* rationalize
racionalnost *n.* rationality
račun *n.* count
račun *n.* receipt
račun *n.* account
računanje *n.* computation
računati *v.t.* compute
računati *v. t.* count
računati *v.t.* reckon
računovođa *n.* accountant
računovodstvo *n.* accountancy

**rad** *n.* labour
**rad** *n.* work
**radan** *a.* painstaking
**rađanje** *n.* nativity
**radije** *adv.* rather
**radijum** *n.* radium
**radikalan** *a.* radical
**radio** *n.* radio
**radio** *n* wireless
**radionica** *n.* workshop
**raditi** *v.i.* labour
**raditi** *v.t.* operate
**raditi** *v.t.* work
**radna soba** *n.* study
**radni sto** *n* desk
**radnik** *n.* labourer
**radnik** *n.* worker
**radnik** *n.* workman
**radnja modistkinje** *n.* millinery
**radno odelo** *n.* smock
**radost** *n.* glee
**radost** *n.* joy
**radostan** *a.* glad
**radostan** *a.* jolly
**radostan** *n.* joyful, joyous
**radovati se** *v.i.* rejoice
**radoznalost** *n* curiosity
**radoznao** *a* curious
**radoznao** *a.* inquisitive
**rafinerija** *n.* refinery
**rahitičan** *a.* rickety
**rahitis** *n.* rickets
**raj** *n.* paradise
**rak** *n.* cancer
**raketa** *n.* rocket
**rame** *n.* shoulder
**ran** *adv* early
**rana** *n* sore
**rana** *n.* wound
**randevu** *n.* rendezvous

**rang** *n.* rank
**rangirati** *v.t.* rank
**ranije** *adv.* before
**ranije** *adv* formerly
**raniji** *a.* prior
**raniji datum** *n.* antedate
**raniti** *v.t.* wound
**ranjiv** *a.* sore
**ranjiv** *a.* vulnerable
**rano** *a* early
**rano detinjstvo** *n.* infancy
**rapir** *n.* rapier
**rascep** *n* cleft
**rascepiti** *v.t.* splinter
**rascepiti** *v.i.* split
**rashladiti** *v.t.* refrigerate
**rashod** *n* expenditure
**rasipan** *a.* prodigal
**rasipan** *a.* profligate
**rasipan** *a.* wasteful
**rasipanje** *n.* wastage
**rasipnik** *n.* spendthrift
**rasipnost** *n.* prodigality
**rasizam** *n.* racialism
**raskalašn** *a.* wanton
**raskalašnost** *n.* profligacy
**raskid** *n.* rupture
**raskinuti** *v.t.* rupture
**raskol** *n.* schism
**raskoš** *n.* luxuriance
**raskoš** *n.* pomp
**raskošan** *a.* lavish
**raskošan** *a.* luxuriant
**raskošan** *a.* sumptuous
**raskrsnica** *n.* intersection
**raskrsnica** *n.* junction
**rasni** *a.* racial
**rasol** *n* brine
**raspadanje** decay
**raspadati** *v. i* decay

**raspaliti** *v.t.* inflame
**raspaljiv** *a.* inflammatory
**raspeće** *n.* rood
**raspitati** *se v.t.* inquire
**raspodela** *n.* allocation
**raspodeliti** *v.t.* apportion
**raspojasan** *a.* licentious
**raspolaganje** *n* disposal
**raspolagati** *v. t* dispose
**raspoloženje** *n.* mood
**raspoloživ** *a* available
**raspon** *n.* span
**raspor** *n.* slit
**raspored** *n.* schedule
**rasporediti** *v.t.* array
**rasporediti** *v. t* co-ordinate
**rasporediti** *v.t.* regiment
**rasporediti** *v.t.* schedule
**rasporiti** *v.t.* slit
**rasprava** *n.* argument
**rasprava** *n.* treatise
**raspraviti** *v. t.* canvass
**raspravljati** *v.t.* argue
**rasprostranjen** *a.* widespread
**raspustiti** *v.t.* prorogue
**rast** *n.* growth
**rastaviti** *v.t.* sunder
**rastavljanje** *n.* decomposition
**rasteretiti** *v.t.* unburden
**rastezanje** *n* stretch
**rastezati** *v.t.* stretch
**rasti** *v.t.* grow
**rasti** *v.t.* wax
**rastojanje** *n* distance
**rastopiti** *v.t.* fuse
**rastopiti** *v.t.* liquefy
**rastopiti** *v.i.* melt
**rastrgnuti** *v.t.* lacerate
**rasturiti** *v.t.* scatter
**rastužiti** *v.t.* sadden

**rastvarač** *n* solvent
**rastvoriti** *v.t* dissolve
**rastvorljiv** *a.* soluble
**rastvorljivost** *n.* solubility
**rasuti** *v. t* disperse
**raščlanjen** *a.* articulate
**rat** *n.* war
**ratarstvo** *n.* husbandry
**ratifikovati** *v.t.* ratify
**ratnik** *n.* warrior
**ratno stanje** *n* belligerency
**ratoboran** *a.* militant
**ratoboran** *a.* warlike
**ratoboran** *a* bellicose
**ratoboran** *a* belligerent
**ratovanje** *n.* warfare
**ratovati** *v.i.* militate
**ratovati** *v.i.* war
**ravan** *a* even
**ravan** *a* flat
**ravan** *n.* plain
**ravan** *a.* plane
**ravnica** *n.* plane
**ravnina** *n* flat
**ravnodušan** *a.* indifferent
**ravnodušnost** *n.* indifference
**ravnopravnost** *n* equal
**ravnoteža** *n* poise
**ravnoteža** *n.* balance
**razaranje** *n* destruction
**razbacati** *v.t.* winnow
**razbesneti** *v. t* enrage
**razbesneti** *v.t.* infuriate
**razbijanje** *n* smash
**razbiti** *v.t.* rout
**razbiti** *v.t.* shatter
**razbiti** *v.t.* smash
**razboj** *n* loom
**razbojnik** *n.* bandit
**razbojnik** *n.* dacoit

razbojnik *n.* thug
razbojništvo *n.* dacoity
razborit *a.* judicious
razborit *a.* prudent
razborit *a.* sage
razboritost *n.* prudence
razdeliti *v.t.* parcel
razdoblje *n.* innings
razdragan *a.* mirthful
razdraganost *n.* mirth
razdražljiv *a.* irritable
razdvajanje *n.* separation
razdvajanje *n.* severance
razglasiti *v.t.* rumour
razgledati *v.t.* view
razgolititi *v.t.* bare
razgovarati *v.t.* converse
razgovor *n* conversation
razgovor *n* talk
razgraničenje *n.* demarcation
razjasniti *v. t* clarify
razjasniti *v. t* clear
razjašnjenje *n* clarification
različit *a* different
različit *a* dissimilar
različit *a* diverse
različit *a.* various
razlika *n* difference
razlika *n* distinction
razlikovati *v. t.* discriminate
razlikovati *v. i* distinguish
razlikovati se *v. i* differ
razlog *n.* reason
razložiti *v. t.* decompose
razmatranje *n* consideration
razmatranje *n* deliberation
razmatrati *v. i* deliberate
razmaziti *v.t.* pamper
razmena *n* exchange
razmena *n.* interchange

razmeniti *v. t* exchange
razmeniti *v.* interchange
razmetanje *n* strut
razmetati se *v.i.* strut
razmišljanje *n* contemplation
razmišljanje *n.* rumination
razmišljati *v. t* contemplate
razmišljati *v.i.* muse
razmišljati *v.t.* ponder
razmnožavanje *n.* proliferation
razmnožiti se *v.i.* proliferate
razmotriti *v. t* consider
raznolik *a.* multifarious
raznolik *n.* multiform
raznolik *a.* varied
raznovrsnost *n.* variety
razočarati *v. t.* disappoint
razonoda *n.* pastime
razoriti *v.i* blast
razoružanje *n.* disarmament
razoružati *v. t* disarm
razrađen *a* elaborate
razraditi *v. t* elaborate
razred *n.* grade
razrokost *v.i.* squint
razrokost *n* squint
razrušiti *v.t.* raze
razum *n.* sanity
razuman *a.* reasonable
razuman *a.* sane
razuman *a.* sensible
razumeti *v.t.* understand
razumevanje *n.* apprehension
razvedriti *v. t* brighten
razvesti *v. t* divorce
razvesti se *v.t.* repudiate
razviti *v. t.* develop
razvod *n* divorce
razvod *n.* repudiation
razvodniti *v. t* dilute

razvodnjen *a* dilute
razvoj *n.* development
razvrat *n* debauchery
razvratan *a.* lewd
razvratnik *n* debauchee
razvratnost *n.* obscenity
razvrstati *v. t* classify
raž *n.* rye
rđa *n.* rust
rđati *v.i* rust
reagovati *v.i.* react
reakcija *n.* reaction
reakcionaran *a.* reactionary
realista *n.* realist
realističan *a.* realistic
realizacija *n.* realization
realizam *n.* realism
realizovati *v.t.* realize
realnost *n.* reality
rebreni *adj.* costal
rebro *n.* rib
recept *n.* prescription
recept *n.* recipe
recesija *n.* recession
reći *n.* say
reći *v.t.* tell
recipročan *a.* reciprocal
recitacija *n.* recitation
recital *n.* recital
recitovati *v.t.* recite
reč *v.t.* say
reč *n.* word
reč *v.t* word
rečenica *n.* sentence
rečit *a* eloquent
rečitost *n* eloquence
rečnik *n* dictionary
rečnik *n.* vocabulary
red *n.* array
red *n.* order

red *n.* queue
red *n.* row
red *n* trim
redak *a.* rare
redak *a.* scarce
redovan *a.* ordinary
redovan *a.* regular
redovno *adv.* ordinarily
referenca *n.* reference
referendum *n.* referendum
refleks *n.* reflex
refleksan *a* reflex
refleksivan *a.* meditative
reflektor *n.* reflector
reflektujuće *a.* reflective
reforma *n.* reform
reformacija *n.* reformation
reformator *n.* reformer
reformisati *v.t.* reform
refren *n.* chorus
refren *n* refrain
regeneracija *n.* regeneration
regenerisati *v.t.* regenerate
region *n.* region
regionalni *a.* regional
registar *n.* register
registar *n.* registry
registracija *n.* registration
registrovati *v.t.* register
regres *n.* recourse
regrut *n.* recruit
regrutovati *v. t* enlist
regrutovati *v.t.* recruit
regulator *n.* regulator
regulisati *v.t.* regulate
rehabilitacija *n.* rehabilitation
rehabilitovati *v.t.* rehabilitate
reka *n.* river
reket *n.* racket
rekla-kazala *n.* hearsay

**reklamacija** *n* reclamation
**rekreacija** *n.* recreation
**rektum** *n.* rectum
**rekvijem** *n.* requiem
**relativan** *a.* relative
**relej** *n.* relay
**relevantan** *a.* relevant
**relevantnost** *n.* relevance
**religija** *n.* religion
**relikvija** *n.* relic
**reljef** *n.* relief
**remek-delo** *n.* masterpiece
**remi** *n.* rummy
**rendgen** *n.* x-ray
**rendgenski** *a.* x-ray
**renesansa** *n.* renaissance
**renome** *n.* renown
**renovirati** *v.t.* renovate
**renta** *n.* annuity
**rentijer** *n* annuitant
**rep** *n.* tail
**repa** *n.* turnip
**repa** *n* beet
**replika** *n.* replica
**reprezentativan** *a.* representative
**reprodukcija** *n* reproduction
**reprodukovati** *v.t.* reproduce
**reproduktivan** *a.* reproductive
**reptil** *n.* reptile
**republika** *n.* republic
**republikanac** *n* republican
**republikanski** *a.* republican
**resa** *n.* fringe
**restauracija** *n.* restoration
**restoran** *n.* restaurant
**restriktivan** *a.* restrictive
**resurs** *n.* resource
**rešenje** *n.* solution
**rešetka** *n.* grate
**rešetka** *n.* lattice

**rešiti** *v.t.* resolve
**rešiti** *v.t.* solve
**retardiranost** *n.* retardation
**retko** *adv.* seldom
**retorički** *a.* rhetorical
**retorika** *n.* rhetoric
**retorta** *n.* crevet
**retrospekcija** *n.* retrospection
**retrospektiva** *n.* retrospect
**retrospektivan** *a.* retrospective
**retуširati** *v.t.* retouch
**reumatizam** *n.* rheumatism
**reumatski** *a.* rheumatic
**revidirati** *v.t.* audit
**revizija** *n.* revision
**revizija** *n.* audit
**revizor** *n.* auditor
**revnost** *n* bigotry
**revnost** *n.* zeal
**revnostan** *a.* zealous
**revolucija** *n.* revolution
**revolucionar** *n* revolutionary
**revolucionaran** *a.* revolutionary
**revolver** *n.* revolver
**rez** *n* cut
**reza** *n* bolt
**rezač** *n.* sharpener
**rezati** *v. t* cut
**rezati** *v.t.* lop
**rezati** *v.t.* trench
**rezbariti** *v. t.* carve
**rezervat** *n.* reservation
**rezervisati** *v.t.* reserve
**rezervni** *a* spare
**rezervni deo** *n.* spare
**rezervoar** *n.* reservoir
**rezervoar** *n.* tank
**rezidentan** *a.* resident
**rezime** *n* abstract
**rezime** *n.* resume

rezime *n.* summary
rezimirati *v.t.* resume
rezimirati *v.t.* summarize
rezolucija *n.* resolution
rezonanca *n.* resonance
rezonantan *a.* resonant
rezultat *n.* result
režanje *n* growl
režanje *n.* snarl
režati *v.i.* growl
režati *v.i.* snarl
režim *n.* regime
riba *n* fish
ribar *n* fisherman
ribizla *n.* currant
ribnjak *n.* pond
ricinusovo ulje *n.* castor oil
rigidan *a.* rigid
rigorozan *a.* rigorous
rika *n.* roar
rikati *v.i.* roar
rikša *n.* rickshaw
rilo *n.* snout
rima *n.* rhyme
rimovati *se v.i.* rhyme
rintanje *n.* toil
rintati *v.i.* toil
ris papira *n.* ream
riskantan *a.* venturesome
ritam *n.* rhythm
ritmičan *a.* rhythmic
ritual *n.* ritual
ritualni *a.* ritual
rivalstvo *n.* rivalry
rizičan *a.* risky
rizik *n.* hazard
rizik *n.* risk
rizikovanje *n* nap
rizikovati *v.t* hazard
rizikovati *v.t.* risk

rob *n.* slave
rob *n.* thrall
roba *n.* commodity
roba *n.* merchandise
roba *n.* ware
robot *n.* robot
robovati *v.i.* slave
roda *n.* stork
rođak *n.* cousin
rođak *n.* relative
rodbina *n.* kin
rođen bogat *adj.* born rich
rođenje *n.* birth
roditelj *n.* parent
roditeljoubistvo *n.* parricide
roditeljski *a.* parental
roditeljstvo *n.* parentage
roditi *v.* born
roditi *v.t* breed
rodni *a.* natal
rog *n.* horn
rog *n.* antler
rogonja *n.* cuckold
roj *n.* swarm
rojalistički *n.* royalist
rojiti se *v.i.* swarm
rok *n.* term
roktanje *v.i.* grunt
roktati *n.* grunt
rolna *n.* roll
roman *n* novel
romanopisac *n.* novelist
romantičan *a.* romantic
romantika *n.* romance
rominjati *v. i* drizzle
roniti *v. i* dive
ronjenje *n* dive
ronjenje *n* plunge
ropski *a.* slavish
ropstvo *n.* slavery

ropstvo *n.* thraldom
ropstvo *n* bondage
ropstvo *n.* captivity
rosa *n.* dew
rotacija *n.* rotation
rotacioni *a.* rotary
rotirati *v.i.* rotate
rotkvica *n.* radish
rov *n.* sap
rov *n.* trench
rožnjača *n* cornea
rt *n.* cape
rub *n.* list
rub *n.* verge
rub *n.* brink
rubin *n.* ruby
rublja *n.* rouble
rublje *n.* laundry
ručak *n.* lunch
ručati *v.i.* lunch
ručka *n.* handle
ručna burgija *n.* wimble
ručni rad *n.* handiwork
ručni zglob *n.* wrist
ručno *a.* manual
ruda *n.* ore
rudar *n.* miner
rudnik *n* mine
ruganje *n* gibe
ruganje *n.* scoff
rugati se *v.i.* gibe
rugati se *v.i.* jeer
rugati se *v.i.* scoff
ruka *n.* arm
rukav *n* sleeve
rukavica *n.* glove
rukavica bez prstiju *n.* mitten
rukopis *n.* manuscript
rukotvorina *n.* handicraft
rukovati *v.t* handle

rukovati *v.t.* wield
rukovoditi *v.t.* superintend
rum *n.* rum
rumen *a.* rosy
rumenilo *n* flush
rumenilo *n* blush
runo *n* fleece
rupa *n* hole
rupa *n.* puncture
rupica *n* eyelet
rupija *n.* rupee
rušenje *n* overthrow
ruševina *n* debris
rutina *n.* routine
rutinski *a* routine
ruža *n.* rose
ružan *a.* ugly
ružičast *a* pink
ružičast *a.* pinkish
ružičast *a.* roseate
ružičnjak, brojanice *n.* rosary
ružnoća *n.* ugliness
rvač *n.* wrestler
rvanje *n.* grapple
rvati se *v.i.* grapple
rvati se *v.i.* wrestle
rzanje *n.* neigh
rzati *v.i.* neigh

# S

sa *prep.* with
sabat *n.* sabbath
sablja *n.* sabre
sabotaža *n.* sabotage
sabotirati *v.t.* sabotage
saće *n.* honeycomb
sačuvati *v.t.* preserve
sačuvati *v.t.* save

| | |
|---|---|
| **sada** *adv.* now | **samouveren** *a.* confident |
| **sada** *conj.* now | **samozadovoljan** *adj.* complacent |
| **sadista** *n.* sadist | **samozadovoljan** *a.* smug |
| **saditi** *v.t.* plant | **san** *n* dream |
| **sadizam** *n.* sadism | **san** *n.* sleep |
| **sadržaj** *n* content | **sanatorijum** *n.* sanatorium |
| **sadržati** *v.t.* contain | **sandala** *n.* sandal |
| **sadržitelj** *n* multiple | **sandalovina** *n.* sandalwood |
| **safir** *n.* sapphire | **sanduk** *n.* crate |
| **saglasan** *a.* agreeable | **sangviničan** *a.* sanguine |
| **saglasnost** *n.* accord | **sanitarni** *a.* sanitary |
| **saglasnost** *n.* conformity | **sanjalački** *a.* shadowy |
| **saharin** *n.* saccharin | **sanjarenje** *n.* reverie |
| **sahrana** *n.* funeral | **sanjati** *v. i.* dream |
| **sahrana** *n.* sepulture | **sankcija** *n.* sanction |
| **sajam** *n.* fair | **sankcionisati** *v.t.* sanction |
| **sakaćenje** *n.* mutilation | **santa leda** *n.* iceberg |
| **sakatiti** *v.t.* mutilate | **saobraćaj** *n.* traffic |
| **sakrament** *n.* sacrament | **saopštenje** *n.* communiqué |
| **sakriti** *v.t* hide | **saopštiti** *v.t.* impart |
| **sakriti se** *v.i.* cower | **saosećajan** *a.* sympathetic |
| **sakriti se** *v.i.* darkle | **saosećanje** *n* compassion |
| **sakrivanje** *n.* hide | **saosećati** *v. t* commiserate |
| **salata** *n.* salad | **saosećati** *v.i.* sympathize |
| **salo** *n.* lard | **sapun** *n.* soap |
| **salon** *n* drawing-room | **sapunast** *a.* soapy |
| **salto** *n.* somersault | **sarađivati** *v.t.* associate |
| **salveta** *n.* napkin | **sarađivati** *v. i* collaborate |
| **sam** am | **sarađivati** *v. i* co-operate |
| **sam** *a.* solo | **saradnik** *n.* companion |
| **sam** *a.* alone | **saradnik** *n.* associate |
| **samac** *n.* single | **saradnja** *n* collaboration |
| **samo** *adv.* only | **saradnja** *n* co-operation |
| **samo što** *conj.* only | **sarkastičan** *a.* sarcastic |
| **samoglasnik** *n.* vowel | **sarkazam** *n.* sarcasm |
| **samoispitivanje** *n.* introspection | **saslušavanje** *n.* interrogation |
| **samostan** *n.* cloister | **saslušavati** *v.t.* interrogate |
| **samostan** *n.* nunnery | **sastanak** *n.* meeting |
| **samoubilački** *a.* suicidal | **sastanak** *n.* tryst |
| **samoubistvo** *n.* suicide | **sastanak u četiri oka** *n.* tete-a-tete |

sastav *n* composition
sastav *n* compound
sastav *n.* texture
sastaviti *v. t* compile
sastaviti *v. t* compose
sastaviti *v. i* compound
sastaviti *v.t.* piece
sastaviti *v.t.* assemble
sastavljač *n.* compounder
sastavni *adj.* component
sastavni *adj.* constituent
sastojak *n.* ingredient
sastojati se *v. i* consist
sasvim *adv.* quite
sat *n.* clock
sat *n.* hour
sat *n.* watch
satelit *n.* satellite
satira *n.* lampoon
satira *n.* satire
satiričan *a.* satirical
satiričar *n.* satirist
satirizovati *v.t.* satirize
saučesnik *n* accomplice
saučešće *n* condolence
sav *a.* all
savest *n* conscience
savestan *a* dutiful
savet *n.* council
savet *n.* counsel
savet *n.* tip
savet *n* advice
savetnik *n.* counsellor
savetovati *v. t.* counsel
savetovati *v.t.* tip
savetovati *v.t.* advise
savez *n.* alliance
saveznik *n.* ally
savijanje *n* bend
savijati *v.t.* crankle

saviti *v.t* fold
saviti *v. t* bend
savitljiv *a.* supple
savladati *v.t.* master
savladati *v.t.* overwhelm
savladati *v.t.* surmount
savremen *a* contemporary
savremen *a.* up-to-date
savršen *a.* perfect
savršenstvo *n.* perfection
sazivač *n* convener
sazivanje *n.* convocation
sazivati *v.t.* convoke
sazrevati *v.i.* ripen
sazvati *v. t* convene
sazvežđe *n.* asterism
sazvežđe *n.* constellation
sažaljenje *n.* pity
sažaljevati *v.t.* pity
sažaljiv *a.* pitiful
sažet *a* summary
sažet *a.* terse
sažeti *v.t* abstract
sažeti *v. t.* compress
scena *n.* scene
scenski *a.* scenic
sebe *pron.* myself
sebičan *a.* selfish
sećanje *n.* recollection
sećanje *n.* remembrance
secesionista *n.* secessionist
seciranje *n* dissection
secirati *v. t* dissect
seći *v. t* chop
seći *v.t.* intersect
seći *v.t.* poll
seći *v.t.* slice
sedam *n.* seven
sedamdeset *n., a* seventy
sedamdeseti *a.* seventieth

sedamnaest *n., a* seventeen
sedamnaesti *a.* seventeenth
sedativ *n* sedative
sedeći *a.* sedentary
sedeti *v.i.* sit
sedište *n.* seat
sedlo *n.* saddle
sedmi *a.* seventh
sedmo- *a* seven
sednica *n.* session
segment *n.* segment
segmentirati *v.t.* segment
segregacija *n.* segregation
seizmički *a.* seismic
sejati *v.t.* sift
sejati *v.t.* sow
sekira *n.* hatchet
sekira *n.* axe
sekiracija *n* vexation
sekretar *n.* secretary
sekretarijat *n.* secretariat (e)
seksualan *a.* sexual
seksualnost *n.* sexuality
sekta *n.* sect
sektaški *a.* sectarian
sektor *n.* sector
sekunda *n* second
sekundaran *a.* secondary
sekvenca *n.* sequence
selektivan *a.* selective
seliti se *v.i.* trek
seljak *n* boor
seljak *n.* peasant
seljak *n* rustic
seljak *n.* villager
seljaštvo *n.* peasantry
selo *n.* village
sem ako *conj.* unless
sem toga *adv.* withal
sem toga *adv* besides

seme *n.* seed
seme *n.* semen
semestar *n.* semester
seminar *n.* seminar
senat *n.* senate
senator *n.* senator
senatorski *a.* senatorial
senatski *a* senatorial
sendvič *n.* sandwich
senf *n.* mustard
senica *n* bower
senilan *a.* senile
senilnost *n.* senility
senior *n.* senior
senka *n.* shadow
seno *n.* hay
sentimentalan *a.* sentimental
senzacija *n.* sensation
senzacionalan *a.* sensational
senzualan *a.* sensual
seoba *n.* transmigration
seoce *n.* hamlet
seoski *a.* rural
seoski *a.* rustic
seosko dvorište *n.* barton
separabilan *a.* separable
sepsa *n.* sepsis
septembar *n.* September
septičan *a.* septic
septička jama *n.* cesspool
serija *n.* series
serija *n* batch
serijski *a.* serial
serpentina *n.* serpentine
sertifikat *n.* certificate
servilan *a.* menial
servilan *a.* servile
servilnost *n.* servility
servis *n.* serve
servisirati *v.t* service

serž *n.* serge
sesti *v.t.* seat
sestra *n.* sister
sestrinski *a.* sisterly
sestrinstvo *n.* sisterhood
setiti se *v.t.* recollect
sever *n.* north
severni *a* north
severni *a.* northerly
severni *a.* northern
severno *adv.* north
severno *adv.* northerly
sezona *n.* season
sezonski *a.* seasonal
sfera *n.* sphere
sferni *a.* spherical
shvatiti *v.t.* apprehend
shvatljiv *a.* intelligible
sićušnost *adv.* smallness
sićušan *a.* tiny
sidrište *n.* moorings
sidro *n.* anchor
signal *n.* signal
signalizirati *v.t.* signal
siguran *a.* safe
siguran *a.* secure
siguran *a.* sure
sigurno *adv.* certainly
sigurno *adv.* surely
sigurnost *n.* safe
sijalica *n.* bulb
sijati *v.i.* glitter
sijati *v.i.* glow
siktanje *n* hiss
siktati *v.i* hiss
sila *n* force
silazak *n.* descent
siledžija *n* bully
siledžija *n.* ruffian
siliti *v.t* force

silom *adv.* perforce
silovanje *n.* rape
silovati *v.t.* rape
silueta *n.* silhouette
simbol *n.* symbol
simboličan *a.* symbolic
simbolizam *n.* symbolism
simbolizovati *v.t.* symbolize
simetričan *a.* symmetrical
simetrija *n.* symmetry
simfonija *n.* symphony
simpatičan *a.* lovable
simpatija *n.* sympathy
simpozijum *n.* symposium
simptom *n.* symptom
simptomatičan *a.* symptomatic
sin *n.* son
singlirati *v.t.* single
sinonim *n.* synonym
sinoniman *a.* synonymous
sinopsis *n.* synopsis
sintaksa *n.* syntax
sintetički *a.* synthetic
sintetika *n* synthetic
sinteza *n.* synthesis
sipati *v.i.* pour
sir *n.* cheese
sirće *n.* vinegar
sirće *n* alegar
sirena *n.* mermaid
sirena *n.* siren
siroče *n.* orphan
siromah *n.* pauper
siromašan *a.* needy
siromaštvo *n.* poverty
sirotinjski kraj *n.* slum
sirotište *n.* orphanage
sirov *a* crude
sirov *a.* raw
sirup *n.* syrup

skandalizovati *v.t.* scandalize
skeč *n.* skit
skele *n.* scaffold
skelet *n.* skeleton
skenirati *v.t.* scan
skepticizam *n.* scepticism
skeptičan *a.* sceptical
skeptik *n.* sceptic
skica *n* draft
skica *n.* outline
skica *n.* sketch
skicirati *v. t* draft
skicirati *v.t.* outline
skicirati *v.t.* sketch
skiptar *n.* sceptre
skitalački *a* vagabond
skitanje *v.t.* ramble
skitati *n* ramble
skitnica *n.* ranger
skitnica *n.* vagabond
sklad *n.* conformity
sklad *n.* consonance
skladan *a.* shapely
skladište *n* cache
skladište *n.* godown
skladište *n.* repository
skladištenje *n.* storage
skladištiti *v.t.* store
sklon *a.* prone
sklonište *n.* shelter
sklonost *n* bent
sklonost *n.* inclination
sklonost *n.* preference
sklonost *n.* proclivity
sklonost *n* affinity
sklop *n.* assembly
skočiti *v. i* hop
skočiti *v.i* jump
skočiti *v.i.* leap
skočiti *v.i.* spring

skok *n.* jump
skok *n* leap
skok *n.* vault
skolastičar *a.* scholastic
skoro *adv.* nearly
skorojević *n.* upstart
skraćenica *n* abbreviation
skraćivanje *n* abridgement
skratiti *v.t.* abbreviate
skratiti *v.t* abridge
skratiti *v. t* curtail
skratiti *v.t.* shorten
skrenuti *v. t* divert
skrenuti *v.t.* shunt
skrenuti *v.t.* switch
skrenuti pažnju *v.* advert
skresati *v.t* volley
skripte *n.* script
skriven *a.* allusive
skrob *n.* starch
skroman *a.* humble
skroman *a.* modest
skromnost *n.* lowliness
skromnost *n* modesty
skroz *adv.* through
skroz *adv.* throughout
skulptura *n.* sculpture
skup *a* expensive
skup *n.* social
skupina *n* cluster
skupljač trofeja *n.* scavenger
skupljanje *v.t.* rally
skupljanje *n.* shrinkage
skupljati se *v.i* troop
skupo *a.* costly
skut *n.* lap
skuter *n.* scooter
slab *a* faint
slab *a* feeble
slab *a.* frail

slab *a.* infirm
slab *a.* weak
slabašan *a.* puny
slabić *n.* weakling
slabina *n.* loin
slabost *n.* malaise
slabost *n.* weakness
slad *n.* malt
sladak *a.* sweet
sladunjav *a.* mawkish
slagalica *n.* puzzle
slagati se *v.t.* accord
slajd *n* slide
slama *n.* litter
slama *n.* straw
slama *n.* thatch
slan *a.* saline
slan *a.* salty
slanina *n.* bacon
slanje u selo *n.* rustication
slanoća *n.* salinity
slast *n* relish
slatkiš *n.* candy
slatkiš *n* sweet
slatkiš *n.* sweetmeat
slatkoća *n.* sweetness
slava *n* fame
slava *n.* glory
slavan *a.* glorious
slavina *n.* tap
slaviti *v. t. & i.* celebrate
slavlje *n.* jubilation
slavlje *n.* celebration
slavljenje *n.* glorification
slavna osoba *n* celebrity
slavuj *n.* nightingale
sledbenik *n* follower
sledbenik *n.* henchman
sledeći *a.* subsequent
sledeći *a.* next

slediti *v.t.* track
sleganje ramenima *n* shrug
slegnuti ramenima *v.t.* shrug
sleng *n.* slang
slep *a* blind
slepi miš *n* bat
slepilo *n* ablepsy
slepilo *n* blindness
slepiti *v.t.* conglutinate
slepo crevo *n.* appendix
slepoočnica *n* temple
slezina *n.* spleen
sličan *a.* like
slične *a.* similar
sličnost *n.* likeness
sličnost *n.* resemblance
sličnost *n.* semblance
sličnost *n.* similarity
sličnost *n.* similitude
slika *n* effigy
slika *n.* image
slika *n.* painting
slika *n.* picture
slikar *n.* painter
slikarev potporni štap *n.* maulstick
slikarski *a.* pictorial
slikati *v.t.* pencil
slikovit *a.* picturesque
slikovito izlaganje *n.* imagery
sloboda *n.* freedom
sloboda *n.* liberty
slobodan *a.* free
slobodan *a* leisure
slobodnjak *n.* yeoman
slobodno vreme *n.* leisure
slobodoumnik *n.* libertine
slog *n.* syllable
sloga *n.* concord
slogovni *n.* syllabic
sloj *n.* layer

| | |
|---|---|
| **slom** *n* breakdown | **smanjiti** *v.t.* reduce |
| **slom** *n* downfall | **smanjiti izdatke** *v.t.* retrench |
| **slon** *n* elephant | **smanjiti se** *v.i* shrink |
| **slonovača** *n.* ivory | **smaragd** *n* emerald |
| **složen** *a* complex | **smatrati** *v.i.* deem |
| **složen** *a* compound | **smatrati za** *v.t.* repute |
| **složiti se** *v.i.* agree | **smeće** *n.* garbage |
| **slučaj** *n.* case | **smeće** *n.* trash |
| **slučajan** *a* accidental | **smeće** *n.* refuse |
| **slučajan** *a.* haphazard | **smeh** *n.* laughter |
| **slučajan** *a.* incidental | **smejanje** `n.` laugh |
| **slučajan** *a.* random | **smejati se** *v.i* laugh |
| **slučajnost** *n.* contingency | **smelost** *n.* daring |
| **sluga** *n* menial | **smena** *n* shift |
| **sluga** *n.* servant | **smeo** *a* daring |
| **slušalac** *n.* listener | **smer** *n* lay |
| **slušati** *v.i.* listen | **smesta** *adv.* straightway |
| **slušni** *adj.* auditive | **smestiti** *v.t* accommodate |
| **slutiti** *v.t.* misgive | **smestiti** *v.t* house |
| **slutnja** *n.* hunch | **smestiti** *v.t.* place |
| **slutnja** *n.* misgiving | **smešan** *n.* funny |
| **slutnja** *n.* omen | **smešan** *a.* hilarious |
| **sluz** *n.* mucus | **smešan** *a.* laughable |
| **sluzav** *a.* mucous | **smešan** *a.* ridiculous |
| **sluznica** *n.* conjunctiva | **smešan** *a.* zany |
| **služavka** *n.* maid | **smešiti se** *v.i.* smile |
| **služba** *n.* service | **smeštaj** *n.* accommodation |
| **službeni** *a.* official | **smetnja** *n* drawback |
| **službenik** *n* clerk | **smicalica** *n.* artifice |
| **službenik** *n* employee | **smiriti** *v. t.* calm |
| **službovati** *v.i.* officiate | **smišljati** *v.t.* plot |
| **služiti se polugom** *v.t.* lever | **smog** *n.* smog |
| **služiti vojsku** *v.i.* soldier | **smokva** *n* fig |
| **smanjenje** *n.* abatement | **smola** *n.* pitch |
| **smanjenje** *n* decrease | **smotati** *v.t.* furl |
| **smanjenje** *n.* reduction | **smotra** *n* muster |
| **smanjiti** *v.t.* abate | **smrad** *n.* stench |
| **smanjiti** *v. t* decrease | **smrad** *n* stink |
| **smanjiti** *v. t* diminish | **smrdeti** *v.i.* stink |
| **smanjiti** *v.t* lessen | **smrt** *n* death |

smrt *n* decease
smrtan *a.* mortal
smrtnik *n* mortal
smrtno *adj.* alamort
smrtonosan *a* deadly
smrtonosan *a.* lethal
snabdeti osobljem *v.t.* staff
snabdeti predgovorom *v.t.* preface
snabdevanje *n* supply
snabdevati *v.t.* supply
snabdevati hranom *v. i* cater
snaga *n* main
snaga *n.* power
snaga *n.* strength
snalažljiv *a.* resourceful
snalažljiv *a.* shifty
snažan *a* forceful
snažan *a.* hefty
sneg *n.* snow
snežan *a.* snowy
snežiti *v.i.* snow
snimati *v.t* film
snob *n.* snob
snobizam *n.* snobbery
snobovski *v* snobbish
snop *n* bundle
snop *n.* sheaf
snop *n* beam
so *n.* salt
soba *n.* room
soba za posete *n.* parlour
socijalistički *n,a* socialist
socijalizam *n* socialism
sociologija *n.* sociology
sočan *a.* juicy
sočan *a.* luscious
sočan *a.* lusty
sočivo *n.* lentil
sodomija *n.* sodomy
sodomit *n.* sodomite

sofa *n.* sofa
sofista *n.* sophist
sofisticiran *a.* sophisticated
sofisticirati *v.t.* sophisticate
sofizam *n.* sophism
sojka *n.* jay
sok *n* juice
sokak *n.* lane
soko *n* falcon
sokolar *n* hawker
sokolovski *adj* accipitral
solarni *a.* solar
solidarnost *n.* solidarity
solista *n.* soloist
soliti *v.t* salt
solo *n* solo
solo *adv.* solo
solventan *a.* solvent
solventnost *n.* solvency
somot *n.* velvet
sonda *n* probe
sonet *n.* sonnet
sortirati *v.t.* size
sortirati *v.t* sort
sos *n.* sauce
sotona *n.* satan
sova *n.* owl
spajalica *n.* staple
spajanje žicom *n.* wiring
spakovati *v. t* encase
spanać *n.* spinach
sparan *a.* muggy
sparan *a.* sultry
spariti *v.t.* pair
spasavanje *n* rescue
spasavanje *n.* salvage
spasenje *n.* salvation
spasitelj *n.* saviour
spasiti *v.t.* rescue
spasiti *v.t.* salvage

spavaćica *n.* nightie
spavač *n.* sleeper
spavati *v.i.* sleep
specifičan *a.* specific
specifikacija *n.* specification
specijalista *n.* specialist
specijalitet *n.* speciality
specijalizacija *n.* specialization
specijalizovati se *v.i.* specialize
spektakl *n.* spectacle
spektakularan *a.* spectacular
spekulacija *n.* speculation
spekulisati *v.i.* speculate
spelovati *v.t.* spell
sperma *n.* sperm
spirala *n.* spiral
spiralni *a.* spiral
spiritista *n.* spiritualist
spiritualizam *n.* spiritualism
spis *n.* writ
spletkariti *v.i.* scheme
spljoštiti *v.t.* laminate
spoj *n.* juncture
spojiti *v. t* couple
spojiti *v.t* link
spojiti *v.t.* merge
spojiti se *v.t.* interlock
spojni *adj.* annectant
spokoj *n.* calm
spokoj *n.* serenity
spokojan *a.* serene
spoljašnji *a.* outward
spoljašnjost *n* outside
spoljni *a* external
spoljni *a.* outer
spoljni *a.* outside
spomenik *n.* monument
spominjanje *n.* mention
spominjati *v.t.* mention
spona *n* brace

spona *n.* link
spontan *a.* spontaneous
spontanost *n.* spontaneity
sponzor *n.* sponsor
sponzorisati *v.t.* sponsor
spor *n* dispute
spor *a* slow
sporadičan *a.* sporadic
sporan *n.* moot
sporazum *n.* compact
sporazum *n.* agreement
sporost *n.* slowness
sport *n.* sport
sportista *n.* sportsman
sportista *n.* athlete
sposoban *a.* apt
sposoban *a.* competent
sposoban za brak *a.* marriageable
sposoban za jemstvo *a.* bailable
sposoban *a.* capable
sposobnost *n* ability
sposobnost *n* competence
sposobnost *n.* acumen
sposobnost *n.* aptitude
sposobnost *n.* capability
spotaći se *v.i.* stumble
spoticanje *n.* stumble
spoznaja *n* cognizance
sprat *n.* storey
sprati *v.i* flush
sprečiti *v.t.* prevent
sprečiti *v.t.* avert
sprej *n.* spray
spreman *a.* ready
spreman *a.* stock
spremno *adv.* readily
spremnost *n.* readiness
spremnost *n.* willingness
spretan *adj.* deft
sprijateljiti se *v. t.* befriend

**sprint** *n* sprint
**sprintati** *v.i.* sprint
**spržiti** *v.t.* parch
**spustiti se** *v.i.* perch
**spuštati se** *v. i.* descend
**sputati** *v.t* fetter
**sputnik** *n.* sputnik
**sraman** *a.* shameful
**sramota** *n* dishonour
**sramota** *n.* infamy
**sramota** *n.* shame
**sramotan** *a* flagrant
**sramotiti** *v.t.* shame
**sramotiti** *v.t.* vilify
**srastanje** *n.* concrescence
**srasti** *v.t.* accrete
**srazmeran** *a.* proportionate
**srce** *n.* heart
**srcolik** *adj.* cordate
**srčani** *adj.* cardiacal
**srdačan** *a* cordial
**srdačno** *adv.* heartily
**srdit** *a.* irate
**srebrno** *a* silver
**srebro** *n.* silver
**sreća** *n.* fortune
**sreća** *n.* happiness
**sreća** *n.* luck
**srećan** *a.* fortunate
**srećan** *a.* lucky
**srećom** *adv.* luckily
**srećan** *a.* happy
**sreda** *n.* Wednesday
**sredina** *n.* mean
**sredina** *n* middle
**sredina** *n.* midst
**sredina leta** *n.* midsummer
**srednjeg roda** *a.* neuter
**srednjevekovni** *a.* medieval
**srednji** *a.* intermediate

**srednji** *a.* median
**srednji** *a* medium
**srednji** *a.* mid
**srednji** *a.* middle
**srednji rod** *n* neuter
**sredovečan** *a.* medieval
**sredstvo** *n* means
**sredstvo za umirenje** *adj* calmative
**sredstvo protiv insekata** *n* repellent
**sresti** *v.t.* meet
**srna** *n* doe
**srna** *n.* roe
**srodan** *a* congenial
**srodan** *a.* akin
**srodnik** *n.* in-laws
**srodstvo** *n.* kinship
**srp** *n.* sickle
**srušiti** *v.t.* overthrow
**srušiti se** *v.i.* topple
**stabilan** *a.* stable
**stabilizacija** *n.* stabilization
**stabilizovati** *v.t.* stabilize
**stabilnost** *n.* stability
**stabla** *n.* stem
**stabljika** *n.* stalk
**stablo** *n.* trunk
**stacionaran** *a.* stationary
**stacionirati** *v.t.* station
**stadion** *n.* stadium
**stado** *n* flock
**stado** *n.* herd
**stagnacija** *n.* stagnation
**stagnirati** *v.i.* stagnate
**staja** *n.* cote
**stajanje** *n.* standing
**stajati** *v.i.* stand
**staklo** *n.* glass
**staklorezac** *n.* glazier
**stalan** *a* constant
**staložen** *a.* sedate

| | |
|---|---|
| **staložen** *a.* staid | **stas** *n.* stature |
| **stampedo** *n.* stampede | **stasala za udaju** *a.* nubile |
| **stan** *n.* apartment | **statičnost** *n.* static |
| **stanar** *n.* inmate | **statika** *n.* statics |
| **stanar** *n.* occupant | **statističar** *n.* statistician |
| **stanar** *n.* tenant | **statistički** *a.* statistical |
| **standard** *n.* standard | **statistika** *n.* statistics |
| **standardan** *a* standard | **statua** *n.* statue |
| **standardizacija** *n.* standardization | **statusa** *n.* status |
| **standardizovati** *v.t.* standardize | **statut** *n.* statute |
| **stanica** *n.* station | **statutarne** *a.* statutory |
| **stanište** *n.* habitat | **stav** *n.* posture |
| **stanje** *n.* plight | **stav** *n.* attitude |
| **stanje, država** *n.* state | **staviti** *v.t.* position |
| **stanovanje** *n.* habitation | **staviti** *v.t.* put |
| **stanovanje** *n.* occupancy | **staviti kasniji datum** *v.t.* post-date |
| **stanovati** *v. i* dwell | **staviti lisice** *v.t* handcuff |
| **stanovište** *n* angle | **staviti na policu** *v.t.* shelve |
| **stanovište** *n.* standpoint | **staviti pod pritisak** *v.t.* pressurize |
| **stanovnik** *n.* inhabitant | **staviti povez preko očiju** *v. t* blindfold |
| **stanovnik** *n* resident | **staviti u džep** *v.t.* pocket |
| **stanovništvo** *n.* populace | **staviti u jamu** *v.t.* pit |
| **stanovništvo** *n.* population | **staviti van zakona** *v.t* outlaw |
| **star** *a.* old | **staviti veto** *v.t.* veto |
| **staratelj** *n* custodian | **stavka** *n.* item |
| **starateljstvo** *v* custody | **staza** *n.* track |
| **starateljstvo** *n.* wardship | **stažirati** *v.t.* intern |
| **starešina** *n* elder | **stečaj** *n.* bankruptcy |
| **starešina** *n.* martinet | **steći** *v.t.* acquire |
| **starešina** *n.* principal | **stega** *n* clamp |
| **starešinstvo** *n.* seniority | **stegnuti** *v.t.* constrict |
| **starije** *a* elderly | **stena** *n* boulder |
| **stariji** *a* elder | **stena** *n.* rock |
| **stariji** *a.* senior | **stenjanje** *v.i.* groan |
| **starinar** *n.* antiquary | **stenjanje** *n.* moan |
| **starinski** *a.* antiquarian | **stenjati** *n* groan |
| **starinski** *a.* antique | **stenjati** *v.i.* moan |
| **staromodan** *a.* outmoded | **stenograf** *n.* stenographer |
| **start** *n* start | **stenografija** *n.* stenography |
| **stas** *n.* physique | **stepa** *n.* steppe |

**stepen** *n.* degree
**stepenik** *n.* stair
**stereotip** *n.* stereotype
**stereotipizirati** *v.t.* stereotype
**sterilan** *a.* sterile
**sterilisati** *v.t.* sterilize
**sterilitet** *n.* sterility
**sterilizacija** *n.* sterilization
**sterling** *n.* sterling
**stetoskop** *n.* stethoscope
**stidljiv** *a.* timid
**stidljiv** *a.* bashful
**stigma** *n.* stigma
**stih** *n.* verse
**stihoklepac** *n.* poetaster
**stihopisac** *n.* rhymester
**stihotvorstvo** *n.* versification
**stil** *n.* style
**stimulans** *n.* stimulant
**stimulisati** *v.t.* stimulate
**stipendija** *n.* scholarship
**stipendista** *n.* scholar
**stisak** *n* grip
**stiskati** *v.t* wring
**stisnuti** *v.t.* grip
**stisnuti** *v.* pinch
**stišati** *v.t.* tranquillize
**stjuard** *n.* steward
**sto** *n.* hundred
**sto** *n.* table
**sto stepeni** *a.* centigrade
**stočna hrana** *n* fodder
**stoga** *adv.* thus
**stogodišnjak** *n* centenarian
**stogodišnji** *adj.* centennial
**stogodišnjica** *n.* centenary
**stoik** *n.* stoic
**stoka** *n.* cattle
**stolar** *n.* joiner
**stolar** *n.* carpenter

**stolarija** *n.* carpentry
**stolica** *n.* chair
**stolica** *n* chaise
**stolica** *n.* stool
**stomačni** *a.* abdominal
**stomak** *n* abdomen
**stomak** *n.* stomach
**stomatolog** *n* dentist
**stonoga** *n.* centipede
**stonoga** *n.* millipede
**stopa** *n.* rate
**stopalo** *n* foot
**stovarište** *n* depot
**stožer** *n.* pivot
**straćara** *a.* shanty
**stradanje** *n.* tribulation
**strah** *n* dread
**strah** *n* fear
**strah** *n.* fright
**strah** *n.* scare
**strah od otv. prostora** *n.* agoraphobia
**strahopoštovanje** *n.* veneration
**strahopoštovanje** *n.* awe
**strahovati** *v.t* dread
**strana** *n.* aside
**strana** *n.* page
**strana** *n.* side
**stranac** *n* foreigner
**stranac** *n.* stranger
**stranac** *a.* alien
**stranački** *a* factious
**strani** *a* foreign
**stranka** *n.* party
**strast** *n.* passion
**strastven** *a.* passionate
**strašan** *a* dire
**strašan** *a* dread
**strašan** *a.* horrible
**strašan** *a.* terrific
**strašno** *a.* fearful

**strateg** *n.* strategist
**strategija** *n.* strategy
**strateški** *a.* strategic
**straža** *n.* sentry
**stražar** *n.* guard
**stražar** *n.* sentinel
**stražnjica** *n* buttock
**strela** *n.* arrow
**strelac** *n.* marksman
**strelac** *n.* archer
**strelast koren** *n.* arrowroot
**strelica** *n.* dart
**stres** *n.* stress
**stric, teča, ujak** *n.* uncle
**strm** *adj.* declivous
**strm** *a.* steep
**strmina** *n* bluff
**strmoglav** *adv.* headlong
**strnjika** *n.* stubble
**strofa** *n.* stanza
**strog** *a.* strict
**strog** *a.* stringent
**strog** *a.* austere
**strogost** *n.* rigour
**strpljenje** *n.* patience
**strpljiv** *a.* patient
**stršljen** *n.* hornet
**stručan** *a* expert
**stručnjak** *n* expert
**strug** *n.* lathe
**strugar** *n.* turner
**strugati** *v.t* grate
**strugati** *v.t.* whittle
**struja** *n* current
**struk** *n.* waist
**struktura** *n.* structure
**strukturni** *a.* structural
**stub** *n.* pillar
**student** *n.* student
**student** *n.* undergraduate

**student medicine** *n.* medico
**studio** *n.* studio
**stvar** *n.* matter
**stvar** *n.* thing
**stvaran** *a.* actual
**stvaranje** *n* creation
**stvarno** *adv.* really
**stvor** *n.* wight
**stvorenje** *n* creature
**stvrdnuti** *v.t.* harden
**sub** *n.* post
**subjekat** *n.* subject
**subjektivan** *a.* subjective
**sublimirati** *v.t.* sublimate
**subota** *n.* Saturday
**subvencija** *n.* subsidy
**subvencionisati** *v.t.* subsidize
**subverzija** *n.* subversion
**subverzivan** *a.* subversive
**sud** *n.* court
**sud** *n.* tribunal
**sudar** *n.* clash
**sudar** *n* collision
**sudar** *n* crash
**sudariti se** *v. t.* clash
**sudariti se** *v. i.* collide
**sudariti se** *v. i* crash
**sudbina** *n* destiny
**sudbina** *n* fate
**suđenje** *n.* trial
**sudija** *n.* arbiter
**sudija** *n.* judge
**sudija** *n.* referee
**sudija** *n.* umpire
**sudija za prekršaje** *n.* magistrate
**suditi** *v.i.* judge
**sudopera** *n* sink
**sudski** *a.* judicial
**sudski izvršitelj** *n.* bailiff
**sudski nalog** *n.* injunction

| | |
|---|---|
| **sudski progon** *n.* prosecution | **suprotan** *a.* reverse |
| **sudstvo** *n.* judiciary | **suprotno** *a* contrary |
| **sufiks** *n.* suffix | **suprotnost** *n* reverse |
| **sufler** *n.* prompter | **suprotstaviti** *v.t.* contrapose |
| **sugestivan** *a.* suggestive | **suprotstaviti** *v. t* contrast |
| **suglasnik** *n.* consonant | **suprotstaviti** *v.t.* counteract |
| **sujeta** *n.* vanity | **suprotstaviti** *v.t.* oppose |
| **sujeveran** *a.* superstitious | **supruga** *n.* wife |
| **sujeverje** *n.* superstition | **supstanca** *n.* substance |
| **suknar** *n* draper | **suptilan** *n.* subtle |
| **suknja** *n.* skirt | **suptilnost** *n.* subtlety |
| **sukob** *n.* strife | **surf** *n.* surf |
| **sukobiti** *se v. i* conflict | **surovost** *n.* barbarity |
| **suma** *n.* sum | **surutka** *n* buttermilk |
| **sumirati** *v.t.* sum | **surutka** *n* curd |
| **sumnja** *n* doubt | **susedni** *a.* adjacent |
| **sumnja** *n.* suspicion | **susedski** *a.* neighbourly |
| **sumnjati** *v. t.* distrust | **suspendovati** *v.t.* suspend |
| **sumnjati** *v. i* doubt | **susresti** *v. t* encounter |
| **sumnjiv** *a.* questionable | **susret** *n.* encounter |
| **sumnjiv** *a.* suspicious | **suša** *n* drought |
| **sumoran** *a.* gloomy | **sušara** *n.* kiln |
| **sumoran** *a.* sullen | **suština** *n* essence |
| **sumornost** *n.* gloom | **suština** *n.* gist |
| **sumpor** *n.* sulphur | **suština** *n.* quintessence |
| **sumporni** *a.* sulphuric | **suštinski** *a* essential |
| **sunce** *n.* sun | **suton** *n* dusk |
| **sunčan** *a.* sunny | **suton** *n* twilight |
| **sunčati** *v.t.* sun | **sutra** *adv.* tomorrow |
| **sunđer** *n.* sponge | **sutrašnji dan** *n.* tomorrow |
| **suočenje** *n.* confrontation | **suv** *adj.* arid |
| **suočiti se** *v.t* face | **suv** *a.* torrid |
| **supa** *n* broth | **suvenir** *n.* souvenir |
| **supa** *n.* soup | **suveren** *a* sovereign |
| **superiornost** *n.* superiority | **suverenost** *n.* sovereignty |
| **superlativ** *n.* superlative | **suvišan** *a* excess |
| **superlativan** *a.* superlative | **suvišan** *a.* redundant |
| **supersoničan** *a.* supersonic | **suviše** *adv.* too |
| **suprotan** *a* adverse | **suvišno** *a.* superfluous |
| **suprotan** *a.* opposite | **suvo** *a* dry |

suvo grožđe *n.* raisin
suza *n.* tear
suzan *a.* tearful
suzbijanje *n.* repression
suzbijanje *n.* suppression
suzbijati *v.t.* suppress
suziti *v.t.* narrow
suziti *v.t.* straiten
svađa *n.* quarrel
svađa *n.* row
svađa *v. i. & n* brawl
svađati se *v.i.* quarrel
svadba *n.* nuptials
svadba *n.* spousal
svadbeni *a.* nuptial
svadljiv *a.* quarrelsome
svadljivac *n.* barrator
svakako *adv.* needs
svaki *a.* any
svaki *a* each
svaki *pron.* each
svaki *a* every
svaki čas *adv.* minutely
svakidašnji *a.* commonplace
svakidašnji *a.* workaday
svariti *v. t.* digest
svečan *a.* ceremonial
svečan *a* festive
svečan *a.* solemn
svečanost *n* festivity
svečanost *n.* solemnity
sveća *n.* candle
svedočanstvo *n.* testimony
svedočiti *v.i.* testify
svedočiti *v.i.* witness
svedok *n.* deponent
svedok *n.* witness
svemir *n.* universe
svemoć *n.* omnipotence
svemoguć *a.* omnipotent

svemoguć *a.* almighty
sveobuhvatan *a* comprehensive
sveprisutan *a.* omnipresent
sveprisutnost *n.* omnipresence
svestan *a* conscious
svestan *a.* aware
svestran *a.* versatile
svestranos *n.* versatility
sveštenica *n.* priestess
sveštenički *a* clerical
sveštenik *n.* priest
sveštenstvo *n* clergy
sveštenstvo *n.* priesthood
svet *n.* globe
svet *n.* world
svetac *n.* saint
svetački *a.* saintly
svetao *a* bright
svetao *a.* lucent
sveti *a.* holy
sveti *a.* sacred
sveti *a.* sacrosanct
svetilište *n.* sanctuary
svetinja *n.* shrine
svetionik *n* beacon
svetiti se *v.t.* avenge
svetkovati *v.t.* solemnize
svetleći *a.* luminous
svetlo *n.* light
svetlucanje *n.* scintillation
svetlucanje *n.* twinkle
svetlucati *v.i.* scintillate
svetlucati *v.i.* twinkle
svetogrdan *a.* sacrilegious
svetogrđe *n.* sacrilege
svetost *n.* sanctity
svetovan *a.* profane
svetovni *a.* mundane
svetovni *a.* worldly
svetski čovek *n.* worldling

sveukupno *adv.* altogether
svezati trakom *v.t* tape
svezati žicom *v.t.* wire
sveznajući *a.* omniscient
sveznanje *n.* omniscience
svež *a.* fresh
svi *pron.* all
svila *n.* silk
svilen *a.* silken
svilenkast *a.* silky
svinja *n.* pig
svinja *n.* swine
svinjac *n.* sty
svinjsko meso *n.* pork
svirati flautu *v.i* flute
svirati na fruli *v.i* pipe
svirep *a* ferocious
svitak *n.* scroll
svitati *v. i.* dawn
svlačiti *v.t.* slough
svlačiti *v.t.* strip
svo *adv.* all
svod *n.* vault
svod *n* arcade
svod *n.* arch
svoja ličnost *n.* self
svoje *a.* own
svojevoljan *a.* wayward
svojina *n.* belongings
svojstvenost *n.* peculiarity
svrab *n.* itch
svraka *n.* magpie
svrbeti *v.i.* itch
svrgnuti *v. t* depose
svrha *n.* purpose
svrstavati *v.t.* assort
svršena učenica *n* alumna

# Š

šafran *n.* saffron
šah *n.* chess
šaht *n.* manhole
šaka *n* hand
šakal *n.* jackal
šal *n.* scarf
šal *n.* shawl
šala *n.* jest
šala *n.* pleasantry
šaliti se *v.i.* jest
šaljiv *a* comical
šaljiv *a.* jocular
šamar *n.* slap
šamar *n* smack
šampion *n.* champion
šampon *n.* shampoo
šamponirati *v.t.* shampoo
šanac *n.* moat
šansa *n.* chance
šapa *n.* paw
šapat *n* whisper
šaputati *v.t.* whisper
šara *n.* mottle
šargarepa *n.* carrot
šarlatan *n* quack
šarm *n.* charm1
šarmirati *v. t.* charm2
šarolik *a.* motley
šator *n.* tent
šav *n.* seam
šav *n.* stitch
ščepati *v.t.* grasp
ščepati *v.t.* nab
ščepati *v.t.* snap
šećer *n.* sugar
šećerni *a.* saccharine

| | |
|---|---|
| **šef** *n* boss | **škodljiv** *a.* pernicious |
| **šegrt** *n.* apprentice | **škola** *n.* school |
| **šema** *n.* scheme | **školarina** *n.* tuition |
| **šepurenje** *n* swagger | **školjka** *n.* conch |
| **šepuriti se** *v.i.* swagger | **školjka** *n.* shell |
| **šesnaest** *n., a.* sixteen | **školjke** *n* barnacles |
| **šesnaesti** *a.* sixteenth | **škorpija** *n.* scorpion |
| **šest** *n., a* six | **škot** *n.* Scot |
| **šesti** *a.* sixth | **škotski** *a.* scotch |
| **šešir** *n.* hat | **škrabanje** *n.* scribble |
| **šetati** *v.i.* walk | **škrabati** *v.t.* scrawl |
| **šetkati se** *v.i.* lounge | **škrabati** *v.t.* scribble |
| **šetnja** *n* walk | **škrabotina** *n* scrawl |
| **ševa** *n.* lark | **škriljac** *n.* slate |
| **šezdeset** *n., a.* sixty | **škripanje** *n* creak |
| **šezdeseti** *a.* sixtieth | **škripati** *v. i* creak |
| **šibati** *v. t.* cane | **škrt** *a.* niggardly |
| **šibati** *v.t* flog | **škrt** *a.* stingy |
| **šibica** *n* match | **škrtica** *n.* niggard |
| **šiling** *n.* shilling | **škrtost** *n.* avarice |
| **šiljak** *n.* spike | **šljiva** *n.* plum |
| **šiljat** *adj.* cultrate | **šljokica** *n.* tinsel |
| **šimpanza** *n.* chimpanzee | **šljunak** *n.* pebble |
| **šina** *n.* rail | **šmrkanje** *n* sniff |
| **šipka** *n.* bar | **šmrkati** *v.i.* sniff |
| **širenje** *n.* propagation | **šofer** *n.* chauffeur |
| **širenje** *n.* spread | **šok** *n.* shock |
| **širina** *n.* latitude | **šokirati** *v.t.* shock |
| **širina** *n.* width | **šolja** *n.* cup |
| **širina** *n* breadth | **šorts** *n. pl.* shorts |
| **širiti** *v.i.* spread | **španac** *n.* Spaniard |
| **širok** *a.* wide | **španijel** *n.* spaniel |
| **širok** *a* broad | **španski** *a.* Spanish |
| **široko** *adv.* wide | **španski jezik, španac** *n.* Spanish |
| **širom** *prep.* throughout | **špijun** *n.* spy |
| **šišarka** *n.* cone | **špijunirati** *v.i.* spy |
| **šiti** *v.t.* seam | **šporet** *n* cooker |
| **šiti** *v.t.* sew | **špric** *n.* syringe |
| **škljocaj** *n.* click | **špricati** *v.i.* spurt |
| **škodljiv** *a.* maleficent | **šraf** *n.* screw |

**šta** *pron.* what
**šta** *interj.* what
**štagod** *pron.* whatever
**štaka** *n* crutch
**štala** *n.* bawn
**štala** *n* stable
**štala** *n.* stall
**štala** *n* byre
**štampa** *n* press
**štampač** *n.* printer
**štamparska greška** *n.* misprint
**štampati** *v.t.* print
**štand** *n.* stand
**štap** *n.* rod
**štap** *n.* stick
**štapić** *n.* wand
**štaviše** *adv.* moreover
**štedeti** *v.t.* spare
**štedljiv** *a.* frugal
**štedljiv** *a.* thrifty
**štednja** *n.* retrenchment
**štednja** *n.* thrift
**štenara** *n.* kennel
**štene** *n.* puppy
**štene** *n.* whelp
**šteta** *n.* damage
**šteta** *n.* harm
**štetan** *a.* injurious
**štetan** *a.* noxious
**štetan uticaj** *n* blight
**štetan** *a.* baleful
**štetočina** *n.* pest
**štićenik** *n.* ward
**štirkati** *v.t.* starch
**štit** *n.* shield
**štititi** *v.t.* patronize
**štititi** *v.t.* shelter
**štrajk** *n* strike
**štrajkač** *n.* striker
**štrcnuti** *v.t.* syringe

**štucanje** *n.* hiccup
**štula** *n.* stilt
**šuga** *n.* scabies
**šuma** *n* forest
**šuma** *n.* woods
**šumar** *n* forester
**šumarak** *n.* coppice
**šumarstvo** *n* forestry
**šumovit kraj** *n.* woodland
**šunjati** *se v.i.* sneak
**šupalj** *a.* hollow
**šupljina** *n.* hollow
**šuškanje** *n* lisp
**šuškati** *v.t.* lisp
**šut** *n.* kick
**šutirati** *v.t.* kick
**švajcarska** *n.* swiss
**švajcarski** *a* swiss
**švercer** *n.* smuggler

# T

**tabak za pisanje** *n* foolscap
**tabati** *v.t* stump
**tabelarni** *a.* tabular
**tabelisanje** *n.* tabulation
**tabla** *n.* panel
**tableta** *n.* tablet
**tabu** *n.* taboo
**tabulator** *n.* tabulator
**tačan** *a* correct
**tačan** *a* exact
**tačan** *a.* punctual
**tačan** *a.* accurate
**tačka** *n* dot
**tačka** *n.* point
**tačno** *adv* due
**tačnost** *n.* punctuality
**tačnost** *n.* accuracy

**tadašnji** *a* then
**taj** *a.* that
**tajan** *adj.* clandestine
**tajanstven** *a.* secretive
**tajfun** *n.* typhoon
**tajna** *n.* secret
**tajni** *a.* secret
**tajni sporazum** *n* collusion
**tajnost** *n.* secrecy
**tak** *n* cue
**takav** *pron.* such
**takmičar** *n* agonist
**takmičenje** *n.* competition
**takmičenje** *n.* contest
**takmičiti se** *v. i* compete
**takmičiti se** *v. t* contest
**takmičiti se** *v. t* emulate
**tako** *adv.* as
**tako** *adv.* so
**tako** *adv.* that
**takođe** *adv.* also
**takođe** *adv.* likewise
**taksa** *n.* toll
**taksa za vezivanje broda** *n.* wharfage
**taksi** *n.* taxi
**taksi** *n.* cab
**takt** *n.* tact
**taktičan** *a.* tactful
**taktičar** *n.* tactician
**taktika** *n.* tactics
**taktilni** *a.* tactile
**talac** *n.* hostage
**talas** *n* billow
**talas** *n.* surge
**talas** *v.i.* surge
**talas** *n.* wave
**talas** *v.t.* wave
**talasanje** *n.* ripple
**talasati** *v.t.* ripple
**talasati se** *v.i* billow

**talasati se** *v.i.* undulate
**talenat** *n.* talent
**talisman** *n.* talisman
**talog** *n.* sediment
**taman** *a* dark
**tamjan** *n.* incense
**tamničar** *n.* jailer
**tamno-crven** *n* crimson
**tamo** *adv.* there
**tamo** *adv.* thither
**tamo** *adv.* yonder
**tamošnji** *a.* yonder
**tanak** *a* flimsy
**tanak** *a.* thin
**tangenta** *n.* tangent
**tanjirić** *n.* saucer
**tanjiti** *v.t.* thin
**tanka voštana sveća** *n* taper
**tanker** *n.* tanker
**tapiserija** *n.* tapestry
**tapkanje** *n* pat
**tapkati** *v.t.* pat
**tapkati** *v.t.* tap
**tarifa** *n.* tariff
**tata** *n* dad, daddy
**tečan** *a* fluent
**tečan** *a.* liquid
**tečnost** *n* fluid
**tečnost** *n* liquid
**teći** *v.i* flow
**teći** *v.i.* stream
**tegla** *n.* jar
**tegoban** *a.* onerous
**tegoban** *a* burdensome
**tehničar** *n.* technician
**tehnički** *n.* technical
**tehnika** *n.* technique
**tehnolog** *n.* technologist
**tehnologija** *n.* technology
**tehnološki** *a.* technological

| | |
|---|---|
| **teista** *n.* theist | **tendencija** *n.* tendency |
| **teizam** *n.* theism | **tenis** *n.* tennis |
| **tekovina** *n* acquest | **tenzija** *n.* tension |
| **tekst** *n.* text | **teokratija** *n.* theocracy |
| **tekstil** *n* textile | **teolog** *n.* theologian |
| **tekstilni** *a.* textile | **teologija** *n.* theology |
| **tekstualni** *n.* textual | **teološki** *a.* theological |
| **tekući** *a* fluid | **teorema** *n.* theorem |
| **tele** *n.* calf | **teoretičar** *n.* theorist |
| **telefon** *n.* phone | **teoretisati** *v.i.* theorize |
| **telefon** *n.* telephone | **teorija** *n.* theory |
| **telefonirati** *v.t.* telephone | **teorijski** *a.* theoretical |
| **telegraf** *n.* telegraph | **tepih** *n.* carpet |
| **telegrafija** *n.* telegraphy | **terapija** *n.* therapy |
| **telegrafisati** *v.t.* telegraph | **terasa** *n.* terrace |
| **telegrafista** *n.* telegraphist | **teret** *n.* load |
| **telegrafski** *a.* telegraphic | **teret** *n.* onus |
| **telegram** *n.* telegram | **teret** *n* burden |
| **telepata** *n.* telepathist | **teret** *n.* cargo |
| **telepatija** *n.* telepathy | **terevenka** *n.* revelry |
| **telepatski** *a.* telepathic | **terijer** *n.* terrier |
| **teleskop** *n.* telescope | **teritorija** *n.* territory |
| **teleskopski** *a.* telescopic | **teritorijalni** *a.* territorial |
| **telesni** *a* corporal | **termalni** *a.* thermal |
| **telesni** *a* bodily | **terminal** *n* terminal |
| **televizija** *n.* television | **terminologija** *n.* terminology |
| **telo** *n* body | **terminološki** *a.* terminological |
| **telohranitelj** *n.* bodyguard | **termometar** *n.* thermometer |
| **tema** *n.* theme | **termos (boca)** *n.* thermos (flask) |
| **tema** *n.* topic | **teror** *n.* terror |
| **tematski** *a.* thematic | **terorisati** *v.t.* terrorize |
| **tematski** *a.* topical | **terorista** *n.* terrorist |
| **temeljan** *a* thorough | **terotizam** *n.* terrorism |
| **temperament** *n.* mettle | **tesati** *v.t.* hew |
| **temperament** *n.* temper | **tesnac** *n.* defile |
| **temperament** *n.* temperament | **tesnac** *n.* ravine |
| **temperamentan** *a.* temperamental | **test** *n* test |
| **temperatura** *n.* temperature | **testament** *n.* testament |
| **ten** *n* complexion | **testera** *n.* saw |

testerisati *v.t.* saw
testirati *v.t.* test
testis *n.* testicle
testo *n* dough
teško koračati *v.i.* plod
teškoća *n* difficulty
teškoća *n.* hardship
tetka, strina, ujna *n.* aunt
tetoviranje *n.* tattoo
tetovirati *v.i.* tattoo
teturanje *n.* stagger
teturati se *v.i.* stagger
teza *n.* thesis
težak *a* difficult
težak *a* gross
težak *a.* hard
težak *a.* tough
težak *a.* trying
težak hod *n.* shuffle
težina *n.* weight
težiti *v.i.* strive
težiti ka *v.i.* gravitate
težiti *v.t.* aspire
težnja *n.* aspiration
tifozan *n.* typhoid
tifus *n.* typhus
tigar *n.* tiger
tigrica *n.* tigress
tih *a.* silent
tijara *n.* tiara
tik *n.* teak
tikva *n.* gourd
tikvan *n.* loggerhead
tim *n.* team
timariti *v.t* groom
time *adv.* thereby
tinejdžer *n.* teenager
tinjati *v.i.* smoulder
tip *n.* type
tipičan *a.* typical

tipkati *v.t.* type
tirada *n.* tirade
tiranija *n.* tyranny
tiranin *n.* tyrant
tiranski *a.* oppressive
tišina *n* hush
tišina *n.* silence
tišina *n.* stillness
titanski *a.* titanic
titularni *a.* titular
tkač *n.* weaver
tkanina *n* cloth
tkanina *n* fabric
tkati *v.t.* weave
tkivo *n.* tissue
tlačitelj *n.* oppressor
tlo *n.* ground
tlo *n.* soil
tmuran *a.* sombre
to *pron.* it
toalet *n.* lavatory
toalet *n.* toilet
tobolac *n.* quiver
tobožnji *a.* would-be
točak *a.* wheel
toga *n.* toga
tolerancija *n.* tolerance
tolerancija *n.* toleration
tolerantan *a.* tolerant
tolerisati *v.t.* tolerate
toljaga *n* cudgel
tom *n.* tome
tona *n.* ton
tona *n.* tonne
toničan *a.* tonic
tonik *n.* tonic
tonzura *n.* tonsure
top *n.* cannon
topao *v.t.* warm
topaz *n.* topaz

topiti *se v.i* thaw
topljenje *n* thaw
toplota *n.* heat
toplota *n.* warmth
topograf *n.* topographer
topografija *n.* topography
topografski *a.* topographical
topola *n.* poplar
toranj *n.* tower
torba *n.* satchel
torba *n.* bag
torbar *n.* marsupial
tornado *n.* tornado
torpedo *n.* torpedo
torpedovati *v.t.* torpedo
torta *n.* cake
tovar *n.* freight
traćiti *v.t.* squander
tradicija *n.* tradition
tradicionalan *a.* traditional
trag *n.* trace
trag *n.* trail
trag *n.* vestige
traganje *n.* quest
tragati *v.t.* quest
tragati *v.t.* trace
tragedija *n.* tragedy
tragičan *a.* tragic
tragičar *n.* tragedian
trajan *a* abiding
trajan *a.* lasting
trajan *a.* permanent
trajanje *n* duration
trajati *v.i.* last
trajekt *n* ferry
trajnica *n.* perennial
trajnost *n.* permanence
traka *n.* ribbon
traka *n.* streamer
traka *n.* strip

traka *n.* tape
trakt *n.* tract
traktat *n* tract
traktor *n.* tractor
trampa *n.* barter
trampiti *v.t.* barter1
tramvaj *n.* tram
trans *n.* trance
transakcija *n.* transaction
transformacija *n.* transformation
transformisati *v.* transform
transkripcija *n.* transcription
transmisija *n.* transmission
transparentan *a.* transparent
transport *n.* transportation
tranzit *n.* transit
trava *n* grass
travnjak *n.* lawn
traženje *n.* requirement
tražiti *v.t.* require
tražiti *v.t.* search
tražiti *v.t.* seek
trbuh *n* belly
trčanje *n.* run
trčati *v.i.* run
trčati za ženama *v.t.* womanize
trebati *v.t.* need
trebovanje *n.* requisition
trebovati *v.t.* requisition
treće *adv.* thirdly
treći *a.* third
trećina *n.* third
trem *n.* portico
trend *n.* trend
trenirati *v.t.* train
trenje *n.* friction
trenutak *n.* instant
trenutak *n.* moment
trenutan *a.* momentary
trenutni *a* current

trenutni *a.* instant
trepavica *n* eyelash
treperenje *n* flicker
treperenje *n.* palpitation
treperenje *n* warble
treperiti *v.t* flicker
treperiti *v.i.* warble
treptati *v. t. & i* blink
tresak *n* slam
treset *n.* turf
tresnuti *v.t.* slam
tresti *v.i.* shake
tresti se *v.i.* quake
tretman *n.* treatment
trezan *a.* sober
trezvenjački *a.* teetotal
trezvenjak *n.* teetotaller
trezvenost *n.* sobriety
trgovac *n* dealer
trgovac *n.* merchant
trgovac *n.* trader
trgovac *n.* tradesman
trgovac konjima *n.* coper
trgovac na malo *n.* retailer
trgovac na veliko *n.* wholesaler
trgovac pisaćim priborom *n.* stationer
trgovački *a* commercial
trgovački *a.* mercantile
trgovati *v.t* market
trgovati *v.i* trade
trgovati *v.i.* traffic
trgovina *n* commerce
trgovina *n.* trade
tri *n.* three
tri *a* three
tricikl *n.* tricycle
tričav *a.* paltry
trideset *n.* thirty
trideset *a* thirty
trideseti *a.* thirtieth

tridesetina *n* thirtieth
trijumf *n.* triumph
trijumfalan *a.* triumphal
trijumfovati *v.i.* triumph
trik *n* trick
trinaest *n.* thirteen
trinaest *a* thirteen
trinaesti *a.* thirteenth
trio *n.* trio
triplikat *n* triplicate
triput *adv.* thrice
triton *n.* merman
trivijalan *a.* trivial
trka *n.* race
trkač *n.* runner
trkati se *v.i* race
trljanje *n* rub
trljati *v.t.* rub
trn *n.* thorn
trnovit *a.* thorny
trobojni *a.* tricolour
trobojnica *n* tricolour
trodelan *a.* tripartite
trofej *n.* trophy
trojstvo *n.* trinity
trokratan *a.* triplicate
trom *n.* laggard
trom *a.* listless
tromesečni *a.* quarterly
tromo se kretati *v.t.* maunder
tron *n.* throne
tronožac *n.* tripod
tropski *a.* tropical
tropski pojas *n.* tropic
trostruk *a.* triple
trošak *n.* expense
trošiti *v. t* consume
trougao *n.* triangle
trougaoni *a.* triangular
trpeti *v.i* abide

trska *n.* cane
truba *n.* trumpet
trubiti *v.i* hoot
trubiti *v.i.* trumpet
trubiti *v. t* blare
trubljenje *n.* hoot
trudna *a.* pregnant
trudnoća *n.* pregnancy
trulež *n.* rot
truliti *v.i.* rot
trunčica *n.* mote
truo *adj* carious
trupa *n* rout
trzaj *n.* jerk
trzaj *n.* lurch
trzanje *n* pluck
trzati *v.t.* tug
trzati se *v.i.* wince
tržište *n* market
tuberkuloza *n.* tuberculosis
tuce *n* dozen
tuča *n* fray
tući se *v.i.* scuffle
tuga *n.* grievance
tuga *n.* melancholy
tuga *n.* sorrow
tugovati *v.t.* grieve
tugovati *v.i.* mourn
tumač *n* exponent
tumaranje *n* stroll
tumarati *v.i.* loiter
tumarati *v.t.* saunter
tumarati *v.i.* stroll
tumor *n.* tumour
tunel *n.* tunnel
tup *a* dull
tup *a.* obtuse
tup udarac *n.* thump
tup *a* blunt
tupiti *v. t.* dull

tura *n.* tour
turban *n.* turban
turbina *n.* turbine
turbulencije *n.* turbulence
turbulentan *a.* turbulent
turista *n.* tourist
turizam *n.* tourism
turnir *n.* tournament
turšija *n.* pickle
tuš *n.* shower
tuširati *v.t.* shower
tutnjati *v.i.* rumble
tutnjava *n.* rumble
tutnjava *n.* thud
tutnjiti *v.i.* thud
tutor *n.* tutor
tužan *adj* melancholy
tužan *a.* sad
tužan *n.* woeful
tužilac *n* claimant
tužilac *n.* plaintiff
tužilac *n.* prosecutor
tužiti *v.t.* sue
tvorac *n* creator
tvorac *n.* maker
tvorac *n.* originator
tvorevina *n* make
tvrđava *n.* citadel
tvrđava *n.* fortress
tvrdica *n.* miser
tvrditi *v.t.* assert
tvrdnja *n* contention
tvrdoća *n.* adamant
tvrdoglav *adj.* asinine
tvrdoglav *a.* headstrong
tvrdoglav *a.* mulish
tvrdoglav *a.* obstinate
tvrdoglav *a.* stubborn
tvrdoglavost *n.* obstinacy
tvrdokoran *a.* obdurate

# U

u *prep.* at
u *prep.* in
u *prep.* into
u *prep.* within
u **blizini** *adv.* near
u **celosti** *adv.* bodily
u **dobroj nameri** *a* bonafide
u **gomili** *adv.* aheap
u **inostranstvu** *adv* abroad
u **izobilju** *adv.* galore
u **kome** *adv.* wherein
u **krivi čas** *a.* inopportune
u **međuvremenu** *adv.* meanwhile
u **obliku uha** *adj.* auriform
u **okviru** *adv.* within
u **pokretu** *adv.* astir
u **poređenju sa** *prep* besides
u **poslednje vreme** *adv.* lately
u **postelji** *adv.* abed
u **potpunosti** *adv.* wholly
u **samoj unutrašnjosti** *a.* innermost
u **snu** *adv.* asleep
u **svakom slučaju** *adv.* anyhow
u **toku** *prep.* pending
u **unutrašnjosti** *a.* inland
**ubediti** *v. t* convince
**ubediti** *v.t.* persuade
**ubeđivanje** *n.* persuasion
**ubedljiv** *adj.* cogent
**ubeležiti** *v.t* file
**ubica** *n.* murderer
**ubijanje** *n.* kill
**ubilački** *a.* murderous
**ubistvo** *n.* homicide
**ubistvo** *n.* murder
**ubiti** *v.t.* kill

**ubiti** *v.t.* murder
**ubiti** *v.t.* slay
**ubiti** *v.t.* assassinate
**ublažavanje** *n.* mitigation
**ublažiti** *v.t.* mince
**ublažiti** *v.t.* mitigate
**ublažiti** *v.t.* moderate
**ublažiti** *v.t.* soften
**ublažiti** *v.t.* soothe
**ublažiti** *v.t.* allay
**ublažiti** *v.t.* assuage
**ubod** *n.* prick
**ubod** *n.* stab
**ubod** *v.t.* sting
**ubosti** *v.t.* lance
**ubosti** *v.t.* prick
**ubosti** *v.t.* stab
**ubrizgati** *v.t.* inject
**ubrizgavanje** *n.* injection
**ubrzanje** *n* acceleration
**ubrzati** *v.t* accelerate
**ubrzati** *v.i.* hasten
**ubrzati** *v.i.* speed
**ubuduće** *adv.* henceforward
**ucena** *n* blackmail
**uceniti** *v.t* blackmail
**ucrtati** *v.t.* map
**ucveliti** *v. t.* bereave
**ucveljenost** *n* bereavement
**učen** *a.* learned
**učenik** *n* disciple
**učenik** *n.* learner
**učenik** *n.* pupil
**učenje** *n.* learning
**učenje napamet** *n.* rote
**učesnik** *n.* participant
**učestalost** *n.* frequent
**učestvovati** *v.i.* partake
**učestvovati** *v.i.* participate
**učešće** *n.* participation

**učetvorostručiti** *v.t.* quadruple
**učiniti** *v.t.* render
**učiniti dragim** *v.t* endear
**učiniti imunim** *v.t.* immunize
**učiniti nepromočivim** *v.t.* waterproof
**učiniti siročetom** *v.t* orphan
**učiniti udovicom** *v.t.* widow
**učiniti vitezom** *v.t.* knight
**učitelj** *n.* preceptor
**učitelj** *n.* teacher
**učiteljski** *a.* tutorial
**učiti** *v.i.* study
**učiti** *v.t.* teach
**učtiv** *a.* mannerly
**učtiv** *a.* polite
**učtiv** *a.* urbane
**učtivost** *n.* courtesy
**učtivost** *n.* politeness
**učtivost** *n.* urbanity
**učvrstiti** *v.t.* steady
**ućutkati** *v.t* muzzle
**ud** *n.* limb
**udaljen** *a* distant
**udar** *n.* coup
**udar** *n.* impact
**udarac** *n* beat
**udarac** *n.* jostle
**udarac** *n.* stroke
**udarac bičem** *n* lash
**udarac bičem** *n* slash
**udarati** *v. t.* beat
**udarati u bubanj** *v.i.* drum
**udariti** *v.t.* punch
**udariti** *v.t.* strike
**udariti** *v.t.* whack
**udariti da poleti visoko** *v.t.* sky
**udariti motkom** *v. i* bat
**udariti o** *v.t.* jostle
**udariti šapom** *v.t.* paw
**udati** *v.t.* marry

**udenuti** *v.t* thread
**udeo** *n.* share
**udisati** *v.i.* inhale
**udoban** *a* comfortable
**udoban** *a.* cosy
**udoban** *adj.* cozy
**udoban** *n.* snug
**udostojiti** *v.t* dignify
**udovac** *n.* widower
**udovica** *n.* widow
**udovoljavanje** *n.* compliance
**udovoljiti** *v. i* comply
**udružen** *a.* associate
**udruženje** *n.* association
**udruživanje** *n.* merger
**udubljen** *adj.* concave
**udubljenje** *n.* recess
**udvaranje** *n.* courtship
**udvarati se** *v. t.* court
**udvarati se** *v.t.* woo
**udvostručiti** *v. t.* double
**udvostručiti** *v. t* duplicate
**udvostručiti** *v.t.* redouble
**ugađanje** *n.* indulgence
**ugađati** *v.t.* indulge
**ugađati** *v.t.* tune
**ugalj** *n* coal
**uganuće** *n.* sprain
**uganuti** *v.t.* sprain
**ugao** *n.* angle
**ugao** *n* corner
**ugaoni** *a.* angular
**ugar** *n* fallow
**ugasiti** *v.t* extinguish
**ugasiti** *v.t.* quench
**uglađen** *a.* sleek
**uglađenost** *n.* nicety
**uglavnom** *adv.* generally
**uglavnom** *adv.* mainly
**ugled** *n.* reputation

ugled *n.* repute
ugledati *v.t.* sight
ugledna ličnost *n.* personage
ugljenik *n.* carbon
ugnezditi *v.t.* nest
ugnjetavanje *n.* oppression
ugnjetavati *v.t.* oppress
ugoditi *v.t.* please
ugostiti *v.t.* banquet
ugovor *n* contract
ugovor *n.* covenant
ugovoriti *v. t* contract
ugravirati *v. t* engrave
ugristi *v. t.* bite
ugriz *n* bite
ugroziti *v. t.* endanger
ugroziti *v.t.* imperil
ugroziti *v.t.* jeopardize
ugroziti *v.t.* peril
ugrušak *n.* clot
ugušiti *v.t.* quell
ugušiti *v.t.* smother
ugušiti *v.t.* stifle
ugušiti *v.t.* strangle
ugušiti *v.t* suffocate
uhapsiti *v.t.* imprison
uhapsiti *v.i.* lag
uhvatiti *v. t.* capture
uhvatiti u mrežu *v.t* mesh
uhvatiti u zamku *v.t.* noose
uhvatiti u zamku *v.t.* snare
uhvatiti u zamku *v.t.* trap
ujarmiti *v.t.* yoke
ujediniti *v.t.* unite
ujediniti se *v.t.* ally
ujedinjenje *n.* unification
ukaljati *v.* asperse
ukalupljen *a.* stereotyped
ukazati *v.t.* indicate
ukidanje *v* abolition

ukinuti *v.t* abolish
ukinuti ograničenje *v.t.* decontrol
ukiseliti *v.t* pickle
ukiseliti *v.t.* sour
uklanjanje *n.* removal
uključen *a.* incorporate
uključiti *v.t.* involve
uključivanje *n.* inclusion
uključivati *v.t.* include
uključivo *a.* inclusive
ukloniti *v.t.* remove
uknjižiti *v. t.* book
ukočen *a.* numb
ukonačiti *v.t.* lodge
ukor *n.* rebuke
ukor *n.* reprimand
ukor *n.* reproof
ukoreniti *v.i.* root
ukorenjen *a.* ingrained
ukoriti *v.t.* reprimand
ukras za nogu *n* anklet
ukras za vrat *n.* necklet
ukrasiti *v.t.* bedight
ukrasiti *v. t* deck
ukrasiti *v. t* decorate
ukrasiti *v.t.* grace
ukrasiti *v.t.* ornament
ukrasiti draguljima *v.t.* jewel
ukrasiti zvezdama *v.t.* star
ukrasna palma *n* areca
ukrasni *a.* ornamental
ukrasti *v.t.* pilfer
ukrasti *v.i.* steal
ukrašavanje *n.* ornamentation
ukratko *adv.* summarily
ukrcano *adv* aboard
ukrcati *v. t.* board
ukrcati *v. t* embark
ukrcati *v.t.* ship
ukršten *a* cross

ukrutiti *v.t.* stiffen
ukupan *a* overall
ukupan *a.* total
ukus *n* flavour
ukus *n.* smack
ukus *n.* taste
ukusan *a* delicious
ukusan *a.* palatable
ukusan *a.* tasteful
ukusan *a.* tasty
ukusan *a.* toothsome
ukuvano voće *n.* preserve
ulaz *n* entrance
ulazak *n* entry
ulaziti *v. t* enter
ulazni *n.* input
ulepšati *v. t* beautify
ulepšavati *v.t.* adorn
ulica *n.* street
uličarka *n.* strumpet
uliti *v.t.* infuse
ulivati *v.t.* instil
ulizica *n.* sycophant
ulizivanje *n.* sycophancy
ulje *n.* oil
uljiti *v.t* oil
uljudan *a.* courteous
ulog *n* stake
ulog *n.* wager
uloga *n.* role
ulov *n.* catch
uloviti *v. t.* catch
uložiti *v.t.* stake
ultimatum *n.* ultimatum
um *n.* mind
umakanje *n.* dip
umakati *v. i.* dabble
umalo *adv.* almost
umanjiti *v.t.* avale
umanjivati *v.t.* minimize

umarati *v.t* fatigue
umeren *a.* moderate
umeren *a.* temperate
umerenost *n.* moderation
umerenost *n.* temperance
umesto *n.* lieu
umešati *v. t* blend
umetak *n.* parenthesis
umetanje *n.* insertion
umetnički *a.* artistic
umetnik *n.* artist
umetnost *n.* art
umetnuti *v.t.* insert
umetnuti *v.t.* sandwich
umiranje *n* die
umirati od gladi *v.i.* starve
umiriti *v.t.* pacify
umiriti *v.t.* quiet
umiriti *v.t.* still
umiriti *v.t.* appease
umirujući *a.* sedative
umnožavati na ciklostilu *v.t* cyclostyle
umnožiti *v.t.* multiply
umnožiti matricom *v.i.* stencil
umočiti *v. t* dip
umor *n* fatigue
umoran *a.* weary
umoriti *v.t. & i* weary
umotati *v.t.* sheet
umreti *v. i* die
umrljati *v. t* blot
unapred oružati *v.t* forearm
unapred smisliti *v.t.* premeditate
unapred *adv.* beforehand
unaprediti *v.t.* advance
unaprediti *v.t* further
unazad *adv.* aback
unazad *adv.* back
unazad *a.* backward
unazad *adv.* backward

**unca** *n.* ounce
**uneti** *u* **zapisnik** *n.* minute
**unezveren** *a.* haggard
**unija** *n.* union
**unionista** *n.* unionist
**uništenje** *n* annihilation
**uništiti** *v. t* destroy
**uništiti** *v.t.* obliterate
**uništiti** *v.t.* wreck
**uništiti** *v.t.* annihilate
**univerzalan** *a.* universal
**univerzalnost** *n.* universality
**univerzitet** *n.* university
**unosan** *a.* lucrative
**unosan** *a.* remunerative
**unovčiti** *v. t.* cash
**unutar** *prep.* inside
**unutra** *adv.* indoors
**unutra** *adv.* inside
**unutra** *adv.* inwards
**unutrašnji** *a.* indoor
**unutrašnji** *adv.* inland
**unutrašnji** *a.* inner
**unutrašnji** *a* inside
**unutrašnji** *a.* interior
**unutrašnji** *a.* intrinsic
**unutrašnji** *a.* inward
**unutrašnjost** *n.* inside
**unutrašnjost** *n.* interior
**unutrašnjost** *n.* midland
**unutrašnjost** *n.* within
**uobičajen** *a* customary
**uobičajen** *a.* usual
**uobičajen** *a.* wonted
**uobličiti** *v.t* figure
**uobraženost** *n* conceit
**upad** *n.* intrusion
**upadljiv** *a.* conspicuous
**upakovati** *v.t.* pack
**upala slepog creva** *n.* appendicitis

**upaljač** *n.* lighter
**upasti** *v.t.* intrude
**upasti** *v.t.* raid
**upetljati** *v. t* entangle
**upisati** *v. t* enrol
**upisati** *v.t.* inscribe
**upisati visoku školu** *v.t.* matriculate
**upiti** *v.t* absorb
**upitni** *a.* interrogative
**upitnik** *n* interrogative
**upitnik** *n.* questionnaire
**uplašen** *a.* afraid
**uplašiti** *v. t* daunt
**uplašiti** *v.t.* frighten
**uplašiti** *v.t.* scare
**uplesti** *v.t.* wreathe
**uplitanje** *n.* interference
**uplitati se** *v.i.* interfere
**uporan** *a.* insistent
**uporan** *a.* persistent
**uporan** *a.* tenacious
**uporan** *a.* untoward
**uporediti** *v. t* compare
**uporedo** *adv* abreast
**uporište** *n.* stronghold
**uposliti** *v.t.* task
**upotreba** *n.* use
**upotrebiti** *v.t.* use
**upotrebljavati** *v.t.* ply
**upoznat** *a* conversant
**upoznati** *v.t.* acquaint
**upozorenje** *n.* admonition
**upozorenje** *n.* warning
**upozoriti** *v.t.* admonish
**upozoriti** *v. t.* caution
**upozoriti** *v.t* forewarn
**upozoriti** *v.t.* warn
**uprava** *n.* administration
**uprava** *n.* governance
**upravljanje** *n* conduct

**upravljanje** *n.* management
**upravljanje** *n.* ruling
**upravljati** *v. t* conduct
**upravljati** *v.t.* govern
**upravljati** *v.t.* manage
**upravljati** *v.i.* navigate
**upravljati** *v.t.* steer
**upravljati** *v.t.* administer
**upravni** *a.* administrative
**upravnik pošte** *n.* postmaster
**upravnik zatvora** *n.* warden
**upravo** *adv.* just
**upravo** *adv* pat
**upražnjeno mesto** *n.* vacancy
**upregnuti** *v.t* harness
**uprkos** *prep.* notwithstanding
**uprljati** *v. t* bemire
**uprljati** *n.* slur
**uprljati** *v.t.* taint
**upropastiti** *v.t.* ruin
**uprošćavanje** *n.* simplification
**upućen** *adj.* conversant
**uputiti** *v.i.* motion
**uputiti** *v.t.* refer
**uputstvo** *n.* tutorial
**ura** *interj.* hurrah
**uragan** *n.* hurricane
**uramiti** *v.t.* frame
**uravnotežiti** *v.t.* balance
**uravnotežiti** *v.t.* sedate
**urbani** *a.* urban
**uređaj** *n* device
**uređaj** *n.* appliance
**uredan** *a.* neat
**uredan** *a.* orderly
**uredan** *a.* tidy
**uredan** *a.* trim
**uređenje** *n.* arrangement
**urediti** *v. t* edit
**urediti** *v.t.* trim

**urediti** *v.t.* arrange
**urednički** *a* editorial
**urednik** *n* editor
**uredno** *n.* orderly
**urednost** *n.* tidiness
**urez** *n.* scotch
**urezati** *v.t.* score
**urin** *n.* urine
**urinarni** *a.* urinary
**urinirati** *v.i.* urinate
**urlati** *v. i* bellow
**urna** *n* urn
**urnebes** *n.* pandemonium
**urođen** *a.* inborn
**urođen** *a.* innate
**urođenici** *n. pl* aborigines
**urođenički** *a.* indigenous
**urođenik** *a* aboriginal
**urođenik** *n* native
**uručiti** *v.t* hand
**usamljen** *a* forlorn
**usamljen** *a.* lone
**usamljen** *a.* lonely
**usamljen** *a.* lonesome
**usamljen** *a.* solitary
**usamljenost** *n.* loneliness
**usamljenost** *n.* solitude
**usavršiti** *v.t.* perfect
**usedelica** *n.* spinster
**usev** *n* crop
**ushićen** *a.* jubilant
**ushićen** *a.* rapt
**ushititi** *v. t* enrapture
**usidrenje** *n* anchorage
**usidriti brod** *v.t* moor
**uska ulica** *n.* alley
**usklađen** *a.* co-ordinate
**uskladiti** *v. t* equate
**uskomešati se** *v.i.* stir
**uskoro** *adv.* presently

**uskoro** *adv.* shortly
**uskoro** *adv.* soon
**uskratiti** *v. t.* debar
**uskrs** *n* easter
**uslov** *n.* proviso
**uslov, stanje** *n* condition
**uslovni** *a* conditional
**uslovni otpust** *n.* parole
**uslovno otpustiti** *v.t.* parole
**uslužan** *adj.* complaisant
**uslužan** *a.* serviceable
**uslužnost** *n.* complaisance
**usmen** *a.* oral
**usmen** *a* viva-voce
**usmeni ispit** *n* viva-voce
**usmeno** *adv.* orally
**usmeno** *adv.* verbally
**usmeno** *adv.* viva-voce
**usmeriti** *v. t* direct
**usna** *n.* lip
**uspavanka** *n.* lullaby
**uspeh** *n.* success
**uspeh** *n.* achievement
**uspešan** *a.* prosperous
**uspešan** *a* successful
**uspeti** *v.i.* succeed
**uspomena** *n.* keepsake
**uspomena** *n.* memento
**uspomena** *n.* reminiscence
**uspon** *n.* ascent
**usporiti** *v.t.* retard
**usporiti** *v.i.* slow
**uspostaviti** *v. t.* establish
**uspraviti** *v. t* erect
**uspravljen** *a* erect
**usredređenost** *n.* concentration
**usredsrediti** *v. t* concentrate
**usta** *n.* mouth
**ustajao** *a.* mouldy
**ustajao** *a.* stale

**ustanak** *n.* uprising
**ustanoviti** *v. t* constitute
**ustanoviti** *v. t.* essay
**ustanoviti** *v.t.* stipulate
**ustati** *v.i.* arise
**ustav** *n* constitution
**ustoličiti** *v. t* enthrone
**ustostručiti** *n. & adj* centuple
**ustuknuti** *v.i.* recoil
**ustupiti** *v.t.* concede
**usuditi** *se v. i.* dare
**usuditi** *se v.t.* venture
**usvajanje** *n* adoption
**usvojiti** *v.t.* adopt
**ušće** *n* confluence
**ušna mast** *n* cerumen
**ušna resa** *n.* lobe
**uštinuti** *v.t* nip
**uštinuti** *v.t.* pinch
**utakmica** *n.* meet
**utaknuti** *v.t.* jack
**uteha** *n.* comfort
**uteha** *n* consolation
**uteha** *n.* solace
**utelovljen** *a.* incarnate
**utemeljenje** *n.* foundation
**utemeljiti** *v.t.* found
**uterivanje u rupu** *n.* gobble
**utešiti** *v. t* comfort
**utešiti** *v.t.* solace
**uticaj** *n.* influence
**uticajan** *a.* influential
**uticati** *v.t.* affect
**uticati** *v.t.* influence
**utičnica** *n.* jack
**utičnica** *n.* socket
**utikač** *n.* plug
**utilitaristički** *a.* utilitarian
**utisak** *n.* impression
**utisnuti** *v.t.* imprint

**utišati** *v.i* hush
**utišati** *v.t.* lull
**utišati** *v.t.* silence
**utočište** *n* haunt
**utočište** *n.* refuge
**utoliti** *v.t.* slake
**utonuti** *v.t.* immerse
**utopija** *n* . utopia
**utopijski** *a.* utopian
**utopiti** *v.i* drown
**utroba** *n.* entrails
**utrostručenje** *n.* triplication
**utrostručiti** *v.t.,* triple
**utučenost** *n* dejection
**utuviti** *v.t.* inculcate
**utvara** *n.* wraith
**utvrđenje** *n.* fort
**utvrditi** *v.t.* fortify
**utvrditi** *v.t.* ascertain
**uvećanje** *v. t* enlarge
**uvek** *adv.* always
**uveličati** *v.t.* magnify
**uvenuti** *v.i.* wither
**uveravati** *v.t.* reassure
**uverenje** *n.* testimonial
**uverenje** *n.* assurance
**uveriti** *v.t.* assure
**uvertira** *n.* overture
**uvesti** *v.t.* induct
**uvesti** *v.t.* introduce
**uvesti** *v.t.* prelude
**uvesti** *v.t.* usher
**uvežbavati** *v.t.* practise
**uvid** *n.* insight
**uviti** *v.t.* twist
**uvo** *n* ear
**uvod** *n.* introduction
**uvod** *n.* prelude
**uvođenje** *n.* induction
**uvodni** *a.* inaugural

**uvodni** *a.* introductory
**uvodnik** *n* editorial
**uvojak** *n.* curl
**uvojak** *n* forelock
**uvojak** *n* lock
**uvoz** *n.* import
**uvoziti** *v.t.* import
**uvreda** *n.* insult
**uvreda** *n.* offence
**uvreda** *n* affront
**uvrediti** *v.t.* affront
**uvrediti** *v.t.* insult
**uvrediti** *v.t.* offend
**uvredljiv** *a.* abusive
**uzajamno dejstvo** *n.* interplay
**uzak** *a.* narrow
**uzalud** *adv.* vainly
**uzaludan** *a.* futile
**uzaludan** *a.* vain
**uzaludnost** *n.* futility
**uzastopan** *a.* successive
**uzastopni** *adj.* consecutive
**uzastopno** *adv* consecutively
**uzbuđenje** *n.* thrill
**uzbuditi** *v. t* excite
**uzbuditi** *v.t.* thrill
**uzbuna** *n* alarm
**uzbuniti** *v.t* alarm
**uzburkati** *v.t.* trouble
**uzda** *n.* rein
**uzda** *n* bridle
**uzdah** *n.* sigh
**uzdahnuti** *v.i.* sigh
**uzdignuće** *n* elevation
**uzdignuće** *n* uplift
**uzdizati se** *v.t.* ascend
**uzdržan** *a.* taciturn
**uzdržati se** *v.i.* abstain
**uzdržavati se** *v.i.* refrain
**uzduž** *adv.* along

**uzengija** *n.* stirrup
**uzeti** *v.t* take
**uzeti kašikom** *v.t.* spoon
**uzgajivač** *n.* grower
**uzica biča** *n.* whipcord
**uzimajući u obzir** *prep.* considering
**uzmaći** *v.i.* recede
**uznemiravanje** *n.* harassment
**uznemiravati** *v. t* disturb
**uznemiravati** *v.t.* harass
**uznemiren** *a* anxiety
**uznemirenost** *n* disquiet
**uznemiriti** *v. t* commove
**uznemiriti** *v.t.* unsettle
**uznemiriti** *v.t.* upset
**uznemiriti se** *v.i* fuss
**uzor** *n.* paragon
**uzorak** *n.* sample
**uzoran** *a.* commendable
**uzorkovati** *v.t.* sample
**uzročan** *adj.* causal
**uzročnost** *n* causality
**uzrok** *n.* cause
**uzrokovati** *v.t* cause
**uzrujanost** *n* agitation
**uzrujanost** *n.* fret
**uzrujati** *v.t.* agitate
**uzrujati se** *v.t.* fret
**uzurpacija** *n.* usurpation
**uzurpirati** *v.t.* usurp
**uzvik** *n* cry
**uzvik** *n* exclamation
**uzvik** *n.* interjection
**uzviknuti** *v.i* exclaim
**uzvišen** *a.* lofty
**uzvišen** *a.* sublime
**uzvišenost** *n* sublime
**uzvraćati** *v.t.* reciprocate
**uzvratiti** *v. t* counter
**užaren** *adv.* aglow

**užaren** *a.* ardent
**užaren** *a* fiery
**užas** *n.* horror
**užasan** *a.* awful
**užasan** *a.* terrible
**uže** *n.* rope
**užina** *n.* snack
**uživanje** *n* delight
**uživanje** *n* enjoyment
**uživati** *v. t.* delight
**uživati** *v. t* enjoy
**uživati** *v.t.* relish
**uživati** *v.i.* bask
**užlebiti** *v.t* groove
**užurban** *a.* hasty

# V

**vagati** *v.t.* scale
**vagati** *v.t.* weigh
**vagina** *n.* vagina
**vagon** *n.* wagon
**vajar** *n.* sculptor
**vajarski** *a.* sculptural
**vakcina** *n.* vaccine
**vakcinacija** *n.* vaccination
**vakcinisati** *v.t.* vaccinate
**vakuum** *n.* vacuum
**validan** *a.* valid
**valjak** *n.* roller
**valjanost** *n* good
**valjati rublje** *v.t.* mangle
**valjati se** *v.i.* wallow
**valuta** *n* currency
**van** *adv.* out
**van** *adv* outward
**vanbračan** *a* bastard
**varalica** *n.* impostor
**varalica** *n.* sharper

varalica *n.* swindler
varalica *n.* trickster
varanje *n.* cheat
varanje *n.* trickery
varati *v. t.* cheat
varati *v.t.* rook
varenje *n* digestion
varijabla *a.* variable
varijacija *n.* variation
varirati *v.t.* vary
variti *v. t.* brew
varka *n* sham
varnica *n.* spark
varničiti *v.i.* spark
varvarski *a.* barbarous
vaška *n.* louse
vat *n.* watt
vatra *n* fire
vatren *a* fervent
vatreno oružje *n.* gun
vaučer *n.* voucher
vazduh *n.* air
vazdušast *adj.* aeriform
vazdušast *a.* airy
vazdušni *a.* aerial
vazdušni duh *n.* sylph
vazektomija *n.* vasectomy
vazelin *n.* vaseline
važan *a* considerable
važan *a.* weighty
važno *a.* important
većina *n.* majority
večan *adj.* eternal
večan *a.* everlasting
veče *n* evening
večera *n* dinner
večera *n.* supper
večeras *adv.* tonight
večerati *v. t.* dine
večit *a.* perpetual

večnost *n* eternity
već *adv.* already
većina *n* most
većinom *a.* most
vegetacija *n.* vegetation
vegetarijanac *n.* vegetarian
vegetarijanski *a* vegetarian
vek *n.* century
vekna *n.* loaf
velelepnost *n.* svečanost
veleprodaja *n.* wholesale
veleprodajni *a* wholesale
veleprodajno *adv.* wholesale
veličanstven *a.* magnificent
veličanstven *a.* majestic
veličanstven *a.* marvellous
veličanstven *a.* palatial
veličanstven *a.* stately
veličanstvenost *n.* grandeur
veličanstvo *n.* majesty
veličati *v. t* exalt
veličati *v. t.* extol
veličati *v.t.* glorify
veličina *n.* magnitude
veličina *n.* size
velignton *n.* wellignton
velik *a.* grand
velik *a* great
velik *a.* large
velik *a* big
velike boginje *n.* smallpox
velikodušan *a.* generous
velikodušan *a.* magnanimous
velikodušnost *n.* generosity
velikodušnost *n.* liberality
velikodušnost *n.* magnanimity
vena *n.* vein
venac *n.* coronet
venac *n* festoon
venac *n.* garland

| | |
|---|---|
| **venac** *n.* wreath | **verzija** *n.* version |
| **venac za glavu** *n* anadem | **veseliti se** *v.i.* frolic |
| **venčanje** *n.* wedding | **veseljak** *n.* spark |
| **venčati** *v.t.* wed | **veselje** *n.* hilarity |
| **ventil** *n.* valve | **veselje** *n.* jollity |
| **ventilacija** *n.* ventilation | **veselje** *n.* merriment |
| **ventilator** *n.* ventilator | **veselost** *n.* gaiety |
| **ventilirati** *v.t.* ventilate | **veselost** *n.* joviality |
| **veo** *n.* veil | **veseo** *a.* cheerful |
| **veoma** *adv* much | **veseo** *a.* gay |
| **veoma** *a.* very | **veseo** *a.* jovial |
| **vepar** *n* boar | **veseo** *a* merry |
| **vera** *n.* creed | **veseo** *a.* sportive |
| **vera** *n* faith | **veslač** *n.* oarsman |
| **veran** *a* faithful | **veslanje** *n* row |
| **veran** *n.* trusty | **veslati** *v.i.* paddle |
| **veranda** *n.* porch | **veslati** *v.t.* row |
| **veranda** *n.* verendah | **veslo** *n.* oar |
| **verati se** *v.i.* scramble | **veslo** *n* paddle |
| **verbalni** *a.* verbal | **vestern** *a.* western |
| **veridba** *n.* betrothal | **vesti** *n.* news |
| **verifikacija** *n.* verification | **vesti** *n. pl.* tidings |
| **verifikovati** *v.t.* verify | **vešala** *n.* . gallows |
| **veriti** *v. t* betroth | **vešt** *a.* proficient |
| **vernost** *n* fidelity | **vešt** *a.* skilful |
| **vernost** *n.* allegiance | **vešt** *a.* adept |
| **verodostojan** *a* credible | **veštački** *a.* artificial |
| **verovanje** *n* belief | **veštica** *n.* hag |
| **verovatan** *a.* probable | **veštica** *n.* witch |
| **verovati** *v.t* trust | **veština** *n.* adept |
| **verovati** *v. t* believe | **veština** *n.* proficiency |
| **verovatno** *a.* likely | **veština** *n.* skill |
| **verovatno** *adv.* probably | **vetar** *n.* wind |
| **verovatnoća** *n.* likelihood | **veteran** *n.* veteran |
| **verovatnoća** *n.* probability | **veteranski** *a.* veteran |
| **verovatnost** *n.* verisimilitude | **veterinarski** *a.* veterinary |
| **verski** *a.* religious | **veto** *n.* veto |
| **vertikala** *n.* perpendicular | **vetrenjača** *n.* windmill |
| **vertikalan** *a.* perpendicular | **vetrovit** *a.* windy |
| **vertikalan** *a.* vertical | **veverica** *n.* squirrel |

| | |
|---|---|
| **vez** *n* embroidery | **vime** *n.* mamma |
| **vez** *n* berth | **vime** *n.* udder |
| **veza** *n* bond | **vinjak** *n* brandy |
| **veza** *n* connection | **vino** *n.* wine |
| **veza** *n.* liaison | **vinova loza** *n.* vine |
| **vezati** *v.t.* knot | **vinuti** *se v.i.* soar |
| **vezati** *v.t.* lace | **violina** *n* fiddle |
| **vezati** *v.t.* tie | **violina** *n.* violin |
| **vezati kablom** *v. t.* cable | **violinista** *n.* violinist |
| **vezati** *v.t* bind | **virenje** *n* peep |
| **vezivanje** *n* deligate | **viriti** *v.i.* peep |
| **vežba** *n.* exercise | **virtuelan** *a* virtual |
| **vežbati** *v. t* exercise | **virus** *n.* virus |
| **vibracija** *n.* vibration | **visak** *n.* lead |
| **vibrirati** *v.i.* vibrate | **visina** *n.* height |
| **vic** *n.* joke | **visina** *n.* altitude |
| **videti** *v.t.* see | **visinometar** *n* altimeter |
| **vidik** *n.* vista | **viski** *n.* whisky |
| **vidikovac** *n* belvedere | **visok** *a.* high |
| **vidljiv** *a.* visible | **visok** *a.* tall |
| **vidljivost** *n.* visibility | **visoko** *adv.* aloft |
| **vidokrug** *n.* purview | **visoko** *adv.* highly |
| **vidovnjak** *n.* seer | **Visost** *n.* Highness |
| **vidra** *n.* otter | **višak** *n* excess |
| **vigvam** *n.* wigwam | **višak** *n* over |
| **vihor** *n.* whirlwind | **višak** *n.* superfluity |
| **vijuganje** *n* wriggle | **višak** *n.* surplus |
| **vijugati** *v.i.* wriggle | **više** *adv* more |
| **vijugati se** *v.i.* zigzag | **više** *adv* over |
| **vijugav** *a.* sinuous | **više** *a* several |
| **vijugav** *a.* zigzag | **više ponuditi** *v.t.* outbid |
| **vika** *n.i.* bawl | **više voleti** *v.t.* prefer |
| **vikanje** *n* yell | **višegodišnji** *a.* perennial |
| **vikar** *n.* vicar | **višestruk** *a.* multiplex |
| **vikati** *v. i* cry | **viši dvorski službenik** *n* chamberlain |
| **vikati** *v.i.* shout | **vitak** *n.* slender |
| **vikati** *v.i.* yell | **vitak** *a.* slim |
| **vila** *n* fairy | **vitalan** *a.* vital |
| **vila** *n.* villa | **vitalnost** *n.* vitality |
| **vilica** *n.* jaw | **vitamin** *n.* vitamin |

viteški *a.* chivalrous
viteštvo *n.* chivalry
vitez *n.* knight
vizija *n.* vision
vizionar *n.* visionary
vizionarski *a.* visionary
vizualizovati *v.t.* visualize
vizuelni *a.* visual
Vlada *n.* government
vladar *n.* ruler
vladar *n.* sovereign
vladati *v.i.* reign
vladati *v.t.* rule
vladavina *n* reign
vlaga *n* damp
vlaga *n.* moisture
vlakno *n* fibre
vlasnički *a.* proprietary
vlasnik *n.* owner
vlasnik *n.* proprietor
vlasništvo *n.* ownership
vlast *n* dominion
vlast *n.* authority
vlastelin *n.* squire
vlastelinski *a.* manorial
vlastelinstvo *n.* manor
vlažan *a* damp
vlažan *adj.* dank
vlažan *a.* humid
vlažan *a.* moist
vlažiti *v. t.* damp
vlažiti *v.t.* moisten
vlažnost *n.* humidity
vlažnost *n.* wetness
vo *n.* ox
voće *n.* fruit
voćnjak *n.* orchard
vod *n.* platoon
vod *n.* squad
vođa *n.* leader

vode *n.* water
vodeni *a.* watery
vodič *n.* guide
voditi *v.t.* guide
voditi *v.t* head
voditi *v.t.* wage
voditi napad *v.t.* spearhead
voditi poreklo *v.t.* originate
vodoinstalater *n.* plumber
vodolija *n.* aquarius
vodonik *n.* hydrogen
vodootporan *a.* waterproof
vodootpornost *n* waterproof
vodopad *n.* waterfall
vođstvo *n.* guidance
vođstvo *n.* leadership
vojni *a.* martial
vojni *a.* military
vojnička truba *n* bugle
vojnik *n.* soldier
vojska *n* military
vojska *n.* army
vojvoda *n* duke
vokalni *a.* vocal
volej *n.* volley
voleti *v.t.* love
volja *n.* volition
volja *n.* will
voljan *a.* willing
voljen *a.* loving
volonter *n.* volunteer
volontirati *v.t.* volunteer
volovska koža *n* buff
volt *n.* volt
vosak *n.* wax
voštana mast *adj.* cerated
voz *n.* train
vozač *n* driver
vozač *n.* motorist
vozilo *n.* vehicle

**voziti** *v. t* drive
**voziti** *v.t.* ride
**voziti bicikl** *v.t.* pedal
**voziti se** *v.i.* motor
**voziti se na jahti** *v.i* yacht
**voziti se u taksiju** *v.i.* taxi
**vožnja** *n* drive
**vožnja** *n* ride
**vrabac** *n.* sparrow
**vraćanje** *n.* recurrence
**vračanje** *n.* witchcraft
**vraćanje u pritvor** *n* remand
**vragolast** *a.* mischievous
**vrana** *n* crow
**vrat** *n.* neck
**vrata** *n* door
**vratar** *n.* porter
**vratar** *n.* usher
**vratilo** *n.* shaft
**vratiti** *v.t.* reclaim
**vratiti** *v.t.* requite
**vratiti se** *v.i.* relapse
**vratiti se** *v.i.* return
**vratiti se** *v.i.* revert
**vratiti se istim putem** *v.t.* retrace
**vratiti u domovinu** *v.t.* repatriate
**vratiti u pritvor** *v.t.* remand
**vratnice** *n.* wicket
**vrba** *n.* willow
**vrbovnik** *n* crimp
**vrebati** *v.i.* lurk
**vrebati** *v.i.* prey
**vreća** *n.* sack
**vreća** *n.* poke
**vrećica** *n.* pouch
**vredan** *a.* industrious
**vredan** *a.* valuable
**vredan** *a* worth
**vredan pažnje** *a.* noteworthy
**vređati** *v.t.* resent

**vrednost** *n.* value
**vrednost** *n.* worth
**vreme** *n.* time
**vreme** *n* weather
**vreme za spavanje** *n.* bed-time
**vremenski** *a.* temporal
**vremenski period** *n.* while
**vreo** *a.* hot
**vresište** *n.* moor
**vreteno** *n.* spindle
**vrh** *n.* peak
**vrh** *n.* summit
**vrh** *n.* tip
**vrh** *n.* top
**vrh koplja** *n.* spearhead
**vrh** *n.* apex
**vrhovni** *a.* supreme
**vrhovni nadzor** *n.* superintendence
**vrhunac** *n.* climax
**vrhunac** *n.* heyday
**vrhunac** *n.* pinnacle
**vrisak** *n* scream
**vrisak** *n.* shriek
**vrištati** *v.i.* scream
**vrištati** *v.i.* shriek
**vrli** *a.* virtuous
**vrlina** *n.* virtue
**vrpca** *n.* string
**vrsta** *n.* kind
**vrsta** *n.* sort
**vrsta** *n.* species
**vrsta baruta** *n.* amberite
**vrsta biljke** *n.* cardamom
**vrsta cigare** *n* cheroot
**vrsta konja** *n.* bayard
**vrsta krojača** *n.* cosier
**vrsta organa** *n.* cornicle
**vrsta ponošanja** *v.t.* condite
**vršalica** *n.* thresher
**vršati** *v.t.* thresh

vrtlog *n* whirl
vrtlog *n.* whirlpool
vrtoglav *a.* giddy
vruć *a.* warm
vrućina *n.* ardour
vrveti *v.i.* teem
vuča *n.* traction
vući *v.t* draw
vući noge *v.i.* shuffle
vuk *n.* wolf
vulgaran *a.* vulgar
vulgarnost *n.* vulgarity
vulkan *n.* volcano
vulkanski *a.* volcanic
vuna *n.* wool
vunena tkanina *n* woollen
vuneni *a.* woollen

# Z

za *prep* for
za divljenje *a.* admirable
za razliku *od prep* unlike
za vreme *prep* during
zabava *n.* entertainment
zabava *n.* frolic
zabava *n.* fun
zabava *n* amusement
zabaviti *v. t* entertain
zabavljati se *v.i.* sport
zabavljati *v.t.* amuse
zabeležiti *v.t.* jot
zabeležiti *n.* log
zabiti *v.t.* nail
zabluda *n* fallacy
zaborav *n.* oblivion
zaboravan *a* forgetful
zaboraviti *v.t* forget
zabosti *v.t.* stick

zabrana *n.* prohibition
zabrana *n.* ban
zabraniti *v.t* bar
zabraniti *v.t* forbid
zabraniti *v.t.* prohibit
zabraniti *v.t.* taboo
zabranjen *a* taboo
zabranjujući *a.* prohibitory
zabraviti *v. t* bolt
zabrinut *a.* solicitous
zabrinut *a.* anxious
zabrinutost *n.* solicitude
zabrljati *v.t.* mull
zabuna *n* confusion
zabušant *n.* shirker
zabušavati *v.t.* shirk
začarati *v.t* bewitch
začepiti *n.* gag
začepiti *v.t.* plug
začeti *v. t* conceive
začeti *v. t* beget
začin *n.* spice
začiniti *v.t.* season
začiniti *v.t.* spice
začuditi *v.t.* astonish
zadatak *n* errand
zadatak *n.* task
zaderati *v.t.* scar
zadesiti *v. t* befall
zadimljen *a.* smoky
zadirati *v. i* encroach
zadirkivanje *n.* banter
zadirkivanje *n.* raillery
zadirkivati *v.t.* banter
zadirkivati *v.t.* rag
zadirkivati *v.t.* tease
zadiviti *v.t.* amaze
zadivljenost *n.* amazement
zadovoljan *a.* content
zadovoljavajući *a.* satisfactory

zadovoljavati *v.i.* suffice
zadovoljiti *v. t* content
zadovoljiti *v.t.* satisfy
zadovoljstvo *n.* content
zadovoljstvo *n* contentment
zadovoljstvo *n.* gratification
zadovoljstvo *n.* pleasure
zadovoljstvo *n.* satisfaction
zadružni *a* co-operative
zadržati *v. t* detain
zadržati *v.t.* retain
zadržati *v.t.* withhold
zadržavanje *n.* retention
zadubljen u misli *a.* pensive
zadužen *a.* indebted
zaduženje *n* debit
zadužiti *v. t* debit
zagađenje *n.* pollution
zagaditi *v.t.* pollute
zagledano *adv.* agaze
zaglibiti *v.i* bog
zagonetka *n.* riddle
zagorčati *v. t* embitter
zagrejati *v.t* heat
zagrliti *v. t.* embrace
zagrljaj *n* embrace
zagubiti *v.t.* misplace
zagušljiv *a.* stuffy
zahtev *n* demand
zahtev *n* request
zahtevati *v. t* claim
zahtevati *v. t* demand
zahtevati *v.t.* necessitate
zahtevati *v.t.* request
zahvalan *a.* grateful
zahvalan *a.* thankful
zahvaliti *v.t.* thank
zahvalnost *n.* gratitude
zahvalnost *n.* thanks
zahvalnost *n.* appreciation

zahvat *n* grasp
zainteresovan *a.* interested
zaista *adv.* indeed
zajam *n.* loan
zajažljiv *a.* satiable
zajednica *n.* community
zajednički *a.* common
zajednički *a.* mutual
zajedničko *adv.* jointly
zajedno *adv.* together
zajedno živeti *v. t* cohabit
zakasneo *a.* overdue
zakasneo *adj.* belated
zaklanjati *v.t.* screen
zaklati *v.t.* slaughter
zakletva *n.* oath
zaključak *n.* conclusion
zaključati *v.t* lock
zaključiti *v. t* conclude
zaključiti *v.t.* infer
zaključivanje *n.* inference
zaključni *a* conclusive
zaklon *n.* lee
zakon *n.* law
zakonit *a.* lawful
zakonitost *n.* legality
zakonodavac *n.* legislator
zakonodavan *a.* legislative
zakonodavstvo *n.* legislature
zakopati *v. t.* bury
zakopčati *v. t.* button
zakovati *v.t.* rivet
zakovica *n.* rivet
zakrčiti *v. t* clutter
zakrčiti *v.t.* ram
zakrpa *n* patch
zakrpiti *v. t* botch
zakrpiti *v.t.* patch
zakucati *v.t.* jam
zakup *n.* lease

| | |
|---|---|
| **zakup** *n.* tenancy | **zameniti** *v.t.* supersede |
| **zakupac** *n.* lessee | **zamenjivati** *v.t.* alternate |
| **zakupiti** *v.t.* lease | **zamerka** *n.* stricture |
| **zalazak** *n* set | **zamisliti** *v.t* fancy |
| **zalemiti** *v.t.* solder | **zamisliti** *v.t.* imagine |
| **zalet** *n* pounce | **zamišljen** *a.* wistful |
| **zaleteti** *se v.i.* pounce | **zamka** *n.* noose |
| **zaliha** *n.* stock | **zamka** *n.* pitfall |
| **zaliti** *v.t.* pitch | **zamka** *n.* snare |
| **zaliv** *n.* gulf | **zamka** *n.* trap |
| **zaliv** *n* bay | **zamoran** *a.* irksome |
| **zalivati** *v.t.* water | **zamoran** *a.* tiresome |
| **zaljubiti** *se v. t* enamour | **zamotati** *v. t* envelop |
| **zaljubljiv** *a.* amorous | **zamotati** *v.t.* wrap |
| **zaloga** *n.* pledge | **zamrsiti** *v.t.* tangle |
| **zaloga** *v.t.* pledge | **zamrznuti** *v.i.* freeze |
| **zalogaj** *n.* morsel | **zamuljiti** *v.t.* silt |
| **zalogaj** *n.* mouthful | **zanat** *n* craft |
| **založiti** *v. t* deposit | **zanatlija** *n.* artisan |
| **založiti** *v.t.* mortgage | **zanatlija** *n* craftsman |
| **založni dužnik** *n.* mortgagor | **zanemariti** *v.t.* neglect |
| **založni verovnik** *n.* mortagagee | **zanemarivanje** *n* neglect |
| **zaluđivati** *v.t.* infatuate | **zanemarljiv** *a.* negligible |
| **zalutao** *a* stray | **zanesenost** *n.* rapture |
| **zalutao** *adv.,* astray | **zanimanje** *n.* occupation |
| **zalutati** *v.i.* stray | **zanimanje** *n.* vocation |
| **zamagliti** *v. t* blear | **zanimljiv** *a.* interesting |
| **zamah** *n.* lunge | **zanovetalo** *v.t.* nag |
| **zamah** *n.* sweep | **zanovetanje** *n.* nag |
| **zamah** *n* whisk | **zanovetati** *v.i.* grumble |
| **zamazati** *v. t.* daub. | **zao** *a* evil |
| **zamazati** *v.t.* smear | **zao** *a.* malignant |
| **zamena** *n.* replacement | **zao** *a.* nefarious |
| **zamena** *n.* substitute | **zao** *a.* wicked |
| **zamena** *n.* substitution | **zaobilaznica** *n* bypass |
| **zamenica** *n.* pronoun | **zaobliti** *v.t.* round |
| **zamenik** *n* deputy | **zaokupiti** *v.t* engross |
| **zameniti** *v. t* commute | **zaokupiti** *v.t.* preoccupy |
| **zameniti** *v.t.* replace | **zaoštriti** *v.t.* point |
| **zameniti** *v.t.* substitute | **zapad** *n.* occident |

zapad *n.* west
zapadni *a.* west
zapadni *adv.* westerly
zapadnjački *a.* occidental
zapadno *adv.* west
zapadno *a.* westerly
zapaliti *v.t* fire
zapaljenje *n.* inflammation
zapaljenje pluća pneumonia
zapaljeno *adv.* aflame
zapaljiv *a.* inflammable
zapamtiti *v.t.* remember
zapanjeno *adv.* agape
zapanjenost *n* daze
zapanjiti *v. t* daze
zapanjiti *v.t* astound
zapečatiti *v.t.* seal
zapečatiti *v.i.* stamp
zapetljan *a.* intricate
zapisati *v.t.* note
zapisati *v.t.* record
zapisničar *n.* recorder
zapisničar *n.* scorer
zapisnik *n.* record
zapleniti *v.t.* sequester
zaplet *n.* plot
zaplet *n.* tangle
započeti *v.t.* initiate
zaposlenje *n* employment
zaposliti *v. t* employ
zaposliti *v.t* hire
zapovednički *a.* authoritative
zapovednik *n* commandant
zaprašiti *v.t.* dust
zapravo *adv.* actually
zapreka *n.* hitch
zapremina *n.* volume
zaprepastiti *v.t.* horrify
zaptivač *n.* gasket
zaraćena strana *n* belligerent

zarada *n.* salary
zaraditi *v.t.* net
zarazan *a* contagious
zarazan *a.* infectious
zaraziti *v.t.* plague
zarđao *a.* rusty
zarez *n* comma
zarez *n.* notch
zarobiti *v.t.* enslave
zarobiti *v. t.* entrap
zarobiti *v. t.* captivate
zarobljen *a.* captive
zarobljenik *n.* captive
zaroniti *v.i.* duck
zaroniti *v.t.* plunge
zaseda *n.* ambush
zaseniti *v. t.* dazzle
zaseniti *v.t.* overshadow
zaseniti *v.t.* shade
zasićenje *n.* saturation
zasijati *v.t* flash
zasipati *v. t* bestrew
zasititi *v.t.* satiate
zasititi *v.t.* saturate
zasladiti *v. t.* candy
zasladiti *v.t.* sugar
zaslepljenost *n.* infatuation
zasluga *n.* merit
zaslužan *a* creditable
zaslužan *a.* meritorious
zaslužiti *v. t.* deserve
zaslužiti *v. t* earn
zaslužiti *v.t* merit
zasnovati *v.t.* base
zastareo *a.* obsolete
zastareo *a.* outdated
zastareo *a.* antiquated
zastati *v.i.* pause
zastava *n* flag
zastava *n.* banner

| | |
|---|---|
| **zastoj** *n* halt | **zauške** *n.* mumps |
| **zastoj** *n.* standstill | **zauvek** *adv* forever |
| **zastoj** *n* stoppage | **zauzdati** *v.t.* rein |
| **zastrašiti** *v. t.* cow | **zauzet** *a* busy |
| **zastrašiti** *v.t.* intimidate | **zauzeti** *v.t.* occupy |
| **zastrašivanje** *n.* intimidation | **zavada** *n.* feud |
| **zastrašivati** *v. t.* bully | **zavaliti se** *v.i.* loll |
| **zastupati** *v.t.* advocate | **zavarak** *n* weld |
| **zastupnik** *n.* attorney | **zavarivati** *v.t.* weld |
| **zastupnik** *n.* proxy | **zavera** *n.* conspiracy |
| **zasvoditi** *v.t.* arch | **zaverenik** *n.* conspirator |
| **zašećeriti** *v.t.* sweeten | **zavesa** *n* curtain |
| **zašiljiti** *v.t.* spike | **zaveštati** *v. t.* bequeath |
| **zašiljiti** *v.i.* taper | **zavet** *n.* vow |
| **zašrafiti** *v.t.* screw | **zavetovati** *v.t.* vow |
| **zaštita** *n.* protection | **zavežljaj** *n.* packet |
| **zaštita** *n.* safeguard | **zavidan** *a* enviable |
| **zaštititi** *v.t.* protect | **zavideti** *v. t* envy |
| **zaštitne naočare** *n.* goggles | **zavidljiv** *a* envious |
| **zaštitni** *a.* preservative | **zavidnik** *n* grudge |
| **zaštitni** *a.* protective | **zavijanje** *n* howl |
| **zaštitnik** *n.* protector | **zavijati** *v.t.* howl |
| **zašto** *adv.* why | **zavirivati** *v.i.* pry |
| **zatajiti** *v.i.* misfire | **zavisan** *a* dependent |
| **zateturati se** *v.i.* lurch | **zavisiti** *v. i.* depend |
| **zatišje** *n.* lull | **zavisnik** *n.* addict |
| **zatvarač** *n.* shutter | **zavisnik** *n* dependant |
| **zatvaranje** *n.* closure | **zavisnost** *n.* addiction |
| **zatvor** *n.* constipation | **zavisnost** *n* dependence |
| **zatvor** *n.* jail | **zavisnost od drugih** *n* anaclisis |
| **zatvor** *n.* prison | **zaviti** *v.t* bandage |
| **zatvoren** *a.* close | **zavođenje** *n.* seduction |
| **zatvorenik** *n.* prisoner | **zavoditi** *n.* seduce |
| **zatvoriti** *v. t* close | **zavodljiv** *a* seductive |
| **zatvoriti** *v.t.* pound | **zavoj** *n.* bandage |
| **zatvoriti** *v.t.* shut | **završetak** completion |
| **zatvoriti** *u* **svetilište** *v. t* enshrine | **završetak** *n* finish |
| **zaustaviti** *v.t.* arrest | **završetak** *n.* termination |
| **zaustaviti** *v.i.* stem | **završiti** *v. t* end |
| **zaustaviti** *v.t.* stop | **završiti** *v.t* finish |

zavrteti *v.i.* spin
zbaciti *v. t* dethrone
zbaciti *v.t.* toss
zbacivanje *n* toss
zbijati šalu *v.i.* joke
zbirka *n.* miscellany
zbogom *interj.* bye-bye
zbogom *interj.* farewell
zbogom *interj.* good-bye
zbogom *interj.* adieu
zbor *n* rally
zbrinuti *v. t* bestow
zbrka *n.* jumble
zbrka *n.* muddle
zbrka *n.* welter
zbrkano *adv.* pell-mell
zbrkati *v.t.* jumble
zbrkati *v.t.* muddle
zbrojiti *v.t.* total
zbuniti *v.t.* nonplus
zbuniti *v.t.* perplex
zbuniti *v.t.* puzzle
zbuniti *v. t.* baffle
zbuniti *v. t* bemuse
zbuniti *v. t* bewilder
zbunjenost *v. t* confuse
zbunjenost *n.* perplexity
zdrav *a.* healthy
zdrav *a.* salutary
zdrav *a.* sound
zdrav *a.* wholesome
zdravica *n.* toast
zdravlje *n.* health
združeno *adj.* conjunct
zebra *n.* zebra
zec *n.* hare
zec *n.* rabbit
zefir *n.* zephyr
zelen *a.* green
zelen *a.* verdant

zelena boja *n* green
zelenaš *n.* usurer
zelenaštvo *n.* usury
zelenilo *n.* greenery
zelenkada *n.* daffodil
zemaljski *a* earthly
zemlja *n.* country
zemlja *n* earth
zemljan *a* earthen
zemljano posuđe *n.* crockery
zemljište *n.* land
zemljotres *n* earthquake
zenit *n.* zenith
zerez *n.* nick
zevanje *n.* yawn
zevati *v.i.* gape
zevati *v.i.* yawn
zgodan *a.* handsome
zgrabiti *v.t.* grab
zgrabiti *v.t.* seize
zgrabiti *v.t.* snatch
zgrada *n* building
zgrešiti *v.i.* trespass
zgrušati *v. t* clot
zgusnuti *v.i.* thicken
zid *n.* wall
zidar *n.* mason
zidarstvo *n.* masonry
zidni *a.* mural
zima *n.* winter
zimovati *v.i* winter
zimski *a.* wintry
zimzelen *a* evergreen
zlatan *a.* golden
zlatar *n.* goldsmith
zlato *n.* gold
zlikovac *n.* villain
zlo *n* evil
zloba *n.* malice
zloba *n.* rancour

zloban *a.* sardonic
zločin *n* crime
zločinac *n.* malefactor
zlokoban *a.* inauspicious
zlokoban *a.* sinister
zlonameran *a.* malicious
zlonamernost *n* animus
zloslustan *a.* ominous
zlostavljanje *n.* abuse
zlostavljanje *n.* mal-treatment
zlostavljanje *n.* molestation
zlostavljati *v.t.* abuse
zlostavljati *v.t.* molest
zloupotreba *n.* misapplication
zloupotreba *n.* misuse
zloupotrebiti *v.t.* misuse
zmaj *n* dragon
zmaj *n.* kite
zmija *n.* serpent
zmija *n.* snake
značaj *n.* importance
značaj *n.* significance
značajan *a.* meaningful
značajan *a.* momentous
značajan *a.* notable
značajan *a.* significant
značajnost *n.* notability
značenje *n.* meaning
značenje *n.* purport
značenje *n.* signification
značiti *a.* mean
značiti *v.t* mean
značiti *v.t.* purport
značka *n.* badge
znak *n.* mark
znak *n.* sign
znak *n.* token
znamenit *a.* signal
znanje *n.* knowledge
znanje *n.* lore

znatan *a* formidable
znatan *a.* substantial
znati *v.t.* know
znoj *n.* sweat
znojenje *n.* perspiration
znojiti *se v.i.* perspire
zob *n.* oat
zodijak *n* zodiac
zona *n.* zone
zonski *a.* zonal
zoolog *n.* zoologist
zoologija *n.* zoology
zoološki *a.* zoological
zoološki *vrt n.* zoo
zora *n* dawn
zora *n* aurora
zračenje *n.* radiation
zračiti *v. i* beam
zračiti *v.t.* radiate
zrak *n.* ray
zrelost *n.* maturity
zreo *a.* mature
zreo *v.i* mature
zreo *a* ripe
zrno *n.* grain
zub *n.* tooth
zubac *n* cog
zubobolja *n.* toothache
zujanje *n.* buzz
zujanje *n* hum
zujanje *n.* whir
zujanje *v.i.* whiz
zujati *v. i* hum
zujati *v. i* buzz
zum *n.* zoom
zumirati *v.i.* zoom
zurenje *n* gaze
zuriti *v.t.* gaze
zvaničnik *n* official
zvanično *adv.* officially

zvano *adv.* alias
zveckanje *n.* jingle
zveckati *v.i.* jingle
zveckati *v.i.* rattle
zvečka *n* rattle
zvekan *n.* soft
zveket *n.* clink
zveknuti *v.i.* smack
zver *n* beast
zverski *a* beastly
zvezda *n.* star
zvezda vodilja *n.* loadstar
zvezdan *a.* starry
zvezdan *a.* stellar
zvezdica *n.* asterisk
zvezdolik *adj.* asteroid
zviždati *v.i.* whistle
zvižduk *n* whistle
zvonik *n.* steeple
zvoniti *v.t.* toll
zvonjava *n* toll
zvono *n* bell
zvrk *n.* whirligig
zvučati *v.i.* sound
zvučni *a.* sonic
zvučnik, govornik *n.* speaker
zvučnost *n.* sonority
zvuk *n* sound
zvuk *n.* tone
zvuk trube *n.* clarion

# Ž

žaba *n.* frog
žaba krastača *n.* toad
žacnuti *v.i* smart
žad *n.* jade
žalba *n.* appeal
žalba *n* complaint

žaliti *v.i.* regret
žaliti *v.t.* rue
žaliti *v.i.* sorrow
žaliti se *v.t.* appeal
žaliti se *v. i* complain
žaliti *v. t* bewail
žaljenje *n* regret
žalost *n.* affliction
žalost *n.* grief
žalostan *a.* grievous
žalostan *a.* lamentable
žalostan *n.* mournful
žalostan *a.* rueful
žalostan *a.* sorry
žamor *n.* murmur
žaoka *n.* sting
žargon *n.* jargon
žargon *n.* lingo
žarišni *a* focal
žbun *n.* shrub
žeđ *n.* thirst
žedan *a.* thirsty
žedan *adj.* athirst
žele *n.* jelly
želeti *v.t* desire
želeti *v.t.* want
želeti *v.t.* wish
železnica *n.* railway
želja *n* desire
želja *n.* wish
željan *a* desirous
željan *a* eager
željan *a.* wishful
željno *adj.* appetent
želudačni *a.* gastric
žena *n* female
žena *n.* woman
ženska košulja *n* chemise
ženski *a* female
ženski *n.* womanish

**ženski manastir** *n* convent
**ženskog** *roda a* feminine
**ženstven** *a* effeminate
**ženstvenost** *n.* womanhood
**žestina** *n* fervour
**žestina** *n.* vehemence
**žestok** *a* fierce
**žestok** *a.* vehement
**žetelac** *n.* haverster
**žetelac** *n.* reaper
**žeti** *v.t.* reap
**žetva** *n.* harvest
**žica** *n.* wire
**žig** *n.* hallmark
**žiganje** *n.* pang
**žir** *n.* acorn
**žirafa** *n.* giraffe
**žitarica** *n.* cereal
**žitni** *a* cereal
**živ** *a.* live
**živ** *a.* vivid
**živ** *a.* alive
**živa** *n.* quicksilver
**živa ograda** *n.* hedge
**živac** *n.* Nerve
**živac** *n* quick
**živahan** *adj* alacrious
**živahan** *a.* animate
**živahan** *a.* living
**živahan** *a.* spirited
**živahan** *a.* sprightly
**živahnost** *n.* alacrity
**živahnost** *n.* vivacity
**živeti** *v.i.* live
**živeti na selu** *v.t.* rusticate
**živi pesak** *n.* quicksand
**živin** *a.* mercurial
**živina** *n.* fowl
**živina** *n.* poultry
**živo** *a.* lively

**život** *n* life
**život** *n* living
**životinja** *n.* animal
**životopisac** *n* bioscope
**žižak** *n.* weevil
**žleb** *n.* groove
**žlezda** *n.* gland
**žongler** *n.* juggler
**žonglirati** *v.t.* juggle
**žrtva** *n.* oblation
**žrtva** *n.* victim
**žrtva nesreće** *n.* casualty
**žrtveni** *a.* sacrificial
**žrtveni jarac** *n.* scapegoat
**žrtvovanje** *n.* sacrifice
**žrtvovati** *v.t.* sacrifice
**žrtvovati** *v.t.* victimize
**žućkast** *a.* yellowish
**žuč** *n* bile
**žudeti** *v.t.* covet
**žudeti** *v.t.* crave
**žudeti** *v.i.* hanker
**žudeti** *v.i.* yearn
**žudnja** *n.* yearning
**žulj** *n* blister
**žumance** *n.* yolk
**žurba** *n.* haste
**žurba** *n* hurry
**žurba** *n.* rush
**žuriti** *v.t.* hurry
**žuriti** *v.t.* rush
**žuriti** *v. t* bustle
**žustar** *adj* brisk
**žut** *a.* yellow
**žut poput šafrana** *a* saffron
**žuta boja** *n* yellow
**žutica** *n.* jaundice
**žvakati** *v. t* chew
**žvakati** *v.t.* masticate
**žvakati** *v.t.* munch